SCIENCE, TECHNOLOG

MW00843790

This book gathers inter-disciplinary and multi-disciplinary perspectives on the effects of today's advances in science and technology on issues ranging from government policy-making to how we see the differences between men and women. The chapters investigate how invention and innovation really take place, how science differs from competing forms of knowledge, and how science and technology could contribute more to the greater good of humanity. For instance, should there be legal restrictions on "immoral inventions?" A key theme that runs throughout the book concerns who is taken into account at each stage and who is affected. The amount of influence users have on technology development and how non-users are factored in are evaluated as the impact of scientific and technological progression on society is investigated, including politics, economy, family life, and ethics.

TODD L. PITTINSKY is a professor in the Department of Technology and Society at Stony Brook University (SUNY), USA, and the Faculty Director of its Undergraduate College of Leadership and Service.

# SCIENCE, TECHNOLOGY, AND SOCIETY

*New Perspectives and Directions*

EDITED BY

## TODD L. PITTINSKY

*Stony Brook University, State University of New York*

CAMBRIDGE
UNIVERSITY PRESS

# CAMBRIDGE
## UNIVERSITY PRESS

University Printing House, Cambridge CB2 8BS, United Kingdom

One Liberty Plaza, 20th Floor, New York, NY 10006, USA

477 Williamstown Road, Port Melbourne, VIC 3207, Australia

314–321, 3rd Floor, Plot 3, Splendor Forum, Jasola District Centre,
New Delhi – 110025, India

79 Anson Road, #06–04/06, Singapore 079906

Cambridge University Press is part of the University of Cambridge.

It furthers the University's mission by disseminating knowledge in the pursuit of
education, learning, and research at the highest international levels of excellence.

www.cambridge.org
Information on this title: www.cambridge.org/9781107165120
DOI: 10.1017/9781316691489

First published 2019

Printed and bound in Great Britain by Clays Ltd, Elcograf S.p.A.

*A catalogue record for this publication is available from the British Library.*

*Library of Congress Cataloging-in-Publication Data*
NAMES: Pittinsky, Todd L.
TITLE: Science, technology, and society : new perspectives and directions / edited by Todd L.
Pittinsky, Stony Brook University, State University of New York.
DESCRIPTION: New York : Cambridge University Press, [2019]
IDENTIFIERS: LCCN 2019012493 | ISBN 9781107165120 (hardback) | ISBN 9781316616895
(paperback)
SUBJECTS: LCSH: Science – Social aspects. | Technology – Social aspects. | Genetic engineering –
Social aspects.
CLASSIFICATION: LCC Q175.5 .S37385 2019 | DDC 303.48/3–dc23
LC record available at https://lccn.loc.gov/2019012493

ISBN 978-1-107-16512-0 Hardback
ISBN 978-1-316-61689-5 Paperback

*For my father, Bernard Pittinsky, who passed on quite a bit of wisdom, but this in particular: whenever I wanted to buy some new gadget, he would ask what I needed to do that I couldn't already do.*

# Contents

# Figures

# Tables

x

# Contributors

JESSICA CAVIN BARNES, *North Carolina State University*

S. KATHLEEN BARNHILL-DILLING, *North Carolina State University*

ROGER BROWNSWORD, *King's College London*

HARRY COLLINS, *Cardiff University*

JASON A. DELBORNE, *North Carolina State University*

ROBERT EVANS, *Cardiff University*

BENOÎT GODIN, *National Institute of Scientific Research*

DAVID HORN, *The Ohio State University*

JENS MAZEI, *TU Dortmund University*

M. GRANGER MORGAN, *Carnegie Mellon University*

NELLY OUDSHOORN, *University of Twente*

TODD L. PITTINSKY, *Stony Brook University*

ELIZABETH A. PITTS, *North Carolina State University*

DOUGLAS SICKER, *Carnegie Mellon University*

DEAN KEITH SIMONTON, *University of California, Davis*

ROBIN WILLIAMS, *University of Edinburgh*

# Acknowledgments

First, thanks to David Repetto, my editor at Cambridge University Press. David saw the potential of this project and stuck by it, even as it evolved into new versions.

I thank Emily Watton, the editorial assistant at Cambridge University Press, for skillfully and diligently working with me to go from word processing documents to the actual book.

John Elder was gracious and masterful, critical and constructive, in helping all of us to sharpen, polish, refine, and enhance our essays to their best versions.

I am grateful for Firman Manda Firmansyah's time and graphics skills in helping with the figures and tables.

Shawn Gaffney provided initial research assistance to identify contributors; the final eclectic, wonderfully diverse, and inclusive collection of authors reflects his insights.

At home, Alexandru and Vladi gave me great encouragement, in this as in all projects, perhaps most profoundly by encouraging me to stay curious about the world – as it is and as it might be.

And of course, I thank the authors who joined me in this exercise, connected initially by nothing more than the pixels making up the email inviting them to contribute. What came together is a diverse array of interests and research programs that together allow us to map – at least, for the moment – our emerging and ever-changing world.

# Prologue

The dramatic advance of science and technology evokes a range of responses. Some see technology diminishing and undermining our society and even our humanity. Others see unbridled potential. What they agree on is that science and technology are profoundly changing our society. Less noted, though, is how profoundly society shapes – or could shape – the course of science and technology.

This collection offers a broad, deep, and accessible set of essays on the interplay between science, technology, and society. It reflects a very broad range of disciplines and an international group of contributors.

Science and technology studies (STS), from its birth in the 1960s, has attracted interest from a wide array of disciplines and subfields. Today, as the pace and power of science and technology become ever more apparent – with consequences literally at our fingertips – interest is exploding.

This increasing interest in the interplay and intersections of science, technology, and society is paralleled by an ever-growing desire – indeed, an imperative – for STS scholarship to make a difference. College educators are trying to devise new core curriculums that will adequately equip students to live comfortably in a world dominated by technology and science. The stakes in our real lives are too high for inquiry and examination to remain in the ivory tower.

Whether you are a professional researcher, eager to understand more about the contours and frontiers of STS, or a general reader drawn to this fascinating domain, or a student in a course, we invite you to dive in. Whether you single out a particular topic or make your way through most or all of the collection, you will be challenged and rewarded with new perspectives and new directions.

# CHAPTER I

# Technically Based Programs in Science, Technology, and Public Policy

*M. Granger Morgan and Douglas Sicker*[*]

## 1.1 Background

In this chapter, we review and discuss academic programs in technology and public policy, focusing on those that are either located in an engineering college or have a strong engineering focus. We consider what constitutes technically focused research in programs melding engineering and policy, where and how this work is done, the focus of these programs at the undergraduate and graduate levels, and the challenges of building and sustaining such programs.

Many academic programs in the United States and elsewhere focus on the *social studies* aspects of science, technology, and public policy. Indeed, most programs listed in the original American Association for the Advancement of Science guide to graduate education in science, engineering, and public policy were in this category (Levey, 1995). Few programs combine deep technical education and understanding with modern social science and policy-analytical skills and knowledge.

Of course, some policy problems related to technology do not require the policy maker or analyst to get "inside the black box" (Rosenberg, 1982), meaning he or she has no need to understand the detailed workings of technology at play. Indeed, for many such problems, spending too much time considering the technical details can be a distraction or lead the analyst astray. However, a subset of policy problems can lead to poor or nonsensical results: those in which the technical details are integral to the policy issue. Table 1.1 illustrates both kinds of problems. Examples of both types of problems involve direct satellite communication in which the technical details are not critical to a solution of the policy problem and in which it is essential to "get inside the black box," for which a reasonable technical solution requires a deep familiarity with the technical details.

---

[*] Morgan (2010, 2011) were used with permission from the publisher.

Table 1.1 *Examples of problems*

| A problem related to technology | A problem in which technical details are centrally important |
|---|---|
| *Delivery of continuing adult education through direct-broadcast satellite to rural India.* To adequately address this problem, the analyst does not need to know much at all about how direct-broadcast satellites work. So long as the analyst knows what the technology costs, who is needed to run it, and similar details, a nontechnical policy analyst can address this problem very well. Indeed, getting too bogged down in the technical details could easily distract the analyst from the central issues. | *Developing India's negotiating positions for an upcoming international conference on reallocated parking orbits for geostationary satellites.* To adequately address this problem, the analyst must have a deep technical understanding of the relative advantage of gain on the ground versus gain on the spacecraft, the likely future cost and performance of microwave amplifiers, and a variety of similar issues. Without such knowledge, the resulting policy conclusions could be seriously misinformed. |

In the United States, most programs in technology and policy date to the early 1970s. One notably earlier high-visibility program was the Harvard Program on Technology and Society, created with a substantial endowment from IBM. This program started in 1964 and ran through 1972 under the direction of philosopher Emmanuel (Manny) Mesthene. The focus was not particularly on policy analysis but rather on technology impacts on society and on technology and social change. The program published a series of high-visibility annual reports but was never successfully integrated into the mainstream of academics at Harvard. Later, a portion of the endowment was used to support the professorship of Louis M. Branscomb, who ran the Science, Technology, and Public Policy Program in the Belfer Center for Science and International Affairs of the Kennedy School at Harvard. In contrast to Mesthene, Branscomb had a much stronger involvement in policy-analytic work, leading to a focus that continues at the Belfer Center today. The Harvard program predated most other programs that started to emerge in its very last years.

In the early 1970s, Arthur Singer at the Sloan Foundation made a series of grants to develop programs in science, technology, and public policy. A few years later, William Blanpied at the National Science Foundation also made a number of grants to build programs in this area. Since the late 1970s, however, no major ongoing foundation or government support has emerged in the United States to build interdisciplinary academic programs in science, technology, and public policy, although foundations, such as the Exxon Education Foundation, have made occasional grants.

Despite limited support, many science and engineering educators have come to recognize the importance of preparing students with rigorous technical backgrounds who are also capable of addressing policy problems in which technical details matter. This has not always been true. In the 1950s and 1960s – and even today on some campuses – the strong postwar tradition of engineering science and education created an environment in which many faculty belittled any activity that was not laden with partial differential equations. Fortunately, recent decades have witnessed a rebalancing of engineering education. However, even today, developing and sustaining programs in technology and policy present numerous challenges:

- Processes for academic promotion and tenure apply traditional disciplinary templates in evaluating junior faculty and give no weight to cross-disciplinary accomplishments and impact in that realm, such as technical policy surrounding energy, environment, information and communications technology, and biomedical engineering issues.
- Few faculty candidates can combine deep technical knowledge and skill with solid modern social-scientific, policy-analytic, and policy-application knowledge and skills.
- Many faculty candidates educated in the more qualitative social sciences, or in social studies of technology, have limited interest in or ability to address policy problems with deep technical content.
- There is difficulty engaging the nature and interests of funding sources and the relative ease of funding.
- Stakeholders lack vision in defining interesting research questions and in being watchful for – and building on – insights that can be generalized in this field.

## 1.2   Building and Sustaining a Program in Technology and Policy

In a conversation I had years ago with physicist Ray Bowers (who, together with chemist Frank Long, started Cornell's program in science, technology, and policy), Bowers spoke about why Mesthene's Harvard Program on Technology and Society had not survived, despite a generous endowment from IBM. Bowers argued that it had not been integrated into the academic fabric at Harvard but rather had been built off to the side. Thus no one was available to defend it "among those with real power in the

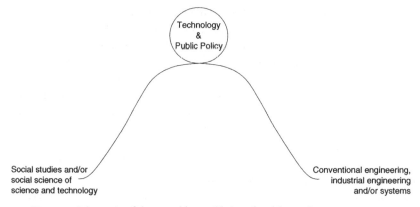

Figure 1.1 Schematic of the unstable equilibrium faced by academic programs in technology and policy. Faculty and administrators must devote continuous attention and energy to keeping the program balanced, that is, with substantial technical content, modern applied social science, and substantive/rigorous policy-analytic methods.

university." Bowers and Long worked to weave science and technology policy into the academic fabric of Cornell University. The Cornell department that grew out of their early efforts, Science and Technology Studies, is now an established department in the College of Arts and Sciences. However, it no longer performs the deep, technically focused policy work that Bowers and Long pioneered.

For a number of reasons, sustaining a program in technology and policy in which technical rigor is integral to the program's education and research involves an unstable equilibrium, illustrated in Figure 1.1. Without continuous effort to maintain the unstable balance, a program will evolve either into more conventional forms of engineering or into social studies of science and technology.

Cornell faculty and administrators applied that continuous effort. When Bowers and Long left the program, a number of excellent nonscientists took their place, including sociologist Dorothy Nelkin and linguist and lawyer Sheila Jasanoff. Walter Lynn continued to contribute a technical perspective while he was still active, but as the program grew and was merged with a program in the history of science, it evolved into a very different kind of effort. Today, the undergraduate major in science and technology studies "aims to further students' understanding of the social and cultural meanings of science and technology" (Cornell University Department of Science and Technology Studies, 2018c, para. 2). Using perspectives and tools "that cross the traditional boundaries of sociology, philosophy, politics, and history," doctoral-level studies in the department treat "science and technology as historical and cultural productions" (Cornell, 2018a, para. 3). The "approach throughout is both descriptive (aimed at understanding how science and technology are accomplished) and normative (e.g., showing where actual practices and professed norms are in conflict)" (Cornell, 2018b, para. 2). Although such work is interesting and important, it is quite different in focus from the pioneering technology-assessment activities of Bowers, Long, and their colleagues on topics such as video telephony and solid-state microwave devices, where deep technical knowledge was applied to substantive policy analysis.

A second way activities that begin in technology and public policy may migrate toward the social studies side of Figure 1.1 is to shift toward conventional public policy. We make no normative argument. Important problems in public policy are either unrelated to technology or concern it but do not require a deep understanding of technical issues.

A third example of a movement away from the unstable equilibrium toward the social studies side of Figure 1.1 is the evolution of the Association of Public Policy and Management (APPAM) and its *Journal of Policy Analysis and Management* (*JPAM*). Individuals at the Sloan Foundation and academics like Charlie Wolf, Pat Crecine, Toby Davis, and Ray Vernon worked intently to include scientists and engineers in the workshops that led to APPAM's creation. Participants made a serious effort to include technical people in the early mix of those involved in the organization. However, over time, most members of the association and most readers of *JPAM* had no deep interest in technical issues. As a result, the technical people shifted their efforts away from APPAM/JPAM to more technically focused societies and journals.

On the right-hand side of the unstable equilibrium in Figure 1.1 is the example of the Department of Technology and Human Affairs at the School of Engineering and Applied Sciences at Washington University. Under the leadership of chemical engineer Robert Morgan,[1] Washington University established the Interdepartmental Program in Technology and Human Affairs in 1971; it grew into a full-fledged department in the engineering school in 1976. Its name was subsequently changed to the Department of Engineering and Policy. The department offered a full range of degrees, from BS to PhD. However, when Morgan stepped down,

---

[1] No relation to the coauthor of this chapter.

the new department head and several deans became interested in issues like midcareer continuing technical education, and the department's new leadership did not devote the necessary attention and energy to sustaining the program, which ultimately collapsed.

In addition to requiring continual balancing of energies from faculty and administrators, programs in technology and policy that have survived and grown have evolved in ways that allowed them to adapt to the strengths and limitations of their host institutions. However, all have faced some common problems, of which the greatest may be finding appropriate faculty who combine strong technical knowledge with well-honed policy analysis skills. The careers of most First-Wave faculty active in this area evolved from traditional roots. Some had already developed strong technical careers, were safely tenured, and had the luxury to move into more interdisciplinary undertakings. In other cases, young faculty took considerable career risks to pursue an intellectual venture they viewed as critically important.

In the Department of Engineering and Public Policy (EPP) at Carnegie Mellon University, where we teach, the strategy has been never to compromise on the technical credentials of new faculty. In some cases, we found faculty candidates who had already built strong backgrounds in technology and policy. A few junior hires had strong technical backgrounds and clear policy interests but little formal or practical policy background. Because Carnegie Mellon actively encourages interdisciplinary work, it has been practical to hire such individuals and develop their policy expertise over time, cultivated by those in leadership positions and by faculty who already have such expertise. Many institutions find it difficult or impossible to do this. However, the situation is changing. Although the pool remains small, in the last fifteen years, EPP has increasingly been able to recruit junior faculty who combine excellent technical skills with strong policy interests and demonstrated accomplishments.

### 1.3    Undergraduate Technology and Policy Programs Offered by Engineering-Based Departments

In the United States and a number of other countries, many engineering undergraduate programs flourish in areas, such as industrial engineering, environmental engineering, and systems engineering, that sometimes touch on issues of public policy. However, we are aware of only a few technically based programs that offer undergraduate degrees in science, technology, and public policy. One of the oldest is the set of double-major programs offered with each of the five traditional engineering departments of Carnegie Mellon's Department of Engineering and Public Policy. We describe these in detail in the section on Carnegie Mellon undergraduate programs in engineering and public policy.

The Department of Management Science and Engineering at Stanford offers a BS degree program that "trains students in the fundamentals of engineering systems analysis to prepare them to plan, design and implement complex economic and technological management systems where a scientific or engineering background is necessary or desirable" (Stanford University, 2018, para. 1). In addition to a set of standard science, mathematics, and engineering core courses, students take accounting, computer science, deterministic optimization, economics, and organizational theory and complete a capstone senior project.

The Department of Technology and Society in the College of Engineering and Applied Sciences at the State University of New York, Stony Brook, offers an undergraduate degree in technology-systems management and a minor. The department describes its program as focusing "on technological advances that shape every facet of modern life. Students develop an understanding of the characteristics, capabilities, and limitations of current and emerging technologies. Successful practices in government, industry, education, and personal life depend on such understanding" (Stony Brook University, 2018a, para. 3). Students take several courses in mathematics and natural sciences and select a cluster of "seven related courses ... in one area of natural science, engineering, applied science or environmental studies" from a traditional department (Stony Brook University, 2018b, para. 6). The department offers a significant number of its own courses in technology-systems management, from which students are expected to select eleven. The department also offers minors in technology-systems management and nanotechnology studies.

The Engineering School at McMasters University in Ontario, Canada, offers a BS program in engineering and society that combines historic analysis, social science, and engineering to "investigate how technology affects society and how in turn society influences the development of technology" (McMaster University, 2018, para. 2).

University College London (UCL) has recently developed an undergraduate minor in engineering and public policy for students in any of the core engineering disciplines. Jason Blackstock, who has been leading efforts to establish an EPP program at UCL, told us that a recent trend in the United Kingdom incorporates *policy exposure* into mainstream undergraduate engineering programs. For example, Blackstock is work-ing with the Royal Academy of Engineering to run some Engineering a Better World programs aimed at UK undergraduate engineers. This program will expose students to sustainable-development goals and help them identify how their capabilities might contribute. Several universi-ties have asked for support to model offerings on UCL's curriculum. Blackstock noted,

> This is definitely not the same as training in technically rigorous engineer-ing-policy analysis, but the trend is starting to generate considerably more interest (most importantly, a pipeline of interested engineering graduates) in graduate degrees that blend technical engineering and policy analyses.

At Delft University of Technology in The Netherlands, the faculty in Technology, Policy, and Management offers a BS program in Technische Bestuurskunde (loosely translated as "systems engineering and policy analysis"). Although the faculty's graduate programs operate in English), the BS program operates in Dutch. In a recent self-assessment prepared for one of the national reviews that all Dutch academic programs receive, faculty at Delft explained:

> The BSc programme *Technische Bestuurskunde* teaches students to analyze systems that are technically, socio-economically and politically complex. Examples include large-scale infrastructures for telecom, transport and energy, or medium-scale systems like business information systems or wind farms. Many disciplines are involved, and therefore the TB curriculum includes subjects ranging from calculus, computational modelling and technology to economics, law and governance.

Some universities, including Ohio State University (John Glenn College of Public Affairs, 2018) and Pennsylvania State University, offer minors in public policy or additional policy coursework for engineering students. Although more abbreviated than a major, these often involve only three to five courses. Dartmouth offers a "major modified with Public Policy" in a "program for the aspiring public servant who realizes it will be useful to understand technology – and for the engineer who realizes that public policy affects which technologies are funded and chosen for development and adoption" (Thayer School of Engineering at Dartmouth, 2018, para. 4). Programs such as the civil engineering program at the University of Michigan (Michigan Engineering, 2018) consider policy issues related to a specific discipline, such as civil or environmental engineering, but nar-rowly tailor these and do not provide the scope of methods or breadth of a full major.

## 1.4 The Undergraduate Program in Engineering and Public Policy at Carnegie Mellon

In contrast with other programs that began with a focus on graduate education, the activity that led to the Department of Engineering and Public Policy at Carnegie Mellon began with an undergraduate program designed to add additional dimensions and skills for engineering students, most of whom go on to conventional engineering careers. EPP now offers undergraduate programs designed to suit the needs of engineering and nonengineering students.

The main undergraduate degree is the EPP double-major program, which earns students a joint degree between EPP and any of the five primary engineering departments: chemical, civil, electrical and computer, mechanical, and materials science. EPP also offers double majors and minors in Science, Technology, and Public Policy for students outside the engineering college who are earning a BS, including students in the Mellon College of Science, the School of Computer Science, and in select majors in Dietrich College. Similar to the double major in engineering and public policy, this new double major is meant to broaden perspectives on a student's primary major and provide additional career skills. Last, for Carnegie Mellon University students outside the College of Engineering, EPP administers the technology and policy minor, designed to allow students to explore the interactions of technology and policy without adding too much to the course requirements in their major curriculum.

Students earn double-major degrees by EPP taking over all the technical and nontechnical elective-course space in the single-major undergraduate curriculum to comprise the second half of the degree. In that elective-course space, all students must take introductory courses in microeconomics and engineering statistics. Then, they select one of several social-analysis electives in the area of decision science; a course in writing and communication (beyond their freshman writing course); at least three "technology-policy" electives, most of which are offered by the department; and a course entitled Applied Methods for Technology-Policy Analysis. They also complete two EPP project courses.

EPP has evolved undergraduate courses and course sequences in areas such as energy systems; air pollution; telecommunication policy; computer security and privacy; management of technical innovation; and risk perception, assessment, and analysis. These are regular technical electives in the College of Engineering (often double-listed in traditional departments as well), open to all students in the college who meet the prerequisites. It is not unusual for a large portion of students in EPP technical elective courses in telecommunication policy to be single majors in electrical and computer engineering. Similarly, many students in EPP courses in air pollution are pursuing single majors such as civil engineering, chemical engineering, or mechanical engineering. This cross-pollination is supported across the college and is very common.

An important feature of the EPP undergraduate curriculum is project courses, run jointly by faculty in the Department of Engineering and Public Policy and the Department of Social and Decision Sciences in the College of Humanities and Social Sciences. The typical course hosts 20 to 25 students. Projects address some real-world problems in technology and public policy, typically with an outside client for whom the work is being done. (See Table 1.2 for examples of recent topics.) The Department has run project courses since 1970. Today, it runs two such projects every semester. Students start the semester with a vaguely defined problem area and various background materials, which they use to define and shape a workable problem. Then, they undertake the necessary analysis to frame and address the problem. Typically, two faculty advisors and two PhD students serve as managers. Over the first few weeks, students work to develop a thorough understanding of the subject and define the focus of the work they propose to do. Approximately halfway through the semester, they make a first formal presentation to an outside review panel who bring various types of expertise and represent differing points of view in the problem area. The review panel assists students by providing critical comments on their structuring of the problem and by suggesting various resources and information sources. At the end of the semester, the students prepare a final written project report of about 100 pages and make a final verbal presentation of their findings and conclusions to the review panel. It is impossible for 20 to 25 people to work on a single problem collaboratively, so much of the work occurs in smaller working groups of four to six students.

Project courses serve several important educational functions. First, they are the venue in which students have an opportunity to assemble various technical and social-analysis components of their education and gain practical experience applying them to a real-world problem. Second, they provide a valuable opportunity for students to develop and refine their verbal, oral, and presentation skills. In the real world of daily engineering practice, these skills are as important for success as core mathematical and quantitative analytical skills. Project courses are rigorous and complex, requiring a great deal of work. However, over the past 20 years, EPP has undertaken three surveys of all of its double-major undergraduate alumni

Table 1.2 *Examples of topics addressed by a number of recent undergraduate technology-policy group project courses in the Department of Engineering and Public Policy at Carnegie Mellon University*

---

Spring 2017: Air Quality Benefits from Vehicle Emissions Testing
Spring 2017: The Future of Emergency Alerts and Warnings
Fall 2016: Pittsburgh Bicycling: An Analysis of City Impacts, Stakeholders, Project
  Prioritization, and Infrastructure Options
Spring 2016: The Kariba Dam
Fall 2015: Police Body Cameras
Fall 2015: Personal Environmental Monitoring
Spring 2015: California's Water Problem: A Survey of New Technical and Social Solutions
Spring 2015: Big Data in the 'Burgh: Evaluating the Impacts of an Open Data Portal in
  Pittsburgh
Fall 2014: Optimal Scheduling for Medical Clinics
Fall 2014: Providing Information to Non-English Speakers during Disasters
Spring 2014: Adaptation in Pittsburgh
Spring 2014: A Plastic Bag Tax for Pennsylvania?
Fall 2013: Local News in Pittsburgh in the Internet Age
Fall 2013: How Clean Is Clean Enough? Public Response to Radioactive Contamination
Spring 2013: What Are the Prospects for Natural Gas Vehicles in the Pittsburgh Region?
Spring 2013: Advancing Wind Energy
Fall 2012: The Locks and Dams Crisis
Fall 2012: Bridging the Digital Divide
Spring 2012: Emergency Messaging with Social Media
Spring 2012: Vehicle Use, Transportation, and Energy Policy

---

*Note.* A full list of past EPP project courses can be found at www.cmu.edu/epp/prospective/undergraduate/epp-project-courses/index.html

and, in all three cases, the strong response has been that "project courses were the single most valuable experience in my four years at Carnegie Mellon," because they teach students how to work in interdisciplinary teams, how to quickly master an entirely new problem domain, how to manage to a schedule, and how to produce a set of professional-quality products.

The college has carefully designed the EPP double-major program to correspond with all traditional engineering undergraduate majors to produce curricula that meet Accreditation Board for Engineering and Technology (ABET) accreditation.[2] Traditionally, when ABET reviews an engineering college, it sends a separate accreditor to visit EPP to

---

[2] ABET is the US program that accredits engineering programs. They explain, "The letters A.B.E. T. stood for Accreditation Board for Engineering and Technology. But over the last 80 years our scope has broadened, and now we [also] accredit Computer Science, Applied Science, and Engineering Technology programs" (ABET, 2018, para. 5).

confirm that compatibility with all traditional majors is in compliance. However, in 2014, EPP became separately accredited through ABET to allow a student to obtain an engineering degree with only a major in EPP (and not including a traditional dual major such as electrical and computer engineering or civil engineering). However, EPP has no intention of allowing students to complete only an EPP degree, because faculty see great value in students having depth in a core discipline in science or engineering.

For a few years, the Engineering Department also offered a single-major accredited degree in engineering and public policy. Students were still required to focus their technical studies in one of the traditional fields of engineering, but did not have to take enough courses to meet the requirements of an accredited degree in that field. The idea was that this broader degree, involving more engineering courses in other fields and more social-analysis content, would offer an effective background for a student who wished to enter a career in a field such as patent law or science and technology journalism. The department graduated a small number of single majors, but each time a student proposed to do a single major, the faculty immediately set out to convince them otherwise, arguing that with "just three more courses you can get a conventional engineering degree ... life is uncertain ... you never know when that might be valuable." After a few years, the faculty decided they did not believe in the single major and stopped offering it.

## 1.5   Graduate Education and Research in Technology and Policy

The Technology and Policy Program (TPP) at the Massachusetts Institute of Technology (MIT) was one of the first master of science (MS) programs in technology and policy and is still one of the largest and most successful. Although students are not required to have an undergraduate background in science or engineering, most do. They take a series of core courses and then take additional technical and social science courses from across the institute. Many students enter the program without support, but because MIT is such a large, diverse institution, they subsequently fan out across the institute to discover and secure a position in a research program of interest, through which they also obtain support.

For many years, one tenure-track faculty member, Richard de Neufville, solely operated TPP, working with a number of instructors supported with soft money. When MIT established its Engineering Systems Division (ESD), TPP became part of the Division and eventually became well-staffed by a number of tenure-track faculty. ESD also offered a PhD program. For a variety of reasons, many traditional engineering faculty at MIT decided ESD needed to change direction. After some extended internal discourse, in 2015 the Institute for Data, Systems, and Society replaced the ESD. The Institute for Data Systems, and Society developed a doctoral program that it describes as (a) driven by problems of societal interest, (b) application-domain driven, (c) involving quantitative methods, (d) relying on real-world data, and (e) engaging the societal aspects of the problem. This program is in early development. TPP remains a strong separate MS program.

At Stanford, the Department of Engineering Economic Systems was one of the first to offer technology and policy MS and PhD degrees, focusing heavily on methodological development in decision analysis. Over the years, it merged with the Department of Operations Research. Later, a second merger occurred with the Department of Industrial Engineering. The resulting department is now called the Department of Management Science and Engineering and has a broader research focus than Engineering Economic Systems originally had.

The Energy and Resources Group at the University of California, Berkeley, offers Master of Arts (MA), MS, and PhD degrees focused primarily on issues of energy and sustainability. Much of the research focuses on very dynamic energy issues that have been unfolding in the State of California. John Holdren founded the program and, while he was still at Berkeley, the Energy and Resources Group addressed issues related to national security.

At Carnegie Mellon, the Department of Engineering and Public Policy has chosen to focus its attention at the graduate level on developing a PhD program designed for students with science and engineering backgrounds. EPP combines technical analysis with social science, economics, and policy analysis to address problems in which knowledge of technical details is critical to decision-making. Current areas of research include the environment and energy; risk analysis and risk communications; information and communications technology; engineering education; and design, organization, and technology change.

EPP also offers an MS in Engineering and Technology Innovation Management (E&TIM) for students with science or engineering backgrounds who wish to develop skills in managing technical projects. The timing is unusual in that courses begin in January and end in December, with a summer internship in the middle. Students can combine this degree with a traditional engineering MS that they begin in the fall semester before starting E&TIM and finish in the spring semester after completing the E&TIM degree.

Other programs have come and gone. Today, several new program show significant promise. For example, at the University of Maryland, the Clark School of Engineering and the School of Public Policy jointly offer an MS in engineering and public policy. Also the Department of Technology and Society in the College of Engineering and Applied Sciences at the State University of New York, Stony Brook, offers BS and MS degrees and recently initiated a PhD program in Technology, Policy, and Innovation.

In addition to US programs defined broadly as working on a range of areas in technology and policy, a much larger number of programs address smaller domains. The University of Colorado has long had an MS program in telecommunications and policy. The many environmental programs include strong ones at the Yale School of Forestry, the Department of Environmental Studies at the University of California, Santa Cruz, and the program in Environmental Science and Engineering at the University of North Carolina. New programs continue to develop; for example, at the Nicholas School at Duke.

In Canada, the University of Calgary set out to build a major program in science, technology, and policy. For various reasons, that effort stalled and is no longer taking new students, although it may be restarted. Also, in Canada, McMaster University has established an MS program in engineering and public policy, and the University of British Columbia at Simon Fraser has technically based policy activities.

Europe has several technically based MS and PhD programs. In the Netherlands, Delft University of Technology's Faculty in Technology, Policy and Management has long offered several MS programs and a PhD. Other Dutch universities have offered similar programs, though less developed and stable, including Eindhoven, Utrecht, and Twente. In Portugal, PhD programs are emerging in engineering and public policy at the Instituto Superior Técnico in Lisbon and the University of Porto. Both collaborate with EPP at Carnegie Mellon.

Several UK universities have long had some technically based policy work, including Cambridge and Oxford. Cambridge offers a master in philosophy in technology policy that was originally developed in collaboration with TPP at MIT. For a while, Oxford hosted a program in engineering, economics, and management, but it closed in the late 2000s. For a while, the MS program in Oxford's Blavatnik School of Government included a mandatory unit on science and public policy. Whether that will continue as a required unit or become optional is unclear.

The Science Policy Research Unit at Sussex initially had quite a strong technical focus, but today is significantly less technical. At the School of Civil Engineering and Geosciences at Newcastle University, the Earth systems science, engineering, and management program does a significant amount of policy work with deep technical content. A number of more specialized programs align with traditional departments and include some attention to policy; these include the Energy Institute at University College London and the Center for Environmental Policy at Imperial College London. The University of Manchester offers a PhD in science, technology and innovation policy. University of College London has recently created a Department of Science, Technology, Engineering, and Public Policy offering MS and PhD degrees. Other parts of the world provide a few programs. For example, the Division of Engineering and Technology Management in the Faculty of Engineering in the National University of Singapore offers a variety of MS programs and is creating a PhD program.

Table 1.3 lists the Web pages of the programs noted in the preceding discussion. (Apologies to any program we missed.)

In these programs, the number of problems falling in the notion that policy problems in which the technical details are of critical importance is enormous. Successful programs have therefore focused on a subset. Rather than adding faculty in unrelated areas, colleges recruit faculty with over-lapping interests, thereby building several discreet focal areas.

The relative ease of securing research support is a factor that often shapes how a program evolves. Although funding does not tend to be a significant problem in an area such as energy or the environment, other areas, such as telecommunications policy, have very little government or private-foundation support. Firms in telecommunications tend to be reluctant to support policy-related work (e.g., on spectrum policy) unless they can be assured that the conclusions and policy recommendations will support their positions. When only a few sources of interested funding exist, it is difficult to amass a balanced portfolio of support. Programs able to attract support from private firms more easily than from the National Science Foundation may focus away from public policy and toward private-sector issues and problems.

## 1.6 Technically Focused Policy Analysis (Science for Policy)

Brooks of Harvard (1964) was careful to always draw a distinction between policy for science and science for policy. This section of the chapter explores what Brooks called science for policy: the analysis of

Table 1.3 *Web addresses of a number of the academic programs in technology and policy*

| Program | Web address |
|---------|-------------|
| Carnegie Mellon University, Department of Engineering and Public Policy | www.cmu.edu/epp |
| Energy and Environmental Systems Group (ISEEE), University of Calgary, Alberta, Canada | www.ucalgary.ca/pubs/calendar/grad/current/energy-environmental-systems-eess.html |
| MPhil in Technology Policy, Judge Business School, Cambridge, UK | www.jbs.cam.ac.uk/programmes/mphil_techpol/index.html |
| Faculty of Technology, Policy, and Management, Delft University of Technology, Netherlands | www.tudelft.nl/en/tpm/ |
| Industrial Engineering and Innovation Sciences, Eindhoven University of Technology, Netherlands | www.tue.nl/en/university/departments/industrial-engineering-innovation-sciences/ |
| IN+ at Instituto Superior Técnico, Lisbon, Portugal | http://in3.dem.ist.utl.pt/ |
| Institute for Data, Systems, and Society and the Program in Technology and Policy, MIT | http://idss.mit.edu/<br>http://tppserver.mit.edu/ |
| SUNY Stony Brook, Department of Technology and Society in the College of Engineering and Applied Sciences | www.stonybrook.edu/est/ |
| Civil Engineering and Geosciences at Newcastle, UK | www.ncl.ac.uk/postgraduate/courses/degrees/civ-eng-geotechnical-engineering-geology-mphil-phd/#profile |
| University of Manchester, Science, Technology, and Innovation Policy | www.manchester.ac.uk/study/postgraduate-research/programmes/list/10323/phd-science-technology-and-innovation-policy/ |
| Division of Engineering and Technology Management, University of Singapore, Singapore | www.isem.nus.edu.sg/ |
| Department of Management Science and Engineering, Stanford University | www.stanford.edu/dept/MSandE/ |
| Faculty of Geosciences, Utrecht University, Netherlands | www.uu.nl/en/organisation/faculty-of-geosciences |
| University College London (UCL), Department of Science, Technology, Engineering, and Public Policy (STEaPP) | www.ucl.ac.uk/steapp |
| UC Berkeley Energy and Resources Group | https://erg.berkeley.edu |
| UC Berkeley Energy, Civil Infrastructure, and Climate Program | www.ce.berkeley.edu/programs/ecic |

Table 1.3 (cont.)

| Program | Web address |
|---|---|
| FEUP Porto, Doctoral Program in Engineering and Public Policy (EPP) | https://sigarra.up.pt/feup/en/cur_geral.cur_view?pv_curso_id=767 |
| University of Sussex, Science and Technology Policy Research program (SPRU) | www.sussex.ac.uk/spru/ |
| University of Colorado, Boulder, Interdisciplinary Telecommunications | www.colorado.edu/itp/ |
| Yale, School of Forestry and Environmental Studies | https://environment.yale.edu |
| UC Santa Cruz, Department of Environmental Studies | http://envs.ucsc.edu |
| University of North Carolina, Environmental Sciences and Engineering | http://sph.unc.edu/envr/environmental-sciences-and-engineering-home/ |
| Duke, Nicholas School of the Environment | https://nicholas.duke.edu |
| McMaster University, Engineering & Society Program | www.eng.mcmaster.ca/engandsoc/ |
| Penn State University, Engineering Design, Technology, and Professional Programs | www.sedtapp.psu.edu |
| Ohio State University, Science, Engineering, and Public Policy Minor | http://glenn.osu.edu/undergraduate/sepp/ |
| Dartmouth, Engineering Science Major Modified with Public Policy | http://engineering.dartmouth.edu/academics/undergraduate/ab/modified/policy/ |
| University of Michigan, Civil and Environmental Engineering | http://cee.engin.umich.edu/academics/undergrad-studies |

policy issues in which the technical details are integral to the issue and drive, or at least should drive, the analysis. As we noted, many problems are *about* technology. These are problems for which a competent policy analyst can do a competent study without deep technical understanding. As in Table 4.1, an analyst need not know anything about the details of how satellites, data, or TV sets function. In contrast, to prepare for a meeting on world radio communication, analysis must rest on a deep understanding of the technologies involved. This latter class of technically focused policy analysis highlights the need for technical policy programs.

## *1.6.1   Typical Analytical Strategies*

Although many of the tools necessary to perform technically focused policy analysis are similar to those of all policy analysis, an important difference is that this form of analysis involves problems in which, if one is to avoid reaching oversimplified or ineffective answers, it is necessary to get "inside the black box" (Rosenberg, 1982) and consider the details of the technical systems involved. A first step in any such analysis is to determine whether the technical details actually matter and, if so, how much detail is pertinent. As Quade (1975) noted, "Good policy analysis should seek to establish the boundaries of the issue under investigation where thought and analysis show them to be and not where off-the-cuff decisions or convention . . . would have them" (p. 4).

Tools for technically focused policy analysis have evolved gradually over many decades. Skilled analysts choose from a large repertoire of analytical tools and methods. Often, they start by building or adopting a static or dynamic model that describes the operation of the physical and social system they are analyzing. Such models may take many forms, ranging from simple formulations based on conservation of mass and energy to closed-form dynamic models of physical processes, ranging from air pollution transformation and dispersion to accounting tools such as input–output models that link to environmental loadings or agent-based models in which system performance is an emergent property of many interacting simple rules or influences. Analysts should keep the analysis simple but adequate to the needs of the problem (Morgan & Henrion, 1999). Because technical people and organizations easily become enamored of model-building, this is often a real-world challenge.

Having developed an appropriate characterization of the relevant physical and social system, most analyses then develop a formal characterization of the preferences of decision makers and apply those in some form of normative assessment, such as cost effectiveness, benefit cost, or probabilistic decision analysis, using either single or multiple attributes to evaluate and compare various policy options. This stage of analysis is typically similar to any form of quantitative policy analysis.

Performing adept policy analysis is as much art as science (Morgan & Henrion, 1999) requiring a deep understanding of the limitations and strengths of the available tools and methods and a willingness and ability to choose strategies and methods that fit the problem. Too often, analysts master only a few specialized tools and use them on whatever problem they encounter. As Maslow (1966) noted, "When the only tool you have is a hammer, every problem begins to resemble a nail" (p. 15). Furthermore, people have become increasingly specialized and their tools are not always applicable beyond a limited scope.

### 1.6.2    Historical Development of Technically Based Policy Analysis Tools

Some of the earliest tools and methods in quantitative policy analysis are those of operations research. These grew from British and US efforts during the Second World War to improve targeting of antiaircraft fire and aerial bombing and to locate and destroy enemy submarines (Little, 2002). These methods were further refined in the postwar period by groups such as the RAND Corporation, first for defense and subsequently for a range of civil applications, such as dispatching fire and police services (Ignall et al., 1975). At Harvard (Raiffa & Schlaifer, 1968) and Stanford (Howard & Matheson, 1977), faculty refined and applied the closely related ideas of optimal statistical decision theory, or decision analysis, to a range of policy problems, largely for private firms, but occasionally for public policy (Howard, Matheson, & North, 1972).

At about the same time, scholars developed methods of technology assessment to anticipate how specific technologies might evolve and with what consequences. Early examples include the work of Cornell's Bowers (Bowers & Frey, 1972), National Academy of Sciences participants (Brooks & Bowers, 1977), and practitioners such as Roy Amara at the Institute for the Future and Joe Coates at the US Congress Office of Technology Assessment.

Conventional tools of engineering analysis, including such simple but powerful ideas as mass and energy balance (Morgan & McMichael, 1981) and more complex strategies such as simulation modeling also became common. However, with the exception of the work of analysts in the decision-analytic tradition, most work in quantitative policy analysis through the 1980s involved deterministic analyses using best estimates (or sometimes upper bounds). When two analyses reached conflicting conclusions, researchers were often unable to determine if those conclusions contradicted each other or both lay within an unstated range of uncertainties.

The language and ideas of microeconomics have become the *lingua franca* of much work in policy analysis, with ideas such as marginal cost and consumer surplus now widely used. Several tools originally developed in economics are now part of the standard repertoire of those who practice quantitative policy analysis. *Cost–benefit analysis* is perhaps the most obvious example (Lave, 1996; Mishan, 1972). Recent years have also seen the application of ideas, such as the use of *options* (de Neufville & Scholtes, 2011; Patiño-Echeverri, Morel, Apt, & Chen, 2007), originally developed in corporate finance.

For more than a century, the characterization and treatment of uncertainty has been an integral part of experimental science. As Sagan (1995) noted, "Every time a scientific paper presents a bit of data, it's accompanied by an error bar – a quiet but instant reminder that no knowledge is complete or perfect." As more professionals whose original training was in experimental science entered the field of policy analysis, that culture gradually transferred (Morgan & Henrion, 1999). For example, as late as the1970s, most analyses performed for the US Environmental Protection Agency contained little or no formal treatment of uncertainty. Today, virtually all such analyses contain at least some quantitative discussion and formal treatment of uncertainty.

Bottom-up *life-cycle analysis* (LCA) has become an increasingly popular tool (Miller & Blair, 1985). To overcome the limits that such analysis can encounter when the boundaries of analysis are drawn too narrowly, researchers have developed an economy-wide approach known as economic input–output (EIO)/LCA (Hendrickson, Lave, & Matthews, 2006). This approach uses an input–output table of the entire economy (the EIO part), such as links to databases on energy use and environmental emissions. EIO/LCA inherently yields only approximate answers, but because it looks across the full economy; it can sometimes identify large impacts that have been overlooked by conventional LCA.

Technically based policy analysts have been slow to incorporate ideas from modern behavioral decision science (Kahneman, Slovic, & Tversky, 1982; Morgan, Fischhoff, Bostrom, & Atman, 2002), although examples are becoming more common (Paté-Cornell & Fischbeck, 1993; Paté-Cornell, Lakats, Murphy, & Gaba, 1997). Application methods from Bayesian inferences are also relatively rare, but growing more common (Small, 2008; Stiber, Small, & Pantazidou, 2004; Wasserman, 2000). Most technically focused policy analysis does a poor job of considering interest-group politics and the political environment in which policy recommendations must be implemented (Pressman & Wildavsky, 1973). Presumably this is because most such analysts have little or no experience in these areas. Improving this situation presents a clear challenge for those engaged in educating future generations of technically focused policy analysts.

### 1.6.3   Who Performs Technically Based Policy Analysis?

Institutions that perform high-quality technically based policy analysis can be classified into five groups:

1 Private-sector firms
2 Consulting firms and think tanks
3 Government mission-oriented agencies
4 Analysis groups whose specific mission is to support government
5 University academic and research programs

**Private-sector firms.** A few large corporations have a tradition of in-house development and use of technically based policy analysis, such as large telecommunications and oil companies. More often, companies commission such analysis from consulting firms, especially in areas such as the application of decision analysis to strategic planning (Howard & Matheson, 1977; Lumina Decision Systems, 2009).

**Consulting firms and think tanks.** Think tanks, including Federally Funded Research and Development Centers such as RAND (Research ANd Development), MITRE, and IDA (Institute for Defense Analyses), have been a primary source of analysis for federal agencies, especially the Department of Defense. Analysis conducted in most nonprofit think tanks, such as Resources for the Future or the Brookings Institution, tend to be heavily economics-based and to involve only modest technical content. However, in some areas, such as environmental regulation or space or telecommunications policy, some of these organizations have developed considerable technical expertise.

**Government mission-oriented agencies.** Government agencies often turn to consulting firms for specific analyses they need. They often use think tanks or the National Research Council (NRC) when the analysis they need is more general in nature. Many think tanks are capable of performing sophisticated modeling and other forms of quantitative policy analysis. The NRC, however, rarely does complex analysis, but is much more likely to synthesize and evaluate work that is already available.

Some mission-oriented federal agencies, such as the Department of Energy, the Environmental Protection Agency, and the Department of Defense, have developed considerable in-house expertise in technically based policy analysis for their own use and to inform broader policy discourse. Such capability is much less common at the state-government level.

**Analysis groups whose specific mission is to support government.** The three organizations created specifically to provide analysis for government entities deserve mention here: the Office of Technology Assessment of the US Congress (OTA), the Congressional Research Service, and the General Accountability Office (GAO).

OTA was established in 1972 to provide independent, technically focused policy analysis for Congress. After struggling for a few years to find a working model, it became a very successful bipartisan analysis group under the leadership of Jack Gibbons (Morgan & Peha, 2003). However, Congress chose to defund it in 1995 after the Republican sweep of both houses. Over time, the Congressional Research Service has begun to build more comprehensive technical analytical capability and to perform assessments that are quite substantive.

As an experiment, beginning in 2002, Senator Bingaman's office explored using the GAO for technology assessment. A small number of such studies have since been produced (US Government Accountability Office, 2002, 2005). Several other efforts re-funded the OTA or created other institutional arrangements to fill what many see as a gap in analytical capability for Congress (Knezo, 2005; Morgan & Peha, 2003).

### 1.6.4    Does Analysis Matter?

Kingdon (1995) articulated a model of the policy process that involves the three parallel streams of processes of problems, policies, and politics. The first and, to a slightly lesser degree, the second, are in the realm of technically based policy analysis. Analysts identify issues that they believe are important problems and perform analysis that clarifies the nature of the problem and suggests possible solutions. Policy entrepreneurs then work to promote related policy strategies and solutions. Occasionally, the broader political agenda shifts so the three streams align and a policy window opens. If, at that moment, good solutions – buttressed by good analysis – are available, analysis can have a significant impact on policy. This was the case, for example, in the decision to adopt an emissions-trading approach to the control of sulfur dioxide. Air pollution experts analyzed the sources, transport, and deposition of sulfur air pollution for many years. In collaboration, economists at CalTech, Resources for the Future, and elsewhere developed ideas about tradable emissions permits. When the Clean Air Act rewrite occurred in a political environment that was not friendly to conventional command-and-control regulation, policy entrepreneurs in Washington, in the Council of Economic Advisers, and elsewhere used technically based policy analysis to promote a market-based solution and were successful (Hahn, 1989; Hahn & Noll, 1982).

Occasionally, analysis performed at just the right moment can have a major impact on an ongoing policy debate. This was the case, for example, when Lave, Hendrickson, and McMichael (1995) demonstrated, at the same time that California was debating requiring the adoption of electric vehicles, that recycling the lead-acid batteries of electric cars would result in more lead released to the environment than if those same cars were fueled with leaded gasoline. However, analysis more commonly has an impact on policy through a slow process of diffusion. Someone performs a small part of the analysis that yields a result. Other analysts see the analysis, get interested, and do related work. Over time, a consensus builds so that ultimately, when decision makers address the issue, they get much the same advice from most experts. At times, this process can be *very* slow. For example, it was over half a century from the time that Ronald Coase and Leo Herzel first showed the advantages of allocating radio-frequency spectrum through auctions to the FCC's eventual adoption of the idea in the 1990s (Coase, 1998; Hazlett, 1998).

This process can be disrupted by political manipulation designed to overemphasize uncertainty in the minds of nonexperts or even to distort and misrepresent the science (Mooney, 2006). The current widespread public confusion over whether climate change is "real" – in the face of many NRC and Intergovernmental Panel on Climate Change assessments – is a clear example of the power of money spent by groups like the Global Climate Coalition to confuse stakeholders and delay action on an important issue. Laws that say, "make it so," or that otherwise ignore physical reality, will not make real problems in technology and public policy disappear any more than the Indiana State House of Representatives could change physical reality when, in 1897, it passed House Bill #246 – by a vote of 67 to 0 – to simplify the value of π to 3.2. The Indiana Senate tabled the "Pi bill" after speaking with a mathematician (Agricultural Economics, Purdue University, 2003).

Clearly, ideology, short-term political interests, or simple ignorance or misunderstanding of the natural world or of engineered systems will, from time to time, lead to senseless and ultimately unrealistic policy outcomes. Although certainly an extreme example, the former Soviet Union is not the only society that has fallen – or will fall – prey to misguided pseudoscientific policies of the sort promoted by the notorious Soviet agrobiologist Trofim Denisovich Lysenko (Joravsky, 1986). The objective of practitioners of careful and balanced technically focused policy analysis is to ensure, whenever possible, that such illogical outcomes are avoided and, when they are not avoided, to work to ensure that realistic policy prescriptions ultimately prevail.

## 1.7  Impacts

No systematic national or international assessment of the educational, research, and public policy impacts of academic programs in technology and policy has emerged, although several programs have conducted limited assessments. Anecdotal evidence suggests that the impacts are large and growing. Virtually all programs have faculty and graduates who have made major contributions in government or private-sector decision-making.

Although it was not our intention to explore this issue in depth here, it is worth pointing out a few high-level impacts. Thanks in large part to work conducted in several programs in technology and policy, current policy-analytical work is much improved in how problems are framed and in the analytical tools used, than was the case just 30 years ago. For example, techniques pioneered in several of these programs – such as decision analysis, the systematic characterization and analysis of uncertainty, and methods in quantitative risk analysis – are now nearly ubiquitous. Perhaps most importantly, the thousands of graduates of programs in technology and policy approach their work in a more encompassing way than their more conventionally educated engineering colleagues.

## REFERENCES

ABET (2018). *Frequently asked questions (FAQ)*. Retrieved from www.abet.org/ /faq/

Agricultural Economics, Purdue University (2003). *Indiana Pi*. Retrieved from www.agecon.purdue.edu/crd/Localgov/Second%20Level%20pages/Indiana_ Pi_Story.htm

Bowers, R., & Frey, J. (1972). Technology assessment and microwave diodes. *Scientific American, 226,* 13–21.

Brooks, H. (1964). The scientific adviser. In R. Gilpin & C. Wrights (Eds.), *Scientists and national policy making* (pp. 73–96). New York, NY: Columbia University Press.

Brooks, H., & Bowers, R. (1977). Technology: Process of assessment and choice. In A. H. Teich (Ed.), *Technology and man's future* (2nd ed., pp. 229–242). New York, NY: St. Martins Press.

Coase, R. H. (1998). Comment on Thomas W. Hazlett: Assigning property rights to radio spectrum users: Why did FCC license auctions take 67 years? *Journal of Law and Economics, 41,* 577–580. https://doi.org/10.1086/467403

Cornell University Department of Science and Technology Studies (2018a). *Academics*. Retrieved from https://sts.cornell.edu/academics

Cornell University Department of Science and Technology Studies (2018b). *Graduate program*. Retrieved from http://sts.cornell.edu/phd

Cornell University Department of Science and Technology Studies (2018c). *Overview*. Retrieved from http://sts.cornell.edu/phd

de Neufville, R., & Scholtes, S. (2011). *Flexibility in design*. Cambridge, MA: MIT Press.

Hahn, R. (1989). Economic prescriptions for environmental problems: How the patient followed the doctor's orders. *Journal of Economic Perspectives, 3*(2), 95–114. https://doi.org/10.1257/jep.3.2.95

Hahn, R. W., & Noll, R. (1982). Designing a market for tradable emissions permits. In W. Magat (Ed.), *Reform of environmental regulation* (pp. 119–146). Cambridge, MA: Ballinger.

Hazlett, T. W. (1998). Assigning property rights to radio spectrum users: Why did FCC license auctions take 67 years? *Journal of Law and Economics, 41*, 529–575. https://doi.org/10.1086/467402

Hendrickson, C. T., Lave, L. B., & Matthews, H. S. (2006). *Environmental life cycle assessment of goods and services: An input-output approach*. New Haven, CT: RFF Press.

Howard, R. A., & Matheson, J. E. (1977). *Readings in decision analysis.*, Menlo Park, CA: SRI International.

Howard, R. A., Matheson, J. E., & North, D. W. (1972). The decision to seed hurricanes. *Science, 176*, 1191–1202. Retrieved from www.warnernorth.net/hurricanes.pdf

Ignall, E. J., Kolesar, P., Swersey, A. J., Walker, W. E., Blum, E. H., Carter G., & Bishop, H. (1975). Improving the deployment of New Your City fire companies. *Interfaces, 5*, 48–61. https://doi.org/10.1287/inte.5.2pt2.48

John Glenn College of Public Affairs (2018). *Science, engineering, and public policy minor*. Retrieved from http://glenn.osu.edu/undergraduate/sepp/

Joravsky, D. (1986). *The Lysenko Affair*. Chicago, IL: University of Chicago Press.

Kahneman, D., Slovic, P., & Tversky, A. (1982). *Judgment under uncertainty: Heuristics and biases*. Cambridge, England: Cambridge University Press.

Kingdon, J. W. (1995). *Agendas, alternative and public policies*. Columbus, GA: Little, Brown.

Knezo, G. J. (2005). *Technology assessment in Congress: History and legislative options* (CRS Report for Congress No. RS21586). Retrieved from http://fas.org/sgp/crs/misc/RS21586.pdf

Lave, L B. (1996). Benefit-cost analysis: Do the benefits exceed the costs? In R. Hahn (Ed.), *Risks costs and lives saved: Getting better results from regulation* (pp. 104–134). Oxford, England: Oxford University Press.

Lave, L. B., Hendrickson, C. T., & McMichael, F. C. (1995). Environmental implications of electric cars. *Science, 268*, 993–995. doi:10.1126/science.268.5213.993

Levey, L. (1995). *Guide to graduate education in science, engineering and public policy.* Washington, DC: American Association for the Advancement of Science. Retrieved from http://grantome.com/grant/NSF/NCSES-8921065

Little, J. D.C. (2002). Philip M. Morse and the beginnings. *Operations Research, 50,* 146–148. doi:10.1287/opre.50.1.146.17799

Lumina Decision Systems (2009). *Who uses Analytica?* Retrieved from http://www.lumina.com/ana/usesofanalytica.htm

Maslow, A. (1966). *The psychology of science: A reconnaissance.* New York, NY: Harper & Row.

McMaster University (2018). *Bachelor of engineering and society: Overview.* Retrieved from www.eng.mcmaster.ca/engphys/programs/degree-options/bengsociety

Michigan Engineering (2018). *Undergraduate degrees and programs.* Retrieved from www.engin.umich.edu/academics/undergraduate-degrees/

Miller, R. E., & Blair, P. D. (1985). *Input–output analysis: Foundations and extensions.* Upper Saddle River, NJ: Prentice Hall.

Mishan, E. J. (1972). *Elements of cost-benefit analysis.* Crows Nest, Australia: George Allen and Unwin.

Mooney, C. (2006). *The Republican war on science.* New York, NY: Basic Books.

Morgan, M. G. (2010). Technology and policy. In D. Grasso & M. Burkins (Eds.), *Holistic engineering education: The dawn of a new era* (pp. 271–281). Berlin, Germany: Springer.

Morgan, M. G. (2011). Technically focused policy analysis. In K. Husbands-Fealing, J. Lane, J. Margurger III, & S. Shipp (Eds.), *The science of science policy: A handbook* (pp. 120–130). Stanford, CA: Stanford University Press.

Morgan, M. G., Fischhoff, B., Bostrom, A., & Atman, C. (2002). *Risk communication: A mental models approach.* Cambridge, England: Cambridge University Press.

Morgan, M. G., & Henrion, M. (1999). *Uncertainty: A guide to dealing with uncertainty in quantitative risk and policy analysis.* Cambridge, England: Cambridge University Press.

Morgan, M. G., & McMichael, F. C. (1981). A characterization and critical discussion of models and their use in environmental policy. *Policy Sciences, 14,* 345–370. doi:10.1007/BF00138489

Morgan, M. G., & Peha J. (Eds.) (2003). *Science and technology advice to the Congress.* New Haven, CT: RFF Press.

Paté-Cornell, M.-E., & Fischbeck, P. S. (1993). PRA as a management tool: Organizational factors and risk-based priorities for the maintenance of the tiles of the space shuttle orbiter. *Reliability Engineering and System Safety, 40,* 239–257. doi:10.1016/0951-8320(93)90063-5

Paté-Cornell M.-E., Lakats, L. M., Murphy, D. M., & Gaba, D. M. (1997). Anesthesia patient risk: A quantitative approach to organizational factors and risk management. *Risk Analysis, 17,* 511–523. doi:10.1111/j.1539-6924.1997.tb00892.x

Patiño-Echeverri, D., Morel, B., Apt, J., & Chen, C. (2007). Should a coal-fired power plant be replaced or retrofitted? *Environmental Science and Technology, 41*, 7980–7986. doi:10.1021/es0711009

Pressman, J. L., & Wildavsky, A. (1973). *Implementation: How great expectations in Washington are dashed in Oakland; or, Why it's amazing that federal programs work at all, this being a saga of the Economic Development Administration as told by two sympathetic observers who seek to build morals on a foundation of ruined hopes.* Berkeley: University of California Press.

Quade, E. S. (1975). *Analysis for public decisions.* Amsterdam, Netherlands: Elsevier.

Raiffa, H., & Schlaifer, R. (1968). *Applied statistical decision theory.* Cambridge, MA: MIT Press.

Rosenberg, N. (1982). *Inside the black box: Technology and economics.* Cambridge, England: Cambridge University Press.

Sagan, C. (1995). The demon-haunted world: Science as a candle in the dark. New York, NY: Random House.

Small, M. J. (2008). Methods for assessing uncertainty in fundamental assumptions and associated models for cancer risk assessment. *Risk Analysis, 28,* 1289–1307. doi:10.1111/j.1539-6924.2008.01134.x

Stanford University (2018). *Stanford engineering: Undergraduate program.* Retrieved from https://msande.stanford.edu/academics/undergraduate-programs

Stiber, N. A., Small, M. J., & Pantazidou, M. (2004). Site-specific updating and aggregation of Bayesian belief network models for multiple experts. *Risk Analysis, 24,* 1529–1538. doi:10.1111/j.0272-4332.2004.00547.x

Stony Brook University (2018a). *Undergraduate: Technological systems management.* Retrieved from www.stonybrook.edu/academics/program-details-undergraduate/index.php?code=tsm&type=description&level=undergrad_bulletin_data#ProgramOverview

Stony Brook University (2018b). *Undergraduate bulletin: Fall 2018–Spring 2019 working copy.* Retrieved from www.stonybrook.edu/sb/bulletin/_workingcopy/academicprograms/tsm/degreesandrequirements.php

Thayer School of Engineering at Dartmouth (2018). *Perspective: Engineering and politics.* Retrieved from https://engineering.dartmouth.edu/magazine/perspective-engineering-and-politics

US Government Accountability Office (2002). *Technology assessment: Using biometrics for border security* (Report No. GAO-03-174). Retrieved from www.gao.gov/assets/160/157313.pdf

US Government Accountability Office (2005). *Technology assessment: Protecting structures and improving communications during wildland fires* (Report No. GAO-05-380). Retrieved from www.gao.gov/assets/160/157597.pdf

Wasserman, L. (2000). Bayesian model selection and model averaging. *Journal of Mathematical Psychology, 44,* 92–107. doi:10.1006/jmps.1999.1278

# CHAPTER 2

# Comparative Studies of Science and Technology

## David Horn

## 2.1 The Work of Comparison

Comparison has been at the heart of a wide variety of disciplinary and interdisciplinary projects in Europe and the United States, especially since the nineteenth century: anthropology, comparative anatomy, comparative linguistics, comparative literature, comparative politics, comparative religion, and so on.[1] Though comparative projects are not restricted to the West or to the modern period, they have functioned, there and elsewhere, in historically and culturally specific ways. In the nineteenth-century West, comparison was often at the heart of efforts to construct or to prop up hierarchies of race, gender, sexuality, and class; to legitimate missionary outreach and colonial government; or to contain the diversity of human histories, cultures, technologies, and forms of knowledge in neat taxonomies and continuous linear narratives.[2] In the later twentieth and early twenty-first centuries, comparison has at times been made to do very different kinds of work: to destabilize hierarchies, to trouble familiar assumptions about identity and difference, to disrupt binary oppositions, or to establish critical distance.[3]

---

[1] On comparison, see Yengoyan (2006) and Felski and Friedman (2013), and especially the pair of essays that open the Felski and Friedman volume: Radhakrishnan (2013) and Friedman (2013). Interestingly, only one essay in these volumes – Adas's critique of diffusionist approaches to the spread of Western science in the colonial world – is explicitly focused on science and technology (Adas, 2006).

[2] For a masterful treatment of this topic, see Adas (1989). In the nineteenth century, Adas noted, "increasingly industrialized European (and North American) cultures *as a whole* were seen to be a separate class, distinct from all others. The polarities were numerous and obvious: metal versus wood; machine versus human or animal power; science versus superstition and myth; synthetic versus organic; progressive versus stagnant. All aspects of culture could be linked to these polarities, to the fundamental dichotomy between industrial and preindustrial societies" (p. 144).

[3] For a discussion of defamiliarization in twentieth-century anthropology, see Marcus and Fischer (1986, esp. Chapter 6). Marcus and Fischer distinguished between "defamiliarization by epistemological critique" and "defamiliarization by cross-cultural juxtaposition." Examples of the latter included Mead (1928), but as of 1986, Marcus and Fischer could find no published examples of the

If it appears that researchers can use comparative studies to pursue diametrically opposed ends, this is because what is sometimes called "the comparative method" (like the scientific method, for that matter) covers a wide variety of projects, approaches, practices, and techniques.[4] Scholars most often talk about the *objects* of comparison, about the *things* they compare: cultures, modes of production, paradigms, assemblages, styles of thinking, impacts, or risks. But we might also distinguish comparisons in other ways; for example, by their end or *telos* – that is, the epistemological, political, and ethical goals they pursue. Comparisons may work to naturalize, legitimize, rationalize, or reinforce; to denaturalize, delegitimize, or make less rational or familiar; to tell stories about progress or regression, accident, or inevitability; or to imagine or critique new technological and political possibilities. The ends of comparison, in this sense, relate closely to questions of stakes. In service of these ends, what we might call a variable tactics of comparison may work to foreground difference, discontinuity, dissonance, change over time, or specificity, or else to foreground similarity, sameness, stability through time, or generic qualities.

Finally, work is required to make things *comparable*: to delimit objects, to draw or erase boundaries; to distinguish what is essential from what is imagined to be secondary or irrelevant, information from noise; to put things into or take them out of a context. We might say that projects of comparison involve not just work but a kind of productive *violence*: severing, trimming, uprooting, forcing together, and cramming into taxonomic boxes. We may overlook this work and this violence when they say things are or are not comparable. (Moreover, a tension exists in our language: to say things are "comparable" is sometimes to affirm that they are *worthy* of comparison – which can itself mean many things – and sometimes to affirm a more or less significant shared *similarity*.) In the end, we cannot compare things simply "as they are"; nor (despite what we may colloquially say) do things "invite" or "warrant" comparison outside the mediations of language and culture. A whole range of practices of abstraction, distinction, distillation, and classification are required to make messy objects like "Ptolemaic cosmology," "Japanese particle detectors," "African traditional thought," and "eugenics" into more or less bounded,

---

"stronger" version they proposed: "an ethnographic project pursued within a domestic context that from its inception has a substantive relationship to some body of ethnography elsewhere" (p. 162).

[4] Of course, it is also possible to eschew comparative work altogether, to find it uninteresting or suspect. For a discussion of disciplinary *hostility* to comparison, see Eilberg-Schwartz (1990), and especially Chapter 4, on the history and possible futures of comparative approaches to the study of religion.

consistent, and stable *things* that can be compared with *other things*. Rather than say things are comparable or incomparable, or that a comparison is warranted or unwarranted, we might instead ask if a comparison is productive or unproductive. But even here, we must always ask, productive of what, for whom, and in relation to what goals?

Comparative ethnographic studies of science and technology have, until recently, been few and far between (see the section entitled The Challenge of Cross-Cultural Comparison) and the potential of comparative work has rarely been theorized in the literature of science and technology studies (STS).[5] This is especially surprising because STS draws on a range of disciplines and interdisciplines (such as anthropology, history, literary studies, media studies, political science, and sociology) that have well-established comparative traditions, and because comparison is central to the work of many scientists and engineers.[6] Indeed, a number of questions that are central to STS might properly be said to *hinge* on comparisons: questions about the nature and distinctiveness of the work scientists and engineers do, about scientific change and technical innovation, about the policing of boundaries between science and other forms of knowledge, about the production of identity and difference, and about the local effects of global processes and regimes of power.

The following outline cannot pretend to be exhaustive, and is limited to work produced by scholars in Europe and the United States. I have organized the discussion along three threads: historical, epistemological, and cultural. These are somewhat arbitrary and intersect in many places; I mean them to give a sense of the work that comparison has done, is doing now, and might do in the future in studies of science and technology. In particular, I want to foreground the ability of careful comparative work to

---

[5] A notable exception is the discussion by Jasanoff (1986, pp. 1–8). By contrast, fields such as literary and religious studies regularly consider the stakes of comparison. On comparative literature, see Bernheimer (1994) and Damrosch (2006), as well as other contributions to *Comparative Critical Studies 3*. On the comparative study of religion, see Smith (1982), as well as the responses in Patton and Ray (2000).

[6] The varied uses of comparison *within* the sciences and engineering are beyond the scope of this essay. A complete treatment would include both explicitly comparative projects (e.g., comparative anatomy, studies of racial and sexual difference, and risk assessment) as well as the uses of metaphor and analogy in scientific work.

On the making of categories of sex and sexuality, see Laqueur (1992), Schiebinger (1987, 1993), Fausto-Sterling (2000), and Terry (1999). On racial categories, see Mansfield and Guthman (2015), Tamarkin (2014), and Harding (1993). On metaphors in science, see Brown (2003), Figlio (1976), Kuhn (1979), and Martin (1987, 1991). For a much earlier treatment of this question, see Fraser Harris (1912). On analogy, see Stepan (1986). For a philosophical treatment of analogic thinking more generally, see Hesse (1966). A narrower discussion of the topic (focused on similarities of structure and form) can be found in Oppenheimer (1958).

open new questions for STS, to challenge and disrupt what we take for granted, and to make it possible to imagine different scientific and technological worlds.

## 2.2  Historical Studies of Science and Technology: Comparison and Discontinuity

Even the most Whiggish histories of science and technology – the kinds that might appear in an introductory science textbook – have an *implicitly* comparative dimension to the extent that, in imagining a steady progress and ineluctable movement toward the present – and beyond this into an imagined future – they constitute the past as prologue, or else characterize it as a time of relative ignorance and error.[7] As Ken Alder (2002) put it, "the scientific winners write the account in such a way as to make their triumph an inevitable outcome of the righteous logic of their cause" (p. 301). Similarly, linear histories of technology, including some Marxist histories, position nonindustrial societies from the past (and from the non-Western present) as *pre-* or *proto*-industrial.[8] J. D. Bernal's *Science in History*, a four-volume work first published in 1954, mapped science in relation to changes in the means of production and the productive relations to which these gave rise. Bernal, an X-ray crystallographer by training, set out to explore the reciprocal influences of science and society – a project he imagined to be in the service of developing more socially responsible forms of science. Bernal shared with many liberal historians the view that science is cumulative and progressive, following a "definite succession" (Bernal, 1969, p. 1:44).[9] Even when such histories are critical rather than optimistic or triumphalist – when, for example, they chart the spread of authoritarian technics at the expense of democratic technics (Mumford, 1964)[10] or when they offer feminist critiques of the changing relations of women and machines (see, e.g., Cowan, 1983; Wajcman, 2004) – they may depend

---

[7] On the idea of Whiggish history, see Butterfield (1931). Ironically, Butterfield's own intervention in history of science adopted a rather Whiggish point of view (Butterfield, 1951). Also see Jardine (2003).

[8] Adas (1989) engaged comparison on two levels: the ways stories told about technology worked to distinguish Europeans from others and the ways these stories changed from one historical context to another.

[9] For Bernal, human history was divisible into distinct stages, each marked by the appearance of some new material technique (stone, bronze, iron, steam, atomic power), which in turn gave rise to (and was changed by) new sciences.

[10] Although not known as a "comparativist," Lewis Mumford frequently used comparison to great effect – for example, in his brief but rightly famous discussion of time reckoning before and after the introduction of the mechanical clock (Mumford, 1934, pp. 12–18).

on staging comparisons between historical moments. But comparison has
a more explicit and disruptive role in histories that emphasize *dis*continuity, that confront pasts and the present to foreground difference, to disrupt
or defamiliarize that which is taken for granted, to highlight contingency
and accident (also see Feyerabend, 1975).

### 2.2.1   Alternative Histories

Joseph Needham (1900–1995), an embryologist and sinologist, used the
history of science and technology in China to challenge the ethnocentrism
of earlier historians of Western science and to call into question their
unilinear narratives. "It has been natural," Needham generously suggested,
"for western Europeans to work backward from modern science and
technology, tracing the evolution of scientific thought to the experiences
and achievements of Mediterranean antiquity." But earlier histories had
betrayed a "bland unconsciousness of even the existence of the contributions of other peoples to the history of man's understanding of his environment" (Needham, 1954, p. 3).[11] As Needham described it, the project
begun in 1938 – to write a systematic history of Chinese scientific thought
and technology – initially centered on this "essential problem": that
"modern science had not developed in Chinese civilization (or Indian)
but only in Europe" (Needham, 1969, p. 190).[12] Here Needham echoed
Max Weber's project on capitalism: for Weber (2001), modern science, like
capitalism, was among the "cultural phenomena" that had appeared "in
Western civilization, and Western civilization only" and that "(as we like to
think) lie in a line of development having *universal* significance and
value."[13] But Needham was quickly led by his studies to another comparative problem: "why, between the first century BC and the fifteenth
century AD, Chinese civilization was much *more* efficient than occidental
in applying natural knowledge to practical needs?" (Needham, 1969,
p. 190). Needham's list of early and world-changing Chinese achievements
was considerably longer than the famous trio of printing, gunpowder, and

---

[11] Needham cited in particular the early nineteenth-century work of William Wheeler.
[12] *Science and Civilization in China*, initiated by Needham, has since come to comprise seven volumes
    made up of twenty-seven books by various authors.
[13] Though "knowledge and observation of great refinement have existed elsewhere, above all in India,
    China, Babylonia, and Egypt," Weber (2001, p. xxviii) wrote, "only in the West does science exist at
    a stage of development which we recognize to-day as valid." Weber built his case for the peculiarity
    of the Western experience through detailed studies of ancient Judaism and the religions of China
    and India.

the magnetic compass cited by Francis Bacon in 1620 as central to the development of the West, and was not limited to the technological (Bacon, 1620, Book 1, aphorism 129). The answer to both questions lay, Needham supposed, in the social, intellectual, and economic structures of the different civilizations. The task of the historian was what he termed a "veritable titration of the culture of East and West" (Needham, 1969, p. 11). Far from seeing the development of Western science as inevitable, Needham was led by study of early Chinese achievements to regard the Western experience as needing a new kind of historical explanation (see also Huff, 2003). By the mid 1950s, the stakes were high:

> Today, though the "white man" may have put down his "burden" and even forgotten about it, are not Europeans, viewing the effects of modern science and technology in the complete transformation of the habitable globe, tempted too often to say to themselves that after all, this began in Europe with Galileo and Vesalius, and to conclude that Wisdom was born with us? (Needham, 1954, p. 9)

Needham modestly offered his history of Chinese science and technology as a "salutary correction of perspective" (p. 9).

### 2.2.2   Toward a Comparative Epistemology

In 1935, Ludwig Fleck (1896–1961) used the history of changing concepts of syphilis (moral, religious, and scientific) to develop a "comparative epistemology" – more precisely, a comparative study of "thought collectives" (*Denkkollektive*) and "thought styles" (*Denkstile*; Fleck, 1979). Fleck imagined cognition as (necessarily) the result of a social activity, so science did not stand outside the social domain or beyond sociological analysis, as others might have assumed (Fleck, 1979, p. 38).[14] For Fleck, comparative epistemology led to a rejection of any distinction between *bad* and *good* thinking and of stories that would chart the gradual displacement of the first by the second (see, for example, the discussion below of Lévy-Bruhl). In place of these, Fleck proposed the comparative study of the varied styles that collectives generate, through time and across disciplines: "A stylistic bond exists between many, if not all, concepts of a period, based on their mutual influence" (Fleck, 1979, p. 9). Styles, in Fleck's formulation, both enable and constrain thinking (precisely because subjects are not

---

[14] Latour (2005, p. 112) argues that Fleck might be considered the "founder of the sociology of science." As Latour reminds us, Fleck accused other sociologists of "an excessive respect, bordering on pious reverence, for scientific facts" (p. 39).

consciously aware of the work of constraint).[15] In science as elsewhere, ways of making sense are obliged to take particular forms that are bounded and discontinuous; concepts may not easily circulate across the epistemological boundaries of collectives. Specialized knowledge does not simply *increase*, according to Fleck, but *changes* and takes historically distinctive forms: the "readiness for one particular way of seeing and acting" gives way to another. The thought style of the modern natural sciences, Fleck argued, has its *own* specificity, characterized by a mood, a reverence to a specific ideal – "the ideal of objective truth, clarity, and accuracy. It consists in the *belief* that what is being revered can be achieved only in the distant, perhaps infinitely distant future; in the *glorification* of dedicating oneself to its service; in a definite *hero worship* and a distant *tradition*" (Fleck, 1979, p. 142). What might previously have been taken as self-evident, projected backward as timeless, or imagined as the inevitable result of a gradual process, Fleck revealed, by a comparative study, to be the contingent style peculiar to a thought collective situated in culture and history.

### 2.2.3    Comparison and Commensurability

In 1962, Thomas Kuhn (1922–1996) published *The Structure of Scientific Revolutions*.[16] Kuhn's study of change in science had its origins in an experience of interdisciplinarity: an "exposure to out-of-date scientific theory and practice that radically undermined [Kuhn's] basic conceptions about the nature of science and the reasons for its special success" (Kuhn, 1970, p. v).[17] Rejecting the versions of the history of science conveyed in textbooks – namely, that science develops by gradually accumulating the discoveries and inventions of individuals – Kuhn argued that no-longer-current views of nature cannot readily be labeled error or superstition, as they were "neither less scientific nor more the product of human idiosyncrasy than those current today" (Kuhn, 1970, p. 2). Here, science's past is no longer figured as error, or as nonscience, but as another *kind* of otherness – a mode of thinking and doing that we no longer take for granted (or could choose to) and that is incommensurate with what has displaced it.

---

[15] Fleck (1979, p. 108) wrote, "It is coercion of the strongest kind, because it appears in the guise of a self-evident necessity and is thus not even recognized as a coercive force."

[16] Kuhn (1970). For contemporary responses to the work, many of which take up issues of comparison and incommensurability, see Lakatos and Musgrave (1970).

[17] At the time of this exposure, Kuhn was helping to teach an experimental course on physics for nonphysicists. Later, he would engage the disciplines of psychology, linguistics, and philosophy as a junior fellow at Harvard. For a recent reappraisal of Kuhn's work that calls productively into question his appreciation of his own historical context, see Fuller (2010).

In fact, Kuhn developed a second kind of comparison, also shaped by his encounter with the humanities and the social sciences. Kuhn (1970) was struck by the notion that, in science, in contrast to humanistic and social-scientific disciplines, certain kinds of debate come to an *end* – that there can be, for extended periods of time, a kind of tacit agreement on funda-mental questions, on what counts as evidence, on the reliability of instru-ments, and on the relevance of certain techniques of measurement. Sciences, he argued – or at least mature versions of them – develop and rely on "paradigms" (p. viii) in ways that art history or psychology do not.[18] As with Fleck's (1979) thought styles, paradigms are always particular or specific: they enable and constrain scientific thinking (indeed, they enable thinking *by* constraining it).[19] On this account, setting *particular kinds* of limits is the condition of possibility of normal science, which Kuhn likened to solving paradigm-specific puzzles or to fitting nature (sometimes vio-lently or blindly) into the conceptual boxes a paradigm provides.[20] When anomalies can no longer be managed in this way and a crisis ensues, one paradigm gives way to another in a moment of revolutionary change.

The distinctiveness of the frameworks that organize fields is most evident, Kuhn suggested, when the assumptions of paradigms are them-selves *compared*; for example, Aristotle's and Galileo's descriptions of the motion of pendulums, or Ptolemy's and Copernicus's assumptions about the movements of celestial bodies. Kuhn argued that shifts in assumptions are neither cumulative nor, strictly speaking, corrective, but rather more like abrupt changes in *world view*: "In so far as their only recourse to that world is through what they see and do, we may want to say that after a revolution scientists are responding to a different world" (Kuhn, 1970, p. 111). Here and elsewhere, Kuhn struggled to find a metaphor that could capture the dislocations that attend scientific revolutions: they are, Kuhn variously suggested, like perceptual (Gestalt) shifts or religious conver-sions, and the proponents of competing paradigms are like the speakers of different languages. But if paradigms can be compared in this sense, Kuhn

---

[18] Ironically, Kuhn's notion of paradigms has frequently been used to make sense of the histories of disciplines *outside* the sciences – fields Kuhn imagined to *lack* the kinds of tacit agreement about fundamentals that paradigms signal and reproduce.

[19] On Kuhn's debt to Fleck, see Kuhn's foreword to Fleck (1979, pp. vii–xi). Latour (2005, p. 112), however, cautions against reading Fleck only through a Kuhnian lens.

[20] Kuhn (1970, p. 64) famously compared scientists' inability to recognize results that are inconsistent with a prevailing paradigm to the kinds of "blindness" revealed by anomalous card experiments conducted by perceptual psychologists: "In science, as in the playing card experiment, novelty emerges only with difficulty, manifested by resistance, against a background provided by expectation."

suggested they cannot readily be measured against one another. Because they do not share assumptions about how the world is put together, divides itself, moves, or can be quantified, competing paradigms may be "incommensurable" and their supporters may be liable to talk past each other: "The competition between paradigms is not the sort of battle that can be resolved by proofs" (Kuhn, 1970, p. 148).[21]

### 2.2.4   Media Environments

Though they fall outside the discipline of history, Marshall McLuhan's (1911–1980) studies of media (and of technologies generally, as the lines between the two are never firmly drawn) depend on historical narratives that seek to disrupt or denaturalize common sense. McLuhan's idiosyncratic coauthored work *The Medium Is the Massage* – a book that, among other things, challenged its own status as a book – set up comparisons of different "media environments," which McLuhan characterized as active and invisible "processes" rather than "passive wrappings" (McLuhan & Fiore, 1981, p. 68). McLuhan's rather fanciful and abstract chronology posited two important shifts: the first from the oral and aural culture characteristic of nonalphabetic societies to a print culture, and the second from print culture to a world structured by "electric" media (principally television). Each shift, on McLuhan's account, produced dramatic – even violent – disruptions: "All media work us over completely . . . they leave no part of us untouched, unaffected, unaltered" (McLuhan & Fiore, 1981, p. 26). For McLuhan, media produced these effects independently of their contents – thus, "the medium is the message." Just as railroads "created totally new urban, social, and family worlds" regardless of what the train cars carried,[22] so the printing press and the television reconfigured social relations in ways that exceeded the meaning of the stories they conveyed (McLuhan & Fiore, 1981, p. 72).[23]

Technologies of the alphabet and print (along with artistic innovations such as perspectival easel painting) contributed, McLuhan argued, to the making of individualism, privacy, detachment, fragmentation, and

---

[21] On discontinuity in the history of science and the philosophical problem of incommensurability, also see Feyerabend (1975). Feenberg (2010) explored the implications of Kuhn's work for theorizing technology and technological histories.

[22] McLuhan (1994, pp. 8–9) made a similar point about the lightbulb, which he described as a medium without content.

[23] See also the comparison between pedestrian and automotive worlds that opens Winner's (1986, pp. 8–9) book. Turkle (2012) took up similar themes in comparing the ways telephones and text messages mediate social relationships.

specialization, whereas electric media promised new kinds of connection and community – a "global village" that returned us to acoustic space and recuperated the "primordial feeling, the tribal emotions from which a few centuries of literacy divorced us" (McLuhan & Fiore, 1981, p. 63). Again, it was comparison – for example, of the experience of reading a book in private with watching John F. Kennedy's funeral on television – that made visible the specific relations of subjects, spaces, and values that were characteristic of particular stages in the history of media, and that opened up for evaluation new political possibilities (as well as attendant dangers).[24] What might to some have seemed natural, or the endpoint of an ineluctable development (individualism, practices of reading, the privileging of vision), was made into the strange (and estranging) effects of a transient technology.

### 2.2.5   Histories of the Present

The discontinuous histories of the human sciences produced by Michel Foucault (1926–1984) arose from an intellectual and political engagement with his own present (France of the 1960s–1980s).[25] Foucault was influenced by the work of philosopher of science Gaston Bachelard and Marxist theorist Louis Althusser (and, in particular, by their attention to epistemological ruptures or breaks (*coupures*)), by George Canguilhem's history of concepts, and by Nietzsche's genealogical method.[26] Foucault referred to his earlier projects as "archaeological" – they sought to excavate the structures of fields of knowledges, the discursive formations or *epistemes* that made thought *possible* in specific historical eras. In *The Order of Things*, an archaeology of human sciences in the West, Foucault mapped the *epistemes* that organized inquiry into nature, language, and the economy in the Renaissance, the "classical era," and modernity (Foucault, 1970). Foucault outlined a discontinuous history, marked by breaks and

---

[24] Electric media, for example, not only made possible the global village, but also "tyrannical womb-to -tomb surveillance" (McLuhan & Fiore, 1981, p. 12). For the (sometimes comparative) study of the politics built into artifacts, see Winner (1986). Winner's analysis owed more to Mumford than to McLuhan and was suspicious of forms of technological determinism, a charge frequently brought to bear on McLuhan's work.

[25] Foucault's work has shaped other recent histories and anthropologies of the human sciences, from psychology and sexology to social hygiene and urban planning. See, for examples, Horn (2003), Inda (2006), Rabinow (1995), Rose (1996), and Terry (1999).

[26] See, for example, Bachelard (1972) and Althusser (1969). On the idea of the "break," also see Balibar (1978). Canguilhem's approach to the history of scientific concepts is sketched out in the essays collected in Canguilhem (1988). For Foucault's elucidation of the genealogical method, see especially Foucault (1978b).

shifts in problems, rationalities, and objects – from the Renaissance problem of mimesis, to the classical problem of representation, to the modern
problem of "man."

In later work, Foucault turned increasingly to a genealogical approach to
produce what he called "histories of the present." Modeled on Nietzsche's
genealogy of morality, these works turned to the past not to seek the *origins*
of the present – at least not in a way that would point to its inevitability – but
to mark the specificity of contemporary articulations of knowledge and
power. The remarkable juxtaposition that opens *Discipline and Punish*
(Foucault, 1977) is perhaps the most vivid example: the extravagant, public
destruction of the body of the would-be regicide Robert-François Damiens
in 1757 is set alongside a schedule from a nineteenth century "house for
young prisoners" that organizes a quite different disposition of bodies,
punishment, and architecture (Foucault, 1977, pp. 3–8). Foucault did not
present this as a story of gradual progress – of the displacement of less
humane by more humane technologies – but as a shift in regimes of truth
and power. Taking its origin in the prison unrest in 1970s France, this history
of the present was meant to make visible and to denaturalize the forms of
disciplinary power that emerge in modernity, spreading well beyond the
prison, and to loosen the hold of a juridical theory of power (centered on the
negative, repressive power of the king) that Foucault argued had misled us
about how power and knowledge operate today. In *The History of Sexuality*,
Foucault (1978a) took up the specificity and strangeness of Western sciences
of sexuality and technologies of the self, and traced the emergence of
biopolitics. In a second volume, Foucault (1985) set up a contrast with
ancient Greece: the point was not that sexuality had not been a problem
for the Greeks, but that it had been a different *kind* of problem. Foucault
proposed a history of "problematizations," of the ways sex (or crime or
madness, for example) were made into particular kinds of scientific and
governmental problems (Foucault, 1985).

## 2.3   Science and Its "Others"

Alongside these historiographical debates, and often in conversation with
them, a range of other scholars raised questions about the specificity of
science and technology – about whether they demand to be known
*differently*, even requiring their own disciplines, or may be studied in the
same ways as other kinds of human social activity. Science has often been
defined in part by what it is imagined *not* to be: irrational, primitive,
religious, subjective, qualitative, cultural, social, or political.

## 2.3.1 Science and "Primitive Thinking"

For many Western historians and anthropologists, it has been important to locate science in relation to other forms of knowledge, both as part of science's prehistory and as part of a contested terrain of ways of thinking and doing during and after colonialism. In *How Natives Think*, published in French in 1910, Lucien Lévy-Bruhl (1857–1939) imagined a fundamental difference between science, characteristic of Western modernity, and "primitive thinking" (Lévy-Bruhl, 1925).[27] For Lévy-Bruhl, if it was true that "there are aggregates of human beings who differ from each other in construction as invertebrate animals differ from vertebrates, a comparative study of the various types of collective mentality is just as indispensable to anthropology as comparative anatomy and physiology are to biology" (pp. 28–29). To bring out the features of primitive thinking, Lévy-Bruhl proposed to compare that mentality with "*our own*, i.e., with that of races which are the product of 'Mediterranean' civilization, in which a rationalistic philosophy and positive science have been developed" (Lévy-Bruhl, 1925, pp. 28–29). For comparative purposes, he suggested, choosing mental types marked by "the greatest differences" had an advantage.

When compared with modern science, Lévy-Bruhl argued, primitive thinking is mystical, illogical or *pre*-logical, and relatively indifferent to the problem of contradiction.[28] The thinking of non-Western others was, he said, marked by a variety of absences, lacks, or incapacities; for example, incapacities for dispassionate observation, speculative thought, and understanding the relations of causes and effects.[29] These deficiencies were not limited to indigenous peoples of Africa and the Americas:

> Chinese scientific knowledge affords a striking example of ... arrested development. It has produced immense encyclopædias of astronomy, physics, chemistry, physiology, pathology, therapeutics and the like, and to our minds all this is nothing but balderdash. How can so much effort and skill have been expended in the long courses of ages, and their product be absolutely nil? (Lévy-Bruhl, 1925, p. 380)

Lévy-Bruhl asked similar questions of Indian science and medicine.

---

[27] The original title was *Les fonctions mentales dans les sociétés inférieures*.

[28] For a more generous reading of Lévy-Bruhl, and an otherwise thoughtful treatment of the relations of magic, science, and religion, see Tambiah (1990).

[29] Lévy-Bruhl rejected the positions of Frazer, Tylor, and other "English anthropologists" who did allow the possibility of a *logic* to "primitive" thinking about spirits. Tylor (1903, pp. 108–109), for example, wrote, "It was no spontaneous fancy, but the reasonable inference that effects are due to causes, which led the rude men of old days to people with such ethereal phantoms their own homes and haunts, and the vast earth and sky beyond. Spirits are simply personified causes."

To the extent that Lévy-Bruhl believed comparative work had something to teach Westerners about *themselves*, it was about the persistence of
the illogical, the mystical, and the irrational in the modern world.
Comparative study "leads us to recognize that the rational unity of the
thinking being, which is taken for granted by philosophers, is
a *desideratum*, not a fact" (Lévy-Bruhl, 1925, p. 386).

### 2.3.2   Magic, Science, and Religion

A variety of anthropological and historical projects can be read as
responses to the provocations of Lévy-Bruhl. In a 1925 essay that compared magic, science, and religion, Bronisław Malinowski (1884–1942;
1954) took on the notion that "primitive man has no sober moods at all,
that he is hopelessly and completely immersed in a mystical frame of
mind" (p. 25). Malinowski posed two questions. First, "has the savage any
rational outlook, any rational mastery of his surroundings?" Drawing
primarily on work in Melanesia, Malinowski found unequivocally that
"the savage" did (p. 26).[30] Second, "can this primitive knowledge be
regarded as a rudimentary form of science?" Here, Malinowski's answer
was more equivocal or guarded[31] and, in the end, the question was made
less urgent by the discovery of two distinct domains of savage reality:
a "profane world of practical activities and rational outlook" that existed
alongside "a sacred region of cult and belief" (pp. 35–36). For
Malinowski, comparison revealed that magic and religion were not the
*antitheses* of science; rather, each had their proper domains, techniques,
and objects. Magic shared with science (but not religion) the goal of
"attainment of practical aims."[32] But together with religion, magic was
proper to the domain of the sacred, whereas science (or "rational knowledge") was proper to the domain of the profane. Malinowski was insistent
on the *specificity* of the work done by alternate forms of knowledge and
technology:

> As a matter of empirical fact the body of rational knowledge and the body of
> magical lore are incorporated each in a different tradition, in a different

---

[30] Malinowski (1954, p. 26) also cited A. A. Goldenweiser to affirm a kind of "primitive" *technical*
expertise: "it would be unwise to ascribe to the primitive mechanic merely a passive part in the
origination of inventions."
[31] "If we applied another criterion yet, that of the really scientific attitude, the disinterested search for
knowledge and for the understanding of causes and reasons, the answer would certainly not be in
a direct negative" (Malinowski, 1954, p. 35).
[32] Malinowski (1954, p. 87) followed Frazer (2012, p. 113) in describing magic as a "pseudo-science."

social setting and in a different type of activity, and all of these differences are clearly recognized by the savages. (Malinowski, 1954, p. 87)[33]

### 2.3.3 Science and "African Traditional Thought"

Robin Horton (b. 1932), a British anthropologist of religion writing in the late 1960s, faulted Western scholars for failing to recognize the equivalents to theoretical thinking in other cultures (Horton, 1967, 1977). Blinded by differences in *idiom*, Horton argued, many had concluded that traditional religious thought was atheoretical and nonempirical. Horton constructed his comparison in a particular way, contrasting "traditional religious thought" and "traditional African thought" with modern Western thought, chiefly with Western science.[34] Horton focused first on "the features common to modern Western and traditional African thought" before turning to the enumeration of differences that "really do distinguish one kind of thought from the other" (Horton, 1977, p. 131). For Horton, explanatory theory, whether in Africa or elsewhere, seeks unity underlying apparent diversity, order underlying apparent disorder, and regularity underlying apparent anomaly. The questions posed by Lévy-Bruhl's (1925) "primitives" are, on this account, not different in *kind* from those posed by Western scientists; only the *idiom* is different. Gods and spirits are, in the explanatory work they do, like atoms and molecules, and the African's explanation of disease is like the physicist's explanation of the atomic bomb:

> Substitute "disease" for "mushroom cloud," "spirit anger" for "massive fusion of hydrogen nuclei," and "breach of kinship morality" for "assemblage and dropping of a bomb," and we are back with the diviner. In both cases reference to theoretical entities is used to link events in the visible,

---

[33] Also see Evans-Pritchard (1937, pp. 63–83). In the famous example of a collapsed granary, Evans-Pritchard countered the presumption that the Azande resorted to witchcraft because they lacked an understanding of cause and effect: "The Zande knows that the supports were undermined by termites and that people were sitting beneath the granary in order to escape the heat of the sun. But he knows *besides* why these two events occurred at a precisely similar moment in time and space. It was due to the action of witchcraft" (p. 70, emphasis added).

[34] Horton has rightly been criticized for flattening differences among African cultures, though later in the essay he focused more specifically on personal fieldwork among the Kalabari. In a similar fashion, Horton made science into a more or less homogenous cultural and historical phenomenon that was broadly characteristic of the West, though in the final sentence of the essay Horton (1977) conceded "the modern Western layman is rarely more 'open' or scientific in his outlook than is the traditional African villager" (p. 171). For an influential critical response to Horton, see Wiredu (1976).

tangible world (natural effects) to their antecedents in the same world (natural causes). (Horton, 1977, p. 136)

These two ways of moving beyond common sense, though not wholly alien to one another, also have their own specificities. For Horton, both are related to (and make analogies to) particular kinds of lived experience, characterized as impersonal in industrial societies and personal in African societies. One effect of this difference, Horton suggested, is the comparative inability of Western medicine to see relations between social disturbances and individual afflictions (Horton, 1977, p. 137). But more broadly, Horton found African cultures to be "closed" in comparison with the "open" cultures of Western science, which he imagined to be marked by a culturally specific attitude: a willingness (*pace* Kuhn) continually to acknowledge the possibility of alternative ways of making sense.[35] Horton followed Evans-Pritchard (and, to some extent, Lévy-Bruhl, 1925) in suggesting that the traditional African "cannot think his thought is wrong" (Evans-Pritchard, 1937, p. 194) and is reluctant to "register repeated failures of prediction," while affirming that science knows no such taboos (Horton, 1977, p. 162). If this seems simply a reaffirmation of the superiority of Western forms of knowledge, Horton also warned of science's dangerous faith in progress and of a loss of "an intensely poetic quality in everyday life and thought" (p. 162).[36]

### 2.3.4   Science and Religion

The opposition of science and religion has not, of course, been limited to comparisons between the West and the non-West. The dichotomy is also a familiar part of the political landscape in the United States and Europe, and of narratives that imagine a history of struggle between scientific knowledge and certain forms of Christianity. Emblematic of this struggle are Galileo's fight with the Catholic Church in seventeenth-century Italy and the ongoing contest between Darwinian biology and certain strains of US Protestantism. At the end of the nineteenth century, White (1832–1918) and Draper (1811–1882) described science as being "at war" with religion (Draper, 1874; White, 1896).[37] A broad range of triumphalist histories have imagined a gradual displacement of religion by science.

---

[35] In the longer version of his essay, Horton (1967) briefly addressed Kuhn's work, but downplayed the blind spots and anxiety that were, on Kuhn's account, associated with anomalous results.

[36] At the end of his essay, Horton (1977) expressed some sympathy for the ways Négritude theorists had characterized the differences between African and Western thought. For an assessment of the limits of science and a call for supplementing the scientific with the poetic, see Césaire (1945).

[37] Also see, for a more recent example of the "conflict" model, Russell (1997).

More recent scholarship has cast doubt on these models, contending instead that religion and science have complex and historically specific relations in different cultural contexts.[38] Historians have challenged the conventional narratives on Galileo and Darwin,[39] whereas scholars of religious studies have explored science in relation to other religious traditions – for example, Islam, Hinduism, and Buddhism (Dallal, 2010; Gottschalk, 2013; Hammerstrom, 2015; Huff, 2003). Bruno Latour (2010) characterized the whole field of "religion and science" as a "comedy of errors," arguing that we misunderstand both science and religion when we regard them as engaged in a territorial dispute:

> I find those disputes – whether there is one or two domains, whether it is hegemonic or parallel, whether polemical or peaceful – equally moot for this reason: They all suppose that science and religion have similar but divergent claims in reaching and settling a territory, either of this world or some other world. I believe on the contrary that there is no point of contact between the two. (p. 110)

Latour was especially suspicious of analyses that hinged on comparisons of belief and knowledge: "*belief is a caricature of religion exactly as knowledge is a caricature of science*" (p. 121, emphasis original).[40]

### 2.3.5 Two Cultures? Science and the Humanities

In a 1959 lecture delivered at Cambridge University, C. P. Snow (1905–1980), a chemist and novelist, identified two "cultures": an "intellectual" (and sometimes "traditional") culture, peopled mostly by British literature professors, and a scientific culture, characteristic especially of physical scientists (Snow, 1964).[41] Between the two, he argued, was a gulf marked by divergent values and mutual misunderstanding. The scientists he interviewed complained of struggling to read novels by Dickens, while the humanists he

---

[38] See, for example, Olson (2006), Brooke (1991), Lindberg and Numbers (1986), and Ferngren (2002). For a popular treatment, see the lively essays in Numbers (2009).

[39] On Galileo, see Biagioli (1993) and Dawes (2016). On Darwin and Darwinism, see Browne (1996), Larson (1997), and Livingstone (2014).

[40] Latour (2010) continued, "Belief is not a quasi-knowledge question *plus* a leap of faith to reach even *further* away; knowledge is not a quasi-belief question that would be answerable by looking directly at things close at hand" (pp. 121–122).

[41] Though it is less often remarked upon, Snow also compared the orientations of scientists and engineers, who again "often totally misunderstand each other." "Pure scientists" like Snow, had mostly been "dim witted" and condescending about engineers and applied science: "We prided ourselves that the science we were doing could not, in any conceivable circumstances, have any practical use" (Snow, 1964, pp. 31–32).

regularly quizzed at cocktail parties could not describe the Second Law of Thermodynamics. "I was asking something," Snow complained, "which is about the equivalent of: *Have you read a work of Shakespeare's*" (Snow, 1964, p. 15, emphasis original).[42] The groups had so little in common "in intellectual, moral and psychological climate" that "instead of going from Burlington House or South Kensington to Chelsea, one might have crossed an ocean" (p. 2). Snow saw the need to bridge or close this gulf as driven primarily by the centrality of industrial technology to modern life and its potential role in addressing growing global inequality.[43] Although the solutions Snow proposed were mostly reforms to national education, the burden to move to the middle seems to have fallen unevenly on the shoulders of humanists, whom he characterized as "natural Luddites." The optimism of scientists, he suggested, was by contrast one "that the rest of us badly need" (Snow, 1964, p. 7).[44]

Since Snow delivered his lecture, a variety of scholars have taken issue with his cultural geography,[45] some asserting, for example, that Western scientists and humanists are imbricated in *one* culture more than they are divided by two.[46] For George Levine (1987), Snow's formulation "implies a distinction that needs to be denied." Science, he argued, "is no more exempt from the constraints of nonspecialist culture than literature is; nor has it ever been" (p. 3).[47] Others, as we will see below, have suggested that science is not a monolithic transnational thing but takes particular shapes in a variety of local circumstances. We are faced, then, not with one culture or two, but many.

### 2.3.6   Science and Pseudoscience

Especially since the nineteenth century, the distinction between "real" and "spurious" science, or between science and pseudoscience, has helped scientists and science historians tell reassuring stories about the relations of knowledge, culture, and power. Pseudosciences have been

---

[42] Ironically, the concept of entropy has had profound consequences in the arts and humanities. See, for example, the discussion in Hayles (1990).

[43] For a different take on the relations of science and the humanities, see Bernal (1946).

[44] By contrast, Snow (1964) found a connection "between some kinds of early twentieth-century art and the most imbecile expressions of anti-social feeling" (p. 8).

[45] The most famous – indeed infamous – critique is that offered by Leavis (1962).

[46] The formation of the Society for Literature, Science, and the Arts (with its journal *Configurations*) is but one example of a new interest in exploring relations *among* what Snow imagined to be worlds apart.

[47] It is not clear that Snow was ever talking about culture in *this* sense.

imagined to require a different kind of accounting than sciences – one that is more about the intrusion of values better left at the laboratory door, about distortion or a bending away from the truth, about a pollution of the objective by the subjective. Put another way, this distinction – and the comparisons it sustains – has allowed human genetics to take its comfortable distance from eugenics, chemistry from alchemy, astronomy from astrology, psychiatry from phrenology, physics from "New Age" claims about the dangers of extra-low-frequency electromagnetic radiation.

A wide variety of historical studies – for example, of eugenics, criminal anthropology, and the sciences of racial hygiene – have sought to trouble this distinction, returning to moments when boundaries were blurred and when the proponents of what we now call pseudoscience held chairs in science departments at prestigious universities and published in the leading journals of medicine, biology, and chemistry (Horn, 2003; Keller, 2010; Proctor, 1988). But the distinction reasserts itself even in some studies that seek to overcome it. The best example, perhaps, is Stephen Jay Gould's *The Mismeasure of Man*: an important history and critique of biological determinism whose title already suggests a tension (between measurement and *mis*measurement, science and something else; Gould, 1996). Gould's study ranged from US craniometry to Italian criminology to French and US studies of IQ. From the outset, Gould (1941–2002) called into question easy binaries, refusing "to contrast evil determinists who stray from the path of scientific objectivity with enlightened antideterminists who approach data with an open mind and therefore see truth." Instead, Gould called the idea that science is an "objective enterprise" a "myth" (p. 53).

But Gould (1996) immediately proposed a new distinction, suggesting that some scientific subjects were "virtually free" from "constraints of fact," in part because they were invested with enormous social importance despite a paucity of "reliable data" (p. 54). Gould could take comfort in the knowledge that biological determinists relied on fallacious reasoning, measured less accurately, and understood statistics poorly; in short, they did science *badly*, even if they were not "bad scientists." Gould may not have called Cesare Lombroso a pseudoscientist, but could not resist calling Lombroso's arguments "scientifically vacuous" (p. 154).

More recently, Andrew Ross (b. 1956) argued that the line dividing science and varieties of New Age thought is not given in advance, but is a contested boundary, actively policed by professional organizations such as the Committee for Skeptical Inquiry (formerly CSICOP), which counted Carl Sagan among its founding members (Ross, 1991).[48] For Ross, New Age sciences and the resistance they provoke were symptoms of a crisis of scientific rationality and materialism at the end of the twentieth century. Ross drew on Latour to reframe the binary of "orthodox" and New Age science as an effect of moves made and networks established in demarcation debates. For Latour (1987), "Irrationality is always an accusation made by someone building a network over someone else who stands in the way" (p. 209). More broadly, Latour insisted on a symmetrical treatment of claims that come to be regarded as rational or irrational, objective or subjective, disinterested or interested, matters of knowledge or matters of belief. The difference between facts and other kinds of claims about the world, Latour argued, has nothing to do with the essential qualities of those statements, or of the people who make them, but with their *fate*, with the strength of networks – built of humans, laboratories, recording devices, animals, and others – that make some claims durable and able to move out into the world, and others less durable and less mobile.

## 2.4  The Challenge of Cross-Cultural Comparison

### 2.4.1  From Implicit to Explicit Comparisons

Beginning in the late twentieth century, a wide variety of scholars sought to move beyond the dichotomies of earlier generations, conducting historical and ethnographic studies of forms of scientific and medical knowledge and technical practice in specific cultural contexts. These have included attention to indigenous knowledges or what used to be counted as *ethno*-astronomies, *ethno*-botanies, or *ethno*-pharmacologies. That prefix has been troubled by efforts to reimagine the sciences of the *West* as ethnosciences – that is, as no less shaped by local languages and cultures.

One of the best examples is the field of medical anthropology; indeed, two of the essays that might be said to mark the coming of age of the field in the 1970s, by George Foster (1976) and Arthur Kleinman (1978), committed medical anthropology to comparative work.[49] More often than not, this has not taken the form of extensive, cross-national comparisons, but has instead relied on detailed ethnographic studies in single sites to make sense of nonbiomedical traditions, of the interactions of these with

---

[48] CSI continues to publish *The Skeptical Inquirer*.
[49] Foster's (1976) binary of "personalistic" and "naturalistic" explanations of disease built on the work of Horton.

biomedicine, or of the ways new medical technologies (e.g., techniques of assisted reproduction) are taken up in varied national contexts.[50] But at the same time that medical anthropology works to make the strange familiar, it also frequently makes the familiar strange. Even if, as Margaret Lock (1993) suggested, anthropologists frequently "implicitly measure local knowledge against the 'facts' of science" (p. 331) and find them wanting, the study of non-Western nosologies, etiologies, ways of imagining the body, and ways of using and resisting new technologies can reveal the cultural and historical specificity of biomedicine's own ways of doing and making sense. This point has been driven home by edited volumes that have, for example, juxtaposed Western and non-Western constructions of affective disorders or variations in the experience and narration of pain (Good, Brodwin, Good, & Kleinman, 1992; Kleinman & Good, 1985), but has been implicit in a wide range of other studies. Paul Farmer's (1992) work on AIDS/*sida* in Haiti has, for example, explored not only the local logics of sorcery and "sent sickness," but also the histories of colonialism and the racialized politics of accusation that have shaped the Haitian experience of disease. Janice Boddy's (1988) study of the therapeutics of trance in a Sudanese village analyzed spirit possession among married women as an effect of overdetermined gender roles, but also called into question the universality of Western taxonomies of psychiatric disorders.

Beyond medical anthropology, a number of recent ethnographic studies examined local instantiations of global technologies. These, too, have often been implicitly comparative, in the sense that they refuse to rely on – or they otherwise challenge – models derived from the experience of the West to make sense of articulations of science and technology with diverse urban and rural communities (Choy, 2011; Coleman, 2017; Masco, 2006; Petryna, 2002; Srinivas, 2001; Wade, López Beltrán, Restrepo, & Ventura Santos, 2014). Comparative cultural and historical studies of scientific discourse have, meanwhile, looked at the playing out of particular scientific and technical projects in multiple cultural contexts (Adams, 1990; Pick, 1993; Porter, 1995; Turda & Gillette, 2014). Donna Haraway, for example, interrupted a story about US primatology in *Primate Visions* with a discussion of primate studies in Japan, India, and Africa to highlight the specificity of the cultural and political work nonhuman primates are called on to do in the United States. Mapping the "biopolitics of a multicultural field," Haraway (1989, pp. 244–278) noted that Japanese primatologists, for

---

[50] See the several volumes authored by Inhorn, most recently in 2015.

example, do not share with their US counterparts a dream of encountering in primates "the untouched heart of nature."

### 2.4.2   Laboratory Lives: The United States and Japan

One of the first projects to undertake a systematic, comparative ethnography of science was Sharon Traweek's *Beamtimes and Lifetimes*, first published in 1988. Building on a then-new interest in laboratory studies,[51] Traweek undertook the difficult work of doing fieldwork in more than one place, living among high-energy physicists at the Stanford Linear Accelerator in California and at the High-Energy Accelerator Research Organization in Japan. Traweek argued that, although US high-energy physicists elaborate and inhabit a culture of "no culture," imagining that what they do stands outside of culture and travels easily across national boundaries, the ways they lived and worked were shaped by their particular historical and cultural contexts, as were those of their Japanese counterparts.[52]

Traweek (1988) was interested in the ways national cultures shape the making of buildings and machines, of research projects, and of physicists themselves.[53] The particle detectors at the center of the work of high-energy physicists were structured by differential access to government funding, by local styles of work, even by aesthetics. "In the features of a detector," she argued, "we can learn to read a group's history, its division of labor, its strategy for discovery" (p. x). A good US detector, Traweek showed, is one that is specialized, modifiable, and always in danger of ceasing to work (a sign that it is on the cutting edge), whereas a good Japanese detector is one built to be multipurpose, reliable, and durable. The machines the workgroups built not only materialized different values, but were also mobilized to do different kinds of work: in the US case, to discover new particles and, in the Japanese case, to collect more refined data on previously discovered particles (Traweek, 1988, p. 71).

Traweek also followed the rites of passage that mark changes in a scientist's status and that reproduce community-specific values. In the US case, for example, "Social eccentricity and childlike egotism were

---

[51] Latour and Woolgar's (1979) path-breaking *Laboratory Life* had appeared in 1979.

[52] Interestingly, Traweek (1988) reported that Japanese physicists – "quite conscious of belonging to an emergent scientific community" (p. 14) – were, on the whole, more interested in cultural differences than their US counterparts.

[53] Latour (1990) faulted Traweek (1988) for reliance on a Durkheimian notion of culture. In later work, Latour (1993) argued that the proper objects of comparison are "nature-cultures."

cultivated displays of commitment to rationality, objectivity, and science" (Traweek, 1988, p. 91). Traweek contrasted the dominant metaphors that organize the workplace in the two laboratories: the *ie* or extended family at the Japanese High-Energy Accelerator Research Organization (where status was "determined by age, not by competition, [and] there is no strict division of labor") and the sports team at the Stanford Linear Accelerator (where the "coach" was empowered to design the team strategies and the team survived only as long as it was "winning" (Traweek, 1988, pp. 148–152). Finally, Traweek used comparison to make sense of the systematic exclusion of women from both physics communities: in the United States, physics was imagined to require competitiveness and women were imagined to be too cooperative, whereas, in Japan, doing good physics was thought to require cooperation and women were imagined to be too competitive (Traweek, 1988, p. 104). But all of this escaped notice, Traweek argued, in a culture of "extreme objectivity: a culture of no culture, which longs passionately for a world without loose ends, without temperament, gender, nationalism, or other sources of disorder – a world outside human space and time" (Traweek, 1988, p. 162).

### 2.4.3   Local Biologies

Margaret Lock (b. 1936; 2002) also constructed a comparison between North America and Japan in *Twice Dead* to explore the divergent histories and contemporary politics of cadaveric organ donation. Although we might have been tempted to explain the differences asymmetrically – by invoking Japanese culture (survivals from an archaic past lurking in Japanese modernity) to account for a failure to embrace new medical possibilities – Lock argued that we need symmetrical explanations that account also for North America's ready acceptance of new ways of being dead and of sustaining life (p. 5). Here, as in earlier work on the non-identity of menopause and *kōnenki* (a term Lock glossed as "change of life"), Lock chose to compare two cultures "saturated with scientific knowledge and its practice," throwing into relief differences in nosologies, in imagined geographies of the body, and in the material experiences of illness and death – what she has called "local biologies" (p. 303).

As Lock documented, in an account that combined cultural history and multisite ethnography, the first heart transplant performed by Christiaan Barnard in South Africa in 1967 led quickly – despite the ethical and medical questions it raised – to an explosion of interest in cadaveric transplantation in the West and to a redefinition of death (brain death) in the United States in

1968. In Japan, however, the transplant performed by Jiro Wada in 1968 was followed by a nearly 30-year moratorium on cadaveric transplants, and brain death was recognized only in 1997. As Lock (2002) observed, we cannot explain this difference by "a Japanese lack of education, technology, skills, or economic resources" (p. 4), nor simply by the controversy that surrounded the Wada case. Instead, both the North American embrace of cadaveric transplantation and Japanese resistance and indifference were effects of local cultures. In each case, transplantation could be read as a constellation of technology (primarily the ventilators that make possible "living cadavers," but also the guns and automobiles that, in the West, assure a steady supply of brain-dead donors), law, gift-giving practices, histories of anatomical dissection, ideas of the body and death, and the trust placed in medical professionals. In the end, each outcome was made to appear equally strange, equally contingent rather than inevitable. It is this challenge to common sense that raised, at least for North American readers of Lock's book, new questions about present and future possible articulations of dead bodies, medical science and technology, and the living.

### 2.4.4    From Comparative Policy Studies to Sociotechnical Imaginaries

Beyond history and anthropology (although, as with much of the work in STS, disciplinary boundaries tend to be porous), a wide range of studies has focused on national and local differences in the regulation of science and technology, on the management of risk, and on political resistance to new scientific and technological regimes. Drawing particularly on the disciplines of comparative politics, policy studies, and sociology of science and technology, many of these studies move beyond assessments of local "impacts," exploring science and technology as what Winner (1986) called "ways of life," with implications for political practice and social justice. Some are implicitly comparative (Baviskar, Sinha, & Philip, 2006; Fonseca & Santos Pereira, 2014; Hecht, 2010), whereas others involve more than one national site.[54] Much of this work has focused on the intersection of technological risk, science, and governmental regulation, and the majority of multisite studies have staged comparisons among Western nations.[55]

---

[54] For some examples, see Brickman, Jasanoff, and Ilgen (1985), Daemmrich (2004), Kelman (1981), and Vogel (1986).

[55] For an early survey of the field that makes a case for the value of comparison, see Jasanoff (1986): "Cross-national analysis helps define the boundaries between the scientific and transscientific aspects of risk management and illustrates the methods that policy makers can adopt in dealing with issues at the borderline of science and politics" (p. 5).

Topics have ranged from the development and deployment of genetic tests for breast and ovarian cancer in the United States and Britain (Parthasarathy, 2007) to antinuclear movements in France and Germany (Nelkin & Pollak, 1982) to drug regulation in Germany and the United States (Daemmrich, 2004).

Sheila Jasanoff developed some of the most sustained comparative projects in a variety of national contexts. Her 2005 study, *Designs on Nature*, compared biotechnology in the United States and Europe (Germany and the United Kingdom). Jasanoff mapped entanglements of knowledge, technical capability, politics, and culture. At the end of study, she suggested that comparison provides a productive "angle of vision" on the relations of science and politics:

> It is not the divine prerogative of producing universally valid principles of knowledge or governance that comparison should strive for. It is to make visible the normative implications of different forms of contemporary scientific and political life, and to show what is at stake, for knowing and reasoning human beings, in seeking to inhabit them. (p. 291)

In *Dreamscapes of Modernity*, Jasanoff and coauthor Sang-Hyun Kim (2015) proposed the comparative study of what they call "sociotechnical imaginaries." Jasanoff defined these as "collectively held, institutionally stabilized, and publicly performed visions of desirable futures, animated by shared understandings of forms of social life and social order attainable through, and supportive of, advances in science and technology" (p. 5).[56] The authors' project was to attend to the subjective and psychological elements of agency and to "the structured hardness" of technological systems and political cultures. Their method of choice was once again *comparison*:

> comparing across social and political structures not only helps to identify the content and contours of sociotechnical imaginaries, but also avoids the intellectual trap of taking as universal epistemic and ethical assumptions that turn out, on investigation, to be situated and particular. (Jasanoff, 2015, p. 24)

The study of these imaginaries has not been limited to national comparisons, but includes attention to local manifestations of transnational processes and to their uneven effects in single national contexts (Bhadra, 2013; Felt, Fochler, & Winkler, 2010; Jasanoff, 2015; Jasanoff & Kim, 2013).

---

[56] For an earlier definition, see Jasanoff and Kim (2009). The authors found the adjective "sociotechnical" better suited to their goal of moving beyond the scientific workplace and its individual actors than Marcus's (1995) closely related concept of "technoscientific" imaginaries.

## 2.5  Conclusion: Comparative Futures

Comparison has been called on to perform a wide variety of work in studies of science and technology: to pursue diverse goals using varied techniques. At the heart of many of these projects has been a desire to describe what science and technology have in common with other forms of human knowledge and human practice and what distinguishes them or gives them specificity. Both questions are in some sense questions about culture, though a consensus hardly exists about what culture is, how it stands in relation to science and technology, or how it might best be studied. Nor is there any guarantee that studies of the cultural embeddedness of ways of knowing and doing will produce particular kinds of results. But, as many of these examples show, comparative studies of science and technology (cross-cultural studies in particular) can be powerful engines to disrupt the taken for granted, loosen the hold of common sense, and imagine new configurations of knowledges, technologies, and ways of life. What other kinds of work may comparison do in twenty-first-century studies of science and technology? What will we choose to bring together and keep separate, in the name of what, and with what at stake?

REFERENCES

Adams, M. B. (1990). Towards a comparative history of eugenics. In *The wellborn science: Eugenics in Germany, France, Brazil, and Russia* (pp. 217–232). Oxford, England: Oxford University Press.

Adas, M. (1989). *Machines as the measure of men: Science, technology, and ideologies of Western dominance.* Ithaca, NY: Cornell University Press.

Adas, M. (2006). Testing paradigms with comparative perspectives: British India and patterns of scientific and technology transfer in the age of European global hegemony. In A. Yengoyan (Ed.), *Modes of comparison: Theory and practice* (pp. 285–318). Ann Arbor: University of Michigan Press.

Alder, K. (2002). The history of science, or, an oxymoronic theory of relativistic objectivity. In L. Kramer & S. Maza (Eds.), *A companion to Western historical thought* (pp. 297–381). Malden, MA: Blackwell. doi:10.1002/9780470998748.ch16

Althusser, L. (1969). *For Marx* (B. Brewster, Trans.). London, England: New Left Books.

Bachelard, G. (1972). *The new scientific spirit* (P. Heelan, Trans.). Boston, MA: Beacon.

Bacon, F. (1620). *Novum organum scientiarum.* Book 2, Aphorism 129.

Balibar, E. (1978). From Bachelard to Althusser: The concept of the epistemological break. *Economy and Society, 7*(3), 27–37.

Baviskar, A., Sinha, S., & Philip, K. (2006). Rethinking Indian environmentalism: Pollution in Delhi and fisheries in Kerala. In J. Bauer (Ed.), *Forging environmentalism: Justice, livelihood, and contested environments* (pp. 189–256). London, England: Routledge.

Bernal, J. D. (1946). *Science and the humanities* [Brochure]. London, England: Birbeck College.

Bernal, J. D. (1969). *Science in history* (4 Vols.). London, England: Watts.

Bernheimer, C. (Ed.) (1994). *Comparative literature in the age of multiculturalism.* Baltimore, MD: Johns Hopkins University Press.

Bhadra, M. (2013). Fighting nuclear energy, fighting for India's democracy. *Science as Culture, 22,* 238–246.

Biagioli, M. (1993). *Galileo, courtier: The practice of science in the culture of absolutism.* Chicago, IL: University of Chicago Press.

Boddy, J. (1988). Spirits and selves in Northern Sudan: The cultural therapeutics of possession and trance. *American Ethnologist, 15,* 4–27.

Brickman, R., Jasanoff, S., & Ilgen, T. (1985). *Controlling chemicals: The politics of regulation in Europe and the United States.* Ithaca, NY: Cornell University Press.

Brooke, J. H. (1991). *Science and religion: Some historical perspectives.* Cambridge, England: Cambridge University Press.

Brown, T. L. (2003). *Making truth: Metaphor in science.* Urbana: University of Illinois Press.

Browne, J. (1996). *Darwin: A biography* (2 Vols.). Princeton, NJ: Princeton University Press.

Butterfield, H. (1931). *The Whig interpretation of history.* New York, NY: Norton.

Butterfield, H. (1951). *The origins of modern science, 1300–1800.* New York, NY: Macmillan.

Césaire, A. (1945). Poésie et connaissance. *Tropiques, 12,* 157–170.

Canguilhem, G. (1988). *Ideology and rationality in the history of the life sciences* (A. Goldhammer, Trans.). Cambridge, MA: MIT Press.

Choy, T. (2011). *Ecologies of comparison: An ethnography of endangerment in Hong Kong.* Durham, NC: Duke University Press.

Coleman, L. (2017). *A moral technology: Electrification as political ritual in New Delhi.* Ithaca, NY: Cornell University Press.

Cowan, R. S. (1983). *More work for mother: The ironies of household technology from the open hearth to the microwave.* New York, NY: Basic.

Daemmrich, A. (2004). *Pharmacopolitics: Drug regulation in the United States and Germany.* Chapel Hill: University of North Carolina Press.

Dallal, A. S. (2010). *Islam, science, and the challenge of history.* New Haven, CT: Yale University Press.

Damrosch, D. (2006). Rebirth of a discipline: The global origins of comparative studies. *Comparative Critical Studies, 3,* 99–112.

Dawes, G. W. (2016). *Galileo and the conflict between religion and science.* New York, NY: Routledge.

Draper, J. W. (1874). *History of the conflict between science and religion.* New York, NY: Appleton.

Eilberg-Schwartz, H. (1990). *The savage in Judaism: An anthropology of Israelite religion and ancient Judaism.* Bloomington: Indiana University Press.

Evans-Pritchard, E. E. (1937). The notion of witchcraft explains unfortunate events. In *Witchcraft, oracles and magic among the Azande* (pp. 63–83). Oxford, England: Clarendon Press.

Farmer, P. (1992). *AIDS and accusation: Haiti and the geography of blame*. Berkeley: University of California Press.

Fausto-Sterling, A. (2000). *Sexing the body: Gender politics and the construction of sexuality*. New York, NY: Basic.

Feenberg, A. (2010). *Between reason and experience: Essays in technology and modernity*. Cambridge, MA: MIT Press.

Felski, R., & Friedman, S. S. (Eds.) (2013). *Comparison: Theories, approaches, uses*. Baltimore, MD: Johns Hopkins University Press.

Felt, U., Fochler, M., & Winkler, P. (2010). Coming to terms with biomedical technologies in different technopolitical cultures: A comparative analysis of focus groups on organ transplantation and genetic testing in Austria, France, and The Netherlands. *Science, Technology, and Human Values, 35*, 525–553.

Ferngren, G. B. (Ed.) (2002). *Science and religion: A historical introduction*. Baltimore, MD: Johns Hopkins University Press.

Feyerabend, P. (1975). *Against method: Outline of an anarchist theory of knowledge*. London, England: New Left Books.

Figlio, K. (1976). The metaphor of organization: An historiographical perspective on the bio-medical sciences of the early nineteenth century. *History of Science, 14*, 17–53.

Fleck, L. (1979). *Genesis and development of a scientific fact* (T. Trenn & R. Merton, Eds.; F. Bradley & T. Trenn, Trans.). Chicago, IL: University of Chicago Press.

Fonseca, P. F. C., & Santos Pereira, T. (2014). The governance of nanotechnology in the Brazilian context: Entangling approaches. *Technology in Society, 37*, 16–27.

Foster, G. (1976). Disease etiologies in non-Western medical systems. *American Anthropologist, 78*, 773–782.

Foucault, M. (1970). *The order of things: An archaeology of the human sciences* (A. Sheridan, Trans.). New York, NY: Vintage.

Foucault, M. (1977). *Discipline & punish: The birth of the prison* (A. Sheridan, Trans.). New York, NY: Vintage.

Foucault, M. (1978a). *The history of sexuality, Vol. 1: An introduction* (R. Hurley, Trans.). New York, NY: Vintage.

Foucault, M. (1978b). Nietzsche, genealogy, history. In D. F. Bouchard (Ed.), *Language, counter-memory, practice: Selected essays and interviews* (pp. 139–164). Ithaca, NY: Cornell University Press.

Foucault, M. (1985). *The use of pleasure* (R. Hurley, Trans.). New York, NY: Vintage.

Fraser Harris, D. (1912). The metaphor in science. *Science, 36*(922), 263–269.

Frazer, J. (2012). *The golden bough* (Vol. 1, 3rd ed.). Cambridge, England: Cambridge University Press.

Friedman, S. S. (2013). Why not compare? In R. Felski & S. S. Friedman (Eds.), *Comparison: Theories, approaches, uses* (pp. 34–45). Baltimore, MD: Johns Hopkins University Press.

Fuller, S. (2010). *Thomas Kuhn: A philosophical history of our time*. Chicago, IL: University of Chicago Press.

Good, M-J. D., Brodwin, P., Good, B. J., & Kleinman, A. (Eds.) (1992). *Pain as human experience: Anthropological perspective*. Berkeley: University of California Press.

Gottschalk, P. (2013). *Religion, science, and empire: Classifying Hinduism and Islam in British India*. Oxford, England: Oxford University Press.

Gould, S. J. (1996). *The mismeasure of man* (Rev. ed.). New York, NY: Norton.

Hammerstrom, E. (2015). *The science of Chinese Buddhism: Twentieth-century engagements*. New York, NY: Columbia University Press.

Haraway, D. (1989). *Primate visions: Gender, race, and nature in the world of modern science*. New York, NY: Routledge.

Harding, S. (Ed.) (1993). *The "racial" economy of science: Toward a democratic future*. Bloomington: Indiana University Press.

Hayles, N. K. (1990). *Chaos bound: Orderly disorder in contemporary literature and science*. Ithaca, NY: Cornell University Press.

Hecht, G. (2010). Hopes for the radiated body: Uranium miners and transnational technopolitics in Namibia. *Journal of African History, 51*, 213–234.

Hesse, M. B. (1966). *Models and analogies in science*. South Bend, IN: University of Notre Dame Press.

Horn, D. (2003). *The criminal body: Lombroso and the anatomy of danger*. New York, NY: Routledge.

Horton, R. (1967). African traditional thought and Western science. *Africa, 37*, 50–71, 155–187.

Horton, R. (1977). African traditional thought and Western science. In B. Wilson (Ed.), *Rationality* (pp. 131–171). Oxford, England: Basil Blackwell.

Huff, T. (2003). *The rise of early modern science: Islam, China and the West* (2nd ed.). Cambridge, England, Cambridge University Press.

Inda, J. X. (2006). *Targeting immigrants: Government, technology, and ethics*. Malden, MA: Blackwell.

Inhorn, M. (2015). *Cosmopolitan conceptions: IVF sojourns in global Dubai*. Durham, NC: Duke University Press.

Jardine, N. (2003). Whigs and stories: Herbert Butterfield and the historiography of science. *History of Science, 41*, 125–140.

Jasanoff, S. (1986). *Risk management and political culture: A comparative study of science in the policy context*. New York, NY: Russell Sage.

Jasanoff, S. (2015). Future imperfect: Science, technology, and the imaginations of modernity. In S. Jasanoff & S.-H. Kim (Eds.), *Dreamscapes of modernity: Sociotechnical imaginaries and the fabrication of power* (pp. 1–33). Chicago, IL: University of Chicago Press. doi:10.7208/chicago/9780226276663.003.0001

Jasanoff, S., & Kim, S.-H. (2009). Containing the atom: Sociotechnical imaginaries and nuclear regulation in the US and South Korea. *Minerva, 47*, 119–146.

Jasanoff, S., & Kim, S.-H. (2013). Sociotechnical imaginaries and national energy policies. *Science as Culture, 22*, 189–196. doi:1080.09505431.2013.786990

Jasanoff, S., & Kim, S.-H. (Eds.) (2015). *Dreamscapes of Modernity: Sociotechnical Imaginaries and the Fabrication of Power.* Chicago, IL: University of Chicago Press.

Keller, E. F. (2010). *The mirage of a space between nature and nurture.* Durham, NC: Duke University Press.

Kelman, S. (1981). *Regulating American, regulating Sweden: A comparative study of occupational safety and health policy.* Cambridge, MA: MIT Press.

Kleinman, A. (1978). Concepts and a model for the comparison of medical systems as cultural systems. *Social Science & Medicine. Part B: Medical Anthropology, 12,* 85–93.

Kleinman, A., & Good, B. (Eds.) (1985). *Culture and depression: Studies in the anthropology and cross-cultural psychiatry of affect and disorder.* Berkeley: University of California Press.

Kuhn. T. (1970). *The structure of scientific revolutions* (2nd ed.). Chicago, IL: University of Chicago Press.

Kuhn, T. (1979). Metaphor in science. In A. Ortony (Ed.), *Metaphor and thought* (pp. 409–419). Urbana: University of Illinois Press.

Lakatos, I., & Musgrave, A. (Eds.) (1970). *Criticism and the growth of knowledge.* Cambridge, England: Cambridge University Press.

Laqueur, T. (1992). *Making sex: Body and gender from the Greeks to Freud.* Cambridge, MA: Harvard University Press.

Larson, E. (1997). *Summer for the gods: The Scopes trial and America's continuing debate over science and religion.* New York, NY: Basic.

Latour, B. (1987). *Science in action: How to follow scientists and engineers through society.* Cambridge, MA: Harvard University Press.

Latour, B. (1990). Postmodern? No, simply Amodern! Toward an anthropology of science. *Studies in History and Philosophy of Science, 21,* 145–171. doi:10.1016/0039-3681

Latour, B. (1993). *We have never been modern.* Cambridge, MA: Harvard University Press.

Latour, B. (2005). *Reassembling the social: An introduction to actor–network theory.* Oxford, England: Oxford University Press.

Latour, B. (2010). "Thou shall not freeze-frame," or, How not to misunderstand the science and religion debate. In *On the modern cult of the factish gods* (pp. 99–124). Durham, NC: Duke University Press.

Latour, B., & Woolgar, S. (1979). *Laboratory life: The social construction of scientific facts.* Beverly Hills, CA: Sage.

Leavis, F. R. (1962). *The two cultures? The significance of C. P. Snow.* Cambridge, England: Cambridge University Press.

Levine, G. (Ed.) (1987). *One culture: Essays in science and literature.* Madison: University of Wisconsin Press.

Lévy-Bruhl, L. (1925). *How natives think* (L. Clare, Trans.). New York, NY: Alfred A. Knopf.

Lindberg, D. C., & Numbers, R. L. (Eds.) (1986). *God & nature: Historical essays on the encounter between Christianity and science.* Berkeley: University of California Press.

Livingstone, D. (2014). *Dealing with Darwin: Place, politics, and rhetoric in religious engagements*. Baltimore, MD: Johns Hopkins University Press.

Lock, M. (1993). The politics of mid-life and menopause: Ideologies for the second sex in North American and Japan. In S. Lindenbaum & M. Lock (Eds.), *Knowledge, power, and practice: The anthropology of medicine and everyday life* (pp. 330–363). Berkeley: University of California Press.

Lock, M. (2002). *Twice dead: Organ transplants and the reinvention of death*. Berkeley: University of California Press.

Malinowski, B. (1954). Magic, science and religion. In *Magic, science and religion and other essays* (pp. 17–92). New York, NY: Doubleday.

Mansfield, B., & Guthman, J. (2015). Epigenetic life: Biological plasticity, abnormality, and new configurations of race and reproduction. *Cultural Geographies, 22*, 3–20.

Marcus, G. (1995). (Ed.). *Technoscientific imaginaries: Conversations, profiles, and memoirs*. Chicago, IL: University of Chicago Press.

Marcus, G., & Fischer, M. M. J. (1986). *Anthropology as cultural critique: An experimental moment in the human sciences*. Chicago, IL: University of Chicago Press.

Martin, E. (1987). *The woman in the body: A cultural analysis of reproduction*. Boston, MA: Beacon.

Martin, E. (1991). The egg and the sperm: How science has constructed a romance based on stereotypical male–female roles. *Signs, 16*, 485–501.

Masco, J. (2006). *Nuclear borderlands: The Manhattan Project in post–Cold War New Mexico*. Princeton, NJ: Princeton University Press.

McLuhan, M. (1994). The medium is the message. In *Understanding media: The extensions of man* (pp. 7–21). Cambridge, MA: MIT Press.

McLuhan, M., & Fiore, Q. (1981). *The medium is the massage: An inventory of effects*. Berkeley, CA: Gingko Press.

Mead, M. (1928). *Coming of age in Samoa*. New York, NY: William Morrow.

Mumford, L. (1934). *Technics and civilization*. New York, NY: Harcourt.

Mumford, L. (1964). Authoritarian and democratic technics. *Technology and Culture, 5*, 1–8.

Needham, J. (1954). *Science and civilization in China* (Vol. 1). Cambridge, England: Cambridge University Press.

Needham, J. (1969). Science and society in East and West. In *The grand titration: Science and society in East and West* (pp. 190–217). Toronto, Canada: University of Toronto Press.

Nelkin, D., & Pollak, M. (1982). *The atom besieged: Antinuclear movements in France and Germany*. Cambridge, MA: MIT Press.

Numbers, R. L. (Ed.) (2009). *Galileo goes to jail and other myths about science and religion*. Cambridge, MA: Harvard University Press.

Olson, R. G. (2006). *Science and religion, 1450–1900: From Copernicus to Darwin*. Baltimore, MD: Johns Hopkins University Press.

Oppenheimer, R. (1958). Analogy in science. *Centennial Review of Arts & Science, 2*, 351–373.

Parthasarathy, S. (2007). *Building genetic medicine: Breast cancer, technology, and the comparative politics of health care.* Cambridge, MA: MIT Press.

Patton, K., & Ray, B. (Eds.) (2000). *A magic still dwells: Comparative religion in the postmodern age.* Berkeley: University of California Press.

Petryna, A. (2002). *Life exposed: Biological citizens after Chernobyl.* Princeton, NJ: Princeton University Press.

Pick, D. (1993). *Faces of degeneration: A European disorder, c. 1848–1918.* Cambridge, England: Cambridge University Press.

Porter, T. M. (1995). *Trust in numbers: The pursuit of objectivity in science and public life.* Princeton, NJ: Princeton University Press.

Proctor, R. (1988). *Racial hygiene: Medicine under the Nazis.* Cambridge, MA: Harvard University Press.

Rabinow, P. (1995). *French modern: Norms and forms of the social environment.* Chicago, IL: University of Chicago Press.

Radhakrishnan, R. (2013). Why compare? In R. Felski & S. S. Friedman (Eds.), *Comparison: Theories, approaches, uses* (pp. 15–33). Baltimore, MD: Johns Hopkins University Press.

Rose, N. (1996). *Inventing our selves: Psychology, power, and personhood.* Cambridge, England: Cambridge University Press.

Ross, A. (1991). New age—A kinder, gentler science? In *Strange weather: Culture, science and technology in the age of limits* (pp. 15–74). London, England: Verso.

Russell, B. (1997). *Religion and science* (2nd rev. ed.). Oxford, England: Oxford University Press.

Schiebinger, L. (1987). Skeletons in the closet: The first illustrations of the female skeleton in eighteenth-century anatomy. In C. Gallagher & T. Laqueur (Eds.), *The making of the modern body: Sexuality and society in the nineteenth century* (pp. 42–82). Berkeley: University of California Press.

Schiebinger, L. (1993). *Nature's body: Gender in the making of modern science.* Boston, MA: Beacon.

Smith, J. Z. (1982). In comparison a magic dwells. In *Imagining religion: From Babylon to Jonestown* (pp. 19–35). Chicago, IL: University of Chicago Press.

Snow, C. P. (1964). *The two cultures and a second look.* Cambridge, England: Cambridge University Press.

Srinivas, S. (2001). *Landscapes of urban memory: The sacred and the civic in India's high-tech city.* Minneapolis: University of Minnesota Press.

Stepan, N. L. (1986). Race and gender: The role of analogy in science. *Isis, 77,* 261–277.

Tamarkin, N. (2014). Genetic diaspora: Producing knowledge of genes and Jews in rural South Africa. *Cultural Anthropology, 29,* 552–574.

Tambiah, S. J. (1990). *Magic, science, religion, and the scope of rationality.* Cambridge, England: Cambridge University Press.

Terry, J. (1999). *An American obsession: Science, medicine, and homosexuality in modern society.* Chicago, IL: University of Chicago Press.

Traweek, S. (1988). *Beamtimes and lifetimes: The world of high energy physicists.* Cambridge, MA: Harvard University Press.

Turda, M., & Gillette, A. (2014). *Latin eugenics in comparative perspective.* London, England: Bloomsbury.

Turkle, S. (2012). *Alone together: Why we expect more from technology and less from each other.* New York, NY: Basic.

Tylor, E. B. (1903). *Primitive culture: Researches into the development of mythology, philosophy, religion, language, art, and custom* (Vol. 2, 4th ed.). London, England: John Murray.

Vogel, D. (1986). *National styles of regulation: Environmental policy in Great Britain and the United States.* Ithaca, NY: Cornell University Press.

Wade, P., López Beltrán, C., Restrepo, E., & Ventura Santos, R. (Eds.) (2014). *Mestizo genomics: Race mixture, nation, and science in Latin America.* Durham, NC: Duke University Press.

Wajcman, J. (2004). *TechnoFeminism.* London, England: Polity.

Weber, M. (2001). *The Protestant ethic and the spirit of capitalism* (T. Parsons, Trans.). London, England: Routledge.

White, A. D. (1896). A history of the warfare of *science* and theology (2 Vols.). New York, NY: Appleton.

Winner, L. (1986). *The whale and the reactor: A search for limits in an age of high technology.* Chicago, IL: University of Chicago Press.

Wiredu, K. (1976). How not to compare African thought with Western thought. *Ch'Indaba*, 2, 4–8.

Yengoyan, A. (Ed.) (2006). *Modes of comparison: Theory and practice.* Ann Arbor: University of Michigan Press.

CHAPTER 3

# On the Origins of Models of Innovation
## Process and System Approaches

*Benoît Godin*

The concept of innovation goes back to ancient Greece (Godin, 2015). The concept of *technological innovation* is more recent. The term emerged after World War II (see Figure 3.1), with a few exceptions before then (e.g., Hansen, 1932; Kuznets, 1929, p. 540; Schumpeter, 1939, p. 289; Stern, 1927, 1937; Veblen, 1915/2006, 118, 128–129). Societies were seen as changing at a faster rate than before, hence the study – and concepts – of economic change, social change, organizational change (and planned change), and technological change. The question was, How can people contribute to this change? That is, how do people accelerate it (or reduce the lag or gap between invention and its application)? How do people direct and orient change toward desired goals? Technological innovation is the answer. Theorists began to study technological innovation as a phenomenon to be understood and provided strategies to firms and policies to governments.

Theorists of technological innovation are as diverse as academics and practitioners themselves. Their theories are equally diverse in the sense that they cover the psychological, social, organizational, and economic dimensions of innovation. One facet that unites theorists is a shared representation of innovation as a *process*. The process approach to the study of innovation stresses the time dimension. Innovation is a chronological process, from the generation of an idea to its application in a practical context: from theory to practice. Innovation is not a thing or a single act, whether of a genius or an entrepreneur, but a sequence of events or a series of activities with a purpose. This representation takes many forms, depending on the discipline. To sociologists, the process moves from (individual) adoption to (social) diffusion; to economists, from invention to commercialization; to management schools, from product development to manufacturing.

By the late 1960s, however, the meaning of *process* had changed. Technological innovation was now a *system*. In the system approach, innovation is called a process, but the process refers to structure rather

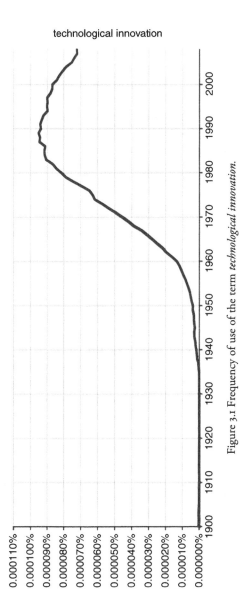

Figure 3.1 Frequency of use of the term *technological innovation*.

than time. The system approach considers institutions or organizations and their interrelations as they contribute to innovation. In general, time is not a fundamental factor in the analysis. Theorists do not explain how a system develops historically and how it evolves over time; rather, they explain how existing systems work.

This chapter looks at the origins of process and system approaches.[1] The literature studied in this chapter makes few references to Schumpeter, the emblematic scholar for writers on innovation, because that seminal author developed no theory of innovation as a process or as a system. This chapter develops the idea that looking at innovation as a process comes from sociologists and economic historians, whereas looking at innovation as a system comes from practitioners and policy-oriented scholars.

## 3.1   Innovation as a Process

If one opens any book on innovation today, one learns that innovation is a process. But what is a process?

### 3.1.1   Prehistory

Innovation is not a concept used in anthropology. Yet in the first half of the twentieth century, anthropologists espoused the idea of process, later used by the theorists of innovation. The very first sketch of the idea emerged as a solution to a controversy in anthropology between advocates of the role of invention and of the role of diffusion in cultural change. This controversy, or rather its resolution, had a strong influence on later understanding of innovation, giving rise to the study of innovation as a sequential process in time.

Early anthropologists classified societies or cultures into types, some more "advanced" than others, and interpreted these types as stages in the evolution of civilization from primitives to barbarians to moderns. How do the stages evolve? How does civilization occur? What is the *process* behind progress? Early anthropologists had two opposing theses. Either civilization arises in one culture and thereafter propagates to other geographical areas (diffusion), or it is the result of parallel and independent developments (invention) in many societies. The controversy placed invention and diffusion in opposition to each other (Smith et al., 1927). Yet both invention and diffusion eventually came to be discussed as stages of a sequence in

---

[1] In the literature on innovation, approaches are usually called *models* (see Godin, 2017).

the process of cultural change (Dixon, 1928; Kroeber, 1923; Linton, 1936; Wissler, 1923).

Sociologists espoused this view, too. A precursor was sociologist Ogburn (1886–1959), a professor at Columbia University. Like the anthropologists, Ogburn made very few uses of the concept of innovation, yet paved the way among sociologists for the idea of the innovation process. In 1922, Ogburn produced *Social Change with Respect to Culture and Original Nature*, asking "why social changes occur, why certain conditions apparently resist change, how culture grows, how civilization has come to be what it is" (Ogburn, 1922, p. v). Ogburn opposed the efforts of anthropologists and others to develop grand theories of change or of evolution by stages, *à la* Spencer. Rather than follow existing biological or anthropological theories, Ogburn concentrated on studying the mechanisms of change. To Ogburn, a central factor or mechanism of social change is technological invention, or "material culture" as he called it, following the usage of anthropologists. "The key to [social] change may be sought in invention, [namely] any new element in culture . . . To understand social change it is necessary to know how inventions are made and how they are diffused" (Ogburn, 1933–1934, p. 331).

Starting with *Recent Social Trends* (US President's Research Committee on Social Trends, 1933), Ogburn began to describe invention as a process that goes through stages. Ogburn suggested many such time sequences that fall into two categories. A first series concerns the process of invention itself: "Invention is a process, beginning with the earliest inception of the idea and proceeding through a definite set of stages to its wide adoption" (Ogburn, 1941, p. 184). Ogburn's colleague, Gilfillan, measured the interval between these stages on three occasions (Gilfillan, 1935, 1952; Ogburn & Gilfillan, 1933) and concluded that, for the most important inventions, the process required from 15 to 50 years, the average being 33 years.

To be sure, Ogburn was not the first to suggest such time sequences. Ogburn had combined a psychological sequence like that of historian Abbott Usher (Usher, 1929/1988) with a sequence on the industrial development of technological products, as first suggested by sociologists (Bernard, 1923), economists (Epstein, 1926), industrialists, and practitioners (e.g., Mees, 1920). Where Ogburn (1941) innovated was in a second series of sequences concerned with the social effects of invention. Again, Ogburn's work contains many chains or time sequences of effects, even slightly different ones in the same article, but they all add up to technology, industry, social institutions, and people. As Ogburn (1937; see also Ogburn, 1936, p. 4) put it, there is a great variety in these sequences; but in the past in many important cases the change occurred first in the technology, which changed the economic institutions, which in turn changed the social and governmental organizations, which finally changed the social beliefs and philosophies. (p. 10)

### 3.1.2 The Diffusion Process

The diffusion of innovation is the ideal subject with which to explore stages. Diffusion is a process that occurs over time and space. Innovations spread from centers, so it was believed in the early sociology of invention, by degrees to other areas. A time sequence or diffusion curve proposed the spread to be slow at first, then accelerating, and finally stagnating or declining (Tarde, 1890/2001). Students of the diffusion of innovation, starting with scholars of agricultural sociology, were very productive in imagining such sequences. Because rural life was a major dimension of society in the nineteenth century, that it was changing completely in the twentieth century, and that governments made many efforts to respond to practical problems and to promote change and modernization, explains why rural sociology took up the study of innovation early (Beal & Bohlen, 1955, 1957; Lionberger, 1960; Ryan & Gross, 1943; Subcommittee on the Diffusion and Adoption of Farm Practices, 1952; Wilkening, 1953).

However, it is Rogers (1931–2004) who got the attention of sociologists with a book that reached a larger public than just rural sociologists. Rogers's book studies the diffusion process by which "an innovation spreads from one individual to another, in a social system, over time" (Rogers, 1962, p. 12). This process has three stages – innovation, diffusion, and adoption (by individuals) – of which the adoption stage is itself composed of the five stages imagined by Beal and Bohlen (1955, 1957).

Rogers (1962) theorized about every concept of innovation used in sociology in subsequent decades (process, innovation, diffusion, adoption, adopters categories, change agent, innovativeness), but above all the concept of innovation as a process over time with stages. Like Ogburn, Rogers imagined many different sequences. Every sequence, until 1976 at least, started with ideas (the mental) that were subsequently refined, then diffused and adopted (the action). Adoption is a "mental process from hearing to final adoption" (Rogers, 1962, p. 76).

### 3.1.3 The Innovation Process

To the sociologist, the diffusion process goes from idea to adoption. Yet the most well-known sequence is that from invention to commercialization;

a sequence that gave rise to the highly popular "linear model of innovation" (Godin, 2017). The first sketch of such a sequence comes from practitioners, such as Holland of the Division of Engineering and Industrial Research of the National Research Council. In a paper written for a book published in 1928 to celebrate the centenary of the American Institute of the City of New York, Holland developed ideas on the *research cycle*. Why, he asked, is research the prime mover of industry? Because it "reduces to the minimum the period between the scientific discovery and mass production." To Holland, "the speeding up of the period of the cycle, the reduction to the minimum of the time lag, is the criterion of the effectiveness of scientific research as an industrial aid" (Holland, 1928, p. 316). As evidence that research reduces the "time lag" between discovery and production, Holland portrayed the development of industries as a series of successive stages, dubbed the "research cycle." It consists of the following seven stages or "steps" (Holland, 1928, pp. 315–316): pure science research, applied research, invention, industrial research (development), industrial application, standardization, and mass production.

Holland's idea of the research cycle is the first explicit framework for the role of basic research in industrial development. Slightly more than 10 years later, such sequences began to proliferate (Furnas, 1948; Maclaurin, 1949; Stevens, 1941). Maclaurin (1907–1959), an economic historian, gave the sequence a theoretical formulation. As head of the Industrial Relations Section of MIT, Maclaurin became interested in "technological change," a precursor to the term *technological innovation*. Maclaurin approached the Committee on Research in Economic History of the Social Science Research Council, itself interested in promoting investigation of the entrepreneur's role in US industry, with a proposal to jointly sponsor an investigation of technological and industrial expansion. Supported by a grant from the Rockefeller Foundation, Maclaurin initiated the first systematic and long-term research program on "The Economics of Technological Change."

In *Invention and Innovation in the Radio Industry*, Maclaurin (1949) offered a historical and current account of how the process of technological innovation took place in the radio industry. Considering the role of fundamental science, Maclaurin described the people of science as not consciously thinking about the commercial possibilities of their research, which was nonetheless vital to industrial development. Furthermore, Maclaurin discussed the role of inventors and the need for entrepreneurial skill, or the capacity to carry through a successful innovation, and for venture capital. To Maclaurin, history suggests a process in five stages:

fundamental research, applied research, engineering development, production engineering, and service engineering. Technological innovation is a sequential process in time, which starts with science (basic research) and whose ultimate stage is commercialization.

In 1951, Maclaurin seized the opportunity of a conference on *Quantitative Description of Technological Change*, organized by the US Social Science Research Council, to derive some general conclusions from ongoing research. Maclaurin suggested that "Schumpeter regarded the process of innovation as central to an understanding of economic growth" but that he "did not devote much attention to the role of science," and proposed "breaking down the process of technological advance into elements that may eventually be more measurable" (Maclaurin, 1953, p. 97). To Maclaurin, "the important point for economic development is that careful study is needed of the institutional arrangements which are most conducive to the flourishing of all the major elements of dynamic growth" (Maclaurin, 1953, p. 98). Maclaurin identified five propensities, or stages, leading to technological innovation, from research to use: pure science, invention, innovation, finance, and acceptance (or diffusion).

### 3.1.4   A Total Process

That innovation as a process became a leitmotif in the 1960s and later. Researchers generally defined and studied the innovation process as a sequence that includes, depending on the writer, two, three, or four phases. A typical sequence would be:

Invention → innovation → diffusion

Practitioners and engineers/managers are versed in the idea of technological innovation as a process. They may even be considered pioneering theorists, though ignored completely in the literature on the "history" of technological innovation, as is Maclaurin. In fact, two discourses on technological innovation emerged in the twentieth century: One, in the early 1960s, comes from natural scientists, policy makers, and the fields of science, technology, and society (STS) and science, technology, and innovation. For them, innovation is the application of science to industry. The issue discussed is the need for research and development (R&D) and qualified human resources. Here, innovation is an article of faith – the ultimate outcome arising out of basic research – and not really theorized about. Policy analyst Pavitt (1963) is the exemplar of such a discourse.

The other discourse comes from practitioners, especially engineers and managers. According to Morton (1913–1971), the engineer at Bell Laboratories who brought the transistor from invention to market and the author of numerous articles and a book on innovation, innovation is a "teamwork between science, engineering, and industry . . . It include[s] the *totality* [my italics] of human acts by which new ideas are conceived, developed, and introduced" (Morton, 1971):

> Innovation is not just one single act. It is not just a new understanding or the discovery of a new phenomenon, not just a flash of creative invention, not just the development of a new product or manufacturing process; nor is it simply the creation of new capital and consumer markets. Rather, innovation involves related creative activity in *all* [Morton's italics] these areas. It is a *connected* process in which many and sufficient creative acts, from research through service, couple together in an integrated way for a common goal . . . By themselves R&D are not enough to yield new social benefits. They, along with capital resources, must be effectively coupled to manufacturing, marketing, sales, and service. When we couple all these activities together, we have the connected specialized elements of a *total* [my italics] innovation process. (pp. 2–3)

Other reproduced Morton's definition of innovation as a total process – including the phrase "total process" itself – regularly in the years following its appearance. These views were part of a widespread discourse among engineers and managers of the time. A symposium sponsored by the US National Academy of Engineering in 1968 concluded, "There appears to be general agreement that the process of successful technological innovation depends on many more factors than the mere generation of scientific and engineering information" (US National Academy of Engineering, 1968). Managers, too, saw innovation as a process. The summary statement of the annual meeting of the Industrial Research Institute on innovation, where over 100 research managers gathered in April 1970, begins with the following "authoritative picture" of innovation: "Innovation is the process of carrying an idea – perhaps an old, well known idea – through the laboratory, development, production and then on to successful marketing of a product . . . The technical contribution does not have a dominant position" ("Top Research Managers," 1970, p. 45).

An influential input into these views came from the US Department of Commerce. In 1964, the US President asked the Department to explore new ways of "speeding the development and spread of new technology" (US Department of Commerce, 1967, p. 1). To this end, Herbert Hollomon, as Secretary for Science and Technology, set up a panel on invention and innovation. Its report was published in 1967 as *Technological Innovation: Its Environment and Management.* The report began by making a distinction between invention and innovation as the difference between the verbs "to conceive" and "to use." To the Department, innovation is a "complex process by which an invention is brought to commercial reality" (US Department of Commerce, 1967, p. 8). R&D is only one step in this process, which also includes R&D, engineering, tooling, manufacturing, and marketing. Using "rule of thumb" figures from the "personal experience and knowledge" of the members of the panel, the Department reported that R&D accounts for only 5 to 10 percent of innovation costs. "It is obvious that research and development is by no means synonymous with innovation" (US Department of Commerce, 1967, p. 9).

The Department paved the way for an influential representation of innovation in the following decades. Policy makers, supported by engineers/managers and scholars, embraced this representation without reservation. Technological innovation is not merely R&D. It is a "total process," an "entire venture," embedded in a "total environment" (US Department of Commerce, 1967, pp. 2, 8, 11, 14).

### *3.1.5   A Contested Concept*

The theorists of innovation were criticized for the linear model of innovation early, particularly for postulating basic research as the initiating factor or stage and for the linearity of the sequence (Langrish, Gibbons, Evans, & Jevons, 1972; Price & Bass, 1969; Williams, 1967). Missing in the criticisms is a historical perspective that takes the inventor of the model (Maclaurin) seriously. Maclaurin (1949) was broadening the discourse of the time on (basic) research leading automatically to technological innovation. Technological innovation is not only the affair of scientists. It includes activities other than basic research as necessary stages. "Advances in science are not automatically translated into advances in the practical arts" (Maclaurin, 1949, p. xiii). Between fundamental research and its applications is a "continuum" or "sequence" of activities or "stages." The critics also forgot that almost every producer and user of the model admits to qualifications. As Morton (1971) put it, "it is useful to talk of the innovation process as if it were an orderly sequence, always remembering that the ordering and timing of the various parts are neither rigid nor done only once" (pp. 19–20). Be that as it may, the criticisms gave rise to the idea of a system of innovation.

## 3.2    Innovation as a System

*System* was a popular concept in the 1950s–1960s, sometimes referenced as *system dynamics*. The concept entered studies of innovation in the 1960s. Many scholars, particularly from management schools but also from international organizations like the Organisation for Economic Co-operation and Development (OECD), began to use a system approach to study decisions and choices regarding science, technology, and innovation.

Over the years, the meaning of *process* changed, or rather, theorists used it in a different sense. In 1967, Havelock from the University of Michigan – a prolific author on knowledge transfer – and Benne wrote "there seem to be two ways to conceptualize [knowledge] utilization: One way is as a system and the other is as a process" (Havelock & Benne, 1967, p. 50). The same is true of studies of innovation in which process means either a sequence of activities in time or a system of organizations and their relationships. To Havelock and Benne, process models study the way in which – or the mechanism by which – knowledge is used (what is going on at each of the exchange points or linkages in the flow structure), using concepts such as relationship, linkage, transfer, exchange, translation, diffusion, and communication. In contrast, system models are concerned with the "flow structure," using concepts such as organization, group, person, agent, position, role, channel, and link (pp. 50, 60).

Such a categorization was commonplace in the 1960s. A few years before Havelock and Benne, sociologist Chin offered a similar typology. The process or "development model" of change, Chin (1961) claimed,

> develops a time perspective which goes far beyond that of the more here and now analysis of a system model." A system model "emphasizes primarily the details of how stability is achieved ... [whereas] the developmental model assumes constant change and development, and growth and decay. (pp. 211–212)

Briefly stated, a process model concerns time – that is, the stages involved in decision-making on action leading to innovation (emergence, growth, and development) – whereas a system model concerns the actors (individuals, organizations, and institutions) responsible for the innovation and with how they interact. A process model is "historical" and a system model is social: one is developmental, the other is functional. Yet the distinction between them is not as clear-cut as it might seem. In a larger sense, both are models of a social process.

## *3.2.1   A System Model*

The system approach to innovation started with reflections on the holistic nature of technological innovation. A system comprises interacting organizations and functions. Morton (1971) helped change the way the process of innovation was understood at the time and in subsequent decades. In the 1960s, Morton brought in a "system model of innovation." "The essential virtue in the systems approach to innovation," Morton claimed, "lies in the parts of the process and their linkages with one another, *not in the sequence* [my italics] in which such linkages are performed" (p. 19). To Morton,

> a system is an integrated assembly of specialized parts acting together for a common purpose ... a group of entities, each having a specialized, essential function. Each is dependent for its system effectiveness upon its coupling to the system's other parts and the external world ... *Parts, couplings,* and *purpose* are the three characteristics which define every system. (pp. 12–13)

To understand this process, Morton (1971) used the "systems approach" of engineers, constructing a "system model of innovation" comprising inter-related parts, namely "people ... coupled together" (pp. 15–16; see Figure 3.2). To Morton, the system approach is similar to the scientific method (analysis into components and synthesis into a system structure): "The innovation process consists in the application of the scientific-systems method in coupled specialized sub-processes ...: basic or applied research, development and design, or manufacturing, sales and service" (pp. 21–22).

## 3.3   A System Approach

In recent years, a new conceptual framework, the *National System of Innovation,* has popularized the system approach. To some scholars, "the notion of national systems of innovation is one of the most important developments to emerge from innovation studies in the last 25 years" (Fagerberg, Martin, & Andersen, 2014, p. 173). Users of this approach suggest the research system's ultimate goal is innovation and that the system is part of a larger system comprising institutional sectors like government, university, and industry, and their environments. The approach also emphasizes that the relationships between the components or sectors of the innovation system are the *cause* of its performance.

Yet this ostensibly recent approach has deep roots in history. The OECD espoused a system approach well before the National Innovation

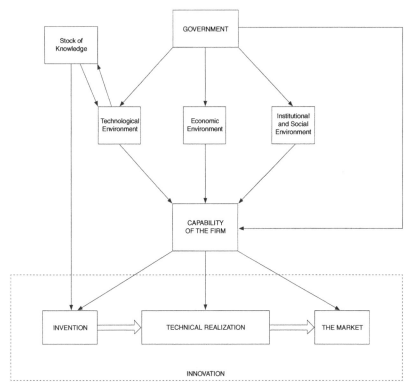

Figure 3.2 Organisation for Economic Co-operation and Development factors influencing innovations.

System framework. The story of that moment is of particular importance to the history of the system approach to innovation. In the 1970s, the OECD developed thoughts on technological innovation as a system comprising four sectors, or components, and embedded in larger environments:

- Sectors: government, university, industry, nonprofit
- Environments: economic, international

Four types of relationship are essential to a performing system. The first is between economic sectors, especially government, university, and industry. The second type of relationship in the system is between basic and applied research. Here, many OECD researchers rejected the idea of technological innovation as a linear process starting with basic research and ending with commercialization. The third type of relationship in the system is among various policy-making government entities. According to the OECD, policy was too fragmented and uncoordinated. The last type of relationship in the system is international cooperation.

The OECD documents produced during and after the 1970s concerned developing a system approach to technological innovation. The innovation system comprises several institutional sectors in relationship to each other and all oriented toward commercialization. The industrial sector was embedded in an economic environment. The government sector comprised various departments whose policies were related but badly coordinated. The university sector had to direct its research potential toward applied or oriented research and develop relationships with industry. Overarching was the OECD as a forum in which countries collaborated to create a new object: science policy. These efforts reached their climax in the 1990s, with the National Innovation System framework.

### 3.3.1   A Contested Concept

The conceptualization of innovation as a system has not gone uncontested. The main criticism concerns the generality of the approach. The proposition that innovation is systemic (a system of related parts) – that everything relates to everything else – resembles theories on social change before the 1970s. Social change is so large a category that many had abandoned the study of change, broadly defined, convinced that little of substance could be built on it.

Another criticism of the system approach is statics. Theorists of innovation typically map systems of innovation and their components and measure factors involved in this system, but rarely look at the dynamics among actors over time or at historical details. In spite of introducing a definition of innovation as a process of activities over time, theorists conducted a static analysis. To be sure, innovation is still called a process, but concerns structure rather than sequence. In this sense, the system approach is often contrasted with the process approach.

A controversy deserves mention. It concerns the origins of the system approach to innovation. Freeman and Lundvall attributed the concept of a National Innovation System to each other. However, both also suggested that economist List (Das Nationale System des Politischen Okonomie, 1841) is the "ancestor" of the concept. To Lundvall (2004), "the basic ideas behind the concept of national systems of innovation go back to Friedrich List" (p. 533). To Freeman and colleague Soete, "List anticipated . . . contemporary theories of national systems of innovation" and the book could even have been titled *The National Innovation System* (Freeman, 1987, p. 99; see also Soete et al., 2009, p. 6). Despite these claims, no tradition of theoretical research on innovation systems arose from List's work.[2] List was initially unknown to (or at least uncited by) Lundvall when writing on a National Innovation System. It is one thing to resuscitate a forgotten author who held similar ideas more than 150 years ago and another to document the rise of a research tradition from that author. Positioning List as a spiritual forefather is rather like looking for a symbolic figure or father figure after the fact. List is an isolated case, a resurrected "ancestor" whose value in the recent literature is to give legitimacy and credibility to the concept of a National Innovation System.

Two conclusions emerge from this story. First, under different terms (system of technological progress, system model, innovating system, innovation system), the concept of innovation system arose in the last few decades – not in the nineteenth century. Second, the idea of an innovation system arose before that of a National Innovation System and before Kline's (1985) much-cited model. Beginning in the 1950s, the concept of a system was applied at the firm level (Morton) and the national level (Mottur, 1968).

A precursor in the use of the process approach and the system approach is certainly the OECD. From 1972 to 1978, it conducted an analysis of national policies to stimulate technological innovation, conducted using two conceptual frameworks. One was according to *time*, as the organization called it, or stages of the innovation process (the linear model of innovation), and the other according to *space*, or the institutions involved in the process of innovation. The OECD used a figure to illustrate each framework, showing institutions are similar to those used today to visualize National Innovation Systems (Organisation for Economic Co-operation and Development, 1972, p. 12; 1978, p. 142; see Figure 3.2).

## 3.4 Conclusion

In 1967, Havelock and Benne suggested that process and system approaches are necessary to the study of what they called *knowledge utilization*:

---

[2] Freeman (1987) used List's work to support an argument for the concept of a National Innovation System, whereas Lundvall argued for an actual linear descent of the concept from List's work.

Knowledge utilization cannot be properly understood without using *both* models. It is obvious that utilizations comes about through the conveyance of information along a complex series of pathways which connect groups and individuals fulfilling many different roles [system] ... Yet, in each interchange – each connection between one person or group and another – a process of communication and influence is going on [process]. (p. 50)

Havelock's message and the OECD study had little impact on scholars of technological innovation, continuing to use the two approaches in isolation from each other. Some scholars denied that a system approach has anything to do with process. Some theorists claimed a change over the last decades, from a process approach to technological innovation to a system approach (e.g., Caraça, Lundvall, & Mendonça, 2009; Rothwell, 1992). In reality, no change has occurred. The process approach continues to be in vogue, although under different names. Some of the most serious and comprehensive writings on the process approach come from management (e.g., Damapour, 2017; van de Ven, Polley, Garud, & Venkataraman, 2008). Yet the process approach competes with a system approach in which the term *process* means a system of interacting organizations or institutions – à la Talcott Parsons – together with a series of factors (as a mechanism) responsible for technological innovation.

Both approaches are fundamental to modern theories of innovation and, in particular, to *models* of technological innovation. To different extents, every theory of innovation, whether psychological, sociological, organizational, or economic, makes use of one or the other approach, as do models of innovation. Process models are usually schematized with boxes and arrows; system models with concentric circles.[3]

This chapter shed new light on the history of theories of innovation. Again and again, scholars from economics and public policy explain the development of theories of technological innovation using contrast between invention as a "black box" and the study of the generation of invention (e.g., Freeman, 1974, pp. 5–17, 27). Another contrast is that between the neoclassical and the evolutionary views (e.g., Nelson, 2009). Neoclassical economists focus on prices and equilibrium to explain firms' (rational) behavior, whereas evolutionary economists consider how firms

---

[3] "The adoption and diffusion processes may be depicted as curves representing activities taking place over a period of time. This analysis of curves of adoption and diffusion will lay the groundwork for the presentation of theoretical models of change" (Havelock, 1969, p. 10.4). "It is useful to visualize a system by drawing a large circle" (Chin, 1961, p. 203), outside of which is the environment. A system model's "special advantage lies in the great ease with which systems can be represented pictorially" (Havelock & Benne, 1967, p. 54).

adapt to changes in their environment. In policy matters, the former is said to explain and justify the government's role in the economy on the basis of market failures whereas the latter considers a more complex set of institutions and rules (e.g., Nelson, 2009; Nelson & Winter, 1974). Some, however, find much less difference between the two traditions than commonly assumed (Schroter, 2009). This chapter documented a fundamental development and distinction. It is more fundamental in the sense that it applies to a larger range of theories of innovation than just economic theories. Approaches to innovation as a process emerged from stories or narratives of a series of events – what some call a "journey."[4] But in the last two decades, a system approach to technological innovation has developed and now competes with a process approach.

## REFERENCES

Beal, G. M., & Bohlen, J. M. (1955). How farm people accept new ideas (Cooperative Extension Science Report No. 15). Ames: Iowa State University Cooperative Extension Service.

Beal, G. M., & Bohlen, J. M. (1957). The diffusion process (Special Report No. 18). Ames: Iowa State University Cooperative Extension Service.

Bernard, L. L. (1923). Invention and social progress. *American Journal of Sociology*, 29, 1–33. doi:10.1086/213560

Caraça, J., Lundvall, B.-A., & Mendonça, S. (2009), The changing role of science in the innovation process: From Queen to Cinderella? *Technological Forecasting & Social Change*, 76, 861–867. doi:10.1016/j.techfore.2008.08.003

Chin, R. (1961). The utility of system models and developmental models for practitioners. In W. G. Bennis, K. D. Benne, & R. Chin (Eds.), *The planning of change: Readings in the applied behavioral sciences* (pp. 201–216). New York, NY: Holt, Rinehart, and Winston.

Damanpour, F. (2017). Organizational innovation. In *Oxford research encyclopaedia – Business and management* (pp. 1–54). Oxford, England: Oxford University Press.

Dixon, R. B. (1928). *The building of cultures*. New York, NY: Charles Scribner.

Epstein, R. C. (1926). Industrial invention: Heroic, or systematic? *Quarterly Journal of Economics*, 40, 232–272. doi:10.2307/1884619

Fagerberg, J., Martin, B. R., & Andersen, E. S. (Eds.) (2014). *Innovation studies: Evolution and future challenges*. Oxford, England: Oxford University Press.

Freeman, C. (1974). *The economics of industrial innovation*. Middlesex, England: Penguin Books.

Freeman, C. (1987). *Technology policy and economic performance*. London, England: Frances Pinter.

---

[4] The innovation journey: initiation, development, and implementation/termination (van de Ven et al., 2008).

Furnas, C. C. (1948). *Research in industry: Its organization and management.* Princeton, NJ: D. van Nostrand.

Gilfillan, S. C. (1935). *The sociology of invention.* Cambridge, MA: MIT Press.

Gilfillan, S. C. (1952). The prediction of technical change. *Review of Economics and Statistics, 34*, 368–385. doi:10.2307/1926864

Godin, B. (2015). *Innovation contested: The idea of innovation over the centuries.* London, England: Routledge.

Godin, B. (2017). *Models of innovation: History of an idea.* Cambridge, MA: MIT Press.

Hansen, A. H. (1932). The theory of technological progress and the dislocation of employment. *American Economic Review, 22*(1), 25–31.

Havelock, R. G. (1969). *Planning for innovation through dissemination and utilization of knowledge.* Ann Arbor, MI: Center for Research on Utilization of Scientific Knowledge (CRUSK), Institute for Social Research, University of Michigan.

Havelock, R. G., & Benne, K. D. (1967). An exploratory study of knowledge utilization. In G. Watson (Ed.), *Concepts for social change* (pp. 47–70). Washington, DC: NTI Institute for Applied Behavioral Science, Cooperative Project for Educational Development.

Holland, M. (1928). Research, science and invention. In F. W. Wile (Ed.), *A century of industrial progress* (pp. 312–334). New York, NY: Doubleday, Doran.

Kline, S. J. (1985). Innovation is not a linear process. *Research Management, 28*(4), 36–45. doi:10.1080/00345334.1985.11756910

Kroeber, A. L. (1923). *Anthropology.* New York, NY: Harcourt, Brace.

Kuznets, S. (1929). Retardation of industrial growth. *Journal of Business History, 2*, 534–560.

Langrish, J., Gibbons, M., Evans, W. G., & Jevons, F. R. (1972). *Wealth from knowledge: Studies of innovation in industry.* London, England: Macmillan.

Linton, R. (1936). *The study of man.* New York, NY: Appleton Century Crofts.

Lionberger, H. F. (1960). *Adoption of new ideas and practices.* Ames: Iowa State University Press.

Lundvall, B.-A. (2004). Introduction to "Technological infrastructure and international competitiveness" by Christopher Freeman. *Industrial and Corporate Change, 13*, 531–539. doi:10.1093/icc/dth021

Maclaurin, W. R. (1949). *Invention and innovation in the radio industry.* New York, NY: Macmillan.

Maclaurin, W. R. (1953). The sequence from invention to innovation and its relation to economic growth. *Quarterly Journal of Economics, 67*, 97–111. doi:10.2307/1884150

Mees, C. E. K. (1920). *The organization of industrial scientific research.* New York, NY: McGraw-Hill.

Morton, J. A. (1971). *Organizing for innovation: A systems approach to technical management.* New York, NY: McGraw Hill.

Mottur, E. R. (1968). *The processes of technological innovation: Conceptual systems model.* Washington, DC: George Washington University's Program of Policy Studies in Science and Technology.

Nelson, R. R. (2009). Building effective "innovation systems" versus dealing with "market failures" as ways of thinking about technology policy. In D. Foray (Ed.), *The new economics of technology policy* (pp. 7–16). Cheltenham, England: Edward Elgar.

Nelson, R. R., & Winter, S. G. (1974). Neoclassical vs. evolutionary theories of economic growth: Critique and prospectus. *Economic Journal, 84,* 886–905. doi:10.2307/2230572

Ogburn, W. F. (1922). *Social change with respect to culture and original nature.* New York, NY: Viking Press.

Ogburn, W. F. (1933–1934). Social change. In E. R. A. Seligman (Ed.), *Encyclopedia of the social sciences* (Vol. 3, pp. 330–334). New York, NY: Macmillan.

Ogburn, W. F. (1936). Technology and government change. *Journal of Business of the University of Chicago, 9,* 1–13.

Ogburn, W. F. (1937). National policy and technology. In U.S. National Resources Committee, *Technological trends and national policy, including the social implications of new inventions* (pp. 3–14). Washington, DC: U.S. Government Printing Office.

Ogburn, W. F. (1941). Technology and planning. In W. F. Ogburn & G. B. Galloway (Eds.), *Planning for America* (pp. 168–185). New York, NY: Henry Holt.

Ogburn, W. F., and S. C. Gilfillan (1933). The influence of invention and discovery. In Recent social trends in the United States (Report of the President's Research Committee on Social Trends; Vol. 1, pp. 122–166). New York, NY: McGraw-Hill.

Organisation for Economic Co-operation and Development (1972). Ad hoc group on industrial innovation (Report No. DAS/SPR/72.32). Paris, France: Author.

Organisation for Economic Co-operation and Development (1978). *Policies for the stimulation of industrial innovation* (Vol. 1). Paris, France: Author.

Pavitt, K. (1963). Research, innovation and economic growth. *Nature, 200,* 206–210. doi:10.1038/200206a0

Price, W. J., & Bass, L. W. (1969). Scientific research and the innovative process. *Science, 164,* 802–806. doi:10.1126/science.164.3881.802

Rogers, E. M. (1962). *The diffusion of innovation.* New York, NY: Free Press.

Rothwell, R. (1992). Successful industrial innovation: Critical factors for the 1990s. *R&D Management, 22,* 221–239. doi:10.1111/j.1467-9310.1992.tb00812.x

Ryan, B., & Gross, N. C. (1943). The diffusion of hybrid seed corn in two Iowa communities. *Rural Sociology, 8,* 15–24.

Schroter, A. (2009). New rationales for innovation policy? A comparison of the systems of innovation policy approach and the neoclassical perspectives (JENA

Economic Research Papers No. 33). Jena, Germany: Max Planck Institute of Economics.

Schumpeter, J. (1939). *Business cycles: A theoretical, historical, and statistical analysis of the capitalist process*. New York: McGraw-Hill.

Smith, G. E., Malinowski, B., Spinden, H. J., & Goldenweiser, A. (1927). *Culture: The diffusion controversy*. New York, NY: W. W. Norton.

Soete, L., Verspagen, B., & ter Weel, B. (2009). *Systems of innovation* (Working Paper No. 2009–062). Maastricht, Netherlands: UNU-MERIT.

Stern, B. J. (1927). *Social factors in medical progress*. New York, NY: Columbia University Press.

Stern, B. J. (1937). Resistance to the adoption of technological innovations. In US National Resources Committee, *Technological trends and national policy* (pp. 33–69). Washington, DC: US Government Printing Office.

Stevens, R. (1941). A report on industrial research as a national resource: Introduction. In National Research Council, Research: A national resource (II): Industrial research (pp. 5–16). Washington, DC: National Resources Planning Board.

Subcommittee on the Diffusion and Adoption of Farm Practices (1952). *Sociological research on the diffusion and adoption of new farm practices: A review of previous research and a statement of hypotheses and needed research*. Lexington: University Kentucky, Kentucky Agricultural Experimental Station and Department of Rural Sociology.

Tarde, G. (2001). Les lois de l'imitation [Statutes of limitation]. Paris, France: Seuil. (Original work published 1890.)

Top research managers speak out on innovation (1970). Research Management, 13, 435–443. doi:10.1080/00345334.1970.11762609

US Department of Commerce (1967). *Technological innovation: Its environment and management*. Washington, DC: US Government Printing Office.

Usher, A. P. (1988). *A history of mechanical inventions*. New York, NY: Dover. (Original work published 1929.)

US National Academy of Engineering (1968). *The process of technological innovation*. Washington, DC: National Academy of Sciences.

US President's Research Committee on Social Trends (1933). *Recent social trends in the United States*. New York, NY: McGraw-Hill.

Van de Ven, A. H., Polley, D. A., Garud, R., & Venkataraman, S. (2008). *The innovation journey*. Oxford, England: Oxford University Press.

Veblen, T. (2006). *Imperial Germany and the Industrial Revolution*. New York, NY: Cosimo. (Original work published 1915.)

Wilkening, E. (1953). *Adoption of improved farm practices as related to family factors* (AES Research Bulletin No. 183). Madison: University of Wisconsin.

Williams, B. R. (1967). *Technology, investment and growth*. London, England: Chapman and Hall.

Wissler, C. (1923). *Man and culture*. New York, NY: Thomas Y. Crowell.

# CHAPTER 4

# The Third Wave of Science Studies

## Harry Collins and Robert Evans

The start of the "Third Wave of science studies" dates to a paper we wrote that was published in April 2002 by the journal *Social Studies of Science* (Collins & Evans, 2002). The paper challenged the idea, then dominant in science and technology studies (STS), that the problems associated with the role of science in policy making could be solved by reducing the influence of scientific experts and giving more rights in these matters to ordinary citizens. The Third Wave paper (hereafter 3Wave) set out a normative theory of expertise that remains consistent with the sociology of scientific knowledge but which can be used to argue against *both* an excessive reliance on science *and* an unrestrained suspicion of expertise. The trick is to turn attention from how truth is made to who is an expert and concentrate on making the "best" decisions rather than the "right" decisions. It can take half a century or more to know what was the right decision, but one can decide on the *best* decision by taking advice from the best experts and experts can be identified in the short term. The speed of politics is faster than the speed of scientific knowledge-making and this means that the best decisions must find a way to combine the expert and the democratic without giving undue influence to either.

In making this case, the Third Wave of science studies draws on and endorses earlier work in STS that showed experience-based experts without formal qualifications can contribute to making the best decisions. 3Wave was not, therefore, written to be controversial, but to make a contribution to thinking about technological decision-making in the public domain and, in particular, to clarify ideas concerning so-called lay expertise. To the authors' surprise, however, it received a hostile reception from the core of the STS community. The main criticism was the mistaken idea that treating expertise as real, and insisting that a range of different expertises are required to make the best policy in each particular case, is a form of technocracy. It was said that this approach denies the role of democratic institutions in technological decision-making in the public domain. But this is not an accurate representation of the initial article or the Third Wave approach in general.

Crucially, the Third Wave takes policy making to be the preserve of politics, with technical expertise, be it from formally qualified experts or citizens with relevant experience, feeding into it where appropriate. Ordinary citizens – that is, those without experience-based expertise – still contribute to technological policy making but do so as citizens, not by pretending to be experts. In the remainder of this chapter, we describe the Third Wave of science studies in greater detail, first summarizing the main elements of the original paper and then setting out more recent developments in what might be thought of as its technical and political wings.

## 4.1   The Third Wave Paper: Studies of Expertise and Experience

To understand what 3Wave was arguing, it helps to understand what it was arguing against. The easiest way to do this is to use the heuristic of "three waves" of science studies that appears in the paper's title and that captures what we see as key transformations in STS theory and practice as they relate to technological decision-making in the public domain.

### 4.1.1   Three Waves of Science Studies

The three-wave sketch of science studies that gives rise to the Third Wave approach is also exceptionally useful for explaining science studies to nonspecialist audiences. The first wave refers to the kind of work done prior to the social constructivist revolution of the 1960s and 1970s; contemporary work that makes the same assumptions as that early work would still be described as a First-Wave approach. Wave 1 science studies typically see science as an epistemically superior practice with a distinctive method that reveals objective truths about nature. From this perspective, relevant sociological questions concern the cultural and institutional settings that can foster this kind of work. For substantive findings of science, sociology can *explain* false science only, because valid science has its own internal logic. Merton's (1973) work on the norms of science is the most well-known example of a First-Wave sociological approach, with the institutional settings that support the norms of communalism, universalism, disinterestedness, and organized skepticism being seen as the ones that most effectively nurture the production of valid science without affecting substantive findings. Where those norms are absent, as in totalitarian states, the scene is set for false science, such as Lysenkoism or the rejection of Einstein's theories (Merton, 1973). Wave 1 sees scientific experts as possessing expertise that is more secure than other forms of knowledge (such as religion, work-based knowledge, or common sense) and that should, therefore, have a determining influence in policy making.

The Second Wave of science studies emerged as a response to the philosophical and social problems of a Wave 1 understanding of science and the wider reconsideration of all kinds of "accepted wisdom" that characterized the 1960s. To start with philosophical concerns, these drew together developments in history and philosophy of science to challenge the naïve realism of Wave 1 and develop a constructivist alternative in which science is treated like any other social institution. One can arrive at this position in many ways, but for STS – and sociology of scientific knowledge in particular – the core concepts are often seen as Wittgenstein's idea of a "form of life," Winch's application of this to the social sciences, and Kuhn's ideas of normal and revolutionary science (Kuhn, 1996; Winch, 1958; Wittgenstein, 1953). The first recognizably STS publication based on this approach is probably Bloor's (1973) paper "Wittgenstein, Mannheim and the Sociology of Mathematics," which would be followed by his 1976 *Knowledge and Social Imagery*. These set out the foundations of what was known as the "strong program" in the sociology of knowledge, including the now-famous four tenets:

1   *Causal,* that is, concerned with the conditions that bring about belief or states of knowledge
2   *Impartial* with respect to truth and falsity, rationality or irrationality, success or failure
3   *Symmetrical* in its style of explanation; the same types of causes would explain, say, true and false beliefs
4   *Reflexive* – in principle, its patterns of explanation would have to be applicable to sociology itself. (Bloor, 1991, p. 7; see also Bloor, 1973)

The crucial changes from Wave 1 are commitments to impartiality and, most importantly, symmetry. Bloor criticized what we call Wave 1 – he did not use the term – for offering no more than a "sociology of error," in which it is only beliefs that come to be seen as "false" that require sociological explanation. "True" beliefs require no such explanation because their warrant is their correspondence with reality; they are believed because they are true. In contrast, under Wave 2, both true and false beliefs require the same kind of sociological explanation, implying that social factors – traditions, interests, biases, and so on – are as much a part of the content of scientific knowledge as they are of religion or any other organized body of knowledge. Collins's (1975) paper "The Seven Sexes: A Study in the Sociology of a Phenomenon, or the Replication of Experiments in Physics," which arose, in part, out of a reading of Winch and Wittgenstein, is probably the first empirical demonstration of a sociology of scientific knowledge approach.

Applying these ideas to the role of science in policy leads to an epistemological leveling-out in which science is no longer the preeminent source of knowledge about the world. Instead, science, through its claims to authoritative knowledge, can now be seen as one of the ways relations of power and domination are reproduced. Promoting social justice thus means demonstrating the legitimacy and rationality of knowledge communities marginalized by science and other elite institutions, thereby linking the philosophical critique of science with more overtly political campaigns for socially responsible science, social justice, and equality. Iconic examples of this work, in which the so-called lay expertise of nonscientific groups is needed to complement or correct mainstream scientific thinking, include Wynne's (1992) study of Cumbrian sheep farmers and Epstein's (1996) study of AIDS treatment activists. Funtowicz and Ravetz (1993), Irwin (1995), Rip, Misa, and Schot (1995), Nowotny, Scott, and Gibbons (2001), Fischer (2009), and Callon, Lascoumes, and Barthe (2011), to name but a few, offer more generalized treatments of the same issue. These ideas remain influential, with Jasanoff writing as recently as 2013 that

> many STS scholars think that the institutions, practices, and products of science and technology should be characterized in new ways not only for the sake of descriptive adequacy and analytic clarity, but also in order to reorder power relationships: for example, to make the exercise of power more reflexive, more responsible, more inclusive, and more equal. (p. 101)

The contribution of this work to technological decision making in the public domain has been to diagnose and correct what, in the 2002 paper, we call the "Problem of Legitimacy": when scientific experts are granted too much authority and allowed to pronounce on issues that go beyond their expertise or data, it destroys the credibility of science. 3Wave accepts that the Problem of Legitimacy is important. As we wrote at the time, the paper was never intended to contradict what had been revealed by Wave 2 either in epistemology or, in the main, politics:

> To save misunderstanding, let us admit immediately that the practical politics of technical decision-making still most often turn on the Problem of Legitimacy; the most pressing work is usually to try to curtail the

tendency for experts with formal qualifications to make ex-cathedra judgements curtained with secrecy. Nevertheless, our problem is not this one. Our problem is academic: it is to find a clear rationale for the expansion of expertise. But a satisfying justification for expansion has to show, in a natural way, where the limits are. Perhaps this is not today's practical problem, but with no clear limits to the widening of the base of decision making it might be tomorrow's. (Collins & Evans, 2002, p. 237)

That said, even at the time this was written, there were straws in the wind indicating the danger of what we called the "Problem of Extension" – the granting of unwarranted legitimacy to the views of those lacking any relevant expertise or experience. These included Thabo Mbeki's refusal to permit the use of AZT to prevent the mother-to-child transmission of HIV and the media's encouragement of popular opposition to vaccines, leading to worrying falls in the uptake of MMR and other vaccines (Boyce, 2007; Laurent-Ledru, Thomson, & Monsonego, 2011; Nattrass, 2012; Sheldon, 2009; Weinel, 2010).

The new approach advocated in 3Wave started from the recognition that knowledge is socially constructed, but argued that this did not license the conclusion that everyone is an expert on everything. Instead, 3Wave argued that the corollary of social constructivism was that extended participation in an expert community – be it of scientists, sheep farmers, or hair dressers – is necessary to gain the tacit knowledge needed to make a legitimate claim to expertise in that domain. Socialization in a domain of expertise is crucial for the transfer of tacit knowledge; socialization is also why, in the case of esoteric communities, the number of experts will be limited and why it is impossible for all citizens to be experts in every domain of practice (Collins & Evans, 2007). Using this principle, it is possible to have a definition of expertise that acknowledges the need for effort but that does not conflate expertise with science or with truth; what is required is extensive experience in the relevant community of practice. This requirement, in turn, suggests that any analysis of technological decision-making in the public domain needs to distinguish between technical areas, where specialist expertise is required – and hence where participation should be restricted to those with relevant experience and tacit knowledge – and those more political questions, where democratic institutions are key and participation is justified through political rights or the sufficiency of everyday, ubiquitous experience and expertise.

Before describing these technical and political phases of technological decision-making in greater detail, we make a few brief points about the 3Wave heuristic. First, the relationship between the Waves differs. Wave 1 is, or at least ought to be, obliterated by Wave 2; the latter supersedes and negates the former as a viable intellectual project in science studies. This is not to say that advocates of the Wave 1 approach do not persist. Indeed, science cannot proceed unless scientists themselves adhere to the Wave 1 approach and even we sociologists generally do our work with a Wave 1 perspective, even when we do not notice it. We justify our university jobs and the associated tenure on the grounds not of our political righteousness but of our technical excellence and superior grasp of social reality. Wave 1 is, in many respects, the foundation of our society. (See Collins's, 2014, *Are We All Scientific Experts Now?* and Collins and Evans's, 2017, *Why Democracies Need Science* for more arguments along these lines.) In contrast, Wave 2 and Wave 3 are compatible and run in parallel, neither undermining or threatening each other. Although they differ, the differences are matters of emphasis and topic – the direction they face – rather than of ontology or epistemology.[1]

## 4.2    Technical and Political Phases

One of the most important distinctions introduced in 3Wave is that between the technical and political phases of technological decision-making. The idea is to distinguish between those aspects of decision-making that require specialist expertise – be it scientific or otherwise – and those in which scientific or other expertise should not be granted any special status. In 3Wave, this is made explicit in the diagram reproduced below (Figure 4.1) summarizing a "typical" controversy. In the top half of the diagram, the technical dimension refers to the expert controversy, with the "core set" identifying the elite scientists and "uncertified experts" referring to the various activist, patient, or community groups that challenge or contest the claims made by scientists. An implied time dimension runs from left to right, with the dotted vertical lines linking the two groups toward the left-hand side of the diagram indicating when the connection should have been made, and the solid lines at the right marking when connection was actually made. The distance between the two lines represents the unnecessary delay caused by the failure to recognize the validity of nonscientific domains of expertise (i.e., the Problem of Legitimacy).

The lower half of the diagram represents the political dimension in which experts – be they scientific or uncertified – have no special status or role. Here the idea is that, where political choices are to be made, they

---

[1] For a summary, see the appendix of Collins and Evans (2007).

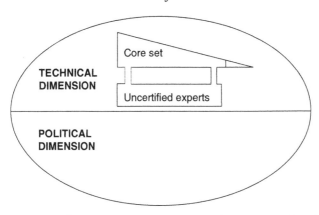

Figure 4.1 Uncertified experts and the core: Relationship between technical and political dimensions in 3Wave. Figure 6 in the original paper (Jasanoff, 2013).

should be informed by relevant expert opinion or advice, such as it is at that time, but that political choice is not, and should not be, reduced to or determined by that expert opinion. Ironically, the position we set out in 2002 – and have been defending ever since – is quite similar to that advocated over a decade later by Brian Wynne, one of our earliest and fiercest critics.

> There are [always] multiple factors in real risk situations, so then the question becomes which of these are relevant for addressing public interest policy outcomes . . . that is not an issue that scientific committees should decide alone. It is a democratic issue, one that should be informed by scientific knowledge but not framed and determined by it. Meanings and concerns should arise within democratic settings articulated through democratic political processes. They should be informed by science, of course, but this is not the same as allowing science to define those public concerns and meanings. There is no reason why something that is democratic and political shouldn't be informed by science. (Antonsen & Nilsen, 2016, p. 37)

The only difference between the position Wynne now endorses and our 2002 position, which he attacked, is that we would say that the "democratic and political" should be informed by expertise rather than science because, as Wave 2 has shown, science is not the only source of expertise.

Defending this difference does, however, require a definition of the two dimensions – technical and political – and this is where Wave 3 does differ from Wave 2. Under Wave 2, the tendency is to blur the boundary between science and politics in describing how scientists do science, whereas under

Table 4.1  *Definition of technical and political phases in*
*3 Wave*

|  |  | Phase | |
| --- | --- | --- | --- |
|  |  | Political | Technical |
| Nature of | Politics | Extrinsic | Intrinsic |
|  | Rights | Stakeholder | Meritocratic |
|  | Representation | By survey | By action |
|  | Delegation | By proxy | Impossible |

Wave 3, the more prescriptive orientation requires that they be distinguished. In 3Wave, we did this most forthrightly in Figure 9 (reproduced herein as Table 4.1), in which we made explicit the differences between the technical and political dimensions, now called the technical and political phases.

The significance of the table is often missed by those who claim that 3Wave is arguing for a return to more technocratic forms of decision-making, reinstating a hard boundary between facts and values. In fact, what Table 4.1 describes is a distinction between two different value systems that characterize the two different – but necessary and complementary – sets of activities needed to take technological decisions in the public domain.

In the technical phase, primarily concerned with propositional questions, the aspiration is to include only those individuals or groups who have sufficient relevant experience to count as experts and to minimize the influence of political concerns on their interactions (Collins & Evans, 2003). Of course, the norms of democracy and the norms of science have a considerable overlap, a relationship set out in Collins and Evans's *Why Democracies Need Science*, but the influence of political disagreements and values should be deliberately minimized in the technical phase (Collins & Evans, 2017; Evans & Plows, 2007). As Wave 2 showed, identifying experts inevitably involves some degree of politics, as does reaching any consensus position, so "intrinsic politics" cannot be eliminated. What makes the technical phase distinctive is the value placed on attempting to reach these outcomes without recourse to overtly political strategies such as making concessions to build a coalition or deliberately seeking to discredit an opponent, which, in the political phase are recognized as legitimate tactics. The standards are different in the political phase; that is the meaning of Row 1 in Table 4.1.

The next rows of the table identify other ways in which the technical and political phases differ. Row 2 is concerned with the basis on which participation in the technical and political phase is granted: in democratic societies those with rights in the political phase are generally thought to be stakeholders, whereas rights in the technical phase are granted to those with merit in the expertise in question. In rows 3 and 4, we show that surveys can be used to gather stakeholders' views and delegates can represent stakeholders, whereas expertise, dependent on tacit knowledge applied in real time to novel situations, can be neither delegated nor summarized in documentary form.

This distinction between technical and political phases not only challenges the tendency of Wave 2 thinking to blur the boundary between science and politics, but also provides a framework to understand how our own and others' work in the Third Wave has developed within its own technical phase. For example, there is now a significant volume of work on the theory, nature, and use of specialist expertise, which is becoming salient among a wider group of specialist audiences outside of science studies.[2] In contrast, the political phase hints at some political norms and values that are important outside the academy, and we have directed much of our most recent work at showing how the two phases can work together. We now discuss both these elements of the Third Wave approach in more detail.

## 4.3 Theorizing Expertise

In a review paper on expertise, Carr distinguishes between expertise as a *performance* and expertise as a *property*. The former sees expertise as "something people do rather than something people have or hold" (Summerson Carr, 2010, p. 18). Wave 2 is firmly in the former camp, seeing expertise as a *relational* phenomenon in which the status and legitimacy granted to expert claims determines whether someone is counted as an expert (Gieryn, 1999). Wave 2, therefore, leads toward descriptive accounts of how expert status is attributed, with the critical edge coming from the implication that the exclusion of nonscientific

---

[2] For indications of the salience of this work, contributions describing it have been invited for inclusion in the *Cambridge Handbook of Expertise and Expert Performance* (2nd ed.); *The Oxford Handbook of Expertise: Research & Application*; and the *Oxford Handbook of Expertise and Democratic Politics*. A succinct summary of the SEE approach that relates it to the second wave and symmetry can be found in the journal *Social Epistemology* (Collins, 2018a).

knowledge communities results in some form of harm: epistemic, political, or physical (Fortun, 2001; Fricker, 2007).

In contrast, Wave 3 sees expertise as an individual capacity developed through participation in a social group. In this context, the central questions are how communities generate expertise and how communities share it. Wave 3 is prescriptive as well as descriptive and contributes to understanding technical controversies through SEE-based analyses of who is or is not an expert. These new understandings have the potential to become interventions in future controversies, should the political will be there. SEE is a social-scientific theory of expertise that can be applied independently of the attributions made by actors in the controversy and that may lead to recommendations that differ from those of the public and of other social scientists (Collins, 2008).

### 4.3.1    Expertise as Social Fluency

The essence of SEE's approach to understanding expertise is the idea of socialization. Although similar in some ways to the "five-stage model" of Dreyfus and Dreyfus, in which a novice starts by self-consciously applying explicit rules and gradually works toward the expert stage to act intuitively, Wave 3 differs from the phenomenological model in that it foregrounds the social embedding of the learner in the language of expert communities (H. L. Dreyfus & Dreyfus, 1986; S. E. Dreyfus, 2004; Collins, 2017). This embedding leads to an apprenticeship model of learning in which the social interactions between the novice and the community of practitioners are the mechanism through which people acquire and transfer knowledge: tacit and explicit but with the emphasis on tacit (Collins, 1974; Lave & Wenger, 1991).

In 3Wave, we illustrated the idea using the example of sociological fieldwork, giving an initial three-level classification of specialist expertise:

1   *No expertise*: the degree of expertise with which the fieldworker sets out – insufficient to conduct a sociological analysis or do quasi-participatory fieldwork
2   *Interactional expertise*: enough to interact interestingly with participants and carry out a sociological analysis
3   *Contributory expertise*: enough to contribute to the science of the field being analyzed (Collins & Evans, 2002, p. 254)

The aim of the example was not to privilege sociological methods or analysis but to illustrate a general point in a way that we thought would make it easy for the journal's readers – principally social scientists – to understand. In fact, we intended the model to generalize to all settings, with an individual's expertise conceptualized as the accumulation of socialization experiences gained from the various groups in which they participate (Collins & Evans, 2015b). Because different individuals participate in different groups and to different degrees, different types of expertise will be based on these different socialization experiences and the distribution of expertise will reflect the availability of these experiences in and between societies (Evans, 2008).

These ideas provide the underlying structure of the Periodic Table of Expertises, which is shown in Figure 4.2 and is one of the foundations of SEE. Working from the top, the first two rows identify the *ubiquitous expertises* and *dispositions* (personal characteristics) found across an entire society that enable socialization to take place. The specialist expertise row identifies the different ways one can engage directly with a knowledge community and the different kinds of expertise that can emerge. The first three categories denote the kinds of understanding that can be achieved without interacting directly with the group, relying solely on published

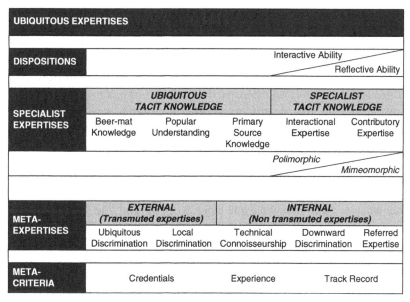

Figure 4.2 The Periodic Table of Expertises. From *Rethinking Expertise*, by H. M. Collins and R. Evans, 2007, Chicago, IL: University of Chicago Press, p. 14. See original text for an explanation of all categories.

material such as magazines, books, academic journals, webpages, podcasts, videos, and so on. As materials become more complex, the reader may acquire more knowledge but, as none of these sources permit any direct interaction with practitioners, readers are unable to acquire any of the tacit knowledge that is unique to that expertise. Thus, the highest levels of expertise cannot be achieved. In contrast, the last two categories – interactional expertise and contributory expertise – do require immersion in the relevant community and, as a result, are the only two that provide the specialist tacit knowledge associated with that domain of practice.

Because high-level expertise is hard to acquire, judging experts in the absence of specialist expertise is inevitable. The meta-expertises row lists some ways one can acquire such expertise: *external* social judgments that are based on widely available social knowledge and make no reference to the content of what is being judged and more informed *internal* judgments that require some familiarity with the expertise in question. The final row identifies criteria that might be used to identify experts, though the more controversial or novel the topic, the harder this will be.

**Applying the Periodic Table of Expertises.** The Periodic Table of Expertises provides a language to describe the kinds of expertise that individuals or groups can legitimately claim and hence provides the basis for making normative claims about who does or does not have expertise (Collins & Evans, 2014a; Coopmans & Button, 2014). For example, the traditional idea of an expert is that of a skilled practitioner. Using Figure 4.2, this corresponds to a contributory expert, and a legitimate claim to this status depends on extensive immersion in the domain of practice. Anyone lacking this degree of socialization cannot justify a claim to contributory expertise.

By emphasizing expertise and experience rather than science and truth, Wave 3's definition of expertise is much wider than typical philosophical or psychological definitions and resolves many philosophical problems such as what happens when experts disagree or when our notion of what is true and what is false changes from place to place and time to time. For instance, understanding homeopathic medicine counts as valuable knowledge in some places but not in others while alchemical knowledge or astrological knowledge used count as true but no longer does; driving a car in the early days of the automobile counted as a high-level expertise but today it does not; speaking French in the UK counts as an expertise but speaking it in France does not; and so on. All these changes present problems for most philosophical and psychological models of expertise, leading some analysts to think the only viable model is an "attributional" one – where who counts as an expert depends solely on other people's assessments. SEE's definition of expertise is realist, however, but does not encounter the problems of the other realist concepts of expertise: it is simply immersion in the community of specialists, irrespective of whether what those specialists believe is seen to be true or efficacious by those outside the community in question. That makes an expertise real, but its degree of *recognition* as an expertise varies from time to time and place to place. The difference between Wave 2 and Wave 3 is that Wave 2 has to accept the existing social classifications of expert and nonexpert whereas Wave 3 is willing to challenge and correct these classifications.

By emphasizing the role of tacit knowledge in the acquisition and sharing of expertise, Wave 3 has implications for interdisciplinarity and teamwork more generally (Collins, 2011). In particular, because interactional and contributory expertises are intimately related to practice, collaborations between social groups may require each to learn new ways of seeing and doing to understand what the other is seeking to achieve and why (Evans & Gorman, 2007; Galison, 1997; Gorman, 2002). Moreover, because what needs to be explained to the other group is usually unpredictable, time and space will need to be created for each to gain some expertise in the other's practices (Fisher et al., 2015).

### 4.3.2  Interactional Expertise and the Imitation Game

Of all the categories in the Periodic Table of Expertises, *interactional expertise* is the most novel and has been the most productive of new thinking.[3] As noted above, the term was first used in 3Wave to describe the expertise that sociological fieldworkers develop following prolonged immersion in the communities they study. The claim was that, even if social researchers do not participate in the full range of group activities (criminologists do not, after all, commit crimes), they can still claim to understand those practices because they can, through extended fieldwork, learn to talk about them in ways their respondents recognize as valid. Immersion in the linguistic culture is key.

Although the term interactional expertise was first used in 2002, the origins of the idea surfaced some years earlier in debates about the nature of artificial intelligence (AI). Phenomenologists, most famously H. L. Dreyfus,

---

[3] For discussions of interactional expertise, see Collins (2004), Collins and Evans (2015a), Collins, Evans, and Weinel (2017), Goddiksen (2014), Plaisance and Kennedy (2014), and Reyes-Galindo and Ribeiro Duarte (2015).

argued that AI would fail because computers do not have human-like bodies, whereas Collins drew on a sociological understanding of knowledge to argue that AI would fail because computers could not be socialized into the relevant community (Collins, 1990, 2018b; H. L. Dreyfus, 1979). According to Collins (drawing on existing arguments in AI), embodiment could not be the crucial factor because many disabled people can talk fluently about – that is, display an understanding of – all kinds of things their bodies would prevent them from experiencing directly (Collins, 1996).

The idea of interactional expertise has opened a new terrain of expertise-related research that has developed the idea in unexpected ways. The initial suggestion was of very few interactional experts; typically, researchers or specialist journalists whose work enabled them to sustain long-term inter-actions with a particular social group. But in interdisciplinary collabora-tions that have a complex division of labor based on some shared understanding, almost all of what each member knows about others' practices will be interactional rather than contributory expertise (Collins, 2011). This, incidentally, resolves the enigma of how it is possible for management of technical domains to work: to understand the domain they are managing and to make recognizably good technical judgments in that domain, managers use interactional rather than contributory expertise (Collins & Sanders, 2007). The same applies to peer review and the like.

Outside workplace settings, the same problem arises for all intergroup relations: how do members of one social group come to understand the experiences of other groups if they do not experience those experiences directly? In some cases, this will occur through representations in the media or other forms of explicit knowledge, with all the attendant risk of misunderstanding. In others, and particularly where genuine understanding is needed, it will be best achieved by talking deeply to members of those groups about their experiences. That said, the difficult and time-consuming process of acquiring a high level of interactional expertise in any domain should not be underestimated; interactional expertise is not an easy solution to any problem (Collins & Evans, 2015a; Plaisance & Kennedy, 2014).

**TheImitation Game.** The idea of interactional expertise gives rise to the bold conjecture that a person with only interactional expertise can speak the language associated with a practice as well as a contributory expert. The Imitation Game method was used to test this claim (Collins & Evans, 2014b; Collins, Evans, Ribeiro, & Hall, 2006; Collins et al., 2015; Evans & Collins, 2010). Based on the Turing Test, a basic Imitation Game consists of three players, illustrated in Figure 4.3.

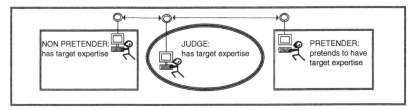

Figure 4.3 Schematic summary of the Imitation Game. From "The Imitation Game and the Nature of Mixed Methods," by H. M. Collins et al., 2015, *Journal of Mixed Methods Research, 21*, p. 513.

One player, drawn from the target group to ensure possession of the necessary contributory expertise, acts as the Judge/Interrogator and creates questions that are sent to the other two players. One of these, the Nonpretender, is also a contributory expert drawn from the target group and answers naturally. The other, the Pretender, is recruited from a different group and asked to answer as if a member of the target group. The Judge/Interrogator then compares the answers and tries to work out which came from the Pretender and which from the Nonpretender. The hypothesis is that, where the Pretender has interactional expertise, the Judge/Interrogator will be unable to distinguish between the two sets of answers. In many Imitation Games, the players – who must be hidden from each other and may be in remote locations – interact through computers using specially built software, but the Game can also be played much more simply over e-mail, using a Postman who conceals the identities, or even with paper and pencil and some screens.[4]

The Imitation Game can be used to explore the content and the distribution of interactional expertise. Research has included "proof of concept" physiological topics such as color-blindness, perfect pitch, and sociological topics such as gender, sexuality and national identity (Collins & Evans, 2014b; Collins et al., 2006; Evans, Collins, Hall, O'Mahoney, & Weinel, in 2019). Methodological work has explored the difference made by playing the Imitation Game with small groups rather than individuals (Evans et al., 2018); other variants are possible (Collins et al., 2015). Of more direct interest to STS practitioners, the game also has been used to explore the extent to which sociological researchers can genuinely

---

[4] A European Research Council Advanced Grant (269463 IMGAME) funded development of the Imitation Game, including the specialized software referenced in this paragraph. A book on the Imitation Game is in preparation for publication by MIT Press.

understand the science they study and the extent to which medical practitioners are able to take a patient's perspective (Collins, 2016; Evans & Crocker, 2013; Giles, 2006; Wehrens, 2014).

The Imitation Game has given rise to a new understanding of representativeness in social science and, in particular, how qualitative research might generalize, despite its typically small sample size (Collins & Evans, 2015b). The argument turns on the idea of uniformity in a population and how uniformity interacts with the kind of sample needed to adequately represent that population. Where uniformity is high, the small, haphazard sample – what we call a probe – used in qualitative research will be representative, as all instances will be identical in the salient dimensions. The standard example is that of natural language speaking, in which any fully socialized individual can demonstrate how the language is used. In contrast, where uniformity cannot be assumed and the research problem is to establish the distribution of some set of characteristics, the large-scale probability samples traditionally favored by quantitative research are the right approach. The link to the Imitation Game is that, in most cases, although Judge/Interrogators and Nonpretenders can be sampled according to *probe* logic; Pretenders should be sampled according to *survey* logic.

### 4.3.3   Three Dimensions of Expertise

In addition to avoiding the normative paralysis created by the descriptive emphasis of Wave 2's relational analysis of expert status, the model of expertise put forward by Wave 3 also provides a flexible alternative to the one-dimensional *stage* models traditionally used in disciplines such as psychology. The theory of expertise used to develop the Periodic Table of Expertises can be seen as operationalizing expertise along three dimensions (Collins, 2013):

1   *Individual accomplishment*: the individual's or group's proficiency in the domain of expertise in question, corresponding to the stage in the stage model of expertise
2   *Esotericity*: the extent to which access to the social collectivity that holds the expertise is open or closed to new members or outsiders
3   *Exposure to tacit knowledge*: how the learner engages with the domain, ranging from addressing only published sources to linguistic interaction to full participation

Figure 4.4 shows the three dimensions. This model allows a much richer description of the types of expertise available and the ways they develop and

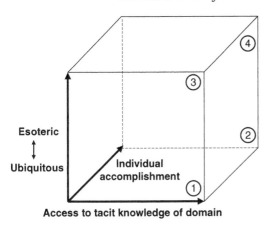

Figure 4.4 Three dimensions of expertise. Adapted from "Three Dimensions of Expertise," by H. M. Collins, 2013, *Phenomenology and the Cognitive Sciences, 12,* p. 257.

spread over time than the one-dimensional view of expertise as the mastery of well-defined skills, such as playing chess. For example, it is possible to see how some expertises, such as natural language speaking, can be ubiquitous whereas others, such as poetic virtuosity, are esoteric. The three-dimensional view also enables individual accomplishment and practice to be set in a broader scheme that suggests what kind of practice is needed; thus, if full mastery means reaching the right-hand edge of the back wall, then practice must involve social interaction with the relevant community because, without this, the tacit knowledge of the domain can never be attained.

### 4.3.4   Summary of the Technical Wing of the Third Wave

The technical wing of the Third Wave program has focused on developing the theory of expertise hinted at in the tripartite division of specialist expertise set out in 3Wave. Over the subsequent decade and a half, SEE's theory of expertise has developed to be more complex, with tacit knowledge and socialization providing the foundational concepts. Building on this are the Periodic Table of Expertises and a number of theoretical and methodological innovations, many of which relate to the idea of interactional expertise.

## 4.4   Expertise in Policy

The starting point for 3Wave was the need to find a solution to the Problem of Extension. The logic of Wave 2 always favors more participation, the rationale being that decisions must always be made more democratic if there is nothing special about science. Although the intention was good, the analysis was flawed as, in many cases, the injustice being committed would be better characterized as an epistemic rather than democratic failure. Specifically, what was denied in many classic case studies of STS was not the democratic rights of citizens but the epistemic claims of what Miranda Fricker (2007) calls "bona fide knowers." What Wave 3 offered that was different was a symmetrical analysis of this epistemic injustice coupled with a recognition that these epistemic concerns were not the only issues that might be raised.

### 4.4.1   Wave 3 and the Role of Citizens

Although 3Wave does acknowledge a role for citizens in the political phase of any technological decision in the public domain, it does not explain or theorize this view in any detail beyond the suggestion that their inclusion should be guided by democratic principles. It may be that this comparative lack of detail enabled critics to see the argument as leading to a defense of technocracy, although, as noted above, from the outset there were clear statements to the contrary in the original and many of the succeeding publications. As Durrant (2011) noted in a detailed analysis of the positions taken by 3Wave and its critics, it is possible to see that, although both are arguing for something that is recognizably democratic, the two sides are drawing on different ideals of democracy. Specifically, 3Wave draws on a Rawlsian notion of political liberalism whereas critics like Jasanoff (2013) and Wynne (1992) typically mobilize the politics of identity.

What this means in practice is that the Third Wave of science studies works with a twin-track model in which citizens' private lives and actions are distinguished from their public political roles and responsibilities, with the latter providing the focus for Wave 3 and its recommendations for the ways citizens and experts should interact. In general terms, Wave 3 argues for a division of labor, based on the recognition that acquiring high-level expertise is difficult and time consuming and therefore cannot reasonably be expected of all citizens in all domains. Instead, systems of scrutiny and deliberation are required that make the best use of available expertise at each stage and ensure that, overall, policy decisions are informed by the relevant expertise while remaining attentive to the views and wishes of citizens.

In setting out where Wave 3 has something distinctive to say, the "sandwich model" shown in Figure 4.5 can be used to identify the

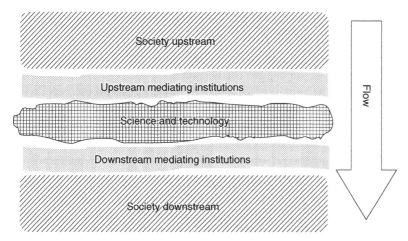

Figure 4.5 Sandwich model of science and society. From *Why Democracies Need Science,* by H. M. Collins & R. Evans, 2017, Cambridge, England: Polity Press, p. 74, Figure 3.3.

various points at which interventions could be made. For simplicity, the diagram shows a single linear progression from upstream concerns, in which framing questions are addressed and priorities set, through the scientific research that might be needed to address these challenges, to the downstream institutions needed to implement and apply the results. In practice, of course, feedback loops exist between all levels and some social groups might dispute or challenge the outcome of each stage.

With these caveats noted, Wave 3 has little new or controversial to say about the importance of upstream mediating institutions. Like many other approaches to STS, Wave 3 recognizes the importance of political processes in framing the questions addressed to experts and its contribution to these debates is mainly to emphasize two points:

1  Framing debates and questions needs to be as open and inclusive as possible to access the full range of possible expert opinion (Collins, Evans, & Weinel, 2016).

2  Where citizens are asked to contribute to such debates, participatory and deliberative methods – in which some degree of learning and interaction can take place – are generally preferable to surveys of public opinion (Evans, 2011; Evans & Plows, 2007).

### 4.4.2    Wave 3 and the Role of Experts

It is in the area labeled "downstream mediating institutions" that Wave 3 makes its most distinctive contribution, setting out the position we call *elective modernism,* arguing that democratic societies should choose to value science despite the limitations identified by Wave 2 of science studies (Collins & Evans, 2017). The argument is twofold. First, it is necessary to explain why expertise that conforms to the values of the technical phase should be preferred to expertise that does not and, second, the mechanism by which this expertise is incorporated into decision-making needs to be specified.

**Why value science?** Although 3Wave does not argue that participation in the technical phase should be restricted to scientists (see Figure 4.5), it does argue that all participants in the technical phase should behave in a "scientific" manner (see Table 4.1; in particular, the requirement that politics should be "intrinsic" rather than "extrinsic"). The question is, why make this condition, given the demonstrable and high-profile failures of science in recent years?

For those operating with a Wave 1 view of science, the answer to this question is obvious: science has a special method that means it is right, or is at least more likely to be right than anything else. Unfortunately, such arguments do not work well after Wave 2 because detailed examinations of science have shown that the epistemological warrant is not nearly as clear as we once thought and, in any case, most sciences are very different from the exemplary success stories of the old model, such as Newtonian and Einsteinian physics and quantum theory. Most sciences continually strive to achieve some clarity concerning a far more recalcitrant and complicated world than those of the very large or very small. In many such sciences, the everyday experience is failure – think of long-term weather forecasting or the econometric modeling of state finances. The alternative put forward by Wave 3 is to focus on the values of science as formative aspirations, by which we mean treating these values as providing the normative framework against which the day-to-day actions of scientists are judged and legiti-mated. In doing so, Wave 3 avoids defining science as an institution characterized by rigid adherence to a set of rules and, instead, sees it as a set of cultural practices characterized by shared sensibilities and values.

In the technical phase, some of the values we take to characterize "acting in a scientific way" include

- Individual honesty and integrity
- Importance of observation and data

- Attempts to corroborate and falsify
- Mertonian norms of communism, universalism, disinterestedness, and organized skepticism
- Duty of clarity in exposition
- Tolerance for dissent
- Continuity with existing knowledge
- Commitment to open-ended inquiry[5]

The reason collectivities that produce knowledge in this way are preferred over those that do not is that this set of values is preferable to any other set of values in determining what to believe about the world. Regardless of how accurate or successful a set of experts has been in the past, it would always be preferable to choose a group who consistently attempted to adhere to the values listed above over those that did not. To see this, one only has to try to imagine a scenario in which one would prefer to take advice from a group that paid no heed to honesty and integrity, made no attempt to refine or test their beliefs against any form of evidence, made a virtue of only recognizing certain groups of people as credible by reference to color or creed, refused to share or disclose information to others, were willfully obscure in public, or suppressed dissent and lurched from fad to fad with no attempt to build a coherent and stable body of explanation.

No epistemic argument is needed to see that the latter scenario is a dystopia and that the Wave 3 approach is to be preferred on moral grounds. It can also be noted, although it is not central to this argument, that the association of these values with science is one reason to defend its role in society: science is to be valued not because it provides more true facts than other institutions or because it generates jobs and new technologies, but because it provides moral leadership (Collins & Evans, 2017).

**How to use expertise.** Returning to the downstream mediating institutions of the sandwich model (Figure 4.5), how should the expert community's outputs be disseminated to and used by the political institutions of the wider society? The answer put forward by Wave 3 is a form of science advice we have called the Committee of the Owls, or simply the *Owls*. This committee would consist of experts drawn from or representing the various specializations involved in whatever controversy was raging, but would also include social scientists familiar with the same controversy and with the nature of science more generally. The use of Owls in the title is intended to convey the way committee members will need to look forward – seeing

---

[5] A full list is available in Collins and Evans (2017).

what their own expertise tells them about the controversy – but also to metaphorically turn their heads 180 degrees and see the same controversy from the perspective of others, including those with whom they might disagree. This includes natural scientists being able to see the world from a social science perspective and social scientists being able to see it from a natural science perspective.

The second distinctive feature of the Owls is that their function is not to tell policy makers or citizens what to do, but rather to provide two distinct pieces of information needed for policy makers or citizens to make informed judgments about how they wish to proceed:

1 A summary of the controversy that identifies the key arguments and their implications, if any, for those involved, including policy makers and other stakeholders. It is important to note that the Owls do not try to resolve the controversy and establish the "truth" about the natural world. Rather, their job is to report a social-scientific fact: the nature of the current technical consensus concerning the issue under debate.

2 They must also report a second social-scientific fact: the grade or degree of consensus among the technical community – where "technical community" includes representatives of all relevant expert communities, including experience-based experts. This might involve pointing to dissenting views but also to their marginality.

Based on these two outputs – the content and strength of consensus – policy makers and citizens would then be free to decide how they want to respond. The only constraint Wave 3 would put on these responses is that they must not distort or misrepresent the report of the Owls. Policy makers would understand that they take a higher risk that needs more justification when they defy a strong consensus and they must not cite a weak consensus as justification for what is, essentially, a political choice. (On this latter point, think of the way claims of supposed consensus among economists have been misused to justify certain political choices!)

**Wave 3 is not technocracy.** It should be clear that Wave 3 is not an argument for technocracy. Political decisions should be informed by appropriate expert advice but not disguised or determined by it. The distinctive way in which Wave 3 approaches these issues is well-illustrated by the example of Thabo Mbeki's decision in the late 1990s not to permit the use of antiretroviral drugs to reduce mother-to-child transmission of HIV in South Africa. At the time – and to explain this decision – Mbeki (as cited in Weinel, 2007) said the following to the second chamber of the South African parliament.

> There . . . exists a large volume of scientific literature alleging that, among other things, the toxicity of this drug [the antiretroviral AZT] is such that it is in fact a danger to health . . . To understand this matter better, I would urge the Honourable Members of the National Council to access the huge volume of literature on this matter available on the Internet, so that all of us can approach this issue from the same base of information. (p. 752)

In reality, no scientific controversy existed outside of the internet: the concerns Mbeki took seriously were no more than the online presence of a fringe group of scientists whose ideas had long been dismissed in the mainstream scientific community.

Why Mbeki made this choice is unclear. Mbeki may have lacked the expertise needed to recognize that no controversy existed or may have had other, more political, reasons for this decision. Perhaps Mbeki did not want South Africa to fall under the thrall of Western pharmaceutical companies; perhaps Mbeki did not think the country could afford the drugs; perhaps Mbeki did not want to give credence to the neocolonialist image of a promiscuous, disease-ridden country. Under Wave 3, these would still be legitimate reasons not to introduce the policy, but these are not the reasons Mbeki gave and, if these were the "real" reasons, the criticism we would make is that justifying the policy by reference to a nonexistent scientific controversy is dishonest and *disempowers the political process*. With a committee like the Owls in place, a future Mbeki would not be able to disguise a political decision as one determined by scientific findings.

The Owls would know that scientific controversies have a certain pattern in which ideas gain or lose credibility over time but do not necessarily disappear completely. Wave 2 shows that human ingenuity is such that determined advocates for a cause can always defend their claim long after it has been rejected by the core set and that, when the mainstream literature becomes closed to them, they publish in the fringe journals or on the internet. This material is what Mbeki was considering and, even if the arguments Mbeki was advising the parliamentarians to read had once had a life in the mainstream literature, their credibility had long since vanished. This is the kind of social science knowledge that the Owls could understand and point out in real time. They could say in such a case, "no real controversy is going on; it is a counterfeit controversy."

A clear distinction exists here between elective modernism and the views of someone like Wynne (1992), who considers that Mbeki was (or at least could be) justified in this decision because:

> he was said by others who were closer to his thinking and speaking, to have been saying, not that there is no causal connection between HIV and AIDS, but something very different and orthogonal to the propositional question in itself – that the causal progression of HIV to full-blown AIDS is strongly exacerbated by poverty, malnutrition, immune-system deficit, bad hygiene and sanitation conditions, and other poverty-related conditions, which extravagantly expensive western commercial drug responses (this was before cheaper but still expensive more local generic drugs were available) advanced by extortionate global corporations would not resolve, but would compete with for investment. He was emphasising his view of the need to focus priority on a different set of salient factors in the multi-factorial situation. It was definitely an arguable position; but it was not a superstitious expression of anti-real beliefs.[6]

Even if this is why Mbeki chose to act in this way, this is not how Mbeki justified it and it is the way people make certain ways of justifying things legitimate that forms the societies in which we live, as what is now called "posttruth" so terrifyingly reveals. It is for this reason that Wave 3 aims to raise the standards by which public officials conduct and justify their actions by arguing that whether the technical consensus is weak or strong, policy makers can always overrule it, but they must explain the political grounds that lead them to choose one side or another and must neither ignore technical advice nor misrepresent it.

### 4.4.3   Summary of the Political Wing of Wave 3

The political wing of the Third Wave principally concerns the use of expert advice in technological decision-making. In arguing for a committee of Owls to provide a new downstream mediating institution, it distinguishes itself from the technological determinism of Wave 1 and the technological populism of Wave 2. Instead, Wave 3 argues for a framework in which a committee of experts, including those from the social sciences, defines the strength and content of expert consensus so this information can be made public. Politicians and other decision makers are then expected to refer to that information when making decisions but are not compelled to follow

---

[6] Wynne (personal communication, March 19, 2008) provides an e-mail exchange between various parties that took place after a talk given in Lancaster University by Evans. We are grateful to Wynne for allowing extracts from this private exchange of communications to be made public.

a strong consensus, as long as the political reasons for doing otherwise are made public.

## 4.5 Conclusions

The Third Wave of science studies, which began with a paper published in 2002, was intended to add some clarity to the debate about technological decision-making in the public domain and to head-off potential problems caused by excessive skepticism about experts. Wave 3 was intended to make the findings of the Second Wave of science studies compatible with a society in which the views of those who know what they are talking about have more weight than the views of those who do not, and where the views of those who cleave to scientific values are given the most respect where technical matters are at stake. If problems of identifying and addressing expertise are not resolved, a dystopia will result. The 2002 paper gave rise to a controversy we did not expect, with prominent scholars in STS misrepresenting its arguments as being a defense of technocracy.

In the more than a decade and a half since the publication of 3Wave, both the technical and political wings of the Third Wave program have developed. On the technical side, the analysis of expertise – SEE – has come to include a detailed categorization of expertise based on the ideas of tacit knowledge and socialization. Of these developments, the identification of interactional expertise – fluency in the language that describes a practice as distinct from mastery of the physical practice itself – has proven particularly important, leading to the development of the research method known as the Imitation Game and new insights into the nature of sampling and its representativeness in social science.

On the political side, there is now a much clearer understanding of the relationships between the Third Wave approach and theories of democracy. Early work focused mainly on refuting unfounded accusations of technocracy, but more recent work has taken a more positive turn, linking SEE with democratic theory, setting out ideas about the role of science in society, and offering a new institution – the Owls – to provide expert advice to citizens and policy makers.

The Third Wave feels, unfortunately, like an idea whose time has come. When 3Wave was first published, the Problem of Extension was seen as something that might arise in the future, with the imagination stoked by the history of the rise of fascism in the 1930s, but with little in the way of immediate relevance. With shocking speed the era of "posttruth" has become all too real, with science studies trying to shrug off any responsibility for the societal change in the status of science, and the need for a rigorous and empirically informed theory of expertise that informs public debate becoming ever more pressing. The future that we didn't want, but whose possibility we felt we had to sketch out, has arrived. If STS scholars want to engage with it and not simply describe it or hide from it there is an immediate need for either the Third Wave of science studies or for better ideas that can do the same job.

## REFERENCES

Antonsen, M., & Nilsen, R. E. (2016). Strife of Brian: Science and reflexive reason as a public project. An interview with Brian Wynne. *Nordic Journal of Science and Technology Studies*, *1*(1), 31–40. doi:10.5324/njsts.v1i1.2124

Bloor, D. (1973). Wittgenstein and Mannheim on the sociology of mathematics. *Studies in History and Philosophy of Science, Part A*, *4*, 173–191. doi:10.1016/0039-3681(73)90003-4

Bloor, D. (1991). *Knowledge and social imagery* (2nd ed.). Chicago, IL: University of Chicago Press.

Boyce, T. (2007). *Health, risk and news: The MMR vaccine and the media: Media and Culture* (Vol. 9). New York, NY: Peter Lang.

Callon, M., Lascoumes, P., & Barthe, Y. (2011). *Acting in an uncertain world: An essay on technical democracy* (G. Burchell, Trans.). Cambridge, MA: MIT Press.

Collins, H. M. (1974). The TEA set: Tacit knowledge and scientific networks. *Science Studies*, *4*, 165–185. doi:10.1177/030631277400400203

Collins, H. M. (1975). The seven sexes: A study in the sociology of a phenomenon, or the replication of experiments in physics. *Sociology*, *9*, 205–224. doi:10.1177/003803857500900202

Collins, H. M. (1990). *Artificial experts: Social knowledge and intelligent machines*. Cambridge, MA: MIT Press.

Collins, H. M. (1996). Embedded or embodied? A review of Hubert Dreyfus' What computers still can't do. *Artificial Intelligence*, *80*, 99–117. doi:10.1016/0004-3702(96)00083-6

Collins, H. M. (2004). Interational expertise as a third kind of knowledge. *Phenomenology and the Cognitive Sciences*, *3*, 125–143. doi:10.1023/B:PHEN.0000040824.89221.1a

Collins, H. M. (2008). Actors and analysts' categories in the social analysis of science. In P. Meusburger, M. Welker, & E. Wunder (Eds.), *Clashes of knowledge* (pp. 101–110). Berlin, Germany: Springer. doi:10.1007/978-1-4020-5555-3_4

Collins, H. M. (2011). Language and practice. *Social Studies of Science*, *41*, 271–300. doi:10.1177/0306312711399665

Collins, H. M. (2013). Three dimensions of expertise. *Phenomenology and the Cognitive Sciences*, *12*, 253–273. doi:10.1007/s11097-011-9203-5

Collins, H. M. (2014). *Are we all scientific experts now?* Malden, MA: Polity.

Collins, H. M. (2016). An imitation game concerning gravitational wave physics. *arXiv:1607.07373v1*. Retrieved from https://arxiv.org/abs/1607.07373

Collins, H. (2017). Interactional expertise and embodiment. In J. Sandberg, L. Rouleau, A. Langley, & H. Tsoukas (Eds.), *Skilful performance: Enacting expertise, competence, and capabilities in organizations* (Perspectives on Process Organization Studies (P-PROS) No. 7, pp. 125–146). Oxford, England: Oxford University Press.

Collins, H. M. (2018a). Are experts right or are they members of expert groups? *Social Epistemology* [Online first]. doi:10.1080/02691728.2018.1546346

Collins, H. M. (2018b). *Artifictional intelligence*. Medford, MA: Polity.

Collins, H. M., & Evans, R. (2002). The third wave of science studies: Studies of expertise and experience. *Social Studies of Science, 32*, 235–296. doi:10.1177/0306312702032002003

Collins, H. M., & Evans, R. (2003). King Canute meets the beach boys: Responses to the third wave. *Social Studies of Science, 33*, 435–452. doi:10.1177/0306312703033007

Collins, H. M., & Evans, R. (2007). *Rethinking expertise*. Chicago, IL: University of Chicago Press.

Collins, H. M., & Evans, R. (2014a). Actor and analyst: A response to Coopmans and Burton. *Social Studies of Science, 44*, 786–792. doi:10.1177/0306312714546242

Collins, H. M., & Evans, R. (2014b). Quantifying the tacit: The imitation game and social fluency. *Sociology, 48*, 3–19. doi:10.1177/0038038512455734

Collins, H. M., & Evans, R. (2015a). Expertise revisited, Part I – Interactional expertise. *Studies in History and Philosophy of Science Part A, 54*, 113–123. doi:10.1016/j.shpsa.2015.07.004

Collins, H. M., & Evans, R. (2015b). Probes, surveys, and the ontology of the social. *Journal of Mixed Methods Research, 11*, 328–341. doi:10.1177/1558689815619825

Collins, H. M., & Evans, R. (2017). *Why democracies need science*. Cambridge, England: Polity Press.

Collins, H. M., Evans, R., Ribeiro, R., & Hall, M. (2006). Experiments with interactional expertise. *Studies in History and Philosophy of Science Part A, 37*, 656–674. doi:10.1016/j.shpsa.2006.09.005

Collins, H. M., Evans, R., & Weinel, M. (2016). Expertise revisited, Part II: Contributory expertise. *Studies in HIstory and Philosophy of Science Part A, 56*, 103–110. doi:10.1016/j.shpsa.2015.07.003

Collins, H. M., Evans, R., Weinel, M., Lyttleton-Smith, J., Bartlett, A, & Hall, M. (2015). The imitation game and the nature of mixed methods. *Journal of Mixed Methods Research, 21*. doi:10.1177/1558689815619824

Collins, H. M., & Sanders, G. (2007). They give you the keys and say "drive it!" Managers, referred expertise and other expertises. *Studies in History and Philosophy of Science Part A, 38*, 621–641. doi:10.1016/j.shpsa.2007.09.002

Coopmans, C., & Button, G. (2014). Eyeballing expertise. *Social Studies of Science, 44*, 758–785. doi:10.1177/0306312714531472

Dreyfus, H. L. (1979). *What computers can't do*. Cambridge, MA: MIT Press.

Dreyfus, H. L., & Dreyfus, S. E. (1986). *Mind over machine: The power of human intuition and expertise in the eyes of the computer.* New York, NY: Free Press.

Dreyfus, S. E. (2004). The five-stage model of adult skill acquisition. *Bulletin of Science, Technology & Society, 4*, 177–181. doi:1177/0270467604264992

Durrant, D. (2011). Models of democracy in social studies of science. *Social Studies of Science, 41*, 691–714. doi:10.1177/0306312711414759

Epstein, S. (1996). *Impure science: AIDS, activism, and the politics of knowledge.* Berkeley: University of California Press.

Evans, R. (2008). The sociology of expertise: The distribution of social fluency. *Sociology Compass, 1*, 281–298. doi:10.1111/j.1751-9020.2007.00062.x

Evans, R. (2011). Collective epistemology: The intersection of group membership and expertise. In H. B. Schmid, D. Sirtes, & M. Weber (Eds.), *Collective epistemology* (pp. 177–201). Frankfurt, Germany: Ontos.

Evans, R., & Collins, H. M. (2010). Interactional expertise and the imitation game. In M. E. Gorman (Ed.), *Trading zones and interactional expertise: Creating new kinds of collaboration* (pp. 53–70). Cambridge MA: MIT Press.

Evans, R., Collins, H. M., Hall, M., O'Mahoney, H., & Weinel, M. (2019). Bonfire Night and Burns Night: Using the Imitation Game to research English and Scottish identities. In D. Caudill, M. E. Gorman, & S. N. Conley (Eds.), *The third wave in the sociology of science: Selected studies in expertise and experience.* New York, NY: Palgrave Macmillan.

Evans, R., Collins, H. M., Weinel, M., Lyttleton-Smith, J., O'Mahoney, H., & Leonard-Clarke, W. (2018). Groups and individuals: Conformity and diversity in the performance of gendered identities. *British Journal of Sociology* [Online first]. doi:10.1111/1468-4446.12507

Evans, R., & Crocker, H. (2013). The imitation game as a method for exploring knowledge(s) of chronic illness. *Methodological Innovations Online, 8*(1), 34–52. doi:1010.4256/mio.2013.003

Evans, R., & Gorman, M. (2007). Trading zones and interactional expertise. *Studies in History and Philosophy of Science, Part A, 38*, 657–666. doi:10.1016/j.shpsa.2007.09.003

Evans, R., & Plows, A. (2007). Listening without prejudice? Re-discovering the value of the disinterested citizen. *Social Studies of Science, 37*, 827–853. doi:10.1177/0306312707076602

Fischer, F. (2009). *Democracy and expertise: Reorienting policy inquiry.* Oxford, England: Oxford University Press.

Fisher, E., O'Rourke, M., Evans, R., Kennedy, E. B., Gorman, M. E., & Seager, T. P. (2015). Mapping the integrative field: Taking stock of socio-technical collaborations. *Journal of Responsible Innovation, 1*, 39–61. doi:10.1080/23299460.2014.1001671

Fortun, K. (2001). *Advocacy after Bhopal: Environmentalism, disaster, new global orders.* Chicago, IL: Chicago University Press.

Fricker, M. (2007). *Epistemic injustice: Power and the ethics of knowing.* Oxford, England: Oxford University Press.

Funtowicz, S. O., & Ravetz, J. R. (1993). Science for the post-normal age. *Futures*, *25*, 739–755. doi:10.1016/0016-3287(93)90022-L

Galison, P. L. (1997). *Image and logic: A material culture of metaphysics*. Chicago, IL: University of Chicago Press.

Gieryn, T. F. (1999). *Cultural boundaries of science: Credibility on the line*. Chicago, IL: University of Chicago Press.

Giles, J. (2006). Sociologist fools physics judges. *Nature*, *442*(7098), 8. doi:10.1038/442008a

Goddiksen, M. (2014). Clarifying interactional and contributory expertise. *Studies in History and Philosophy of Science Part A*, *47*, 111–117. doi:10.1016/j.shpsa.2014.06.001

Gorman, M. E. (2002). Levels of expertise and trading zones: A framework for multidisciplinary collaboration. *Social Studies of Science*, *32*, 933–938.

Irwin, A. (1995). *Citizen science: A study of people, expertise, and sustainable development: Environment and society*. London, England: Routledge.

Jasanoff, S. (2013). Fields and fallows: A political history of STS. In A. Barry & G. Born (Eds.), *Interdisciplinarity: Reconfigurations of the natural and social sciences* (pp. 99–118). London, England: Routledge.

Kuhn, T. S. (1996). *The structure of scientific revolutions* (Vol. 14, 2nd ed.). Chicago, IL: University of Chicago Press.

Laurent-Ledru, V., Thomson, A., & Monsonego, J. (2011). Civil society: A critical new advocate for vaccination in Europe. *Vaccine*, *29*, 624–628. doi:10.1016/j.vaccine.2010.11.004

Lave, J., & Wenger, E. (1991). Situated learning: Legitimate peripheral participation. Cambridge, England: Cambridge University Press.

Merton, R. K. (1973). *The sociology of science: Theoretical and empirical investigations*. Chicago, IL: University of Chicago Press.

Nattrass, N. (2012). *The AIDS conspiracy: Science fights back*. New York, NY: Columbia University Press.

Nowotny, H., Scott, P., & Gibbons, M. (2001). *Re-thinking science: Knowledge and the public in a age of uncertainty*. Cambridge, England: Polity.

Plaisance, K. S., & Kennedy, E. G. (2014). A pluralistic approach to interactional expertise. *Studies in History and Philosophy of Science, Part A*, *47*, 60–68. doi:10.1016/j.shpsa

Reyes-Galindo, L. I., & Ribeiro Duarte, T. (2015). Bringing tacit knowledge back to contributory and interactional expertise: A reply to Goddiksen. *Studies in History and Philosophy of Science Part A*, *49*, 99–102. doi:10.1016/j.shpsa.2014.10.005

Rip, A., Misa, T. J., & Schot, J. (Eds.) (1995). *Managing technology in society*. London, England: Pinter.

Sheldon, T. (2009). Dutch public health experts refute claims that human papillomavirus vaccination has health risks. *BMJ*, *338*, b1109–b1109. doi:10.1136/bmj.b1109

Summerson Carr, E. (2010). Enactments of expertise. *Annual Review of Anthropology*, *39*, 17–32. doi:10.1146/annurev.anthro.012809.104948

Wehrens, R. (2014). The potential of the imitation game methods in exploring healthcare professionals' understanding of the lived experiences and practial challenges of chronically ill patients. *Health Care Analysis*, *23*, 253–271. doi:10.1007/s10728-014-0273-8

Weinel, M. (2007). Primary source knowledge and technical decision-making: Mbeki and the AZT debate. *Studies in History and Philosophy of Science Part A*, *38*, 748–760. doi:10.106/j.shpsa.2007.09.010

Weinel, M. (2010). Technological decision-making under scientific uncertainty: Preventing mother-to-child transmission of HIV in South Africa (Unpublished doctoral dissertation). Cardiff University. Retrieved from http://orca.cf.ac.uk /55502/

Winch, P. (1958). *The idea of a social science and its relation to philosophy: Studies in philosophical psychology*. London, England: Routledge.

Wittgenstein, L. (1953). *Philosophical investigations* (G. E. M Anscombe, Trans.). Oxford, England: Blackwell.

Wynne, B. (1992). Misunderstood misunderstanding: Social identities and public uptake of science. *Public Understanding of Science*, *1*, 281–304. doi:10.1088/0963-6625/1/3/004

# CHAPTER 5

# Legal Regulation of Technology

## Supporting Innovation, Managing Risk, and Respecting Values

### Roger Brownsword

## 5.1 Background

Legal and regulatory responses to emerging technologies vary from one technology to another, from one legal system to another, and from one time to another. Although under some legal systems, the response to a particular technology might be restrictive, under others it might be permissive; even facilitative. Sometimes the regulatory focus is a novel process; at other times, it is a novel product or a particular use or application. Some regulatory cultures tend to be precautionary, others tend to be proactionary, and others respond case by case, providing no simple pattern or stock response.

Different technologies, moreover, elicit different kinds and different degrees of concern. Fukuyama (2002) famously expressed deep moral concern about millennial developments in human biotechnology (that threatened to compromise human dignity), but much less concern about the possible threats to privacy and equality presented by information technology. For some, the deepest and most urgent concern is reserved for technologies – whether bio, nano, nuclear, synbio, geoengineering, or the like – that might kill us all (see, e.g., Annas, Andrews, & Isasi, 2002). In response to such concerns, sometimes public consultation abounds before new laws are introduced, but other times see little or no public engagement, again, with no simple pattern or standard operating procedure.

Generally, regulators do not try to anticipate the development of a new technology; rather, they address new technologies only when they must. Regulators, for example, made no attempt to create a special regulatory space for the development of the internet. Computing and engineering experts were largely left to self-regulate by articulating their own technical standards and codes of practice

(Zittrain, 2008). By the time lawmakers realized that some specific regulatory intervention (to some extent facilitative, to some extent restrictive) might be appropriate, the basic technological infrastructure was already in place. Although this might have seemed to be the law being slow to respond, it reflects one side of the so-called Collingridge (1980) dilemma; namely, that it is difficult for regulators to respond to a new technology until they have a sense of its benefits and risks. The other side of the dilemma is that, by the time regulators do respond, it might be too late to control the technology.

Where the law is called on to respond to a new technology – perhaps in a test case with a claim for compensation, lawmakers often attempt to subsume the new phenomenon in traditional categories and continue to apply existing principles. Such an attempt emerged in the early days of e-commerce, when legislators commonly thought the rules governing off-line transactions should simply be applied to online transactions. Although in principle, online transactions should be treated as legally valid contracts, it is far from clear that online contexts for consumer transactions are materially similar to the offline context (Brownsword, 2018). At times, such subsumption will not do, and some doctrinal adjustments must ensue. For example, in the latter part of the nineteenth century, the United States and the United Kingdom had parallel (but apparently independent) responses to industrialization, as new forms of regulatory criminal offenses were introduced (Sayre, 1933). At around the same time, in Sweden, following a railway accident in 1864 in which seven people died and eleven were seriously injured, with no realistic claim for compensation – the train driver being in no position to satisfy a personal tort claim – Parliament received a petition to respond to the special needs created by the operation of the railways (Friberg & Dufwa, 2010). Just as criminal law needed some adjustment to respond to the health and safety risks presented by dangerous new technologies, arrangements to compensate the victims of accidents needed to be revised. In place of more traditional responsibilities and liabilities predicated on the reasonableness of behavior, of fault, and of intent, a new regulatory approach focuses on the acceptable management of risk.

In this light – and thinking about the use of robot carers – consider the following hypothetical notion suggested by Weaver (2014):

> Suppose the Aeon babysitting robot at Fukuoka Lucle mall in Japan is responsibly watching a child, but the child still manages to run out of the child-care area and trip an elderly woman. Should the parent be liable for that kid's intentional tort? (p. 89)

If we respond to this question by trying to subsume the situation in traditional tort law principles, the answer will probably be determined by whether it is judged to be fair, just, and reasonable to hold the parents liable in these particular circumstances. If, however, robot carers represent a new danger in shopping malls or other public places, then this may be a case for strict liability (not requiring proof of a failure to take reasonable care). Or, taking a distinctly modern view, before retailers, such as Aeon, are to be licensed to introduce robot babysitters and before parents are permitted to make use of robocarers, a collectively agreed scheme of compensation should be developed, should something "go wrong." In the agreed risk-management package, the liability of the parents might be fault-based or strict or it might be that some scheme of social insurance funds compensation (cf. Hubbard, 2014). The point is that the regulatory response is a matter of risk management, not a matter of attributing blame or stigmatizing individuals.

Given the prospect of robots being employed in many capacities, regulators may need to respond sector by sector (addressing, say, robot carers in one piece of law and autonomous vehicles in another) or in an across-the-board manner. Certainly, precedents exist for the adoption of relatively ambitious general legislative frameworks, for example, to regulate assisted conception or to set out general principles of data protection. One problem with this approach, however, is that the legislative process is slow and, because the technology keeps changing, the legislation is always a work in progress. Even if the legislation connects reasonably well to the state of the technology at the time of its enactment, it will not take long to start losing connection. For example, in Europe, the Data Protection Directive (Directive 95/46/EC) was already far behind the state of the technology when enacted (see Swire & Litan, 1998). After years of tortuous negotiation, the General Data Protection Regulation (Regulation [EU] 2016/679) will replace the Directive. However, just as the new regulation was being finalized, it became apparent that a huge leap forward in machine learning and artificial intelligence made the regulation seem likely to suffer the same immediate obsolescence as the Directive.

Although the regulation might be outpaced by technological developments, its Article 25 recognizes the potential to use technological designs and defaults to serve as data protection. In other words, legislators appreciated that new technologies might themselves be regulators. In the twenty-first century, regulatory reliance on technological management has become increasingly prevalent. Already, for example, it is clear that the health and safety risks presented by modern transport systems will be managed, not by common law penal or compensatory rules, but by various kinds of technological fixes evolving into fully automated systems that take human operators out of the equation. Indeed, some commentators anticipate the creation of "an economy which, for all purposes, is planned not by bureaucrats or CEOs but by the technostructure" (Ezrachi & Stucke, 2016, pp. 32–33).

To engage with this variety of responses and regulatory tools, it is helpful to think about the "regulatory environment" in which new technologies emerge. In this environment, traditional areas of the law might play some part, but will often coexist with bespoke legislative frameworks, with a plurality of less-formal norms, and with measures of technological management. Although the regulatory environment for each technology will reflect a mix of local politics, preferences, and priorities, three generic desiderata arise, or, at any rate, these are desiderata for communities where citizens expect to enjoy the benefits of innovation but also expect technologies to be safe and applied in ways that respect fundamental values. Here, regulators face a triple demand:

- Support rather than stifle beneficial innovation
- Provide acceptable management of risks to human health, safety, and the environment
- Respect fundamental community values (such as privacy and confidentiality, freedom of expression, liberty, justice, human rights, and human dignity)

The challenges of these three demands reside in the tensions *between* them and the tensions hidden *in* them.

### 5.1.1   Support Rather than Stifle Beneficial Innovation

Regulators will find that, although the innovation lobby will argue for light-touch regulation, for strong intellectual property rights, for tax breaks, for subsidies (such as the US HITECH program for digital health; Wachter, 2015, Chapter 2), and so on, other parties will argue that proper ex ante risk assessments and precautions must be in place and adequate regulatory oversight might be needed to protect fundamental values such as respect for human rights and human dignity. A further view demands a "proportionate" response by regulators, weighing the burden on innovators (and, possibly, the delayed public enjoyment of benefits) against community concerns for safety and respect for values. This assessment, of course, simply restates the challenge without resolving it.

Tensions *between* the demands aside, each of the demands hinges on a deeply contested concept. In the case of this first demand, what kind of innovation is *beneficial?*: Beneficial to whom, beneficial in meeting whose needs, beneficial relative to which human interests? Beneficial when? At once, in the next 5 years, or at some unspecified time in the future?

### 5.1.2 *Provide for an Acceptable Management of Risks to Human Health and Safety and the Environment*

For the second demand, what is an *acceptable* risk? Notoriously, the view of professional risk-assessors differs from the lay view in characterizing a technology as "low risk" (inviting a leap to "safe") as long as the likelihood of the harm is low, even though anyone would see the harm in the question as extremely serious. (e.g., a commercial air crash is very rare but typically deadly.) Moreover, how is risk distributed? Who benefits and who bears the risk (M. Lee, 2009)?

### 5.1.3 *Respect Fundamental Community Values (Such as Privacy and Confidentiality, Freedom of Expression, Liberty, Justice, Human Rights, and Human Dignity)*

Last, which values (and which particular conception of a value) are guiding principles? Which value system does one support: one based on rights, one based on duties, or one geared toward maximizing utility (Brownsword, 2003)? If based on rights, then which rights (negative only or negative and positive, libertarian or liberal welfare, and so on)? If on duties, then which duties (e.g., Kantian or communitarian)? If on utility, then which variant (act or rule, ideal or actual, and so on)? If, instead, society is guided directly by values such as privacy or human dignity, liberty or justice, equality or solidarity, then which of the many conceptions of these values are to be taken as the reference standard (Beyleveld & Brownsword, 2001; Brownsword, 2017c; Duwell, Braavig, Brownsword, & Mieth, 2014)?

Following is a discussion of each of these three desiderata. After that is discourse on the use of technological management as a strategy for regulating the risks presented by new technologies and by human agents. I consider new approaches to regulating new technologies as well as new technologies as instruments to regulate older kinds of antisocial conduct. Finally is deliberation on the significance of maintaining the preconditions for human social existence. Quite simply, in the rapidly changing context of a range of emerging technologies, the preservation of these infrastructural conditions must be treated as an overriding policy objective for regulators (Brownsword, 2017b).

## 5.2 Supporting Beneficial Innovation

Beneficial innovation does not come from nowhere; it is not manna from heaven. Regulators must nurture and support research and development (Butenko & Larouche, 2015). Creating the right regulatory environment, with effective incentives for innovation, might involve some modification of intellectual property law, competition law, the tax and subsidy regime, and so on. Moreover, regular calls for "light-touch" or "better" or "proportionate" or "targeted" regulation will ensue. In short, "overregulation" is to be avoided; regulators should not set an unnecessary obstacle course for researchers.

Other will resist these calls: those who are concerned that the technologies might endanger human health and safety or the environment and those who are concerned that, danger or safety notwithstanding, the new technologies are incompatible with such fundamental values as human rights, human dignity, liberty, equality, and justice. Where health and safety or the environment are of concern, calls for "precaution" will abound (which might well involve more than a light-touch regulatory intervention) and where fundamental values are a concern, calls for even stronger red-line intervention will emerge.

Speaking of such tensions, Gregory Mandel (2009) nicely captures the dilemma:

> Emerging technology governance must traverse a fine line. Insufficient protection could lead to excessive or unknown human health and environmental risks and undercut public confidence. Excessive regulation could limit the development of an extremely promising technology and foreclose potentially great social, health, environmental, and economic benefits. This combination of vast potential benefits and uncertain risks presents unique and difficult challenges. All stakeholders, however, have significant incentives to develop a protective and well-defined governance structure. (p. 82)

In today's debates about the responsibilities of such "shared economy" operators as Uber and Airbnb and those who use their platforms, some advocate a light-touch approach (European Commission, 2016) and others express concern about the health and safety risks that might arise when Uber drivers work long hours and properties rented on Airbnb might not be subject to fire checks. Of course another concern surfaced that these platform operators, by flying below the standard regulatory radar, are competing unfairly with those taxis and hotels that are burdened by the costs of regulatory compliance.

Among the incentivizing instruments at regulators' disposal, intellectual property rights are central. The question of whether copyright has much incentivizing effect is moot (Heald, 2014), but no doubt the recognition of this form of proprietary right incentivizes commercial enterprises to acquire the relevant rights and to enforce them against infringers; witness the infringement claims brought by big media copyright holders against peer-to-peer file sharers and the platforms that enabled them. By contrast, general agreement exists that patents do have an incentivizing effect and that, without them, pharmaceutical companies in particular would find it hard to raise the funds to finance research and development. Nevertheless, two significant lines of argument oppose the patent regime. One is that the grant of patents is actually counterproductive to the objective of incentivizing beneficial innovation. The other is that the grant of patents fails to pay sufficient attention to whether an invention is compatible with fundamental values (Brownsword, 2014a).

The argument that patents are counterproductive hinges on a cluster of claims: that the system privileges upstream researchers who are first to the patent office over downstream researchers; that patent offices tend to grant patents that are overbroad; and that patent offices can be too quick to grant patents on products or processes of no obvious utility (Nuffield Council on Bioethics, 2002a). To the extent that these claims can be understood, it can be argued that prospective downstream researchers, faced by a thicket of patents and needing to negotiate licenses, might be discouraged from undertaking their research. In this way, the system is not fully faithful to its commitment to encourage beneficial research and innovation. Indeed, patent regimes are clearly dysfunctional if "instead of being a reward for inventors who place private information into the public domain, [they] become a means of recycling public information as private monopolies" (Drahos, 2002, p. 165).

The US Supreme Court's decision in the *Myriad Genetics* case (*Association for Molecular Pathology v. Myriad Genetics, Inc.*) stands out as a recent example of the law taking note of these arguments. The question in that case was whether, in the terms of §101 of the US Patent Act, the locating, sequencing, and isolating of the BRCA1 and BRCA2 genes amounted to a new and useful "composition of matter" or whether it was simply the discovery of a naturally occurring phenomenon. If the former, claims relating to the relevant sequences were patent-eligible; if the latter, no matter how brilliant the discovery, they would not be patentable. When, some years ago, the claims were first examined, patents were granted, which put Myriad in the position of a monopolist ability to file patent-infringement suits against anyone undertaking Breast Cancer Gene (BRCA) testing without its license. With the validity of these patents now called into question, the Supreme Court faced striking a delicate balance between maintaining (upstream) incentives that might lead to useful invention and avoiding impediments to the (downstream) flow of information that might be essential for other beneficial invention. The Court compromised by holding that the primary sequences were merely discoveries of naturally occurring sequences and thus were not patentable; however, the so-called cDNA sequences, which Myriad had constructed and which were not found in nature, were patent-eligible.

The argument that patents can create a tragedy of the anticommons, inhibiting further research and development, is not the only criticism of the present system. Debate also ensues about the extent to which it should be a condition of patentability that the claimed products or processes – novel, inventive, and useful though they might be – are compatible with fundamental values. Generally, patent regimes do not explicitly make compliance with fundamental values a condition of patentability, although moral judgments can enter through concepts such as the utility of the claimed invention. In the landmark case of *Diamond v. Chakrabarty* (1980), the majority of US Supreme Court members paved the way for the patenting of modern biotechnologies by taking a liberal approach to the kind of processes and products for which intellectual property rights might be claimed. Of course, a liberal policy in the patent office does not necessarily provide a comprehensive view; if public funding for morally controversial biotechnological research is withheld – as has happened in the United States and Europe – then, in practice, this can restrict opportunities for researchers.

By contrast with other major patent regimes, European patent law *explicitly* excludes immoral inventions. Article 53(a) of the European Patent Convention provides that an invention is not to be treated as patentable if, despite its originality, its commercial exploitation would be contrary to *ordre public* or morality. When the European Patent Office (EPO) first received modern biotechnological inventions – in the Harvard Onco-mouse application, which concerned a mouse that was genetically engineered to serve as a test animal for cancer research[1] – objectors argued

---

[1] Decision Once-mouse/Harvard, July 14, 1989 (OJ EPO 11/1989, 451; [1990] 1 EPOR 4. Initially, the examiners did not see the application as raising an issue under Article 53(a). It was only when the case was referred to the Board of Appeal that the centrality of Article 53(a) was recognized: see EPO Decision T 19/90 (OJ EPO 12/1990, 476; [1990] 7 EPOR 501).

that patents should not be granted on the relevant processes and products because this would be contrary to morality. For patent examiners who disclaimed any ethical expertise, it might have been tempting to refer the question to an expert ethics committee; instead, the examiners assumed responsibility for interpreting and applying the morality exclusion. Initially, the EPO took a utilitarian approach (giving considerable weight to the promised benefits of the particular bioinventions) and then marginalized the moral exclusion by treating it as applicable only where, in effect, granting a patent would be inconceivable from any moral viewpoint (Beyleveld & Brownsword, 1993).

At much the same time that the EPO was struggling with the Harvard Onco-mouse application, the European Commission in Brussels was trying to develop a new legal regime for patenting biotechnology (Beyleveld, Brownsword, & Llewelyn, 2000). Ostensibly, the proposed regime was a trade measure, designed to harmonize the patenting rules across the European single market. However, as soon as the draft Directive reached the European Parliament, it was clear that the issues could not be confined in this way, with an alliance of politicians protesting that the Commission's quest for a common position went far beyond matters of trade (Porter, 2009). As members of the alliance saw it, the question of whether a particular sequence of the human genome might be treated as patentable subject matter was not so much economic as fundamentally ethical and cultural.

Patent law in Europe thus found itself in the eye of a political storm. One view (favored by many political and industrial interests) was that Europe has too large a commercial stake in the biotechnology sector to be putting obstacles in the way of patentability. In other words, it was argued that the patent regime needed to be geared to encouraging research and development in modern biotechnologies and, crucially, investment in the Europe-based biotechnology sector. For their own reasons, patent practitioners, too, aligned themselves with the view that patent law should stick to the usual technical questions of originality, innovation, and the like, leaving moral debates to others. However, ranged against these views, a variety of constituencies – animal welfarists, environmentalists, dignitarians, and others – joined forces to insist that patent law should not facilitate the biotechnological revolution without taking a hard look at its ethical and cultural implications.

After an extended but unsuccessful attempt to reach agreement on the terms of the draft Directive, it was withdrawn. However, following the behind-the-scenes discussion, a new draft was introduced that duly became

Directive 98/44/EC on the Legal Protection of Biotechnological Inventions. At the heart of the Directive, Article 6(1) – in terms that closely resemble those of Article 53(a) of the European Patent Convention – sets out a general moral exclusion against patentability as follows: "Inventions shall be considered unpatentable where their commercial exploitation would be contrary to *ordre public* or morality; however, exploitation shall not be deemed to be so contrary merely because it is prohibited by law or regulation." This was supplemented by Article 6(2), which provides the following:

> On the basis of paragraph 1 (i.e., Article 6[1]), the following, in particular, shall be considered unpatentable:

(a)  processes for cloning human beings;
(b)  processes for modifying the germ line genetic identity of human beings;
(c)  uses of human embryos for industrial or commercial purposes;
(d)  processes for modifying the genetic identity of animals which are likely to cause them suffering without any substantial medical benefit to man or animal, and also animals resulting from such processes.

Article 6(2) draws on a number of Recitals, one of which, Recital 38, makes it clear not only that the list of four processes/uses was not intended to be exhaustive but also that inventions should simply be regarded as unpatentable where they compromise human dignity (Beyleveld et al., 2000).

More than a decade later, in 2011, the interpretation of the Directive – and specifically the exclusion in Article 6(2)(c) concerning research using human embryos – was tested before the European Court of Justice (the CJEU) in the *Brüstle* case (*Oliver Brüstle v. Greenpeace*). Briefly, the CJEU, responding to a reference from the German Federal Court of Justice, ruled that innovative stem-cell research conducted by Oliver Brüstle was excluded from patentability by Article 6(2)(c) – or, at any rate, it was excluded to the extent that Brüstle's research relied on the use of "base materials" derived from human embryos that were, in the process, necessarily terminated. Inevitably, the underlying tensions in the Directive – between a liberal permissive patenting paradigm in relation to inventive work involving the human genome and a restrictive conservative patenting paradigm in relation to research using human embryos – were brought to the surface. Whereas the EPO's marginalization of the morality exclusion favored the interests of those states that took a liberal approach, the CJEU's dignitarian interpretation of the Directive not only favored a conservative approach, but also imposed that approach on all member states. Predictably, this outcome provoked concerns about the impact on invest-ment in research in Europe and claims that the CJEU had exceeded its authority, as well as objections to the legitimacy of the restrictive dignitar-ian interpretation of the Directive (Plomer, 2012).

In *Brüstle*, the CJEU found itself caught between a liberal rock and a dignitarian hard place (Brownsword, 2014b). The European legislative institutions had been unable to find a common position and the eventual legalized Directive was a pragmatic compromise, giving liberals something of what they wanted (the possibility of patenting inventive work involving the human genome) while giving the dignitarians some of the restrictions they wanted (particularly concerning the protection of human embryos). In effect, the CJEU did little more in *Brüstle* than uphold the dignitarian side of the compromise rather than "fudging" the issue or, even more provocatively, defying the Directive and siding with the liberals.

In addition to the legal question of patentability, *Brüstle* raised complex questions about the competence and authority of patent examiners, courts, and legislatures to engage with disputes that raise deep moral divisions. Litigation in a case such as *Brüstle* – which ostensibly relates to patents – becomes "a theatre for the re-enactment of moral and religious disputes between secular and religious forces divided on the value of human 'life'" (Plomer, 2015, p. 24). Given that the Directive at issue in *Brüstle* was the best attempt that European legislative bodies could make at resolving this dispute, one might entertain some doubts about the adequacy not only of courts but also of legislatures in addressing such issues.

## 5.3 Acceptable Management of Risk

Where individual human agents, A and B, balance the benefits and risks associated with some new technology, they might well form different views. For example, while A might judge that it is of interest to spend time on social networking sites, B might judge otherwise; while A might judge that it is worth spending money on a personal digital assistant, B might judge otherwise, and so on. A and B might or might not prove to be good judges of what is in their own long-term interests, but the fact that individuals make different assessments of this kind is not, in itself, a matter for regulatory concern.

However, if A takes the risk while B enjoys the benefit, should regulators be concerned? Not necessarily. For example, A might be an altruist who is happy to give blood or donate an organ for the benefit of B or to volunteer for a research study strictly for the benefit of others. In the United Kingdom, for instance, about 500,000 people have freely agreed to participate in UK Biobank (2017), largely on the basis that the resource (of medical and lifestyle data, together with biosamples) will assist health care researchers in ways that will benefit future generations. Provided that such assistance is free and not encouraged by a false prospectus, this is fine. If, however, the project has undeclared commercial interests or if researchers may exploit the project commercially (which may not be fully understood by donors or participants), this might well prompt a withdrawal of support or even provoke litigation – whether to claim a share in the commercial proceeds or to prevent such commercialization (Brownsword, 2009).[2]

Where, as is often the case, new technologies are socially and economically disruptive, some persons bear the risks and losses while others capture the benefits (Wolff, 2010). For example, although consumers worldwide might welcome the benefits of Instagram, the many Kodak employees who lost their jobs when the company closed down might take a different view (Keen, 2015, pp. 87–88). Similarly, where new automated technologies affect the employment market, mixed reviews may arise not only from those who directly experience the losses compared to those who benefit from cheaper goods or services, but also from macroeconomists who try to assess whether, in the longer term, the disruptive effects are positive or negative relative to the overall economic well-being of the community (Dau-Schmidt, 2017).

Although regulators might see no need to interfere with many individual (informed) prudential judgments, in some cases they cannot evade action. For example, suppose – to take a provocative hypothetical suggested by Tran (2015, p. 159) – that 3D printing technologies are proposed to "cloneprint" some extinct mammals. Individuals who judge the benefits and risks of this proposal relative to animals, the environment, and humans are likely, as Tran points out, to be guided by whether their dispositions are "animal-friendly" or "environment-friendly" – or, indeed, "human friendly." Generalizing this hypothetical case, regulatees will look to regulators to set appropriate standards – for the sake of human health and safety, the welfare of animals, and the integrity of the environment – for the research, development, and application of "risky" technologies (such as nuclear reactors, particle accelerators, synthetic biology, or nanotechnologies – and, possibly,

---

[2] For well-known cases, see *Moore v. Regents of the University of California* (51 Cal. 3d 120; 271 Cal. Rptr. 146; 793 P.2d 479) and *Greenberg v. Miami Children's Hospital Research Institute* 208 F. Supp. 2d Series 981, July 8, 2002.

3D printers). This is not usually understood as a demand for zero risk but, rather, as an expectation that regulators set standards that manage risk at an acceptable level (European Group on Ethics in Science and New Technologies, 2007, para. 4.2.3). However, what constitutes an acceptable risk depends on how one calculates the costs and benefits and how they are distributed. Although Agent A, who is highly risk-averse, might judge – prudentially – that synthetic biology should be prohibited or at least subjected to a moratorium, Agent B, who is a biotechnological entrepreneur, might take a radically different view.

Where a regulatory position needs to be taken, how should regulators respond to such a plurality of views? In a democracy, a process of public engagement is a reasonable expectation, before a position is taken. Before settling on a legal framework, a process must, in the spirit of deliberative democracy, seek a reasonable position; in this case, a position that reflects a reasonable view about an acceptable level of risk.

However, engaging the public on questions concerning emerging technologies is far from straightforward. For example, how is society to cope with extremely variable levels of public understanding of the technology? How is society to distill attitudes toward a particular technology from a medley of predispositions to science, technology, commerce, and so on? How is society to overcome the public's suspicion of stakeholders in the technology? Reflecting on the public debate on genetically modified (GM) foods in the UK, Jasanoff (2005) suggested that it

> underscored a dilemma confronting state efforts to democratise the politics of new and emerging technologies: on the one hand, interacting only with identifiable stakeholders may simply strengthen the traditionally cozy relations between business and government; on the other hand, the public that needs to be engaged in broader debates about the pros and cons of technology is elusive and, in the absence of reliable precedents, hard to engage in deliberations whose very authenticity and purpose are widely questioned. (p. 129)

How might these obstacles be overcome? An influential report on nanotechnologies by the Royal Society and the Royal Academy of Engineering (2004, para. 38) recommended that (a) dialogue and engagement should occur early – before critical decisions about the technology become irreversible or "locked in"; (b) dialogue should be designed around clear and specific objectives; (c) sponsors should publicly commit to taking account of the outcome of the engagement process; (d) dialogue should be properly integrated with other related processes of technology assessment; and (e) resourcing for the dialogue should be adequate (see, too, Nuffield

Council on Bioethics, 2012). Even with attention to these matters, however, doubts may arise about how fully the public engages and, of course, it is difficult to immunize a citizen jury against the influence of the media – particularly when headlines that accentuate a technology's benefits or risks make good copy.

Assuming, though, that members of the public can adequately engage, their prudential calculations are likely to vary and, concomitantly, their preferred regulatory responses will be at different points of the spectrum from prohibition to permission to promotion. Still, in a democracy, this is the stuff of politics. Decisions made today can be revised tomorrow and, although this might not be the ideal way to accommodate the variety of self-interested views, it is a civilized way of living with pluralism. Accordingly, even if the realization of deliberative democracy is challenging, it appeals as the right approach.

Conflicting assessments of risk and benefit are not only a challenge for national regulators; they can also spill over into international trade, illustrated by the dispute between a number of GM-exporting countries and Europe that eventually came to a head before a World Trade Organization Disputes Panel in *European Communities – Measures Affecting the Approval and Marketing of Biotech Products*.[3]

In a case such as *Biotech Products*, the relevant General Agreement on Tariffs and Trade provisions (especially in the Sanitary and Phytosanitary Agreement) channel the disputants toward arguments based on scientific evidence (R. Lee, 2005). Where, as in *Biotech Products*, the science relating to the safety of GM crops is contested, how can the matter be resolved? An innocent response is that the question should be determined by reference to the view supported by "sound science," taken to be a neutral and reliable arbiter. However, for many commentators on the practice and politics of science, this is a naïve view. Science simply is not like that; scientists reasonably disagree with one another, not just about the ultimate questions, but about matters of methodology, relevance, and focus. Science is never going to be theory-neutral (that is the whole point of the enterprise) and we might wonder whether it can ever be "value-neutral." For example, a fundamental divide exists between a regulatory approach that focuses on the safety of the end product (as tends to be the case in North America) and one that focuses on the safety of the process (as tends to be the case in Europe). If scientists on opposing sides of the Atlantic can make different

---

[3] WT/DS291/23 (United States), WT/DS292/17 (Canada), and WT/DS293/17 (Argentina), August 8, 2003.

safety judgments, each regarded in its own territory as sound science, then "sound science" simply cannot serve as a neutral court of appeal. In turn, the question of whether, say, GM crops or meat from cloned cattle or novel nanofoods are "safe" cannot have a straightforward answer.

In the case of GM crops, European attitudes involve a mix of prudential and precautionary judgments with some profound moral concerns. Irrespective, then, of whether disputes such as that in *Biotech Products* are remitted to the court of "sound science," the question remains of how far the international trading community can permit local culture to create its own special rules for market access. In *Biotech Products*, the Panel's line is that, where a level of scientific uncertainty leaves room for legitimate disagreement, those states that prefer to take a risk-averse approach are allowed, at least provisionally, to do so; in contrast, where little room exists for scientific doubt, members are not to be encouraged to dress up their moral objections as if they are concerns about safety. Objecting that one does not want to gamble on GM crop safety is one thing; objecting to GM crops on moral grounds is something else.

## 5.4 Respecting Fundamental Values

Each community with moral aspirations will subscribe to a number of fundamental values, often enshrined in high-level constitutional instruments. These values offer some guidance on how the community understands its aspiration to do the right thing. These values help specify *what* counts as a "legitimate" interest of oneself and of others and *who* counts as a relevant "other"; for example, whether unborn fetuses, future generations, or animals count as relevant others when we make an ethical judgment.

Notably, in the much-debated UNESCO Universal Declaration on Bioethics and Human Rights 2005 – addressed, in the words of Article 1, to "ethical issues related to medicine, life sciences and associated technologies" – we find a heroic attempt to set a global framework for bioethics. Thus, immediately after Article 4, which emphasizes (in a utilitarian way) the maximization of benefit and the minimization of harm, is a run of articles that highlight the importance of individual autonomy (Article 5) and consent (Article 6), requiring respect for privacy and confidentiality (Article 9). Moreover, demands pepper the Declaration with demands that human dignity should be respected, a prominent example being Article 3(1), which enjoins that "human dignity, human rights and fundamental freedoms are to be fully respected."

In this ethical cocktail, three ingredients dominate, each with its criterion for doing the right thing. According to one view, the right thing is acting in accordance with one's *duties,* another has it that one should always respect the *rights* of others, and a third advocates the maximization of a good such as utility. One can articulate each view in many ways, specifying different goods or goals, different rights, and different duties. Nevertheless, in principle, this matrix governs the basic pattern of ethical debate, whether the technological focus be biotechnology (and bioethics), information and communication technology (and cyberethics), nanotechnology (and nanoethics), neurotechnology (and neuroethics), or something else.

Although, in principle, the matrix sets the pattern, in practice, the pattern is not always fully expressed in debates about the ethics of new technologies. Often, the debate is only a two-sided with utilitarian cost-benefit calculations set against human rights considerations. In general, leaving aside major safety concerns, utilitarians will assert the "green light" ethics of proceeding while human rights theorists will take an "amber light" approach, insisting that the technological traffic pause (to ensure rights clearance) before proceeding. Elsewhere, though, is a three-way articulation of the matrix, the key substantive positions being utilitarian, human rights, and duty-based dignitarian. In this distinctive bioethical triangle is a dignitarian alliance taking issue with utilitarians and human rights advocates, as was the case with the negotiation of Directive 98/44/EC on the patentability of modern biotechnologies (see Supporting Beneficial Innovation above). Although the latter two can sometimes find a common position, it is much more difficult to reach an accommodation with dignitarians. According to the dignitarian ethic, some technological applications are categorically and nonnegotiably unacceptable. In this sense, of the three ethical perspectives, only the duty-based dignitarian view is genuinely "red light" (Brownsword, 2006).

Somewhat confusingly, advocates of human rights and duty-driven dignitarians make recurrent appeals to human dignity. For the former, human dignity (qua empowerment) underpins human rights; for the latter, human dignity (qua constraint) sets limits to human autonomy and to adoption of new technologies (Beyleveld & Brownsword, 2001; Brownsword, 2013). Thus, one should be slow to treat notions commonly found in ethical arguments – such as "harm to others," "informed consent," "precaution," and "proportionality" – as neutral as they may sound. Rather, one should read such ideas through the lens of a particular substantive articulation of the matrix. Also, one should not expect too much of ethical experts. Policy makers and regulators who seek advice from such experts can be told how the plurality plays out in relation to a particular issue, but the plurality cannot be easily dissolved. In practice, coopting ethical experts promises to improve the quality of the regulatory process; it might well be that the most acceptable response to ethical pluralism (as to prudential pluralism) is to invest in the integrity of the process. Indeed, during the time that Amy Gutmann chaired the US Presidential Commission for the Study of Bioethical Issues, its approach was precisely to encourage informed debate about emerging technologies in the spirit of deliberative democracy.

Currently, many ethical questions arise about the development of smart machines (such as the Aeon babysitting robot discussed in the introduction) that might take over a range of responsibilities hitherto held by people. Where responsibilities involve life-and-death decisions, as might be the case with autonomous vehicles and lethal autonomous weapons systems, an acute concern emerges about the ethics of letting the machine decide (Bhuta, Beck, Geiss, Liu, & Kress, 2016; Wallach, 2015, pp. 213–219, 229–231).

With reference to autonomous vehicles, how might such a vehicle address the kind of dilemma presented by the trolley problem (where one option is to kill or injure one innocent human and the only other option is to kill or injure more than one innocent human) or by the tunnel problem (where the choice is between killing a passenger in the vehicle and killing a child – or a neighbor's dog – outside the vehicle). Predictably, no sooner had it been reported that Uber was going to run a pilot test with driverless taxis in Pittsburgh than people raised these precise questions. How might society respond?

First, the particular moral dilemma presented by the trolley problem (at any rate, in the version I described) is open to only two plausible answers. A moralist will either say that killing just the one person is clearly the lesser of two evils and is morally required; or an alternative is to argue that, because the loss of one innocent life weighs as heavily as the loss of many innocent lives, neither option is better than the other, from which it follows that killing just the one person is neither better nor (crucially) worse, morally speaking, than killing many. Accordingly, if autonomous vehicles are programmed to minimize the number of humans who are killed or injured, this is either right in line with one strand of moral thinking or, following the other, at least no worse than any other programming. Someone would oppose such a design who argued that the vehicle should be set up to kill more rather than fewer humans. Barring some quite exceptional circumstances, that, surely, is not a plausible moral view.

Second, if autonomous vehicles were designed to minimize human deaths or injuries, it is hard to believe that human drivers, acting on their on-the-spot moral judgments, would do any better overall. Confronted by a trolley scenario, with little or no time to make a moral assessment of the situation, human drivers would act instinctively and – insofar as they formed any sense of the right thing to do in the particular situation – would surely try to minimize the loss of life (Bonnefon, Shariff, & Rahwan, 2016). What other defensible response could there be?

Third, even if – at least in the case of autonomous vehicles – a reasonably straightforward resolution of the trolley problem exists, more difficult cases may also exist. For example, the dilemma in the tunnel problem is to choose between sacrificing one innocent passenger in an autonomous vehicle or killing an innocent child outside the vehicle. One might suggest that, because autonomous cars present a new and added risk, those who travel in them should be sacrificed. However, this is a case about which moralists might reasonably disagree. In such cases, Carr (2015) asks, "Who determines what the 'optimal' or 'rational' choice is in a morally ambiguous situation? Who gets to program the robot's conscience? Is it the robot's manufacturer? The robot's owner? The software coders? Politicians? Government regulators? Philosophers? An insurance underwriter?" (p. 186).

In the absence of philosopher kings, the best society can expect is that autonomous vehicles will be programmed to reflect the terms of the social license agreed by the members of the community in which they will operate. In such communities, agents will have an opportunity to formulate and express their own moral views as they negotiate and debate the license. Already, the Open Roboethics Initiative is exploring imaginative ways to crowd-source public views on acceptable behavior by robots, even in relation to such everyday questions as whether a robot should give way to a human or vice versa (Moon et al., 2016).

Turning to lethal autonomous weapons, it is important to recognize a radically different context. Tragic accidents may ensue with automated transport systems, but they do not systematically degrade conditions for human social existence. Anyone who doubts the catastrophic impact of modern warfare on the military and civilian populations need only glance at the state of the commons in the war zones of the Middle East. It follows that it is quite difficult to justify engaging in such systematic destructive activities unless they (and the deployment of lethal weapons) can be shown to be quite clearly the lesser of two evils in defense of the basic preconditions for human social existence (see my concluding remarks). Even subtracting lethal autonomous weapons systems from the arsenal, warfare is still likely to be ethically problematic.

That said, what should society decide about moral concerns that focus on leaving autonomous weapons systems to make life-and-death decisions without a human being in control at the time such decisions are made? Arguably, this is not the right focus for the present concern. Rather, the question should be whether humans have designed the machine in such a way that, when the machine takes life, this is in line with the considered moral judgment of the designers and of the communities that endorse the use of such machines. Provided this is the case, humans can have no objection as they are abdicating their moral responsibilities or delegating moral decision-making to a machine. But, of course, the proviso is a critical one. New technologies should not be left to make important decisions without authorization granted by a proper social license.

## 5.5 Technological Management

Regulators might respond to new technologies by enacting legislation or they might favor a more flexible type of standard or, indeed, a less-formal type of governance. Flexibility truly comes at the price of rule-predictability. Less-formal governance garners obvious concerns about leaving it to industry or to the professions to self-regulate. For example, society may have concerns that self-regulation will not be open and inclusive and will be guided exclusively by self-interest. People understand good governance, by contrast, to be transparent, inclusive, accountable, and consistent with the public interest. Barring some oversight to these criteria, many will see the regulatory environment as deficient.

Cutting across these relatively familiar issues of top-down regulation, bottom-up regulation, or coregulation is an emerging issue concerning the choice between regulation by rules or standards and regulation by technological management, raising some puzzling questions for legal scholars. In particular, questions emerge about when and why it is appropriate to employ normative (rule-like) instruments and when to rely on technological management and design. As Jasanoff (2016) recently suggested, even though "technological systems rival legal constitutions in their power to order and govern society ... there is no systematic body of thought, comparable to centuries of legal and political theory, to articulate the principles by which technologies are empowered to rule us" (pp. 9–10).

In other words, reinventing and refocusing jurisprudence must ensure its lines of inquiry better align with the challenges and opportunities presented by today's technologies (Brownsword, 2017a).

As noted, the new General Data Protection Regulation recognizes the possibility of designing privacy protection into the technology. However, 20 years ago Reidenberg (1997–1998) and Lessig (1999, Chapter 7) famously pointed out that entities might deploy "code" and similar technological features with regulatory intent (as when manufacturers embed digital-rights management in a product or a process). Broadening and developing this critical insight is the paradigmatic case of such technological management as that having the following features:

- R, a regulator, has a view about whether regulatees should be required to do X, are permitted to do it, or are prohibited from doing it (the underlying normative view).
- R's view could be expressed in the form of a rule or standard that requires, permits, or prohibits the doing of X (the underlying rule or standard).
- Instead, R uses (or directs others to use) technological management.
- R's intention is to translate the underlying normative view into a practical design that ensures that regulatees do or do not do X (according to the underlying rule).
- The outcome is that regulatees find themselves in environments in which the immediate signals relate to what they can and cannot be do – to possibilities and impossibilities – rather than to the underlying normative pattern of what ought or ought not to be done.

Where these features are present, R intends that the use of some technology, rather than the use of a rule or standard, will channel the behavior of regulatees in a particular way. When entities use technologies, such as closed-circuit television surveillance or DNA profiling, in support of the rules of criminal law, this is a step toward technological management. However, such assistive uses of technology fall short of the kind of forcing or excluding effect contemplated by full-scale technological management. Although some might contest the proposition that "code is law," it is hard to deny that code or other technologies that are intentionally applied with a hard-edged regulatory purpose represent a species of regulation. This presents a whole new agenda for jurists.

First, questions abound about the significance of the "complexion" of the regulatory environment (Brownsword, 2011). Where regulation takes the form of rules, regulatees might comply (or not comply) with the rules for prudential, moral, or mixed reasons. However, faced with regulation by technological management, regulatees have no choice but to comply. They might independently judge that, given the choice, they would comply for prudential, moral, or mixed reasons; but, in fact, they do not have the choice. This possibility seems to have implications for the autonomy of agents and – as moralists would see it – for the conditions required for agents freely to do the right thing.

Second are various "ideals" that are, if not intrinsic to the legal enterprise, at least associated with best practice. At the head of this list are the Rule of Law and the ideal of legality (Brownsword, 2016b). Referencing the well-known Fullerian (Fuller, 1969) principles of legality and, concomitantly, the notion of the Rule of Law as the publication (promulgation) of rules and then the congruent administration of those rules, the question is whether – and, if so, how – these principles might stretch across to technological management. On the face of it, Fullerian principles presuppose *rules*: that is, they stipulate that the rules should be published, that the rules should be prospective, that the rules should be clear and relatively constant, that the rules should not be contradictory, and so on. Indeed, they seem to be particularly focused on the rules of criminal law (or other duty-imposing rules). If this is correct, then perhaps, in an era of technological management, the ideal of legality remains relevant but its focus shifts to the processual public-law values of transparency, accountability, inclusive participation, and the like, together with the controls exerted by background fundamental values (such as compatibility with respect for human rights and human dignity). In this way, although the zone regulated *directly* by traditional legal rules might shrink, the significance of the authorizing rules of law and the ideal of legality (as a check on technological management) remains.

Third, if we assume a major technological impingement on the way people transact and interact in the future, attention switches to the fate of those bodies of law – contract law, tort law, and criminal law in particular – that have hitherto regulated such activities. For example, if smart cars make many traffic laws redundant and if technological management in hospitals and workplaces ensures patients and employees are safe, how much of criminal law and the law of negligence are sidelined? Where society relies on technological management for health and safety, "regulatory" criminal law will be largely displaced. Given that this body of law features strict and absolute liability offenses – where it is not a necessary condition for the commission of the offense that the act in question (such as polluting a waterway) is done to put human health and safety at risk – and, in consequence, is a body of law about which one may not feel entirely comfortable, perhaps its displacement is no bad thing (Sayre, 1933). Arguably, moral concerns heighten only where it is the classical crimes of intent that are disrupted. Certainly, people have little or no enthusiasm for the adoption of absolute liability in relation to core (or, as some would have it, "real" or "true") crimes; but if the rules that specify such central criminal offenses could be rendered redundant by preventive technological measures, should ethicists or legal scholars support or oppose this (Brownsword, 2016a)?

Again, if the technological infrastructure for transactions is such that commerce becomes largely a conversation between machines, what does this mean for the leading principles of contract law and for a jurisprudence that is heavy with case law from earlier centuries (Brownsword, 2018)? Rather than being an occasion for the celebration of new forms of contract, does this signify "the end of contracts" (Zuboff, 2015, p. 86)? Similarly, when so many of our future transactions and interactions will take place in environments that are data gathering and data giving, what does this signify for the laws of privacy, confidentiality, and data protection? Are people's informational interests to be reduced to a balance of acceptable risks and desired benefits? Should society support the use of "privacy by design" (Hildebrandt, 2015)?

Fourth, if there is some possibility of effective biomanagement of human conduct, yet more questions emerge. Thus far, although advances in biotechnologies have received at least as much attention as developments in information and communication technologies, their penetration into daily life has been much more modest and their utility as regulatory instruments much less obvious. Genetics and genomics are extremely complex. Even if genetic researchers make major strides, the chances are that for some time, *behavioral* genetics will be extremely primitive (Nuffield Council on Bioethics, 2002b). However, with another 100 years of research and development, the story might be different (Wilson, 2015). If so, and if biomanagement operates through internal signaling mechanisms that we (humans) know to be operative but of which we are individually not conscious, a new internal dimension arises to the regulatory environment. In such a regulatory environment, signals will be "external" to regulatees and to which they will respond, but also signals will be "internal." To engage with such a world, one will need to frame inquiries by reference to a regulatory environment that has not only normative and nonnormative dimensions, but also external and internal dimensions.

Fifth is the question with which we started: Does sticking with the rule of rules (and standards) have some virtue, rather than resorting to a technological fix? Might rules that are less effective than technological management nevertheless have some virtues? For example, is there virtue when rules do not, in practice, reach compliance? This possibility leaves a gap that can be productively exploited by conscientious objectors and civil disobedients (Morozov, 2013). Even straightforward acts of noncompliance can stimulate reflection on the acceptability of background rules. To this extent, deviance is not entirely dysfunctional. Concomitantly, might leaving some room for self-regulation have virtue, in the way, for instance, that some groups might then have space to develop their own workable standards of neighborliness and reasonableness (Ellickson, 1991)? Furthermore, one might doubt that technological management is capable of reflecting the nuances that can be built into the drafting of rules (inviting interpretation and, concomitantly, offering some space for discretionary application that is responsive to the particular circumstances). The use of technological management may entail risk that excludes too many non-technically expert people who cannot meaningfully participate in the process. Finally, one might wonder whether technological management might, in practice, be resistant to easy change or amendment to the extent that rules are provisional, reviewable, and revisable interventions.

## 5.6 Concluding Remarks

Regulators and their communities have much to ponder. At many levels, new technologies are disruptive. Nevertheless, one set of fixed bearings exists: No matter how advanced a community of humans is technologically, it is imperative that regulators maintain the preconditions for human social existence itself. Quite simply, the terms and conditions of any regulatory (or social) license for new technologies should protect, preserve, and promote the following:

- The essential conditions for human existence (given biological needs)
- The generic conditions for human agency and self-development
- The essential conditions for the development and practice of moral agency

Moreover, these are imperatives for regulators in all regulatory spaces, whether international or national, public or private. Responsibilities for the commons have no exemptions or exceptions; these principles are truly cosmopolitan (Brownsword, 2008, Chapter 7; 2010).

In the first instance, regulators should take steps to protect, preserve, and promote the natural ecosystem for human life. Starting with the maintenance of the so-called planetary boundaries (Raworth, 2017, pp. 43–53; Rockström et al., 2009), regulators need to prevent the occurrence of – or, at any rate, minimize the damage caused by – human-initiated existential threats, for example, threats presented by ozone-depleting chemicals, dangerous pathogens, the proliferation of nuclear weapons, and (arguably) large particle accelerators and colliders (Wallach, 2015, pp. 1–7). Secondly, the conditions for meaningful self-development and agency need to be constructed (largely in the form of positive support and negative restriction) with sufficient trust and confidence in one's fellow agents, together with sufficient predictability to plan, operating in a way that is interactive and purposeful rather than merely defensive. What is dystopian about Orwell's (1949/1954) *1984* and Huxley's (1932/2007) *Brave New World* is not that human *existence* is compromised but that human *agency* is compromised. We can appreciate, too, that today's dataveillance practices, as much as *1984*'s surveillance, "may be doing less to deter destructive acts than [slowly to narrow] the range of tolerable thought and behaviour" (Pasquale, 2015, p. 52). Third, conditions must exist for the moral development of agents and for opportunities to practice moral agency. In other words, the context for human interactions and transactions needs to leave open the possibility for agents freely to do the right thing.

The point about these three essential tenets is that they are conceived as precompetitive or preconflictual. The tensions – the competing demands, purposes, and priorities – that characterize much social life are all to come. These critical preconditions (whatever they are agreed to be) are, by definition, neutral, as between one human and another, between one agent and another, and between one agent with moral aspirations and another (or between one moral viewpoint and another). These preconditions are a "commons" that reflect the needs of all humans, irrespective of their particular projects and plans as agents and their particular moral beliefs. If, during the course of deliberative democratic debate, anyone proposes that some new technology be licensed to operate in ways that might compromise any of these compulsory conditions, regulators should treat such a proposal as wholly "unreasonable." Of course, determining the nature of these conditions will not be a mechanical process and I do not assume it will be without its points of controversy.

That said, clearly each human agent is a stakeholder in the commons that protects the essential conditions for human existence, aligned with the generic conditions of agency. These conditions must, therefore, be respected. Beyond these conditions, agents may debate their differences about the balance of benefit and risk associated with new technologies and about how they should do the right thing in characterizing the benefits and distributing the risks. In other words, although respect for the commons' conditions is binding on all human agents, these conditions do not rule out the possibility of prudential disagreement and moral contestation. A fundamental challenge for regulators in these transformative times is to protect the commons' conditions against dangerous technologies while facilitating the articulation of social licenses for technologies that are divisive but not, in this sense, dangerous.

Finally, securing the preconditions for human social existence should not be considered the end of the matter. These are *pre*conditions – they set the stage – but it is for different groups of humans to articulate their relationships, collective and individual, with emerging technologies. As ever, legal responses to emerging technologies will vary as they reflect different regulatory cultures in conjunction with the plurality of prudential and moral judgments of particular communities.

## REFERENCES

Annas, G. J., Andrews, L. B., & Isasi, R. M. (2002). Protecting the endangered human: Toward an international treaty prohibiting cloning and inheritable alterations. *American Journal of Law & Medicine, 28*, 151–178.

Association for Molecular Pathology v. Myriad Genetics, Inc., 569 US 576 (2013).

Beyleveld, D., & Brownsword, R. (1993). *Mice, morality and patents*. London, England: Common Law Institute of Intellectual Property.

Beyleveld, D., & Brownsword, R. (2001). *Human dignity in bioethics and biolaw*. Oxford, England: Oxford University Press.

Beyleveld, D., Brownsword, R., & Llewelyn, M. (2000). The morality clauses of the Directive on the Legal Protection of Biotechnological Inventions: Conflict, compromise, and the patent community. In R. Goldberg & J. Lonbay (Eds.), *Pharmaceutical medicine, biotechnology and European law* (pp. 157–181). Cambridge, England: Cambridge University Press.

Bhuta, N., Beck, S., Geiss, R., Liu, H-Y., & Kress, C. (Eds.) (2016). *Autonomous weapons systems: Law, ethics, policy*. Cambridge, England: Cambridge University Press.

Biobank. (2017). *About*. Retrieved from www.ukbiobank.ac.uk/about-biobank-uk/

Bonnefon, J.-F., Shariff, A., & Rahwan, I. (2016). The social dilemma of autonomous vehicles. *Science, 352*, 1573–1576. doi:10.1126/science.aaf2654

Brownsword, R. (2003). Bioethics today, bioethics tomorrow: Stem cell research and the dignitarian alliance. *Notre Dame Journal of Law, Ethics and Public Policy, 17*(2), 15–51. Retrieved from https://pdfs.semanticscholar.org/98ae/1999 aabf0d9cec3168acebf12cef007cf120.pdf

Brownsword, R. (2006). Cloning, zoning, and the harm principle. In S. McLean (Ed.), *First, do no harm* (pp. 527–542). Aldershot, England: Ashgate.

Brownsword, R. (2008). *Rights, regulation and the technological revolution*. Oxford, England: Oxford University Press.

Brownsword, R. (2009). Property in human tissue: Triangulating the issue. In M. Steinman, P. Sykora, & U. Wiesing (Eds.), *Altruism reconsidered: Exploring new approaches to property in human tissue* (pp. 93–104). Aldershot, England: Ashgate.

Brownsword, R. (2010). Regulatory cosmopolitanism: Clubs, commons, and questions of coherence (TILT Working Paper No. 18). Tilburg, Netherlands: Tilburg University.

Brownsword, R. (2011). Lost in translation: Legality, regulatory margins, and technological management. *Berkeley Technology Law Journal, 26*, 1321–1365.

Brownsword, R. (2013). Human dignity, human rights, and simply trying to do the right thing. In C. McCrudden (Ed.), *Understanding human dignity* (pp. 345–358). Oxford, England: British Academy/Oxford University Press.

Brownsword, R. (2014a). Patents and intellectual property rights. In D. Moellendorf & H. Widdows (Eds.), *The handbook of global ethics* (pp. 354–367). London, England: Routledge.

Brownsword, R. (2014b). Regulatory coherence—a European challenge. In K. Purnhagen & P. Rott (Eds.), *Varieties of European economic law and regulation: Essays in honour of Hans Micklitz* (pp. 235–258). New York, NY: Springer.

Brownsword, R. (2016a). *Law as a moral judgment: The domain of jurisprudence, and technological management*. In P. Capps & S. D. Pattinson (Eds.), *Ethical rationalism and the law* (pp. 109–130). Oxford, England: Hart.

Brownsword, R. (2016b). Technological management and the rule of law. *Law, Innovation and Technology, 8*, 100–140. doi:10.1080/17579961.2016.1161891

Brownsword, R. (2017a). Field, frame and focus: Methodological issues in the new legal world. In R. van Gestel, H. Micklitz, & E. Rubin (Eds.), *Rethinking legal scholarship* (pp. 112–172). Cambridge, England: Cambridge University Press.

Brownsword, R. (2017b) From Erewhon to Alpha Go: For the sake of human dignity should we destroy the machines? *Law, Innovation and Technology, 9*, 117–153. doi:10.1080/17579961.2017.1303927

Brownsword, R. (2017c). Law, liberty and technology. In R. Brownsword, E. Scotford, & K. Yeung (Eds.), *The Oxford handbook of law, regulation and technology* (pp. 41–68). Oxford, England: Oxford University Press.

Brownsword, R. (2018). The e-commerce directive, consumer transactions, and the digital single market: Questions of regulatory fitness, regulatory disconnection and rule redirection. In S. Grundmann & I. Kull (Eds.), *European contract law in the digital age* (Vol. 3). Cambridge, England: Intersentia. Retrieved from https://oigus.ut.ee/sites/default/files/oi/brownsword.pdf

Butenko, A., & Larouche, P. (2015). Regulation for innovativeness or regulation of innovation? *Law, Innovation and Technology, 7*, 52–82. doi:10.1080/17579961.2015.1052643

Carr, N. (2015). *The glass cage.* London, England: Vintage.

Collingridge, D. (1980). *The social control of technology.* New York, NY: Frances Pinter.

Dau-Schmidt, K. G. (2017). Trade, commerce, and employment: The evolution of the form and regulation of the employment relationship in response to the new information technology. In R. Brownsword, E. Scotford, & K. Yeung (Eds.), *The Oxford handbook of law, regulation and technology* (Chapter 43). Oxford, England: Oxford University Press. doi:10.1093/oxfordhb/9780199680832.013.64

Diamond v. Chakrabarty, 447 US 303 (1980).

Drahos, P. (2002). *Information feudalism: Who owns the knowledge economy?* London, England: Earthscan.

Duwell, M., Braavig, J., Brownsword, R., & Mieth, D. (Eds.) (2014). *Cambridge handbook of human dignity.* Cambridge, England: Cambridge University Press.

Ellickson, R. C. (1991). *Order without law.* Cambridge, MA: Harvard University Press.

European Commission (2016). *Communication from the Commission to the European Parliament, the Council, the European Economic and Social Committee and the Committee of the Regions: Online platforms and the digital single market: Opportunities and challenges for Europe.* Retrieved from https://eur-lex.europa.eu/legal-content/EN/TXT/?uri=CELEX:52016DC0288

European Group on Ethics in Science and New Technologies (2007). *Opinion on the ethical aspects of nanomedicine* (Opinion No. 21). Brussels, Belgium: European Commission.

Ezrachi, A., & Stucke, M. E. (2016). *Virtual competition.* Cambridge, MA: Harvard University Press.

Friberg, S., & Dufwa, B. W. (2010). The development of traffic liability in Sweden. In M. Martin-Casals (Ed.), *The development of liability in relation to technological change* (pp. 190–227). Cambridge, England: Cambridge University Press.

Fukuyama, F. (2002). *Our posthuman future.* London, England: Profile Books.

Fuller, L. L. (1969). *The morality of law* (Rev. ed.). New Haven, CT: Yale University Press.

Heald, P. (2014). How copyright keeps works disappeared. *Journal of Empirical Legal Studies, 11*, 829–866. doi:10.2139/ssrn.2290181

Hildebrandt, M. (2015). *Smart technologies and the end(s) of law.* Cheltenham, England: Edward Elgar.

Hubbard, F. P. (2014). "Sophisticated robots": Balancing liability, regulation, and innovation. Florida Law Review, 66, 1803–1872. Retrieved from https://scholarcommons.sc.edu/cgi/viewcontent.cgi?article=2027&context=law_facpub

Huxley, A. (2007). *Brave new world.* London, England: Vintage Books. (Original work published 1932.)

Jasanoff, S. (2005). *Designs on nature.* Princeton, NJ: Princeton University Press.

Jasanoff, S. (2016). *The ethics of invention.* New York, NY: W. W. Norton.

Keen, A. (2015). *The Internet is not the answer*. London, England: Atlantic Books.

Lee, M. (2009). Beyond safety? The broadening scope of risk regulation. *Current Legal Problems, 62,* 242–285. doi:10.1093/clp.62.1.242

Lee, R. (2005). GM resistant: Europe and the WTO Panel dispute on biotech products. In J. Gunning & S. Holm (Eds.), *Ethics, law and society* (Vol. 1, pp. 131–140). Aldershot, England: Ashgate.

Lessig, L. (1999). *Code and other laws of cyberspace*. New York, NY: Basic Books.

Mandel, G. N. (2009). Regulating emerging technologies. *Law, Innovation and Technology, 1,* 75–92. doi:10.1080/17579961.2009.11428365

Moon, A., Calisgan, E., Bassani, C., Ferreira, F., Operto, F., Veruggio, G. . . . Van der Loos, H. F. M. (2016). The open roboethics initiative and the elevator-riding robot. In R. Calo, A. M. Froomkin, & I. Kerr (Eds.), *Robot law* (pp. 131–162). Cheltenham, England: Elgar.

Morozov, E. (2013). *To save everything, click here*. London, England: Allen Lane.

Nuffield Council on Bioethics (2002a). *The ethics of patenting DNA*. London, England: Author.

Nuffield Council on Bioethics (2002b). *Genetics and human behaviour: The ethical context*. London, England: Author.

Nuffield Council on Bioethics (2012). *Emerging biotechnologies: Technology, choice and the public good*. London, England: Author.

Oliver Brüstle v. Greenpeace eV, ECJ C-34/10 (2011).

Orwell, G. (1954). 1984. London, England: Penguin Books. (Original work published 1949.)

Pasquale, F. (2015). *The black box society*. Cambridge, MA: Harvard University Press.

Plomer, A. (2012). After Brüstle: EU Accession to the ECHR and the future of European patent law. *Queen Mary Journal of Intellectual Property, 2,* 110–135. doi:10.4337/qmjip.2012.02.01

Plomer, A. (2015). *Patents, human rights and access to science*. Cheltenham, England: Edward Elgar.

Porter, G. (2009). The drafting history of the European biotechnology directive. In A. Plomer & P. Torremans (Eds.), *Embryonic stem cell patents* (pp. 3–26). Oxford, England: Oxford University Press.

Raworth, K. (2017). *Doughnut economics*. London, England: Random House Business Books.

Reidenberg, J. R. (1997–1998) Lex informatica: The formulation of information policy rules through technology. *Texas Law Review, 76,* 553–593. Retrieved from https://pdfs.semanticscholar.org/7f22/c171859ac1885ae9afa3afc3373f197aa133.pdf

Rockström, J., Steffen, W., Noone, K., Persson, A., Chapin, F. S., III, Lambin, E., . . . Foley, J. (2009). Planetary boundaries: Exploring the safe operating space for humanity. *Ecology and Society, 14,* 32. Retrieved from www.ecologyandsociety.org/vol14/iss2/art32/

Royal Society and the Royal Academy of Engineering (2004). Nanoscience and nanotechnologies: Opportunities and uncertainties (RS Policy Document No. 19/04). London, England: Author.

Sayre, F. B. (1933). Public welfare offences. *Columbia Law Review, 33,* 55–88.

Swire, P., & Litan, R. (1998). *None of your business: World data flows, electronic commerce and the European privacy directive.* Washington, DC: Brookings Institution Press.

Tran, J. L. (2015). To bioprint or not to bioprint. *North Carolina Journal of Law and Technology, 17,* 123–178. Retrieved from http://ncjolt.org/wp-content/uplo ads/2015/10/Tran_Final.pdf

Wachter, R. (2015). *The digital doctor.* New York, NY: Mc-Graw Hill Education.

Wallach, W. (2015). *A dangerous master.* New York, NY: Basic Books.

Weaver, J. F. (2014). *Robots are people too.* Santa Barbara, CA: Praeger.

Wilson, D. (2015). *Genetics, crime and justice.* Cheltenham, England: Edward Elgar.

Wolff, J. (2010). Five types of risky situation. *Law, Innovation and Technology, 2,* 151–163. doi:10.5235/175799610794046177

Zittrain, J. (2008). *The future of the Internet.* New Haven, CT: Yale University Press.

Zuboff, S. (2015). Big other: Surveillance capitalism and the prospects of an information civilization. *Journal of Information Technology, 30,* 75–89. doi:10.1057/jit.2015.5

CHAPTER 6

# The Social Shaping of Technology (SST)

## Robin Williams

The social shaping of technology (SST) was one of the new analytical frameworks articulated in the 1980s that sought a more effective conceptualization of the relationship between technology and society.

MacKenzie and Wajcman (1985) coined the SST concept in their 1985 edited collection, *The Social Shaping of Technology: How the Refrigerator Got Its Hum*. They observed,

> Social scientists have tended to concentrate on the "effects" of technology, on the "impact" of technological change on society. This is a perfectly valid concern, but it leaves a prior, and perhaps more important, question unasked and therefore unanswered. What has shaped the technology that is having "effects"? What has caused and is causing the technological changes whose "impact" we are experiencing? (p. 2)

SST brought together scholars from various academic traditions who were concerned about the social implications of technological change for health, the quality of life, jobs, the environment, and so on, but who wanted not just to monitor those *impacts* but also to inquire about what is giving rise to the technology that was having those impacts. These researchers wanted to open up "the 'black-box' of technology ... to allow the socioeconomic patterns embedded in both the content of technologies and the processes of innovation to be exposed and analysed" (Williams & Edge, 1996, p. 866).

This intellectual project of SST emerged through a critique of *technological determinism* (TD). This is the theory of the relationship between technology and society – prevalent in much public discourse on technology – that "technology is ... an independent factor, and that changes in technology cause social changes" (MacKenzie & Wajcman, 1985, p. 4). In their 1996 review of SST, Williams and Edge noted that TD, by portraying technology as emerging through some inner technical or economic logic and having determinate social impacts, "did not problematise technological change, but limited the scope of enquiry to monitoring the social adjustments it saw as being required by technological progress" (Williams & Edge, 1996, p. 866). The growing array of SST studies challenged such TD views, showing that technology is

> a social product, patterned by the conditions of its creation and use. Every stage in the generation and implementation of new technologies involves a set of choices between different technical options. Alongside narrowly "technical" considerations, a range of "social" factors affect which options are selected – thus influencing the content of technologies, and their social implications. (Williams & Edge, 1996, p. 866)

SST is thus a theory of the reciprocal relations between technology and social context. Rejecting traditional conceptions that treat these as separate, SST studies seek to capture the "complex interactions between social relations and technologies" (Williams & Edge, 1996, p. 880), conceived as mutual shaping.

The concept of the mutual shaping of technology and society, articulated initially by feminist SST writers (Berg & Aune, 1994; Cockburn & Ormrod, 1993), has achieved wide currency. Many SST scholars wanted to reach out not only to academic audiences but also to policy players, practitioners, and lay actors and to engage with technology policy and practice (Sørensen & Williams, 2002), informing the choice of the metaphor of social shaping, which was more accessible than the language of social constructivism. In comparison to other analytic traditions in technology studies, SST gave particular emphasis to the influence not just of the social setting, but also of material factors in patterning the content, direction, and outcomes of technological change (McLoughlin, 1999). This emphasis is one reason for the distinct interdisciplinary focus in much SST research.

Initial scholars articulated SST according to a relatively simple template for analyzing how its social context and the values and interests of powerful actors shaped the form of technology (and its societal consequences). The enormous array of empirical studies SST has inspired has extended the exploration of the interplay between technology and society across diverse technical fields and areas of human activity. More particularly, SST has provided an opportunity to unpick the detailed processes of sociotechnical change. The purview of SST research has extended from a focus on actors and settings of technology design/development to include contexts of implementation and use and to highlight the role of diverse intermediaries and users. This chapter charts these developments.

This intellectual journey, which Russell and Williams (2002) characterized as from SST Mark I to SST Mark II, accompanied the elaboration of an array of concepts to capture particular moments, settings, and processes, in turn offering new opportunities to understand and intervene in sociotechnical change. Recent work attempted to develop richer analytical templates that engage with the intricate processes by which technologies develop and become socially embedded, involving many actors across multiple settings and extended timeframes. Finally, I explore how three of these – the social learning (Sørensen, 1996), multilevel (Rip & Kemp, 1998), and biography of artifacts and practices (Pollock, Williams, & Procter, 2003) perspectives – seek an evolutionary understanding that attends to the contingent, local dynamics of innovation processes, and to the broader patterning of sociotechnical change (Bijker, 2007).

### 6.1  The Origins of the Social Shaping of Technology Perspective

Attention to the social implications of advances in science and technology (S&T) grew sharply during the 1960s and 1970s, driven by increasing awareness of their unintended consequences – notably the potential health and environmental hazards of industrial chemicals and radioactive materials that added to longstanding concerns about nuclear weapons and military technology. The falling costs and consequent increasing industrial application of microelectronics in the 1970s sparked an intensive discussion, colloquially described as "the new technology debate," about the consequences of technological change in the workplace for jobs, skills and the quality of working life.

Social scientists previously paid only limited attention to these domains. Many appeared ready to accept the jurisdictional claims of scientists and engineers to exclusive understanding of their technical realms, often portrayed as standing outside society. As a result, much of the early analysis of the social implications of S&T came not from social scientists but from scientists and engineers who had begun to critically appraise some of the negative implications of modern S&T (Rose & Rose, 1976a, 1976b). This appraisal was evinced in the UK by the formation of the British Society for Social Responsibility in Science and the emergence of a Radical Science Movement in many US and European universities (Bell, 2015).

Perhaps the starting point was Carson's (1962) book *Silent Spring*, documenting environmental damage from the uncontrolled use of pesticides. This book, coupled with longstanding concern about the military applications of science and technology, was the start of a number of critiques of

S&T practices and their implications for different spheres of human activity. Thus, feminists inquired into the consequences of new reproductive and medical technologies, often developed by male medical specialists for the women who used them (Faulkner & Arnold, 1985). Difficulties encountered in transferring Western technologies to less-developed countries inspired calls for more appropriate technologies (Schumacher, 1973). Others inquired into the consequences of automation for skill and autonomy in the work-place (Braverman, 1974; Noble, 1984). The resulting labor-process theory revisited the nineteenth-century analyses by Marx and other political econ-omists of the industrialization and mechanization of work. Here (and else-where), synergies of interest were established with parallel strands of historical research, exemplified by the work of Hughes (1986).

These various strands of critical inquiry initiated the idea that the social context (including economic and political interests, values, and culture) might shape the content of S&T (knowledge, artifacts, and practices), often accompanied by the suggestion that alternative approaches were possible. The latter underpinned organized attempts to promote, for example, human-centered technologies for the workplace (Green, Owen, & Pain, 1993; Rauner, Rasmussen, & Corbett, 1988) and technologies appropriate for developing countries.

Departing from the post-Enlightenment belief in science as a progressive force that could analyze and resolve social problems, these writers challenged prevalent portrayals of technology as benign or neutral and argued that special interests and values could shape technology. Thus, as Winner (1980) argued, "technology was political." Artifacts could be put together, consciously or unconsciously, in ways that favored some actors and outcomes over others. This, Winner termed "Technical Arrangements as Forms of Order ... instances in which the invention, design, or arrangement of a specific technical device or system becomes a way of settling an issue in a particular community" (p. 123). Winner contrasted these with "Inherently Political Technologies ... that appear to require, or to be strongly compatible with, particular kinds of political relationships" (p. 123) and that would only emerge in certain kinds of society.

The concern to demonstrate the ways social factors shaped technology led SST theorists to engage critically with two features of TD: it treats the trajectory of technology development as a self-evident process of improve-ment, perhaps following a simple technical or economic logic, and it portrays particular technologies as requiring or strongly compatible with particular kinds of social relations (Williams & Edge, 1996). By portraying technology as a driver of social change, TD arguments paradoxically remove the form of technology – the content of technological artifacts and practices – from social-scientific investigation (and also, let me note, from public enquiry) and limit the scope of investigation to monitoring processes of technological change and the consequent social adjustments.

This critique of TD explained the goals of the SST Perspective.[1] In their concern to refute TD and demonstrate the scope for choice in technological development, many early SST studies took as a template instances in which two competing technological solutions emerged at first and then one was subsequently selected and another displaced. Thus, MacKenzie and Wajcman's (1985) edited collection foregrounds excerpts from two important studies:

1  Schwartz Cowan's (1983) work on domestic labor and technology included a study of how the electric compression refrigerator replaced the gas absorption refrigerator because the large corporations making electrical goods had greater economic power and resources than the small and fragmented gas-appliance manufacturers.
2  Noble's (1984) study of machine-tool automation in the postwar United States, in which numerical control replaced the initial programming solution – the record playback system, which captured and reproduced the craft worker's skill in using a machine tool – such that engineers with programming skills rather than craft workers would prepare the program. This was part of an agenda – shared by the US Air Force sponsors, Massachusetts Institute of Technology engineers, and US engineering firms developing and using machine tools – to centralize capacity and reduce managerial dependence on workforce skills.

These cases strikingly demonstrate the existence of *choice* in technology development and provide an opportunity to examine the factors bearing on these dramatic choices.[2] They support the SST precept that the success of one option over others is never simply a "technical matter," but is shaped by an array of economic, cultural, and political factors. Subsequent studies extended the focus of SST inquiry from the factors shaping technology design/development to include the ways technologies were implemented and consumed/used. These studies demonstrated scope for choice at "every stage in the generation and implementation of new technologies"

---

[1]  This historical resort to the critique of deterministic frameworks, though compelling when SST emerged and effective as a means of communicating the underpinning of its concerns, may be less relevant today when deterministic accounts are less prevalent.
[2]  Though, as Russell noted, perhaps no less significant is the suppression of alternatives (Russell & Williams, 1988; Weber, 2014).

(Williams & Edge, 1996, p. 866). SST thus conceived technology development as a garden of forking paths. Although the initial "new technology debate" centered on the impacts of technology, appreciation of the wide array of players involved and the complex interactions across the various stages of technological change mandated against this term, with its tacit implication that particular technologies had determinate impacts. SST rejected as essentialist such TD accounts of the technology–society relationship. The outcomes of technological change depended rather on multiple choices and were only fully established when a technology was implemented and used (Williams, 2006).

Pinch and Bijker's (1984) concept of *interpretive flexibility* (perhaps also cross referenced to Chapter 19, "Social Construction of Technology [SCOT] Methodology") highlighted the multiple meanings and uses of artifacts. Writers from a discourse theoretic background took this argument further and proposed one should view "technology as text" (Woolgar, 1991, p. 22) or as a "script" (Akrich, 1992, p. 208). Although favored readings might be inscribed, multiple readings were possible. Woolgar (1991) argued against privileging one representation of the capacities and consequences of a technology over another. This "ontological relativist" position provoked the so-called guns and roses debate. Grint and Woolgar's (1991, p. 367) argument that "technical capacity is essentially indeterminate" was countered by computer-scientist Kling (1992, p. 362), who observed that "It's much harder to kill a platoon of soldiers with a dozen roses than with well-placed high-speed bullets." Grint and Woolgar, in an endearing attack of self-awareness, conceded that their "arguments become increasingly counter-intuitive; seemingly absurd" (p. 378).

In contrast, SST analysts, particularly the first generation of scholars who had moved into the field with backgrounds in science and engineering, gave sustained attention to what has subsequently come to be termed *materiality* (Hutchby, 2001; Wyatt, 1998) and the *affordances* of technology (Gibson, 1979), constraining as well as enabling particular outcomes. For SST scholars, "technology matters" (MacKenzie & Wajcman, 1999, p. 3). In contrast, writers with a discourse theoretic background had difficulty integrating materiality into their analysis (a difficulty that forced actor network theorists (ANT; see Callon, 1986) to seek the inelegant solution of portraying electrons and mollusks as actors). Reviewing this debate, McLoughlin (1999) suggested that the key test of a metaphor may be its ability "to cross the boundary between source and target domains" (p. 114).

Here, SST researchers sought more inclusive modes of theorization linked to efforts to build broader collaborations (Sørensen & Williams,

2002). SST sought from the outset to engage with issues of S&T policy and practice, hand in hand with a sustained concern – also traced back to its critical roots (including, for example, links to the Science Shop Movement; Bell, 2015) – to discuss the implications of its research with wider audiences, including practitioners, policy makers, and, perhaps most particularly, wider lay publics affected by S&T. SST scholars consequently have been keen to communicate their findings to other groups. One illustration was the choice of terminology by the initial proponents of SST, who favored the metaphor of social shaping rather than social construction. The terminology of social construction brings considerable and often unhelpful intellectual baggage (Williams & Edge 1996, p. 866). This burden became apparent in the so-called Science Wars (McLoughlin, 1999, p. 117) when the emergence of simplistic versions of social constructivism, which portrayed all knowledge claims as equal, provoked fierce criticism from leading figures in the scientific community, opposed to such relativistic treatments of scientific knowledge. MacKenzie and Wajcman (1999, p. xvi) explicitly favored the metaphor of social shaping, as it was less likely than social construction to be misunderstood.

Today, the social-shaping metaphor has achieved wide currency in STS. Researchers from a variety of analytical traditions broadly align with a view of the mutual shaping of technology and society or similar conceptions such as *coproduction* (Jasanoff, 2004) and *coevolution* (Rip & Schot, 2002; Russell & Williams, 2002).

## 6.2   SST and the 1980s Flowering of Technology Studies

SST was one of a number of analytical perspectives that emerged during the 1980s as a growing research community sought to develop more systematic accounts of the technology–society relationship. In the UK and elsewhere, the "new technology debate" stimulated a growth in social science research funding and attracted scholars from a variety of backgrounds, including an influx of a group of scholars from the proximal field of sociology of scientific knowledge, who proclaimed themselves as the "new sociology of technology" (Bijker, Hughes, & Pinch, 1988). I note in particular here the *Social Construction of Technological Systems* (Pinch & Bijker, 1984) and actor network theory (Callon, 1986; Latour, 1987).

A lively discussion emerged between these traditions. It is helpful to review these debates, as they clarify the relationship between these perspectives and highlight matters of enduring concern in the field of S&T studies.

These contributions shared criticism of TD and other perspectives that portrayed technology as outside of society. Historian Hughes (1986) noted the "seamless web" of technical and social factors, exemplified in study of Edison's design of the first electric lighting systems by the trade-off between the cost of copper (economic laws) and its resistance (physical laws). It became axiomatic across analytical traditions in technology studies that matters were "sociotechnical"; likewise, technical specialists must inevitably be "heterogeneous engineers" (Law, 1988, p. 44), grappling with the twin obduracies of materials and social relationships. MacKenzie and Wajcman (1999), in the second edition of *The Social Shaping of Technology*, specifically acknowledge this contribution from ANT in challenging the separation of "the technical" and "the social," noting "it is mistaken to think of technology and society as separate spheres influencing each other: technology and society are mutually constitutive" (p. 23).

Despite these and other broad areas of agreement, researchers also differed. Sharp controversies arose in the early stages of this debate, particularly regarding the theorization and influence of broader social relations. Early ANT writers were resolutely skeptical about existing social-scientific explanation in the operation of social structures; for example, concerning gender or class. They portrayed such theorization as presuming that outcomes can simply be *read off* structural influences/interests (e.g., Callon & Latour, 1981; Latour, 1988). ANT instead sought to account for developments in observable interactions across networks of actors.

Social relations writers replied that this focus on observable behavior leaves researchers poorly equipped to address absences, marginalization, the suppression of alternatives, and other "socially constructed constraints on choice" (Russell & Williams, 1988, p. 2). By turning their backs on social-scientific analyses of class, gender, and so on, these scholars also jettisoned these analyses' sensitizing concepts that alerted researchers to otherwise assumed differences. Feminist analysts drew attention to the consequent failure of early ANT to notice the marked absence of women from key arenas of S&T decision-making (Cockburn & Ormrod, 1993), coupled with an unreflexive focus that did not attend to the notion that scientists and engineers, at the center of their case studies, were typically educated males with an elite background in developed economies (Winner, 1993).

ANT accounts emphasized the transformatory potential of individual technical specialists (e.g., Latour, 1983, 1987) and their ability to transcend existing paradigms and create new institutions. Indeed, Latour (1988) introduced the concept of Sartrean engineers to explicitly portray these individuals as somehow free from the constraints of their past history. Such a perspective has difficulties in addressing the constraining effects of preexisting socioeconomic structures and culture.

Social relations theorists accordingly criticized these microsociological, actor-centric accounts for their neglect of sharp inequalities in access to knowledge and resources between diverse actors' and social groups' inequalities that are deeply rooted in the broader social and economic fabric and that conditioned their ability to be actors (Russell, 1986; Russell & Williams 1988). Feminist analyst Cockburn (1992), though recognizing the contribution of ANT, criticized its "incomplete representation of the historical dimensions of power" (p. 35).

Researchers hurled similar criticisms at the social construction of technology model, which sought to explain developments through the interactions of "relevant social groups" (Pinch & Bijker, 1984, p. 414) for failing to theorize the influence of broader settings (Russell, 1986; Russell & Williams, 1988). Bijker (1993) responded to these criticisms by introducing the concept of *technological frame* to account for material and nonmaterial structures that can influence sociotechnical design.

These early controversies were seen as a source of "creative tension" (Williams & Edge, 1996, p. 869) in these strongly overlapping fields of inquiry. Subsequent contributions to the field, reviewed by Sørensen and Williams (2002), appeared less inclined to take polarized positions and more willing to explore complementarities between traditions. The success of what has come to be described as "laboratory studies" (exemplified by Latour, 1987) in capturing the complex sets of interactions involved in developing novel scientific and technological practices, convinced even social relations scholars interested in structural influences of the value of detailed study, conducted with powerful archival or ethnographic tools. At the same time, elements of "convergence" (Russell & Williams, 2002, p. 35) could be identified across many subsequent conceptual developments in this very dynamic field that sought to attend to local contexts of interaction and the influence of broader settings (Rip, Misa, & Schot, 1995); particularly the meso level of interaction between organizations (Sørensen & Levold, 1992). The context is no longer treated as a "fixed backdrop" (Russell & Williams, 2002, p. 60); instead, dynamic conceptualizations engage with stability and dynamism, structure and contingency (Bijker, 2007).

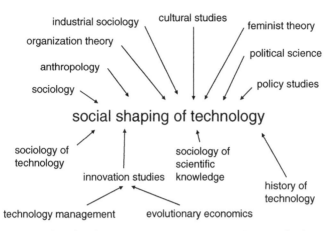

Figure 6.1 Analytical traditions contributing to the social shaping of technology perspective. Graphic by Stewart Russell, summarizing Williams and Edge (1996).

## 6.3 The Development of the SST Perspective

### 6.3.1 SST as a "Broad Church"

SST scholars described themselves as having a perspective rather than a theory. Unlike contributions from the sociology of scientific knowledge, which typically revolved around particular theoretical positions, SST theorists did not seek to align themselves with particular epistemological commitments, but instead conceived the theory as a "broad church" (Williams & Edge, 1996, p. 865). As Figure 6.1 shows, SST drew on a variety of intellectual resources and traditions, united by a commitment to detailed investigation of the processes of technological change.[3]

A rapidly growing body of research was informed by the SST perspective (Dierkes & Hoffmann, 1992), applying it in a wide range of empirical settings (McLoughlin, 1999; Westrum, 1991) extending from an initial focus on workplace and commercial organizations to the home and to settings of everyday life including defense (MacKenzie, 1990) and national energy and information infrastructures (Kubicek, Dutton, & Williams, 1997).[4]

---

[3] As MacKenzie and Wajcman (1999, xvi, preface to the second edition) noted, "If the idea of the social shaping of technology has intellectual or political merit, this lies in the details: in the particular ways in which technology is socially shaped."

[4] Thus Haddon's list of *Social Shaping of Technology* references had over 150 entries (LSE Media and Communications, 2017).

The social shaping of technology was adopted as one of the first social science programs (actions) supported under the European Cooperation in Science and Technology (COST) collaboration program. The COST A4 Action addressed "the impact of the social environment on the creation and diffusion of technologies."[5] A series of international research workshops was organized covering social shaping in different societal and technological settings that resulted in a range of edited collections as well as subsequent European research projects. These projects addressed, variously, "The Car and Its Environments" (Sørensen, 1994b), *Domestic Technology and Everyday Life* (Berg & Aune, 1994), "The Social Shaping of Inter-Organisational Network Systems and Electronic Data Interchange" (Williams, 1995), "The Social Shaping of Computer-Aided Production Management and Computer Integrated Manufacture" (Clausen & Williams, 1997), *The Social Shaping of Information Superhighways* (Kubicek et al., 1997), "Domesticating the World Wide Webs of Information and Communication Technology" (on Telematics in rural areas; Hetland & Meyer-Dallach, 1995), and "Gender, [Information and Communication Technologies] ICTs and Everyday Life" (Frissen, 1998).

The work of COST A4 helped the SST perspective spread rapidly across Europe. A survey of the development of social-shaping research in Europe highlighted the growth of research centers studying SST, particularly in northern Europe (Cronberg & Sørensen, 1995a), and its extension elsewhere with the growth of the European research area (Sørensen, 1999). The differing combinations and strengths of the various disciplines contributing to SST in particular centers and regions resulted in an array of approaches that exhibited "similar concerns" but "different styles" (Cronberg & Sørensen, 1995b, p. 1).

International comparative studies provided an opportunity to explore how differing social settings shaped the development and implementation of technologies. In addition to deriving insights from studies in Europe and other Organisation of Economic Co-Operation and Development nations, SST research explored differences in how technologies, developed indigenously or transferred, were implemented and used in the more sharply contrasting settings of East Asia, Latin America, and Africa.

---

[5] European Cooperation in Science and Technology (2017), provides a partial record of the activities and outputs of COST 4, which began in 1992 and culminated in a "focused study," conducted over 1998–2000.

Burgeoning research across various sociotechnical domains also promoted analysis of the sociotechnical specificity of innovation processes. The dynamics of innovation and the influence of different actors over the rate and direction of technological change varied enormously across settings. These differences rested in the uneven malleability of material systems and in institutional arrangements (Collingridge, 1992; Slayton & Spinardi, 2016; Tait & Williams, 1999).

Sustained engagements arose in some areas between SST and social science specialisms in particular domains of activity; for example, a productive interaction between SST studies of the design and implementation of ICTs and work from media and communication studies (see, e.g., Lievrouw & Livingstone, 2009) and information systems and human–computer interaction (Wilson & Howcroft, 2002). The latter stimulated conceptual development, for example, in relation to the emergence of information infrastructures – systems of IT systems emerging over extended timeframes with multiple users and uses (Monteiro & Hanseth, 1996).

### 6.3.2 The Evolution of the SST Perspective: From Mark I to Mark II

Sustained conceptual development in SST and in technology studies more generally accompanied the rapid growth of empirical research. A study sponsored by COST A4 reviewed these developments (Sørensen & Williams, 2002). Though the proliferation of empirical studies and of concepts to explain developments in particular settings had not been matched by efforts to systematize understanding and develop consensus about theory and methodology, some common elements emerged (Russell & Williams, 2002), constituting a shift from SST Mark I to Mark II.

Some of the earliest critical analyses of technology built on a simple account of the relationship between interests and values in design settings, the content of designed artifacts, and the outcomes when that technology was implemented. These analyses risked offering an *essentialist* account of the technology–society relationship in which technology was a simple reflection of interests that it helped to reproduce when it was used (as noted, for example, by Wajcman, 1991, in relation to gender and technology). In early SST studies, the "range of actors, institutions and other agencies focussed upon ... was relatively small and the relationships between elements, therefore, more or less straightforward," but, as McLoughlin (1999, p. 128) noted, "subsequent social shaping research has developed a far more complex and differentiated understanding of the web of relationships involved."

Though early SST and other technology studies could be criticized for giving undue attention to technology developers and initial technological design (Russell, 1986; Russell & Williams, 1988), the scope of SST studies subsequently extended to include the implementation, consumption, and use of technologies, initially noted in relation to workplace technologies in which the implementation setting was seen as an arena in which supplier offerings were unpicked and reinvented to match local exigencies. Fleck (1988) described these processes as *innofusion,* discussed below.

Fleck's work highlighted the scope for actors concerned with the implementation and use of artifacts to appropriate supplier offerings selectively and use them in ways other than those anticipated in the design (e.g., Fleck, Webster, & Williams, 1990; Noble, 1984). This insight was complemented by some striking historical studies showing how consumers thoroughly transformed technologies like the phone (Fischer, 1992) and the motor car (Kline & Pinch, 1994). Mackay and Gillespie (1992) accordingly argued the need for SST research to engage with the consumption of technologies. A growing array of studies explored the appropriation and consumption of technologies in the home and other settings of everyday life (du Gay, Hall, Janes, Mackay, & Negus, 1997; Schwartz Cowan, 1983; Silverstone & Hirsch, 1992) and highlighted the active role of consumers (Sørensen, 1994a).

### 6.3.3　The Shift from SST Mark 1 to SST Mark II

These empirical and conceptual developments led to a progressive reworking of the SST perspective from MacKenzie and Wajcman's (1985) original account. The initial template of social shaping, exemplified by Noble's (1984) analysis of the automation of machine tools, with its simple array of actors aligned around the selection of numerical control in preference to record playback technology, does not provide a good template for the complex arrays of actors and settings found when we analyze factors impinging on the development, implementation, and use of technologies today. Technologies and the institutional settings in which they arise are more complex and intricate. Beyond the individual-development laboratory, innovation of contemporary technologies, such as mobile phones, is distributed along extended chains of intermediate and final producers, consumers, and regulators, and standardization and other intermediaries coupling technology supply and use (Stewart, Shen, Wang, & Graham, 2012).

SST, in criticizing prevalent "linear models of innovation," rejected episodic accounts of innovation as restricted to initial research and development in the firm (Fleck, 1988, p. 1; Tait & Williams, 1999). SST explored how innovation continues through technology implementation to use and may feed into future supply. Technologies thus evolve over multiple product cycles and over extended timescales. The future of a technology is tested, contested, and worked out across a number of locales and timeframes. Whereas initial SST accounts focused on particular artifacts, current analytical frameworks conceive technology as complex assemblages (Koch, 2007) involving heterogeneous elements (component technologies, practices, and visions of use) developing in tandem, each with its particular history and dynamics.[6]

These changing ways of understanding and analyzing technology can be seen as constituting what Russell and Williams (2002) described as SST Mark II. A variety of approaches have emerged, seeking more effective conceptualization of the processes and outcomes of technological innovation (see, for example, the various approaches reviewed in Sørensen & Williams, 2002). Some also attempt to provide methodological templates and some to identify opportunities for intervention.

In the next section, I highlight three sets of analytical developments: the social learning perspective, which follows most immediately from the preceding discussion; the multilevel perspective (MLP); and the biography of artifacts and practices perspective.

## 6.4 The Further Development of SST

### 6.4.1 The Social Learning Perspective

The social learning perspective, proposed by Sørensen (1996), was an extension to SST analyses, considering the reflexive efforts of actors involved in these complex and dispersed processes of learning and struggling as new technological capabilities were developed, adapted to, and incorporated in the detailed fabric of social life. Social learning is not a narrow cognitive process but one involving negotiation and practical activity: "a combined act of discovery and analysis, of understanding and meaning, and of tinkering and the development of routines" (Sørensen, 1996, p. 6).

---

[6] Thus Koch (2007, p. 427) suggested that enterprise-resource-planning systems need to be understood as assemblages including "communities of software companies, customers, professional associations, various kinds of hardware and software, procedures implementation, practices and rhetoric spanning time and space."

In addition to proposing a more acute focus on the reflexive and adaptive processes of the individuals and organizations involved, the social learning perspective seeks to engage the extended range of actors and locales in which innovation takes place. Two parallel sets of analytic developments in SST research support this framework: *innofusion* and *appropriation/domestication.*

**Innofusion.** Fleck's (1988; Fleck et al., 1990) innofusion concept draws attention to the experimentation that takes place in the contexts in which supplier offerings are implemented, through the (often unplanned) struggle to get the artifact to work and be productive in a particular organizational and technological setting. In this process, complex artifacts, such as corporate ICT solutions, may need to be disassembled, adapted, and reconfigured. The technology may be further elaborated and reinvented during its implementation and use. These local innovations may feed into future technology supply (Fleck, 1988; Fleck et al., 1990). Innofusion thus constitutes a potentially important innovation resource that is becoming increasingly recognized, for example, with the spread of open models of innovation (von Hippel, 2001).

**Appropriation/domestication.** Workplace studies examined how organizations and their members needed to "appropriate" industrial technologies (Clark, 1997, p. 29), to discover and exploit their affordances (Hutchby, 2001), building on Arrow's (1962) observation that organizations learned to use machinery more productively through extended trial-and-error processes of "learning by doing." Supplier ICT solutions are necessarily generic; their offerings cannot precisely cater to the specific practices of particular organizations and groups. They thus require a creative effort by users to develop new routines and practices to make the system useful and – through what are known as workarounds (Pollock, 2005) – to compensate for deficiencies.

Powerful parallels emerged between the efforts documented in these implementation studies of industrial technologies and the broadly homologous work done by voluntary users to adopt and embed personal technologies into their everyday lives. Silverstone and Hirsch (1992, p. 25) applied the concept of *domestication* to examine how technologies were introduced into these physical and symbolic spaces – the "moral economy" of the household – and integrated into household routines. Lie and Sørensen (1996) extended this concept beyond the domestic setting to reference processes of taming or "bringing technology in from the wild" (p. 2).

In further elaborating the social learning perspective, Williams, Stewart, and Slack (2005) highlighted these two linked circuits (innofusion and appropriation/domestication) – culminating in the evolution of artifacts and their societal embedding – as the twin processes of sociotechnical change, particularly relevant to analyzing the design, implementation, and use of IT applications. Sørensen (1996) also began to differentiate specific types of social learning processes. In addition to learning by doing/using, these include *learning by interacting*. Here Sørensen extended the innovation systems concept of the learning economy, which highlights the contribution of supplier–user coupling and knowledge flows (Andersen & Lundvall, 1988). Direct-supplier–user links took on a growing intermediary role by actors who found ways to extract knowledge from particular contexts and apply it productively elsewhere (Stewart & Hyysalo, 2008).

When new technologies are introduced and appropriated, governments and private actors must find ways to ensure proper and appropriate use of their products (Silverstone & Hirsch, 1992; Williams et al., 2005). Sørensen (1996) proposed the concept of *learning by regulation* to describe this process of encouraging beneficial uses and restricting others.

The social learning perspective aligns with new approaches to technology development that highlight the need for experimentation and new ways of engaging with users, including the widespread resort to "living labs" (Ballon & Schuurman, 2015, para. 1) safe spaces in which lay and specialist users can engage playfully with the affordances of novel artifacts. The social learning perspective has also, for example, promoted a radical change in efforts to deploy ICTs to meet the needs of developing countries (Heeks, 2002, 2009).

### 6.4.2   The Multilevel Perspective

The MLP emerged from the influential program of research by Rip and colleagues (1995) at the University of Twente. In addressing the challenges of modulating the direction and outcomes of technological change, they sought to capture the local dynamism and the influence of broader contexts. For the latter, they applied concepts of technology regime and selection environment (Nelson & Winter, 1977) from evolutionary economics. Thus Schot (1992), examining the scope for promoting cleaner technology, argued that the "technology regime" at the time, based on unsustainable energy resources, constituted a "selection environment" (p. 39) that might inhibit and weed out greener innovations. Kemp, Schot, and Hoogma (1998) suggested that strategic niche management might be needed to be protect promising (e.g., greener) but immature innovations until their performance had improved such that they could compete in the market. Rip and Kemp (1998) wove these studies into a more general framework. The MLP examines how changes at the niche level might, if successful, enable shifts in the broader settings of sociotechnical regimes; changes at regime level might, in turn, contribute to change at the highest level – the sociotechnical landscape. Despite being criticized for offering an unduly simplified schema, in contrast to the empirical complexity of real innovation journeys, the MLP has been applied in a range of empirical analyses. Its concepts have been geared to conveying the implications of SST research to policy audiences. The MLP has, in some contexts, gained wider recognition as a tool for intervention, particularly in managing transitions to environmental sustainability (Geels, 2011).

### 6.4.3   The Biography of Artifacts Perspective

The changing empirical settings of innovation and related conceptual developments also call into question established research designs and methodologies in STS. Laboratory studies (following Latour, 1987) demonstrated the value of ethnographic methods and the rich accounts they could yield of engagement with technologies. For many scholars, single-site ethnographies became the default methodological choice. However, such short-term, local studies were poorly equipped to address today's technologies, such as highly complex ICTs that emerged through activities of ever-growing global arrays of innovation players across long highly segmented chains supplying intermediate and complementary products. The growth of complex systems of ICT systems – information infrastructures that are developed and unfold over many sites and extended durations – challenge studies of particular settings of technology design or implementation/use, adopted for the study of discrete technologies (Monteiro & Hanseth, 1996).

Local ethnographies, though favored by interactionist analysts, are temporally and spatially bounded and seem increasingly inadequate in such contexts. ANT frameworks allowed wider research journeys, but their "flat ontologies" and simple methodological nostrums such as "follow the actor" (Latour, 1987, p. 12) left unanswered key methodological questions about the choice of which actors to follow. Different accounts would emerge depending on which actors began (Sørensen & Levold, 1992). Different starting positions/viewpoints for research (e.g., technology design or of implementation) yield different understandings of an organizational technology, with some actors foregrounded and others not (Kaniadakis, 2012).

The timescales of technology development, implementation, and use are far longer than the durations of typical research projects (Williams et al., 2005); very few studies engage with both in tandem. However, researchers may wish to extrapolate forward from observations of particular innovation moments and locales.[7] Some researchers appear to have been tempted to infer from snapshot studies of engineering laboratories how particular design choices will impinge on future users (e.g., Woolgar, 1991).

A long-term series of studies of the long biography of the development, implementation, and use of enterprise systems (Pollock, Williams, & Procter, 2003) allowed Williams and Pollock (2012) to explore how choices about the timing, starting point and scope of an investigation shift what can be discovered. Snapshot studies of the implementation of enterprise-wide solutions – studies typically undertaken in the immediate aftermath of adoption, when organization members were struggling to adapt their working methods to the standard sets of business processes in the generic software packages – have led to critical portrayals of these technologies. Such views are hard to reconcile with their widespread adoption and with the perception, once these complex technologies had become embedded, that the organization could not function without them (Williams & Pollock, 2012). Building on these insights, Pollock and Williams (2009) proposed the biography of artifacts perspective to provide more effective analytical templates and to guide research-design choices. Pollock and Williams called for new approaches to analysis and investigation that can attend to the multiple settings and temporalities of sociotechnical change. Rather than resort to particular research designs by default, it will be necessary to adapt the methodology to the phenomenon being investigated and the goals of the study. This will require pragmatic choices about where to focus detailed examination and reflection on the consequences of those choices. This approach, helpfully extended by Hyysalo (2004) to include *practices*, provides tools with which analysts can develop and reason about strategies to link various

---

[7] The presumption that we can extrapolate the world from detailed research at a single site has been criticized by Pollock and Williams (2009, p. 196) as an instance of the "fairy cake theory of the universe" – propounded in Adams's (1979) *Hitchhiker's Guide to the Galaxy* trilogy – which suggests that "since every piece of matter in the Universe is in some way affected by every other piece of matter in the Universe, it is in theory possible to extrapolate the whole of creation – every galaxy, every sun, every planet, their orbits, their composition, and their economic and social history from, say, one small piece of fairy cake" (p. 198).

local studies to generate an adequate account of the evolution of an artifact biography.

## 6.5 Conclusion

SST emerged among a group of scholars who wished to subject the pathways, content, and social implications of technology artifacts and practices to critical scrutiny. The idea of the mutual shaping of technology and social relations provided an effective analytical template and paved the way for the huge expansion of empirical research in technology studies over the subsequent three decades. The concern of SST researchers from the outset to engage with the content of technical artifacts and practices also encouraged productive interdisciplinary collaborations with technical specialists, in some cases informing attempts to contribute to technology development. Many SST scholars also sought to intervene in technology and innovation policies and explored ways to make their insights relevant to policy makers, innovation communities, and wider publics. This intellectual project continues and, as shown, exhibits continuing dynamism, with the elaboration of new conceptual and methodological frameworks to better capture modern technologies and their societal insertion. New vistas emerge, evinced by MacKenzie's dramatic move, with Michel Callon and others, to establish the field of "social studies of finance," applying their intellectual tools to analyze how theories and artifacts reshape the operation of financial markets (MacKenzie, 2006, p. ix) in what might be seen as a new sociology of finance.

This observation occasions a final comment. Today, scholars have moved away from their initial orientation around particular foundational positions. In the richer conceptual environment, the different traditions have engaged and profoundly reshaped one another.

## REFERENCES

Adams, D. (1979). *The hitchhiker's guide to the galaxy: A trilogy in five parts.* London, England: William Heinemann.

Akrich, M. (1992). The de-scription of technical objects. In W. Bijker & J. Law (Eds.), *Shaping technology—Building society: Studies in sociotechnical change* (pp. 205–244). Cambridge, MA: MIT Press.

Andersen, E. S., & Lundvall, B.-Å. (1988). Small national systems of innovation facing technological revolutions: an analytical framework. In C. Freeman & B.-Å. Lundvall (Eds.), *Small countries facing the technological revolution* (pp. 9–36). London, England: Pinter.

Arrow, K. J. (1962). The economic implications of learning by doing. *Review of Economic Studies, 29,* 155–173. doi:10.2307/2295952

Ballon, P., & Schuurman, D. (2015). Living labs: Concepts, tools and cases. *Info, 17*(4). doi:10.1108/info-04-2015-0024

Bell, A. (2015). Science for the people! *Mosaic: The Science of Life* [blog]. Retrieved from https://mosaicscience.com/story/science-people

Berg, A.-J., & Aune, M. (1994). The domestication of telematics in everyday life. *Proceedings of the COST A4 Workshop Domestic technology and everyday life—Mutual shaping processes* (Vol. 1). Luxembourg: Office for Official Publications of the European Community.

Bijker, W. E. (1993). Do not despair: There is life after constructivism. *Science, Technology, & Human Values, 18,* 113–138. doi:10.1177/016224399301800107

Bijker, W. E. (2007). Dikes and dams, thick with politics. *Isis, 98,* 109–123. doi:10.1086/512835

Bijker, W., Hughes, T., & Pinch, T. (Eds.) (1988). *The social construction of technological systems: New directions in the sociology and history of technology.* Cambridge, MA: MIT Press.

Braverman, H. (1974). *Labor and monopoly capital: The degradation of work in the twentieth century.* New York, NY: Monthly Review Press.

Callon, M. (1986). Some elements of a sociology of translation: Domestication of the scallops and the fishermen of St Brieuc Bay. In J. Law (Ed.), *Power, action and belief: A new sociology of knowledge?* (pp. 196–223). London, England: Routledge.

Callon, M., & Latour, B. (1981). Unscrewing the big Leviathan: How actors macrostructure reality and how sociologists help them to do so. In K. D. Knorr-Cetina & A. V. Cicourel (Eds.), *Advances in social theory and methodology: Toward an integration of micro- and macro- sociologies* (pp. 277–303). Boston, MA: Routledge.

Carson, R. (1962). *Silent spring.* London, England: Houghton Mifflin.

Clark, P. (1997). Appropriating administrative interventions: Decision episode framework. In C. Clausen & R. Williams (Eds.), *The social shaping of computer-aided production management and computer integrated manufacture: Proceedings of the COST A4 workshop* (Vol. 2, pp. 49–62). Luxembourg: Office for Official Publications of the European Community.

Clausen, C., & Williams, R. (Eds.) (1997). *The social shaping of computer-aided production management and computer integrated manufacture:* Proceedings of the COST A4 workshop (Vol. 2). Luxembourg: Office for Official Publications of the European Community.

Cockburn, C. (1992). The circuit of technology: Gender, identity and power. In R. Silverstone & E. Hirsch (Eds.), *Consuming technologies: Media and information in domestic spaces* (pp. 32–47). New York, NY: Routledge.

Cockburn, C., & Ormrod, S. (1993). *Gender and technology in the making.* Thousand Oaks, CA: Sage.

Collingridge, D. (1992). *The management of scale: Big organizations, big decisions, big mistakes.* London, England: Routledge.

Cronberg, T., & Sørensen, K. H. (Eds.) (1995a). *Similar concerns, different styles? Technology studies in Western Europe.* Luxembourg: Office for the Official Publications of the European Communities.

Cronberg, T., & Sørensen, K. H. (Eds.) (1995b). Similar concerns, different styles? A note on European approaches to the social shaping of technology. In *Similar concerns, different styles? Technology studies in western Europe* (pp. 1–23). Luxembourg: Office for Official Publications of the European Communities.

Dierkes, M., & Hoffmann, U. (Eds.) (1992). *New technology at the outset: Social forces in the shaping of technological innovations.* New York, NY: Westview.

du Gay, P., Hall, S., Janes, L., Mackay, H., & Negus, K. (1997). *Doing cultural studies: The story of the Sony Walkman.* London, England: Sage.

European Cooperation in Science and Technology (2017). *Action A4.* Retrieved from www.cost.eu/COST_Actions/isch/A4

Faulkner, W., & Arnold, E. (Eds.) (1985). *Smothered by invention: Technology in women's lives.* London, England: Pluto Press.

Fischer, C. (1992). *America calling: A social history of the telephone to 1940.* Berkeley: University of California Press.

Fleck, J. (1988). *Innofusion or diffusation? The nature of technological development in robotics* (Edinburgh PICT Working Paper No. 7). Edinburgh, Scotland: University of Edinburgh.

Fleck, J., Webster, J., & Williams, R. (1990). The dynamics of IT implementation: A reassessment of paradigms and trajectories of development. *Futures, 22,* 618–640. doi:10.1016/0016-3287(90)90131-Z

Frissen, V. (Ed.) (1998). Gender, ICTs and everyday life: Mutual shaping processes. In Proceedings from the COST A4, *Granite workshop* (pp. 7–35). Luxembourg: Office for Official Publications of the European Community.

Geels, F. W. (2011). The multi-level perspective on sustainability transitions: Responses to seven criticisms. *Environmental Innovation and Societal Transitions, 1*(1), 24–40. doi:10.1016/j.eist.2011.02.002

Gibson, J. J. (1979). *The ecological approach to perception.* London, England: Houghton Mifflin.

Green, E., Owen, J., & Pain, D. (Eds.) (1993). *Gendered by design? Information technology and office systems.* London, England: Taylor & Francis.

Grint, K., & Woolgar, S. (1991). Computers, guns, and roses: What's social about being shot? *Science, Technology & Human Values, 17,* 366–380. doi:10.1177/016224399201700306

Heeks, R. (2002). E-government in Africa: Promise and practice. *Information Polity, 7,* 97–114. doi:10.3233/IP-2002-0008

Heeks, R. (2009). *The ICT4D 2.0 manifesto: Where next for ICTs and international development?* (Development Informatics Group Paper No. 42). Manchester, England: Institute for Development Policy and Management.

Hetland, P., & Meyer-Dallach, H.-P. (Eds.) (1995). Domesticating the World Wide Webs of information and communication technology: Making the global village local. In *Proceedings of COST A4* (Vol. 7, p. 31). Luxembourg: Office for Official Publications of the European Community.

Hughes, T. P. (1986). The seamless web: Technology, science, etcetera, etcetera. *Social Studies of Science, 16*, 281–292. doi:10.1177/0306312786016002004

Hutchby, I. (2001). Technologies, texts and affordances. *Sociology, 35*, 441–456. doi:10.1177/S0038038501000219

Hyysalo, S. (2004). *Uses of innovation: Wristcare in the practices of engineers and elderly*. Helsinki, Finland: Helsinki University Press.

Jasanoff, S. (2004). Ordering knowledge, ordering society. In S. Jasanoff (Ed.), *States of knowledge: The co-production of science and social order* (pp. 13–45). London, England: Routledge.

Kaniadakis, A. (2012). ERP implementation as a broad socio-economic phenomenon: The agora of techno-organisational change. *Information Technology & People, 25*, 259–280. doi:10.1108/09593841211252543

Kemp, R., Schot, J., & Hoogma, R. (1998). Regime shifts to sustainability through processes of niche formation: The approach of strategic niche management. *Technology Analysis & Strategic Management, 10*, 175–196. doi:10.1080/09537329808524310

Kline, R., & Pinch, T. (1994). Taking the black box off its wheels: The social construction of the American rural car. In K. Sørensen (Ed.), *The car and its environments—The past, present and future of the motorcar in Europe* (pp. 69–92). Luxembourg: Office for the Official Publications of the European Communities.

Kling, R. (1992). Audiences, narratives, and human values in social studies of technology. *Science, Technology, & Human Values, 17*, 349–365. doi:10.1177/016224399201700305

Koch, C. (2007). ERP—A moving target. *International Journal of Business Information Systems, 2*, 426–443. doi:10.1504/IJBIS.2007.012544

Latour, B. (1983). Give me a laboratory and I will raise the world. In M. Knorr-Cetina & M. Mulkay (Eds.), *Science observed* (pp. 141–170). London, England: Sage.

Latour, B. (1987). *Science in action: How to follow scientists and engineers through society*. Cambridge, MA: Harvard University Press.

Latour, B. (1988). How to write "The Prince" for machines as well as machinations. In B. Elliott (Ed.), *Technology and social process* (pp. 20–43). Edinburgh, Scotland: University of Edinburgh Press.

Law, J. (1988). The anatomy of a socio-technical struggle: The design of the TSR 2. In B. Elliott (Ed.), *Technology and social process* (pp. 44–69). Edinburgh, Scotland: University of Edinburgh Press.

Lie, M., & Sørensen, K. H. (Eds.) (1996). *Making technology our own? Domesticating technology into everyday life*. Boston, MA: Scandinavian University Press.

Lievrouw, L., & Livingstone, S. (2009). *Introduction*. In L. Lievrouw & S. Livingstone (Eds.), *New media* (pp. 1–18). London, England: Sage.

LSE Media and Communications (2017). *Social shaping of technology references*. Retrieved from www.lse.ac.uk/media@lse/WhosWho/AcademicStaff/LeslieHaddon/ShapingRefs.aspx

Mackay, H., & Gillespie, G. (1992). Extending the social shaping of technology approach: Ideology and appropriation. *Social Studies of Science, 22,* 685–716. doi:10.1177/030631292022004006

MacKenzie, D. (1990). *Inventing accuracy: A historical sociology of nuclear missile guidance.* Boston, MA: MIT Press.

MacKenzie, D. (2006). *An engine, not a camera: How financial models shape markets.* Cambridge, MA: MIT Press.

MacKenzie, D., & Wajcman, J. (Eds.) (1985). *The social shaping of technology: How the refrigerator got its hum.* Milton Keynes, England: Open University Press.

MacKenzie, D., & Wajcman, J. (Eds.) (1999). *The social shaping of technology* (2nd ed.). Buckingham, England: Open University Press.

McLoughlin, I. (1999). *Creative technological change: The shaping of technology and organisations.* London, England: Routledge.

Monteiro, E., & Hanseth, O. (1996). Social shaping of information infrastructure: On being specific about the technology. In W. J. Orlikowski, G. Walsham, M. R. Jones, & J. I. Degross (Eds.), *Information technology and changes in organizational work* (pp. 325–343). Boston, MA: Springer.

Nelson, R. R., & Winter, S. G. (1977). In search of a useful theory of innovation. *Research Policy, 6,* 36–76. doi:10.1016/0048-7333(77)90029-4

Noble, D. F. (1984). *Forces of production: A social history of industrial automation.* Oxford, England: Oxford University Press.

Pinch, T., & Bijker, W. (1984). The social construction of facts and artefacts: Or how the sociology of science and the sociology of technology might benefit each other. *Social Studies of Science, 14,* 399–441. doi:10.1177/030631284014003004

Pollock, N. (2005). When is a work-around? Conflict and negotiation in computer systems development. *Science, Technology, and Human Values, 30,* 496–514. doi:10.1177/0162243905276501

Pollock, N., & Williams, R. (2009). *Software and organisations: The biography of the enterprise-wide system—or how SAP conquered the world.* Abingdon, England: Routledge.

Pollock, N., Williams, R., & Procter, R. (2003). Fitting standard software packages to non-standard organisations: The "biography" of an enterprise-wide system. *Technology Analysis & Strategic Management, 15,* 317–332. doi:10.1080/0953732031000160504

Rauner, F., Rasmussen, L., & Corbett, M. (1988). The social shaping of technology and work: Human-centred CIM systems. *AI and Society, 2,* 47–61. doi:10.1007/BF01891442

Rip, A., & Kemp, R. (1998). Technological change. In S. Rayner & E. L. Malone (Eds.), *Human choice and climate change: An international assessment* (Vol. 2, pp. 327–400). Washington DC: Batelle Press.

Rip, A., Misa, T. J., & Schot, J. (Eds.) (1995). *Managing technology in society: The approach of constructive technology assessment.* London, England: Pinter.

Rip, A., & Schot, J. W. (2002). Identifying loci for influencing the dynamics of technological development. In K. H. Sørensen & R. Williams (Eds.), *Shaping* technology, guiding policy: Concepts, spaces and tools* (pp. 145–162). Aldershot, England: Edward Elgar.

Rose, H., & Rose, S. P. R. (Eds.) (1976a). *The political economy of science: Ideology of/in the natural sciences.* London, England: Macmillan.

Rose, H., & Rose, S. P. R. (Eds.) (1976b). *The radicalisation of science, ideology of/in the natural sciences.* London, England: Macmillan.

Russell, S. (1986). The social construction of artefacts: A response to Pinch & Bijker. *Social Studies of Science, 16,* 331–346. doi:10.1177/030631278601600208

Russell, S., & Williams, R. (1988). *Opening the black box and closing it behind you: On micro-sociology in the social analysis of technology* (PICT Working Paper No. 3). Edinburgh, Scotland: University of Edinburgh.

Russell. S., & Williams, R. (2002). Social shaping of technology: Frameworks, findings and implications for policy, with glossary of social shaping concepts. In K. H. Sørensen & R. Williams (Eds.), *Shaping technology, guiding policy: Concepts, spaces and tools* (pp. 37–132). Aldershot, England: Edward Elgar.

Schot, J. (1992). Constructive technology assessment and technology dynamics: The case of clean technologies. *Science, Technology, & Human Values, 17,* 36–57. doi:10.1177/016224399201700103

Schumacher, E. F. (1973). *Small is beautiful: A study of economics as if people mattered.* London, England: Blond & Briggs.

Schwartz Cowan, R. (1983). *More work for mother: The ironies of household technology from the open hearth to the microwave.* New York, NY: Basic Books.

Silverstone, R., & Hirsch, E. (Eds.) (1992). *Consuming technologies: Media and information in domestic spaces.* London, England: Routledge.

Slayton, R., & Spinardi, G. (2016). Radical innovation in scaling up: Boeing's Dreamliner and the challenge of socio-technical transitions. *Technovation, 47,* 47–58. doi:10.1016/j.technovation.2015.08.004

Sørensen, K. H. (1994a). Adieu Adorno: The moral emancipation of consumers. In A.-J. Berg & M. Aune (Eds.), *Domestic technology and everyday life—mutual shaping processes* (Vol. 1, pp. 157–169). Luxembourg: European Commission DGXIII Science Research and Development.

Sørensen, K. H. (1994b). *The car and its environments—The past, present and future of the motorcar in Europe.* Luxembourg: Office for the Official Publications of the European Communities.

Sørensen, K. H. (1996). *Learning technology, constructing culture: Socio-technical change as social learning* (STS Working Paper No. 18/96). Trondheim, Norway: University of Trondheim, Centre for Technology and Society.

Sørensen, K. H. (1999). Similar concerns, different styles? Technology studies in Europe (Vol. II). Luxembourg: Office for the Official Publications of the European Communities.

Sørensen, K., & Levold, N. (1992). Tacit networks, heterogeneous engineers and embodied technology. *Science, Technology, & Human Values, 17,* 13–35. doi:10.1177/016224399201700102

Sørensen, K. H., & Williams, R. (Eds.) (2002). *Shaping technology, guiding policy: Concepts, spaces and tools.* Aldershot, England: Edward Elgar.

Stewart, J. K., & Hyysalo, S. (2008). Intermediaries, users and social learning in technological innovation. *International Journal of Innovation Management, 12*, 295–325. doi:10.1142/S1363919608002035

Stewart, J. K., Shen, X., Wang, C., & Graham, I. R. (2012). From 3G to 4G: Standards and the development of mobile broadband in China. *Technology Analysis & Strategic Management, 23*, 773–788. doi:10.1080/09537325.2011.592284

Tait, J., & Williams, R. (1999). Policy approaches to research and development: Foresight, framework and competitiveness. *Science and Public Policy, 26*, 101–112. doi:10.3152/147154399781782536

Von Hippel, E. (2001). Innovation by user communities: Learning from open-source software. *MIT Sloan Management Review, 42*(4), 82–86.

Wajcman, J. (1991). *Feminism confronts technology*. Oxford, England: Polity Press.

Weber, K. M. (2014). The success and failure of combined heat and power (CHP) in the UK, Germany and the Netherlands: Revisiting Stewart Russell's perspective on technology choices in society. *Science & Technology Studies, 27*, 15–46. Retrieved from https://sciencetechnologystudies.journal.fi/article/view/55313/18145

Westrum, R. (1991). *Technologies and society: The shaping of people and things*. Belmont, CA: Wadsworth.

Williams, R. (Ed.) (1995). The social shaping of inter-organisational network systems and electronic data interchange. In *Proceedings of the InternationalCOST A4 conference* (pp. XX–XX). Luxembourg: Office for Official Publications of the European Community.

Williams, R. (2006). Compressed foresight and narrative bias: Pitfalls in assessing high technology futures. *Science as Culture, 15*, 327–348. doi:10.1080/09505430601022668

Williams, R., & Edge, D. (1996). The social shaping of technology. *Research Policy, 25*, 865–899. doi:10.1016/0048-7333(96)00885-2

Williams, R., & Pollock, N. (2012). Moving beyond the single site implementation study: How (and why) we should study the biography of packaged enterprise solutions. *Information Systems Research, 23*, 1–21. doi:10.1287/isre.1110.0352

Williams, R., Stewart, J., & Slack, R. (2005). *Social learning in technological innovation: Experimenting with information and communication technologies*. Aldershot, England: Edward Elgar.

Wilson, M., & Howcroft, D. (2002). Re-conceptualising failure: Social shaping meets IS research. *European Journal of Information Systems, 11*, 236–250. doi:10.1057/palgrave.ejis.3000437

Winner, L. (1980). Do artifacts have politics? *Daedalus, 109*(1), 121–136. Retrieved from https://transitiontech.ca/pdf/Winner-Do-Artifacts-Have-Politics-1980.pdf

Winner, L. (1993). Upon opening the black box and finding it empty: Social constructivism and the philosophy of technology. *Science, Technology, & Human Values, 18*, 362–378. doi:10.1177/016224399301800306

Woolgar, S. (1991). The turn to technology in social studies of science. *Science, Technology, & Human Values, 16*, 20–50. doi:10.1177/016224399101600102

Wyatt, S. (1998). *Technology's arrow: Developing information networks for public administration in Britain and the United States*. Maastricht, Netherlands: Universitaire Pers Maastricht.

CHAPTER 7

# Placing Users and Nonusers at the Heart of Technology

## Nelly Oudshoorn

Technologies need users. The machines built from waste materials, salvaged metal, and discarded clothing by the Swiss artist Jean Tinguely may be the only machines intended explicitly not to be used or produce anything. Inspired by Dadaism and the anticapitalist movement of the early 1960s, Tinguely aimed to "free machines" from their "slavery" in the mass production of consumer goods (Menil & Alexandre, 1980). These machines were made to disrupt the static presentation of art in conventional museums at that time and to destruct rather than produce anything (Stedelijk Museum, 2017).[1] However, most machines are intended to produce consumer goods, and both depend on users. It is thus no surprise that users are an important theme in science and technology studies (STS). Criticizing a determinist linear view of technology that portrayed users as passive consumers, STS scholars have convincingly shown that users play an active role in all phases of technological development, from design to implementation and use. Users can contribute to stabilizing – or destabilizing – new technologies, modifying existing technologies, and developing technologies themselves (Hyysalo, Elgaard Jensen, & Oudshoorn, 2016; Oudshoorn & Pinch, 2003; Pfaffenberger, 1992; Rohracher, 2005; Sørenson & Williams, 2002; Von Hippel, 2005; Voss et al., 2009; Williams, Slack, & Stewart, 2005). In this chapter, I discuss recent developments in the study of users and nonusers to illustrate the wide variety of ways people act as agents of sociotechnical change. In the first two sections, I describe conceptual approaches developed in specific topical fields at the intersections of STS, innovation studies, and the sociology of the body. The chapter concludes with a discussion of recent developments in research on nonusers.

---

[1] Interestingly, a few of Tinguely's machines could actually be used. To criticize the elitist position of art in society, Tinguely made do-it-yourself drawing machines to invite the public to make art themselves (Stedelijk Museum, 2017).

## 7.1    Changing User–Producer Relations

### *7.1.1    From Configuring Users to Producing Creative Collaborators*

The increased interest in studying users in STS over the past two decades might seduce one into thinking that the active user is a recent figure who emerged around the time of the development of the internet. Although information and communication technologies have been important in facilitating and coshaping the agency of users, the rise of the internet is clearly not the first time users have been major actors in producing technology. To understand how history matters, I suggest considering the changing sociotechnical landscapes in which user–producer relations emerge. To understand these dynamic changes, I go back to the early nineteenth century.[2] In those days, most goods were produced in one-person shops that facilitated close personal contact between users and producers. This intimacy broke, however, with the modernization of industry. Mass production created a sociotechnical landscape in which industrial infrastructures largely replaced small shops specializing in hand-crafted production and an increasing number of links emerged between users and producers. Designers became dependent not on their personal contact with users, but on product and sales departments and numerous dealers who would eventually link to users.

The production of standardized goods was certainly cheaper, but was also poorly tailored to the needs of users. In the early twentieth century, major players in industry, particularly car manufacturers in the United States, became aware of the problems caused by the widening gap between designers and users, resulting in a first attempt to reconnect them: the introduction of marketing and consumer research (Pantzar & Ainamo, 2004).[3] Industry began to use various scientific methods to gain knowledge about users' preferences and willingness to buy their products. Other efforts to reconnect designers and users that emerged in the early twentieth century were in the fields of industrial design, human factors, and ergo-nomics, which aimed to improve the aesthetic quality and usability of mass-produced goods (Benton, 2000; Meister, 1999). The two world wars made industry aware of how important it was that increasingly complex

---

[2] In this analysis of the changing sociotechnical landscapes, I drew from the introductory chapter of Hyysalo et al. (2016).

[3] Of course, the history of the emergence of consumer and marketing research and ergonomics is much richer than I can describe here. For a more detailed account of the rise of these fields, see Benton (2000), Hyysalo et al. (2016), Meister (1999), and Pantzar and Ainamo (2004).

weapons be used effectively (McRuer & Krendel, 1959), encouraging manufacturers to study how people used their other products. Industry now aimed to design products that fit the cognitive and physical properties of users, largely through further development of the principles of work optimization introduced by Taylor (1911). Manufacturers used this knowledge to design products that were better fitted for use and would increase users' willingness to buy. This industrial strategy can best be described as configuring the user: a process of "defining the identity of putative users, and setting constraints upon their likely future actions" (Woolgar, 1991, p. 59). Most importantly, the way designers configured users only encouraged those forms of use intended by the designer. Users were not helped – or even allowed – to develop their own creative and productive capabilities, but rather were mainly disciplined to follow the scripts inscribed in the technologies (Akrich, 1992).

To be sure, this disciplining approach did not restrain users from developing their own responses to mass-produced goods. In the first decades of the twentieth century, people still commonly repaired, mended, and rebuilt the industrial products they used, particularly in the countryside and among the working class in cities (Kline, 2000). US farmers, for example, became famous for rebuilding their cars to make them useful for many other purposes on the farm, thereby extending their intended use (Kline & Pinch, 1996).[4] However, prior to the 1970s, producers were blind to users' situated use and their creative skills in domesticating and inventing technologies. This only changed with the emergence of two radically different design strategies: participatory or collaborative design and human-centered design. Collectively, they emphasized that industry, rather than approaching users as *objects* that it needs to understand better in order to increase sales, should consider users as *subjects* to learn from and collaborate with (Bannon, 1991; Hyysalo et al., 2016, p. 9).

This shift in design approaches can only be understood in the context of major changes in the sociotechnical landscape of the 1970s. The collaborative approach largely emerged in Scandinavia in the late 1970s, where trade unionists began to engage with specific design and implementation projects in firms to design technologies that accounted for the workers' interests and skills. Trade unions developed this strategy in reaction to the implementation of new production technologies that threatened to

---

[4] See Douglas (1987), Fischer (1992), and Martin (1991) for other accounts of how users reinvented mass-produced products such as the telephone and the radio. Equally important, users developed new technologies, such as the airplane, and continued to improve its characteristics (Gardiner & Rothwell, 1985).

make workers redundant or would deskill their work (Asaro, 2000, p. 267). Equally important, the antiauthoritarian social movement in the 1970s inspired collaborative designers to develop a political vision of user–producer relations that emphasized the notion that democratic societies should not delegate design processes to technical elites but should gain control over the development of science and technology (Hyysalo et al., 2016, p. 11). This vision was concretized by developing hundreds of collaboration setups, methods, and techniques for productive interaction between users and designers (Bødker, Kensing, & Simonsen, 2004). Many techniques developed in collaborative design have been adopted by the field of user-centered design, later called human-centered design, that emerged in the 1970s to study human–computer interactions and introduced new interaction design principles to better fit digital technologies to users. The key contribution of this field has been to normalize the view that technologies should be developed in the context of use before and during dissemination (Hyysalo et al., 2016, p. 12).

All these developments contributed to a crucial shift in the ways designers configured users. Instead of disciplining users to use a technology in the way it was intended by the designers, design strategies now aimed to configure users to play an active, creative role in the making of new technologies. This "new production of users" (Hyysalo et al., 2016) can be considered one of the major characteristics of the sociotechnical landscape of the twenty-first century. Users are no longer merely configured as consumers but as collaborators with significant productive capabilities. Producing productive users has become a key objective of industrial strategizing. For many companies, involving users in design has become a normalized part of their business. These strategies may include inviting users to propose specific design ideas (Lego and Ducati) or creating forums in which users help each other learn (or change) how to use products (eBay and Microsoft).

Importantly, the productive role of users in the twenty-first century is not restricted to collaborating with industry. As in the previous century, users have created their own spaces for mending and building technologies. Fab labs, makerspaces, hacker communities, the emergence of citizen science, and the counterexpertise of patient organizations all testify to the creativity and sociotechnical skills of people who try to take the development of technology into their own hands (Callon & Rabeharisoa, 2003; Hatch, 2013; Irwin, 1995; Maxigas, 2012; Oost, Verhaegh, & Oudshoorn, 2009; Thomas, 2002). The contemporary sociotechnical landscape is thus not only characterized by new strategies to produce active users, but also by new forms of production by users themselves. Understanding the dynamics of these new configurations, including their ambivalences, tensions, and controversies, is an important topic for future STS research.

### 7.1.2   *Technologies Inside Bodies: Users as Passive Again?*

One of the core interests in studying users has been to understand how human agency is shaped by and shapes technology. However, most user studies focused almost exclusively on technologies external to the body. Although cyborgs (fusions of bodies and technologies) have existed for some time – examples include people with pacemakers or hip or knee implants – new and emerging human-enhancement technologies have introduced and will introduce many more, including people with brain implants, nanochips, and spinal-cord stimulation (Dalibert, 2014, 2016; Nordmann, 2007; Sandberg & Bostrom, 2006). These eventualities call for a better understanding of the agency of these hybrid bodies and present a crucial and complex challenge to understanding the agency of users.[5] Whereas external devices are inscribed with scripts that invite people to act in specific ways, technologies inside bodies seem to delegate much less agency to their users. People with implants cannot decide when, where, or how to use them. Although one can decide to stop taking medicines, they cannot switch off a device implanted in their body. In contrast to the finite and limited temporal interactions between users and technologies that characterize external devices, implants introduce continuous, inextricably intertwinements between technologies and bodies. Most of these permanent technologies incorporate programs of action that delegate no agency to users in how to interact with the implanted devices (Oudshoorn, 2015, 2016; Verbeek, 2008). They do not configure the user but, as they merge with it, the body.

But even in the absence of programs of action, are people with implants really so passive? Because theories of medication (Ihde, 1990; Latour, 2005) conceptualized the interactions between humans and technologies as finite and limited temporal events, technologies inside bodies invite society to reconceptualize human–technology relations (Dalibert, 2014, 2016; Lettow, 2011; Verbeek, 2008).[6] How can human agency be understood

---

[5] This section largely rests on current research on pacemakers and defibrillators by Oudshoorn (2015, 2016).

[6] Most notably, Ihde's (1990) widely used typology of human–technology relations only includes technologies external to the body, although Verbeek (2008) has extend this categorization by adding cyborg relations.

when technologies move under the skin? At first sight, the concept of cyborgs seems to be a useful heuristic because it emphasizes the merging of bodies and technologies (Haraway, 1985). Although Haraway's (1985) important work on cyborgs has inspired many scholars to address the fusion of humans and machines, feminist scholars have criticized the latter studies for conceptualizing the cyborg merely as a linguistic or metaphorical entity (Sobchack, 2006). Whereas Haraway's cyborg is rooted in a material semiotic approach, the linguistic turn in cultural and literary studies, as well as in STS, has made the cyborg into a discursive entity. This approach to cyborgs is problematic because it neglects the material, lived experiences of people with their technology-enhanced bodies. Feminist scholars therefore stressed the importance of rematerializing the cyborg. Instead of considering how science fiction or other cultural products depict hybrid bodies, feminist scholars aim to account for the materiality of intimate, lived relations between bodies and technologies to understand how people learn to live as cyborgs (Alaimo & Hekman, 2008; Dalibert, 2014, 2016; Lettow, 2011; Oudshoorn, 2015, 2016). Conceptualizing cyborgs as material realities rather than discursive entities changes the focus from how they are represented to what one actually has to do to keep one's hybrid body alive.

To discuss some of the conceptual approaches developed by feminist scholars, I use the case of one of the "old" cyborgs: people with pacemakers and implanted cardioverter defibrillators. These internal devices consist of small, battery-powered generators that give electric pulses to the heart when the heartbeat is too slow (pacemakers) or too fast (defibrillators). Physicians prescribe them to people diagnosed with serious heart-rhythm disturbances when medicines are ineffective; thus, they are a treatment of last resort. A useful heuristic introduced to study the materiality of intimate, lived relationships between bodies and implants is to look at the sensory experiences of people living with these devices (Jones, 2006). This focus on how people sense the reconfigured materiality of their hybrid bodies enables understanding of how internal devices may introduce new bodily sensations.

People with pacemakers and defibrillators, for example, may not only sense and endure the electric pulses and shocks that countermand or take over their heartbeats but also hear beeps when the device's battery is dying. It is not always easy to distinguish these critical beeps from those of many other electronic devices, such as cell phones and smoke detectors. Learning to listen and discriminate between these various beeps is crucial; as one US heart patient put it, "That little beep could be telling you something" (ICD

User Group, 2011). These sounds create an awareness of the existence and fragility of hybrid bodies that can cease to function if one does not detect the beeps and get to the clinic in time in matters of life and death. Heart patients must play an active role in sustaining their technologically trans-formed bodies (Oudshoorn, 2015). This research adds to other STS studies that emphasize the relevance of including multiple senses – taste, hearing, smell, and touch – as important but often overlooked ways of knowing (Pinch & Bijsterveld, 2012; Rice, 2010; Shapin, 2012).

Understanding the agency and fragility of cyborgs is important because technologies inside bodies dramatically transform the vulnerability of bodies, introducing new forms of vulnerability. The irreversibility of implants and their very location introduces new forms of vulnerability that are not yet addressed in the STS literature:[7] vulnerability as an internal rather than external threat and as harm one may try to anticipate but can never escape (Oudshoorn, 2016). These new forms of vulnerability are important to study because they introduce forms of agency that may differ from ways of coping with the harm introduced by technologies external to the body. One cannot try to avoid such a risk by no longer using the device because they cannot remove it themselves, nor can they avoid such a risk by staying away from it, as they might avoid living near a nuclear plant.

An illustrative example of these new forms of vulnerability and related coping techniques is the inappropriate shocks from defibrillators that can result from fractured leads or improper adjustment. Although heart patients cannot prevent such malfunctions or escape their psychological and physical harm, they actively engage in sensing and taming the unwanted agency of faulty machines. They not only use their sensory experiences to tell the difference between appropriate and inappropriate shocks, but some patients also use magnets to stop unneeded shocks, a drastic procedure they copied from ambulance personnel who use mag-nets to deactivate defibrillators (Oudshoorn, 2016). By appropriating technical devices that had been used exclusively by emergency staff, people with defibrillators developed a new coping strategy creating a new techni-que – that is, a new coping strategy – to regain some form of control over the devices in their bodies. Anticipating the proper and improper working of implants thus constitutes a new kind of invisible labor (Star & Strauss, 1999) that is crucial to keeping a hybrid body alive; an invisible labor of anticipating the proper functioning of implants, which did not exist prior

---

[7] See, for example, the recent book *Vulnerability in Technological Culture*, in which the authors only address technologies external to the body (Hommels, Mesman, & Bijker, 2014).

to the introduction of these technologies and has not been addressed in the STS and medical literature. Summarizing, I conclude that technologies inside bodies are an important site to further explore new forms of user agency and vulnerability.

## 7.2  Nonusers and Selective Use

Despite extensive literature on users, nonusers have drawn less attention. However, in the past decades, several STS scholars began to study nonuse. What these studies share is that they go beyond dominant discourses portraying nonuse as a deficiency or a regressive irrational attitude toward modernity and describing nonusers in negative terms, such as laggards, have-nots, and drop-outs. Instead, much work has been devoted to reconceptualizing nonuse and nonusers. Wyatt and colleagues introduced a categorization of nonusers, considering voluntary and involuntary aspects of nonuse (Wyatt, 2003; Wyatt et al., 2002). They identified voluntary nonusers as *rejectors,* who have stopped using a technology because they find it expensive, boring, or too frustrating, or because they have alternatives, and *resisters,* who never adopted a technology because they did not want to. This view of nonuse as a self-reflective, significant act rather than a deficiency or an irrational act (Oudshoorn, 2011) has prompted research on user–technology relations to investigate how people make deliberate, careful choices concerning the use of a specific technology. Benjamin (2016), for example, described how African Americans who visited a sickle-cell clinic were quite skeptical of the tendency to over-prescribe certain therapies and doubted their efficacy; a practice Benjamin dubbed informed refusal. Because involuntary nonuse is important as well, Wyatt and colleagues introduced categories of the *expelled,* who have stopped using the technology because they have lost institutional access to it or can no longer afford it, and the *excluded,* who, for a variety of reasons, never had access to it. An example of the former are people whose electricity was cut off because they could no longer pay the bill (Summerton, 2004).

Scholars outside the field of STS have made important contributions to reconceptualizing nonuse. To convince colleagues in informatics and the creative industries of the relevance of taking nonusers' perspectives into account in designing human–computer interfaces, Satchell and Dourish (2009) introduced a taxonomy with six varieties of nonuse. Although some – such as active resistance, disinterest, lagging adoption, and disenfranchisement (the last taking the form of barriers to entry or to continued use) – are already familiar, the authors also distinguished forms of nonuse often overlooked by other scholars. Disenchantment, for example, refers to people who are reluctant to use a particular new technology because they are afraid that their familiar world will disappear. Studying these nonusers provides an opportunity to understand the tacit, moral routines threatened by the introduction of new technologies (Kiran, Oudshoorn, & Verbeek, 2015). Another interesting concept, displacement, refers to people who do not use a technology themselves but depend on others who do; for example, people in rural villages, particularly in developing regions, do not have phones but rely on relatives or neighbors who do (Parikh & Lazowska, 2006).

Recent scholarship encourages reflecting on the very notions of use and nonuse. As Baumer and other researchers in the field of information and computer science have argued, making a binary distinction between use and nonuse may not always be a useful way to understand how people relate to a technology (Baumer et al., 2013; Derthick, 2014; Loder, 2014). Although Wyatt and colleagues (2002) introduced concepts that escape this dualistic approach with concepts such as rejectors, the excluded, and the expelled, dominant policy and engineering discourses and many studies of nonuse still rely on such a dichotomy. This dualistic perspective does not allow for certain nuances in the ways people interact with technologies, which may take the forms of use and nonuse in different social contexts, daily routines, and phases of life. Baumer et al. and Loder therefore suggested replacing the binary distinction between use and nonuse by investigating "the blurry space" between them (Baumer et al., 2013, p. 3265; Loder, 2014). In this approach, use and nonuse are not considered fixed opposites but attributes of a practice (Weiner & Will, 2016). Concepts such as "negotiated use" (Loder, 2014, p. 2) and "selective use" (Oudshoorn, 2008, p. 281) exemplify this more dynamic approach to studying how people relate to technologies.

This approach to nonuse raises important questions for understanding human–technology relations. How does nonuse in its various forms and practices shape the development and implementation of new technologies? How do nonusers articulate a morality that is challenged by a new technology? How does the primacy of use and the neglect of nonuse in design and innovation policy create and reify claims of novelty, modernity and innovation? These urgent questions need to be addressed in STS research.

## REFERENCES

Akrich, M. (1992). The de-scription of technical objects. In W. Bijker & J. Law (Eds.), *Shaping technology—Building society: Studies in sociotechnical change* (pp. 205–244). Cambridge, MA: MIT Press.

Alaimo, S., & Hekman, S. (2008). Introduction: Emerging models of materiality in feminist theory. In *Material feminisms* (pp. 1–19). Bloomington: University of Indiana Press.

Asaro, P. M. (2000). Transforming society by transforming technology: The science and politics of participatory design. *Accounting, Management and Information Technologies, 10*, 257–290. doi:10.1016/S0959-8022(00)00004-7

Bannon, L. (1991). From human factors to human actors: The role of psychology and human-computer interaction studies in system design. In J. Greenbaum & M. Kyng (Eds.), *Design at work: Cooperative design of computer systems* (pp. 25–44). Hillsdale, NJ: Lawrence Erlbaum.

Baumer, E., Adams, P., Khovanskaya, V. D., Liao, T. C., Smith, M. E., Sosik, V. S., & Williams, K. (2013). Limiting, leaving, and (re)lapsing: An exploration of Facebook non-use practices and experiences. In R. Grinter, T. Rodden, P. Aoki, E. Cutrell, R. Jeffries, & G. Olson (Eds.), *Proceedings of the SIGCHI Conference on Human Factors in Computing Systems* (pp. 3257–3266). New York, NY: Association for Computing Machinery.

Benjamin, R. (2016). Informed refusal: Towards a justice-based bioethics. *Science, Technology, & Human Values, 41*, 967–990. doi:10.1177/0162243916656059

Benton, C. (2000). Design and industry. In M. Kemp (Ed.), *The Oxford history of Western art* (pp. 380–383). Oxford, England: Oxford University Press.

Bødker, K., Kensing, F., & Simonsen, J. (2004). *Participatory IT design: Designing for business and workplace realities*. Cambridge, MA: MIT Press.

Callon, M., & Rabeharisoa, V. (2003). Research "in the wild" and the shaping of new social identities. *Technology in Society, 25*, 193–204. doi:10.1016/S0160-791X(03)00021-6

Dalibert, L. (2014). Posthumanism and somatechnologies: Exploring the intimate relations between humans and technologies (Unpublished doctoral dissertaton). University of Enschede.

Dalibert, L. (2016). Living with spinal cord stimulation: Doing embodiment and incorporation. *Science, Technology, & Human Values, 41*, 635–659. doi:10.1177/0162243915617833

Derthick, K. (2014). *Exploring meditation and technology to problematize the use or non-use binary*. Paper presented at the Refusing, Limiting, Departing-Workshop@CHI. Retrieved from http://nonuse.jedbrubaker.com/wp-content/uploads/2014/03/KatieDerthick-StudyingNonUse-CHI2014-WorkshopSubmission-FINAL.pdf

Douglas, S. J. (1987). *Inventing American broadcasting, 1899–1922*. Baltimore, MD: Johns Hopkins University Press.

Fischer, C. S. (1992). *America calling: A social history of the telephone to 1940*. Berkeley: University of California Press.

Gardiner, P., & Rothwell, R. (1985). Tough customers: Good designs. *Design Studies, 6*, 7–17. doi:10.1016/0142-694X(85)90036-5

Haraway, D. (1985). Manifesto for cyborgs: Science, technology and socialist feminism in the 1980s. *Socialist Review, 80*, 65–108. Retrieved from https://monoskop .org/images/4/4c/Haraway_Donna_1985_A_Manifesto_for_Cyborgs_Science_ Technology_and_Socialist_Feminism_in_the_1980s.pdf

Hatch, M. (2013). *The maker movement manifesto: Rules for innovation in the new world of crafters, hackers, and tinkerers.* Columbus, OH: McGraw-Hill Education.

Hommels, A., Mesman, J., & Bijker W. E. (Eds.) (2014). *Vulnerability in technological cultures: New directions in research and governance.* Cambridge, MA: MIT Press.

Hyysalo, S., Elgaard Jensen, T., & Oudshoorn, N. (Eds.) (2016). *The new production of users: Changing involvement strategies and innovation collectives.* London, England: Routledge.

ICD User Group (2011). *Remote monitoring: Access for everyone but patients* [blog]. Retrieved from http://icdusergroup.blogspot.com/

Ihde, D. (1990). *Technology and the lifeworld: From garden to earth.* Bloomington: Indiana University Press.

Irwin, A. (1995). *Citizen science: A study of people, expertise and sustainable development.* London, England: Routledge.

Jones, C. A. (2006). The mediated sensorium. In C. A. Jones (Ed.), *Sensorium: Embodied experience, technology, and contemporary art* (pp. 5–49). Cambridge, MA: MIT Press.

Kiran, A. H., Oudshoorn, N., & Verbeek, P. P. (2015). Beyond checklists: Toward an ethical-constructive technology assessment. Journal of Responsible Innovation, 2, 5–19. doi:10 .1080/23299460.2014.992769

Kline, R. R. (2000). *Consumers in the country: Technology and social change in rural America.* Baltimore, MD: Johns Hopkins University Press.

Kline, R., & Pinch, T. (1996). Users as agents of technological change: The social construction of the automobile in the rural United States. *Technology and Culture*, 37, 763–795. doi:10 .2307/3107097

Latour, B. (2005). *Reassembling the social: An introduction to actor-network theory.* Oxford, England: Oxford University Press.

Lettow, S. (2011). Somatechnologies: Rethinking the body in philosophy of technology. *Techné: Research in Philosophy and Technology, 15*, 110–117. doi:10.5840/techne201115211

Loder, C. (2014). Negotiating space between use and non-use. In *Proceedings of the ACM CHI 2014 workshop.* Retrieved from http://nonuse.jedbrubaker.com/wp-content/uploads/2014/03/Loder_nonuse.pdf

Martin, M. (1991). *Hello central? Gender, technology and culture in the formation of technology systems.* Montreal, Canada: McGill-Queens University Press.

Maxigas, P. (2012). Hacklabs and hackerspaces—Tracing two genealogies. *Journal of Peer Production*, 2. Retrieved from http://peerproduction.net/issues/issue-2/ peer-reviewed-papers/hacklabs-and-hackerspaces/

McRuer, D. T., & Krendel, E. S. (1959). The human operator as a servo system element. *Journal of the Franklin Institute, 267,* 511–536. doi:10.1016/0016-0032(59)90091-2

Meister, D. (1999). *The history of human factors and ergonomics.* Mahwah, NJ: Lawrence Erlbaum.

Menil, F., de (Director), & Alexandre, M. (Producer) (1980). *Tinguely: A kinetic cosmos* [Documentary film]. United States: FPM Foundation for the Arts.

Nordmann, A. (2007). If and then: A critique of speculative nanoethics. *NanoEthics, 1,* 31–46. doi:10.1007/s11569-007-0007-6

Oost, E., van, Verhaegh, S., & Oudshoorn, N. (2009). From innovation community to community innovation: User-initiated innovation in wireless Leiden. *Science, Technology, & Human Values, 34,* 182–205. doi:10.1177/0162243907311556

Oudshoorn, N. (2008). Diagnosis at a distance: The invisible work of patients and health-care professionals in cardiac telemonitoring technologies. *Sociology of Health & Illness, 30,* 272–295. doi:10.1111/j.1467-9566.2007.01032.x

Oudshoorn, N. (2011). *Telecare technologies and the transformation of healthcare.* Houndmills, England: Palgrave Macmillan.

Oudshoorn, N. (2015). Sustaining cyborgs: Sensing and tuning agencies of pacemakers and ICDs. *Social Studies of Science, 45,* 56–76. doi:10.1177/0306312714557377

Oudshoorn, N. (2016). The vulnerability of cyborgs: The case of ICD shocks. *Science, Technology, & Human Values, 41,* 767–793. doi:10.1177/0162243916633755

Oudshoorn, N., & Pinch, T. (Eds.) (2003). *How users matter: The co-construction of users and technology.* Cambridge, MA: MIT Press.

Pantzar, M., & Ainamo, A. (2004). Nokia, the surprising success of textbook wisdom. *Comportamento Orgnizational e Gestao, 19*(1), 71–86. Retrieved from http://repositorio.ispa.pt/bitstream/10400.12/4774/1/COG,%2010(1),%2071–86.pdf

Parikh, T. S., & Lazowska, E. D. (2006). Designing an architecture for delivering mobile information services to the rural developing world. In *Proceedings of the International Conference of the World Wide Web* (pp. 791–800). Edinburgh, Scotland: Association for Computing Machinery. doi:10.1145/1135777.1135897

Pfaffenberger, B. (1992). Technological dramas. *Science, Technology, & Human Values, 17,* 282–312. doi:10.1177/016224399201700302

Pinch, T., & Bijsterveld, K. (Eds.) (2012). *The Oxford handbook of sound studies.* Oxford, England: Oxford University Press.

Rice, T. (2010) Learning to listen: Auscultation and the transmission of auditory knowledge. *Journal of the Royal Anthropological Institute, 16,* 41–61. doi:10.1111/j.1467-9655 .2010.01609.x

Rohracher, H. (Ed.) (2005). *User involvement in innovation processes: Strategies and limitations from a socio-technical perspective.* Munchen, Germany: Profil.

Sandberg, A., & Bostrom, N. (2006). Converging cognitive enhancements. *Annals of the New York Academy of Sciences, 1093,* 201–227. doi:10.1196/annals.1382.015

Satchell, C., & Dourish, P. (2009). Beyond the user: Use and non-use in HCI. In *Proceedings of the 21st annual conference of the Australian Computer-Human*

Interaction Special Interest Group: Design: Open 24/7 (pp. 9–16). New York, NY: Association for Computing Machinery. doi:10.1145/1738826.1738829

Shapin, S. (2012). The sciences of subjectivity. *Social Studies of Science, 42,* 170–184. doi:10 .1177/0306312711435375

Sobchack, V. (2006). A leg to stand on: On prosthetics, metaphor, and materiality. In M. Smith & J. Morra (Eds.), *The prosthetic impulse: From a posthuman presence to a biocultural future* (pp. 17–41). Cambridge, MA: MIT Press.

Sørenson, K., & Williams, R. (Eds.) (2002). *Shaping technology, guiding policy: Concepts, spaces and tools.* Cheltenham, England: Edward Elgar.

Star, S. L., & Strauss, A. (1999). Layers of silence, arenas of voice: The ecology of visible and invisible work. *Computer Supported Work, 8,* 9–30. doi:10.1023/ A:1008651105359

Stedelijk Museum (2017). *Jean Tinguely: Machine spectacle* [Exhibition catalog]. Amsterdam, Netherlands: Author.

Summerton, J. (2004). Do electrons have politics? Constructing user identities in Swedish electricity. *Science, Technology, & Human Values, 29,* 486–511. doi:10.1177 /0162243904264487

Taylor, F. W. (1911). *The principles of scientific management.* New York, NY: Harper.

Thomas, D. (2002). *Hacker culture.* Minneapolis: University of Minnesota Press.

Verbeek, P.-P. (2008). Cyborg intentionality: Rethinking the phenomenology of human-technology relations. *Phenomenology and the Cognitive Sciences, 7,* 387–395. doi:10 .1007/s11097-008–9099-x

Von Hippel, E. (2005). *Democratizing innovation.* Cambridge, MA: MIT Press.

Voss, A., Hartswood, M., Procter, R., Rouncefield, M., Slack, R. S., & Büscher, M. (Eds.) (2009). *Configuring user-designer relations: Interdisciplinary perspectives.* London, England: Springer.

Weiner, K., & Will, C. (2016). Users, non-users and "resistance" to pharmaceuticals. In S. Hyysalo, T. Elgaard Jensen, & N. Oudshoorn (Eds.), *The new production of users: Changing involvement strategies and innovation collectives* (pp. 273–297). London, England: Routledge.

Williams, R., Slack, R., & Stewart, J. (2005). *Social learning in technological innovation—Experimenting with information and communication technologies.* Cheltenham, England: Edgar Elgar.

Woolgar, S. (1991). Configuring the user: The case of usability trials. In J. Law (Ed.), *A sociology of monsters: Essays on power, technology and domination* (pp. 57–102). London, England: Routledge.

Wyatt, S. (2003). Non-users also matter: The construction of users and non-users of the Internet. In N. Oudshoorn & T. Pinch (Eds.), *How users matter: The co-construction of users and technologies* (pp. 67–81). Cambridge, MA: MIT Press.

Wyatt, S., Graham, T., & Terranova, T. (2002). They came, they surfed, they went back to the beach: Conceptualising use and non-use of the Internet. In S. Woolgar (Ed.), *Virtual society? Technology, cyberbole, reality* (pp. 23–40). Oxford, England: Oxford University Press.

# CHAPTER 8

# Scientific Community

## Dean Keith Simonton

Early philosophers of science, such as Francis Bacon and René Descartes, often viewed scientific inquiry as a largely individualistic enterprise. The individual needed only apply the appropriate method – whether empirical induction or logical deduction – to obtain valid knowledge or "truths" about the natural world. Although such investigators still expected to share their discoveries through publication, even publication started out as a largely individualistic activity, the discoverer arranging for communication through regular book publishers. Bacon and Descartes communicated their main ideas through monographs, as did Nicolaus Copernicus, Galileo Galilei, Johannes Kepler, and other pioneers of the scientific revolution. The dissemination of scientific findings lacked any systematic social organization. In this way, science, or rather what was then called "natural philosophy," did not differ that much from other forms of writing, such as literature or theology.

The individualistic nature of scientific practice began to change substantially in the seventeenth century with the advent of societies and journals devoted to the communication of new discoveries (Gibson, 1982). This transformation is perhaps best illustrated by the founding of the Royal Society of London in 1660. Although other scientific organizations had been founded earlier, most notably in Italy, the Royal Society can be considered the oldest entity of its kind still in existence. In addition to providing a focal point for the exchange of knowledge, in 1665 the organization's first secretary, Henry Oldenburg, took the critical step of launching the *Philosophical Transactions*, likely the first and oldest journal devoted exclusively to the propagation of the latest results produced in Britain and the rest of the scientific world. In addition to helping make the journal article a central means of communication, *Transactions* implemented an early version of peer review, allowing for the professional certification of the knowledge claims reported in the journal. Because the published articles included the date the manuscripts were submitted to the editor, the journal also facilitated the assignment of priority to dis-coveries. *Transactions* thus acquired a critical social function in validating rival claims, an especially important task throughout the history of modern science (Merton, 1957). In all, the Royal Society thus served the scientific community at large, not just particular discipline specialists.

Of course, the conversion of science from an individual to a social activity did not end with the emergence of scientific societies and peer-reviewed journals. Another major development, in the twentieth century, was the increasingly collaborative nature of science, manifested in the substantial increase in the number of coauthors of scientific papers (Price, 1986). These coauthorships increased largely due to the rise of "Big Science" in the form of grant-funded research laboratories replete with doctorates, postdoctorates, graduate students, and technicians. Any discussion of these collaborative relationships would take us well beyond the focus of this chapter; namely, the scientific community. Below, I treat four principal topics associated with that subject: conceptions, norms, consensus, and stratification.

## 8.1   Conceptions

A *scientific community* is a somewhat loose concept that can be defined multiple ways. In the broadest terms, a scientific community is any net-work of scientists who exchange information about science. That exchange can be formal or informal and can include scientific knowledge or policy. Such communities can operate at separate levels of specialization and can involve distinct forms of organization.

In the case of specialization, a minimal community might be defined as all the individuals making up a given scientific specialty. These are the scientists who read each other's publications and cite any significant findings from those publications in their own publications, thereby forming a citation network. Historian and scientometrician Price (1963) referred to these groups as an *invisible college,* a term originally used to describe the natural philosophers who had gathered around English chemist Robert Boyle prior to the founding of the Royal Society (see also Crane, 1972). Making assumptions about how much published research a specialist can keep up on over the course of an active career, Price estimated that the invisible college would include about 100 researchers. This is likely an underestimate because Price assumed that the 100 scientists would produce 100 articles each, when a more realistic figure is an average of 3.5 each (Wray, 2010). When making allowance for this lower mean, the size of research specialties can be expanded to 250–600 scientists. Actually, given that the bulk of research in most scientific disciplines is generated by research teams rather than individuals (Hull, 1988), the revised estimate might be bumped to a still larger figure, given that such teams often consist of two or more scientists who claim expertise in the same or similar specialties – yet all appearing as coauthors on the same publication. Even so, an upper limit remains on the size of any specialty. When a specialty gets too large, it tends to partition into subspecialties, although this process need not be the only one responsible for the advent of new specialties (Wray, 2005).

A scientific community can also be defined at a yet more general level of specialization. Certainly most scientists will identify with a particular discipline, having earned their degrees in an academic discipline rather than in a research specialty. Although no single researcher can possibly read all publications generated by members of a discipline, many can claim some familiarity with current movements, owing to the publication of broad research reviews, often provided by the organizations to which the researcher belongs, such as the Association for Psychological Science and its journal *Perspectives on Psychological Science*. Moreover, some scientists exhibit interests that extend to science in general and thus belong to societies that are even more inclusive. Examples include the British Science Association and the American Association for the Advancement of Science. The journals published by such organizations often provide general overviews of the latest scientific advances. Scientists thus become aware of the research frontiers in specialties to which they themselves could never possibly contribute.

As noted at the beginning of this chapter, the scientific community need not be exclusively defined by substantive specialization. Science is a diverse enterprise that can entail other goals besides the discovery of new knowledge or techniques. These alternative goals include science education and public policy. The former might seek out means to recruit and retain underrepresented groups among active researchers whereas the latter might involve the dissemination of informed positions on such issues as vaccination or climate change. In addition to special sections of scientific societies often devoted to these practical ends, independent organizations can also emerge, such as the Union of Concerned Scientists, founded in 1969 in the United States. However, because membership in the Union of Concerned Scientists can include nonscientists as well as scientists, it may better illustrate the concept of the "epistemic community," consisting of people who share a commitment to the scientific approach to practical problems (Haas, 1992).

To keep this chapter within reasonable bounds, I restrict the concept of a scientific community to professional scientists engaged in contributing to scientific knowledge and methods. Most often, that restriction operates with respect to either the specialty or the discipline rather than to science as a whole. It is rare for a scientist to contribute to a discovery or invention so potent that it eventually affects multiple disciplines. Such contributions are perhaps most likely to appear in mathematics, such as the development of the calculus as a universal approach to analyzing natural phenomena.

## 8.2 Norms

Most communities must operate under certain general expectations about the most appropriate and inappropriate behaviors of their members. Without such societal or cultural norms, the community may not only fail to achieve its fundamental goals, but may even fail to maintain itself as a community. In the specific case of science, these norms should ensure that scientists behave in a manner consistent with the aim of accumulating enduring knowledge about natural phenomena. Presumably these scientific norms would distinguish practitioners from others who might otherwise be mistaken for scientists, especially those who promulgate pseudoscience (Kaufman & Kaufman, 2018). But what are these scientific norms that keep scientists in line with science? Merton (1942, 1973), the pioneer in the sociology of science, first addressed this question. Yet as would be expected, Merton did not have the final word on the issue.

### 8.2.1 *Mertonian Scientific Norms*

Merton (1942) began by introducing the general concept:

> The ethos of science is that affectively toned complex of values and norms which is held to be binding on the [scientist]. The norms are expressed in the form of prescriptions, proscriptions and permissions ... [that] are legitimatized in terms of institutional values. These imperatives, transmitted by precept and example and reenforced by sanctions, are in varying degrees internalized by the scientist. (p. 116)

Moreover, specific imperatives should be those that realize the "institutional goal of science [which] is the extension of certified knowledge" (p. 117). Merton inferred that the following four norms fulfill this function:

1 *Universalism*: This norm "finds immediate expression in the canon that truth-claims, whatever their source, are to be subjected to *preestablished*

*impersonal criteria*: consonance with observation and with previously confirmed knowledge" (p. 118, emphasis original). The universalism imperative stands in stark contrast to a particularism that would consider a scientist's gender, ethnicity, nationality, religion, socioeconomic class, and even personality as somehow relevant in judging the merit of an invention or discovery. Science is an equal-opportunity enterprise: a community of individuals with the same dedication to discovering scientific truths.

2  *Communism*: This term is to be taken "in the non-technical and extended sense of common ownership of goods," implying that the "substantive findings of science are a product of social collaboration and are assigned to the community," thereby representing "a common heritage in which the equity of the individual producer is severely limited" (p. 121). Even an eponymous theory or law, such as Boyle's Law, cannot be considered the property of the scientist who earns the credit. In this sense, science operates differently from technology, for in the latter domain, inventors can attain patents that allow them exclusive rights to benefit from their conceptions.

3  *Disinterestedness*: Scientists are expected to contribute to shared enterprise rather than engage in personal gain or aggrandizement at the expense of the scientific community. Merton was quite struck by the "virtual absence of fraud in the annals of science, which appears exceptional when compared with the record of other spheres of activity" (p. 124). Fraud elevates the individual by undermining the main purpose of science. For this reason, fraudulent results are quickly condemned by the community of peers.

4  *Organized skepticism*: The final norm of the scientific community is the "suspension of judgment until 'the facts are at hand' and the detached scrutiny of beliefs in terms of empirical and logical criteria" (p. 126). As Merton noted, organized skepticism has "periodically involved science in conflict" with other forms of human social activity when science makes inroads into the latter. Science then provides a severe challenge to religious, political, and economic institutions.

Curiously, Merton's (1942) original formulation of the four scientific norms came to an abrupt halt after devoting just two paragraphs to the fourth norm. As a consequence, the interrelations among the norms and their relations with the aims of science were less than fully articulated. Perhaps this truncated treatment reflects the author's somewhat limited aspirations for presenting the main arguments. The essay merely accomplished what Merton was trying to achieve at the time.

### 8.2.2 Post-Merton Critiques

Merton's four norms did not build on any thorough logical analysis or original empirical inquiry, but rather represented speculations founded on various intellectual sources (Turner, 2007). Not surprisingly, then, subsequent scholars responded to Merton's norms in diverse ways. Many merely speculated themselves about how to modify the terminology; for example, by replacing "communism" with "communality" or "communalism" or by shortening "organized skepticism" to "skepticism." Others have added norms such as "originality," "independence," and "openness" (Anderson, Ronning, DeVries, & Martinson, 2010). Speculations can pile on speculations!

An alternative approach, naturally, is to tackle the question by collecting actual empirical data regarding the norms to which scientists themselves claim to subscribe. An early example of this approach involved intensive interviews of Apollo moon scientists (Mitroff, 1974). In opposition to Mertonian norms emerged a parallel set of counternorms such as particularism, solitariness, interestedness, and organized dogmatism. Where Merton's (1942) norms reflected the scientific community, counternorms ensued from the individualistic side of science. A much later empirical inquiry, based on a national survey and focus groups, found that norms and associated counternorms had to be augmented by still more norms (Anderson et al., 2010). Last, even when empirical investigation concentrates solely on Mertonian norms, researchers may find they do not all carry equal weight for the practicing scientist. For example, a Web-based survey of academics found that communism far surpassed either universalism or disinterestedness in importance (Macfarlane & Cheng, 2008). In short, the empirical data present a much more complex picture of how norms actually function in the scientific community.

Finally, it is conceivable that the primary function of the putative norms is not normative at all. They might, for instance, be "better conceived as vocabularies of justification, which are used to evaluate, justify and describe the professional actions of scientists, but which are not institutionalised within the scientific community in such a way that general conformity is maintained" (Mulkay, 1976, pp. 653–654). This justification function is most prominent when the scientific community takes stands on controversial policy issues, with norms placing scientists on higher ground than their opponents. The debates over climate change well illustrate this supposed rhetorical advantage. Whether scientists actually adhere to those ideals can then become the subject of a second level of controversy.

The upshot is this: Although Merton (1942) raised an important issue regarding the role of norms in the scientific community, subsequent research has yet to converge on a final statement regarding those norms, including their number, names, and functions.

## 8.3   Consensus

A key expectation regarding the scientific community is that scientists tend to reach strong consensus concerning the main substantive questions and theoretical issues that define their discipline and concerning the methodological techniques to address those questions and issues. Indeed, a discipline that lacked any such consensus would be less likely to be considered a "science," or at least less likely to be considered a "hard science." Put differently, a discipline lacks discipline when scientists working in the same field can take discrepant, even antithetical positions on theory, method, and data.

I now scrutinize The operation of consensus in scientific communities with respect to three divergent manifestations: the hierarchy of the sciences, research paradigms, and multiple discoveries and inventions.

### 8.3.1   Hierarchy of the Sciences

In the previous section, I alluded to the commonplace distinction between the "hard" and "soft" sciences (e.g., Hedges, 1987; Smith, Best, Stubbs, Archibald, & Roberson-Nay, 2002). The idea that not all scientific disciplines are equally "scientific" goes at least as far back as French philosopher Comte (1839–1842/1855), who ordered the main empirical sciences of the day from the "inorganic" (astronomy, physics, and then chemistry) to the "organic" (physiology or biology) and then to "social physics" (or sociology). The basis for this hierarchical arrangement involved increasing complexity of the discipline's core phenomena and decreasing generality or abstractness of its central concepts and increasing dependence on disciplines earlier in the hierarchy. The word "earlier" has historical meaning, too, for Comte believed the hierarchy also reflected the order in which disciplines became bona fide "positive" sciences. Ironically, despite the notion that positivism advocated an empiricism as the source of all knowledge, Comte never provided an empirical test of this hierarchical arrangement.

The first such empirical test did not come until much later, in a 1983 study published by S. Cole (1983), one of Merton's more productive students in the sociology of science (see also S. Cole, 2004). Yet interestingly, Cole did not use the same criteria to test the hierarchical ordering that Comte (1839–1842/1855) used to hypothesize it in the first place. Instead, S. Cole (1983) posited that "sciences at the top of the hierarchy presumably display higher levels of consensus and more rapid rates of advancement than those at the bottom" (p. 111). None of S. Cole's measures directly assessed either empirical complexity or conceptual generality. Indeed, the overwhelming majority of tests used measures of disciplinary consensus. That said, the degree of consensus exhibited in any science should be inversely related to its complexity. Scientists who study complex phenomena are like the proverbial "blind men and an elephant," each gabbing a different small part of the whole and thus coming to contradictory views of the entire animal. In contrast, those who investigate simpler phenomena would be like blind men who are studying a snake and can attain a stronger consensus regarding its morphology. The greater generality of concepts would also encourage greater consensus because scientists would describe empirical phenomena in a shared nomenclature and theoretical terminology: Compare the periodic table of elements in chemistry with the taxonomy of living forms in biology! Therefore, the criteria that S. Cole actually applied can be considered reasonable proxies for the criteria Comte used to formulate the initial hierarchy.

Unfortunately, S. Cole (1983) concluded no evidence supported the expected hierarchy. Instead, S. Cole identified divergent orderings, the specific arrangement depending on the specific empirical criteria applied. Even so, S. Cole did not actually implement the most appropriate statistical analyses, instead relying exclusively on scanning the raw data. In contrast, subsequent research provided firm evidence for a hierarchy, especially when augmenting S. Cole's measures (Simonton, 2004, 2015). The two inorganic sciences, physics and chemistry, are clustered at the top; the two organic sciences, biology and psychology, appear in the middle; and sociology shows up at the bottom as the single representative of the social sciences.

Significantly, the sciences at the top exhibit the most consensus, such as agreement in peer and expert evaluations regarding the relative contributions of various scientists to the discipline, including earlier peer recognition of the work of younger scientists (S. Cole, 1983; Simonton, 2015). Moreover, higher placement positively aligns with higher conceptual precision (Schachter, Christenfeld, Ravina, & Bilous, 1991) and certainty (Suls & Fletcher, 1983) as well as a higher ratio of laws to theories (Roeckelein, 1997) and greater prominence of graphs (Smith et al., 2002): associations that probably, like consensus, correspond to Comte's (1839–1842/1855) criteria of complexity and generality. Likewise, citations in sciences at the top concentrate on the most current literature (S. Cole, 1983) and knowledge accumulates much more quickly, increasing the obsolescence rate at the leading edge of research (McDowell, 1982). It takes less time for work conducted at the frontier to become incorporated into the discipline's core knowledge, such as that defined by textbooks. In addition, survey results indicated that sciences at the top are rated as more "hard" than those at the bottom (Smith et al., 2002); subjective judgments fit the objective data. As another objective indication of the softness of the lower end of the hierarchy, scientists in the hard sciences are much *less* likely to confirm their research hypotheses, a curious consequence that implies that the soft sciences offer more latitude for confirmation bias to contaminate published research (Fanelli & Glänzel, 2013). The greater susceptibility to confirmation bias also helps explain why disciplines like psychology suffer from replication problems, making it much more difficult to accumulate established knowledge (Open Science Collaboration, 2015). Hard sciences differ from soft sciences in other critical ways, discussed in the next two sections.

In the meantime, I make two final points. First, although Figure 8.1 depicts a single hierarchy, that hierarchy is confined to the "pure" empirical sciences, as was the case in Comte's original conception (1839–1842/1855). Nonempirical disciplines like mathematics are omitted, along with applied empirical disciplines such as medicine and engineering. Most likely, such sciences would have their own hierarchy, orthogonal to the one depicted in the figure, creating a two-dimensional representation of hierarchies (Hemlin, 1993; Klavans & Boyack, 2009).

Second, the hierarchical arrangement seen in the figure indicates that the social characteristics of a discipline, which are an essential characteristic of its scientific community, can be ascribed partly to the attributes of the subject matter. In particular, low-consensus domains align with more complex phenomena than high-consensus domains. Because these social characteristics would probably influence the recruitment and retention of scientists with dispositions most compatible with that domain, scientists in the hard sciences should, in general, have different personalities and backgrounds from those in the soft sciences, and that is, in fact, the case

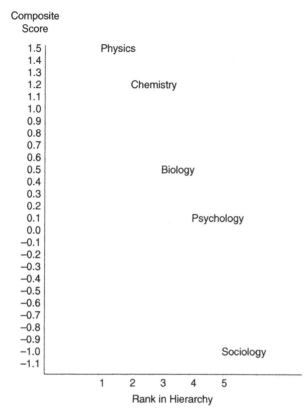

Figure 8.1 The scientific disciplines of physics, chemistry, biology, psychology, and sociology placed in the Comtean hierarchy of the sciences. The horizontal axis specifies the rank, and the vertical axis signifies the quantitative score on a composite measure that includes the magnitude of disciplinary consensus. From "Psychology's Status as a Scientific Discipline: Its Empirical Placement within an Implicit Hierarchy of the Sciences," by D. K. Simonton, 2004, *Review of General Psychology, 8*, p. 74.

(Simonton, 2009). To illustrate, a psychometric inquiry that directly compared chemists with research psychologists found that the latter were "more Bohemian, introverted, unconventional, imaginative and creative in thinking and behavior" (Chambers, 1964, p. 17). Presumably, psychologists are the type of people who would be more accepting of a low-consensus domain like psychological science. Indeed, a feedback loop could exist: their more unconventional dispositions might directly interfere with the attainment of consensus!

## 8.3.2    Research Paradigms

A discipline's placement in the hierarchy shown in Figure 8.1 positively correlates with a yet unmentioned contrast: differences in paradigm development (Ashar & Shapiro, 1990; Simonton, 2015). Measurement of paradigm development comprised three measures: (a) "the average length in words of dissertation abstracts in each field," (b) "the average length in pages of dissertations in each field," and (c) the "length of [the] chain of prerequisite courses in each field" (Ashar & Shapiro, 1990, p. 130), as described in a typical university catalog. The first two are negative indicators, the third positive. Hence, sciences at the top of the hierarchy feature shorter dissertation abstracts, shorter dissertations, and longer chains of course prerequisites (see also Fanelli & Glänzel, 2013). Although the authors did detail the meaning of these three indicators, having borrowed them from other applied studies, these indicators clearly assess the extent to which a discipline is *codified*, where "codification refers to the consolidation of empirical knowledge into succinct and interdependent theoretical formulations" (Zuckerman & Merton, 1972, p. 303). The conceptual precision and established laws that also align with placement at the top of the hierarchy facilitate this consolidation.

Although Kuhn by not mentioned by name in Ashar and Shapiro (1990), the composite measure of paradigm development obviously refers to the concept of paradigms articulated in the classic *The Structure of Scientific Revolutions* (Kuhn, 1970, see also Kuhn, 2012). According to Kuhn (1970), a paradigm means that

> some accepted examples of actual scientific practice – examples which include law, theory, application, and instrumentation together – provide models from which spring particular coherent traditions of scientific research. These are the traditions which the historian describes under such rubrics as "Ptolemaic astronomy" (or "Copernican"),
> "Aristotelian dynamics" (or "Newtonian"), "corpuscular optics" (or "wave optics"), and so on. The study of paradigms, including many that are far more specialized than those named illustratively above, is what mainly prepares the student for membership in the particular scientific community with which he will later practice … [Scientists] whose research is based on shared paradigms are committed to the same rules and standards for scientific practice. That commitment and the apparent consensus it produces are prerequisites for normal science, i.e., for the genesis and continuation of a particular research tradition. (pp. 10–11)

Here, "normal science" plainly represents what was earlier identified as "hard" science at the top of the Comtean hierarchy. Normal science is predicated on a strong consensus regarding theory, methods, and findings that guides what Kuhn called "puzzle-solving" research.

The relation among consensus, paradigms, and hierarchical placement became even more evident when Kuhn (1970) discussed disciplines at the "pre-paradigmatic" phase. Such sciences lack any theoretical, methodological, or substantive consensus. Facts may accumulate without any coherent meaning and a discipline may be fragmented into rival schools or systems. However, if sufficiently fortunate, a scientist can become an exemplar who provides the basis for a paradigm that eventually gathers enough adherents to generate a genuine consensus, at which juncture, a normal science emerges. Until that point, the discipline can only be considered a soft science residing near or at the bottom of the hierarchy.

Yet transformations can continue after a discipline becomes a hard science. In Kuhn's (1970) model, the puzzle-solving inquiries that drive normal science can yield anomalies that do not easily fit in paradigmatic theory. If a sufficient number of important anomalies accumulate, the discipline may enter a crisis stage in which consensus starts breaking down because scientists differ in how best to resolve inconsistencies, for example, by offering divergent post hoc explanations. Nonetheless, with luck, a scientist may offer an entirely new paradigm that resolves the contradictions and thereby initiates a scientific revolution or "paradigm shift." Kuhn argued that these scientific revolutionaries occupy a peripheral status in the scientific community they revolutionize. "Almost always the men who achieve these fundamental inventions of a new paradigm have been either very young or very new to the field whose paradigm they change" (p. 90). In line with this claim, psychological research showed that scientific revolutionaries in the hard sciences have personalities and backgrounds more similar to scientists in the soft sciences, making them true outsiders (Simonton, 2009). In any event, as the new paradigm becomes established, a revitalized normal science arises and the cycle potentially can continue.

In some respects, one can view this Kuhnian cycle as a more dynamic version of the static Comtean hierarchy. In the latter case, consensus inversely relates to complexity, where complexity can be considered a relatively stable feature of the science – making consensus a stable attribute as well. But from a Kuhnian perspective, because complexity is not stable, neither can consensus be so. The preparadigmatic phase of the discipline is too riddled with random data with multiple theoretical interpretations, so consensus is low. With the advent of a paradigm, all important data become subsumed under an overarching theory with precisely defined concepts and methods; consensus increases with decreased complexity.

Nevertheless, should practitioners of this normal science begin to encounter anomalies, the discipline increases in complexity – with the accumulation of unexplained facts or post hoc explanations for those facts – and consensus then declines. The main qualification to this picture is that the state of the discipline should not descend too far down the hierarchy. When classical Newtonian physics began to encounter anomalies toward the end of the nineteenth century, it did not revert to the preparadigmatic physics that existed prior to Galileo, Descartes, and Newton. An empirically compromised paradigm is still much better than no paradigm at all. Most scientists will not even reject an old paradigm until an obviously superior paradigm has already appeared, and even then it may take the younger generation to make the shift (Stewart, 1986; Sulloway, 2014). As Planck (1949) observed, "A new scientific truth does not triumph by convincing its opponents and making them see the light, but rather because its opponents eventually die, and a new generation grows up that is familiar with it" (pp. 33–34; see Hull, Tessner, & Diamond, 1978; Levin, Stephan, & Walker, 1995). Consequently, the ordinal position of the sciences in the Comtean hierarchy in all likelihood remains highly stable: physics, chemistry, biology, psychology, and sociology.

### 8.3.3   Multiple Discovery and Invention

Two final and intimately related correlates of a discipline's placement in the Figure 8.1 graph remain to be discussed. First, scientists working in disciplines higher up in the hierarchy are more prone to experience research anticipation, discovering their work has been or soon will be "scooped" by another scientist (Hagstrom, 1974; Simonton, 2015). Indeed, at the upper end of the hierarchy, researchers will more often terminate a line of investigation to avoid the possibility of wasting further hard work. Second, scientists working higher up in the hierarchy are more likely to participate in a *multiple* discovery or invention (Ogburn & Thomas, 1922; Simonton, 2015). A multiple occurs when two or more scientists or inventors develop the same idea independently and even simultaneously, or nearly so (Lamb & Easton, 1984; Merton, 1961b). Two well-known examples include the independent invention of calculus by Isaac Newton and by Gottfried Leibniz and the independent proposal of a theory of evolution by natural selection by Charles Darwin and by Alfred Russel Wallace. Researchers have recorded hundreds of such multiples (Merton, 1961b; Ogburn & Thomas, 1922; Simonton, 1979). Anticipated duplication and actual duplication represent two aspects of the same underlying phenomenon. Although the phenomena of anticipation and multiples are extremely complex (Simonton, 2010), this chapter requires only that I focus on three implications for understanding scientific communities.

First, such events are manifestly a direct repercussion of disciplinary consensus. In high-consensus sciences, where most scientists have undergone fairly standardized academic training and thus subscribe to the same overriding paradigm, the odds will increase that two or more researchers will decide to investigate the same problem (Simonton, 2010). Then, by chance alone, anticipations and even outright multiples are likely to emerge (Merton, 1961a). In a way, enough redundancy exists among separate researchers or research teams that the entire specialty can operate like a "parallel processing" computer system (Kornfeld & Hewitt, 1981; also see Hull, 1988). In low-consensus disciplines, however, researchers cannot even agree on the most important questions to be addressed. Pursuing the same problem then becomes extremely unlikely. Hence, multiples are common in physics and chemistry, but very unusual in psychology and sociology.

Second, events such as anticipation and multiples betray inefficiencies in communication networks in the scientific community that delay the dissemination of a new discovery or invention (Brannigan & Wanner, 1983). It is telling, for example, that in a sample of 264 multiples, 20 percent took place in a 1-year interval and 18 percent in a 2-year interval, yet 34 percent required a decade or more before the final duplicate appeared (Merton, 1961b). Indeed, Gregor Mendel's discovery of genetic laws were not rediscovered until more than a third of a century had passed. Many multiples might not have appeared at all if communication made more scientists aware that they are en route to being scooped, and over the course of recent history, communication has become ever more rapid. Presentations at scientific conferences, the circulation of reprints, telephone conversations, and eventually the emergence of the almost instantaneous internet – with e-mail, Listservs, and posting sites – accelerated the exchange of knowledge. Not surprisingly, then, the temporal interval between first and last instance in a multiple has shrunk over time (Brannigan & Wanner, 1983). Communication has become so fast that multiples have to be virtually simultaneous to occur at all. Additionally, the number of participants in a multiple – what has been called the multiple's *grade* – has also declined over time (Brannigan & Wanner, 1983). It now has become rare for more than two claimants to declare the same discovery and invention, whereas higher grades used to be more common. For instance, Mendel's genetic laws were rediscovered by *three* independent scientists, making that discovery a Grade 4 multiple. Quadruplets like that are rather unlikely today.

Third and last, multiples – like discoveries and inventions in general (e.g., Schaffer, 1986) – can be considered social constructions rather than objective and simple events requiring no further validation or interpretation. Indeed, multiples are more likely to be the products of social construction than are singletons: the instances in which a given contribution appears to have only a single discoverer or inventor (see Merton, 1961b). The reason is that rival claims are seldom identical (Constant, 1978; Patinkin, 1983; Schmookler, 1966). As a consequence, the scientific community must reach consensus about whether two or more contributions count as a multiple. This consensus may be negotiated through contentious priority disputes in the case of discoveries (Merton, 1957) and through patent litigation in the case of inventions (Schmookler, 1966), but the final consensual judgment may not even correspond to the perspectives of the scientists or inventors whose individual reputations are at stake.

To offer a specific example, nuclear magnetic resonance was independently and simultaneously observed by Bloch, Hansen, and Packard at Stanford and by Purcell, Torrey, and Pound at Harvard. In time, this supposed multiple would lead the heads of these two teams, Felix Bloch and Edward Mills Purcell, to share the Nobel Prize in Physics. Yet despite the fact that physicists "have come to look at the two experiments as practically identical," Purcell once observed, "when Hansen first showed up [at our lab] and started talking about it, it was about an hour before either of us understood how the other was trying to explain it" (Zuckerman, 1977, p. 203). The identity of their respective discoveries was not immediately obvious to the discoverers themselves and thus had to be worked out through information exchange and translation. In the end, the two separate discoveries merged into a single multiple.

Such social construction plays a lesser role in the anticipation phenomenon, for in that case, researchers themselves often make the decision that the outcome of their efforts will be anticipated. Naturally, if journal editors and peer reviewers decide that the hapless researcher has just reinvented the wheel, that anticipation assessment enters the realm of social construction. If the author of the rejected manuscript disagrees with that evaluation, it may or may not be possible to convince the editor and reviewers otherwise. The validity of the supposed equivalence then becomes subject to negotiation. In any case, the multiples phenomenon, like the hierarchy of the sciences and like disciplinary paradigms, illustrates the central place of consensus in the scientific community. Not only are multiples more likely when strong paradigmatic consensus exists, but that consensus is ultimately required to decide whether a multiple has actually occurred.

## 8.4 Stratification

Communities are rarely completely egalitarian. Even in hunter–gatherer cultures, some will enjoy higher status than others and such stratification becomes even more conspicuous as the society's population increases (Carneiro, 1970). Similarly, notwithstanding the supposed influence of Mertonian norms like universalism, communism, and disinterestedness, scientific communities manage to make adequate provision for the elevation of their elite scientists above run-of-the-mill researchers. The most elite of these possess names so highly recognizable that they are easily identifiable with a single name, such as Copernicus, Newton, Lavoisier, Gauss, Darwin, Pasteur, Pavlov, and Einstein. At the same time, a large majority dominate the scientific community, reaching nowhere near that level of name recognition; many, if not most, might be considered nonentities even in their specialties. In short, the scientific community as a whole and each specialty in it are highly heterogeneous in apparent merit. Here I examine this merit heterogeneity by addressing two related questions: How do we gauge variation in scientific status? and What are the sources of that variation?

### 8.4.1 Variation in Scientific Status

One way to assess how scientists differ in their standing is to assess their relative productivity: their output of contributions to the scientific enterprise. When books were the primary vehicles for scientific communication, it made little sense to compare the productivity of scientists by counting publications. Years of original research might be consolidated into a single volume, such as William Gilbert's *De Magnete* (1600). The difference between an elite scientist and a more ordinary one would have to rest more on the quality of their publications than their quantity. Even a scientist as great as Newton published only two books, the *Principia* and the *Optiks* (assuming that his *Queries* attaches to the latter). However, once the journal article became the prime vehicle for the communication of scientific knowledge, it eventually became the foundation for more fine-grained measures of productivity, yielding the publication counts that have become such a prominent feature of modern science. Although this practice can be easily criticized as mere "bean counting," emphasizing quantity over quality, productivity measures provide a reasonable place to begin any inquiry into the comparative merit of scientists in the scientific community.

I start with two general observations about productivity. First, and most obvious, scientists differ immensely in their lifetime output. At one extreme are those who never publish a single journal article, not even the results of their doctoral dissertation (e.g., Anwar, 2004; Bloom, 1963; Hutchinson & Zivney, 1995). At the other extreme are those who publish dozens, even hundreds (Simonton, 2004). To illustrate, consider the following publication records of some historic scientists: Charles Darwin, 119; Herman von Helmholtz, 229; Johannes Müller, 285; Sigmund Freud, 330; Albert Einstein, 607; Augustin Cauchy, 789; Leonard Euler, 856; and Arthur Cayley, 995 (Bringmann & Balk, 1983). Second, this variation has a distribution that departs considerably from the commonplace "normal" or Gaussian distribution (i.e., the "bell-shaped" curve; see O'Boyle & Aguinas, 2012; Walberg, Strykowski, Rovai, & Hung, 1984). Leaving aside those who publish nothing, the modal lifetime output is a single publication; the output monotonically declines thereafter in a decelerating function (Price, 1986). This highly skewed curve has been replicated so many times that it has been described by two laws: Lotka and Price (see Allison, Price, Griffith, Moravcsik, & Stewart, 1976). According to the first, if $n$ is total output, the number of scientists with $n$ publications is inversely proportional to $n^2$, yielding the inverse power function $f(n) = c/n^2$, where $c$ is a constant, dependent on the discipline (Egghe, 2005; Lotka, 1926). According to the second law, if $k$ equals the number of scientists publishing in a discipline, then the square root of $k$ gives the number who account for *half* of all publications (Price, 1986; Simonton, 2004). Thus, if $k = 100$, then just ten scientists produced half of the total output. One striking implication of the Price Law is that a discipline should become more elitist as it increases in size (Simonton, 2010). If $k = 100$, then 10 percent of scientists in the field dominate the publications, but if $k = 400$, then just twenty scientists, or merely 5 percent, can claim the same dominance. Conversely, those at the bottom of the distribution contribute amazingly little to the discipline's total publications: The bottom half of the productivity distribution may produce only about 15 percent of all research (e.g., Dennis, 1954, 1955).

Admittedly, here I glossed over numerous complications, such as how to differentially weight monographs versus short notes or adjust for coauthorships (Furnham & Bonnett, 1992). Another problem, however, is more worth our attention: publications can vary enormously in their impact on science. A standard approach to assessing such impact is to use the total number of citations a publication receives in the professional literature (Garfield, 1987). Because a very large percentage of publications are never cited, this measure can help weed out low-quality contributions (e.g., Redner, 1998). Although various extraneous factors contaminate citations, such as self-citations and contrasts across scientific specialties, these contaminants can be ameliorated with sufficient methodological precautions, making the total citations received by a scientist's lifetime publications a reasonable indicator of total impact (J. Cole & Cole, 1971; Lindsey, 1989; Moravcsik & Murugesan, 1975). Although several procedures exist for compiling a scientist's citations, current research lends some support to the *h*-index (Ruscio, Seaman, D'Oriano, Stremlo, & Mahalchik, 2012), which equals the number of publications cited at least *h* times (Hirsch, 2005). This index has the advantage that it integrates quantity and quality into a single number. That said, it not only discriminates against mass producers who publish much uncited work, but also against researchers who invest heavily in fewer manuscripts, and as a result make only a few highly cited contributions.

As might be anticipated, the distribution of total citations is far more elitist than the distribution of total publications: Whatever the limits on how much a single scientist can publish in a lifetime, the citations that those publications can receive are virtually unlimited. A single "citation classic" can earn thousands – even tens of thousands – of citations. For instance, according to Google Scholar, the paper Einstein coauthored with Podolsky and Rosen in 1935 to challenge the completeness of quantum-mechanics has been cited at least 15,000 times. More importantly, those scientists whose total citations place them in the upper tail of the extremely skewed distribution have a much greater likelihood of being recognized with prestigious awards and honors (e.g., Feist, 1993; Inhaber & Przednowek, 1976; Myers, 1970; Simonton, 1992a). For example, citations predict recipients of the Nobel Prize (Ashton & Oppenheim, 1978). Because productivity highly correlates with citations and because citations highly correlate with professional recognition, exceptional productivity, impact, and recognition define the elite in any scientific community (see also Grosul & Feist, 2014; Rodgers & Maranto, 1989).

One final point about recognition: honors and awards themselves stratify from the least to the most significant (Carson, Peterson, & Higgins, 2005; S. Cole & Cole, 1967) along two dimensions: from a narrow specialty to an entire discipline and from local to national to international. Although these two dimensions can sometimes mesh – Nobels grant international recognition for contributions to an entire science, such as physics or chemistry – others can entail one or the other form of distinction. For example, scientists can receive international awards for major achievements in a narrow specialty if that specialty has international importance. Likewise, mathematicians can receive local awards for accomplishments, even if those accomplishments have not yet attained national or international acclaim. Nevertheless, the crème de la crème among the elite are most likely to get supreme honors in both dimensions: widely recognized contributions to an entire science or at least to a highly valued specialty in a high-status science. Given the extremely low base rates, Noble laureates are the genuine scientific elite (Zuckerman, 1977).

To sum, the scientific community – and any specialty in that community – is conspicuously stratified in a scientist's publications, citations, and recognition. Science is not an egalitarian enterprise. Those at the top constitute an extremely select group.

### 8.4.2   Sources of Status Variation

The conclusion that ended the last section cannot stand without asking whether a scientist's standing in the community is merit-based. Ideally, stratification reflects each scientist's actual contribution to science without any intrusion of extraneous factors. What is the evidence that such is the case?

On one hand, empirical reason exists to believe that status as a scientist rests in actual achievement. First, the internal qualities of articles, rather than external factors such as the author's status, mostly determine citations to single articles (Shadish, Tolliver, Gray, & Gupta, 1995; Stewart, 1983). In fact, the citation impact of an article appears to depend so markedly on the article's intrinsic merit that articles a scientist publishes immediately after a high-impact article are most likely to have no impact whatsoever (Sinatra, Wang, Deville, Song, & Barabási, 2016), with no carry-over effect. Indeed, elite scientists not only publish more highly cited articles than their less distinguished colleagues, but also publish many more poorly cited articles (J. Cole & Cole, 1972). Second, when the unit of analysis switches from the publication to the scientist, the empirical literature shows that prolific, high-impact scientists differ systematically from their less productive and less influential colleagues (Simonton, 2003). For instance, they display distinctive research programs in which they study core phenomena in considerable breadth and depth rather than superficially flitting from topic to topic (Feist, 1997; Simonton, 1992a). In addition, such scientists exhibit personality characteristics associated with highly creative people, such as greater openness to experience (Feist, 2014; Simonton, 2013). Hence, it seems that a scientist's status likely rests on bona fide accomplishments.

In contrast, findings also suggest that a certain amount of arbitrariness intrudes on the identification of elite scientists. Particularly relevant is the research on what Merton called the Matthew Effect, an idea inspired from the Gospel passage that says "For unto every one that hath shall be given, and he shall have abundance: but from him that hath not shall be taken away even that which he hath" (Merton, 1968, p. 58). One manifestation of this effect is the cumulative-advantage model of productivity (Allison, Long, & Krauze, 1982; Allison & Stewart, 1974; Price, 1976). Even if scientists were all equal in their ability to produce publishable articles, the high rejection rates for top-tier journals implies that, in the first round of submissions, not all early career scientists will prove equally successful. By the luck of the draw, those who get acceptances have their continued productivity reinforced, whereas those who get rejections have their productivity discouraged. With sufficient submission cycles, the initial pool can stratify to a highly prolific elite and a much larger group of far-less-productive scientists. Thus, egalitarian potential converts into extreme inequality in achievement.

Moreover, this stratification of research productivity has consequences for professional mobility. Those with earlier successes ascend to top research universities, whereas those on the slower track more likely end up in institutions, such as liberal arts colleges, that emphasize teaching and service (Allison & Long, 1987, 1990; Crane, 1965). This contrast not only accentuates the divergence in career trajectories, but also leads to other critical distinctions down the line, such as grant funding, research awards and honors, and high-status professional positions, such as election to the presidency of a scientific society (S. Cole & Cole, 1967; Feist, 1993; Simonton, 1992a). Of course, such scientists will more likely become gatekeepers who help decide the fates of younger colleagues entering the scientific-reward system (Crane, 1967; Lindsey, 1976).

Although cumulative advantage might appear to undermine the correspondence between merit and status in the scientific community, at least it does not impose a direct bias that undermines the basic norm of universalism. Anybody who is fortunate enough to get off the blocks first is just more likely to win the race. More pernicious is the potential intrusion of biases linked with gender, ethnicity, religion, and other demographic variables that should, according to universalism, be irrelevant. Of these, the impact of gender bias has received the most attention in research (Eagly & Miller, 2016). Although the substantive issues are extremely complex, empirical results suffice to show that the scientific community does not operate in an ivory tower isolated from the prejudices of the larger society. These prejudices may impinge at any point in the pipeline from early education and professional training to eventual scientific attainment.

## 8.5 Conclusion

This chapter provides an overview of what researchers have learned about the scientific community. Starting with various conceptions of that community, especially differentiated by specialty or discipline, the review then examined in some detail the operation of scientific norms, the magnitude and impact of consensus, and the conspicuous stratification of scientists in the community. The treatment touched on such topics as the hierarchy of the sciences, research paradigms, multiple discovery and invention, social constructivism, the Lotka and Price laws, the Matthew Effect and cumulative advantage, and the intrusion of societal biases such as gender. Although the issues raised remain complex and incompletely resolved, the research suffices to demonstrate how science does not and cannot operate as a purely individualistic enterprise. Indeed, even the greatest scientific geniuses are necessarily embedded in a rich social network (Simonton, 1992b). The so-called lone genius in science is the exception, not the rule.

## REFERENCES

Allison, P. D., & Long, J. S. (1987). Interuniversity mobility of academic scientists. *American Sociological Review, 52,* 643–652. doi:10.2307/2095600

Allison, P. D., & Long, J. S. (1990). Departmental effects on scientific productivity. *American Sociological Review, 55,* 469–478. doi:10.2307/2095801

Allison, P. D., Long, J. S., & Krauze, T. K. (1982). Cumulative advantage and inequality in science. *American Sociological Review, 47,* 615–625. doi:10.2307/2095162

Allison, P. D., Price, D. S., Griffith, B. C., Moravcsik, M. J., & Stewart, J. A. (1976). Lotka's law: A problem in its interpretation and application. *Social Studies of Science, 6,* 269–276. doi:10.1177/030631277600600205

Allison, P. D., & Stewart, J. A. (1974). Productivity differences among scientists: Evidence for accumulative advantage. *American Sociological Review, 39,* 596–606. doi:10.2307.2094424

Anderson, M. S., Ronning, E. A., DeVries, R., & Martinson, B. C. (2010). Extending the Mertonian norms: Scientists' subscription to norms of research. *Journal of Higher Education, 81,* 366–393. doi:10.1353/jhe.0.0095

Anwar, M. (2004). From doctoral dissertation to publication: A study of 1995 American graduates in library and information sciences. *Journal of Librarianship and Information Science, 36*, 151–157. doi:10.1177/0961000604050565

Ashar, H., & Shapiro, J. Z. (1990). Are retrenchment decisions rational? The role of information in times of budgetary stress. *Journal of Higher Education, 61*, 123–141. doi:10.1080 /00221546.1990.11775101

Ashton, S. V., & Oppenheim, C. (1978). A method of predicting Nobel Prize winners in chemistry. Social Studies of Science, *8*, 341–348. doi:10.1177/030631277800800306

Bloom, B. S. (1963). Report on creativity research by the examiner's office of the University of Chicago. In C. W. Taylor & F. X. Barron (Eds.), *Scientific creativity: Its recognition and development* (pp. 251–264). New York, NY: Wiley.

Brannigan, A., & Wanner, R. A. (1983). Multiple discoveries in science: A test of the communication theory. *Canadian Journal of Sociology, 8*, 135–151. doi:10.2307/3340123

Bringmann, W. G., & Balk, M. M. (1983). Wilhelm Wundt's publication record: A re-examination. *Storia e Critica della Psichologia, 4*(1), 61–86.

Carneiro, R. L. (1970). Scale analysis, evolutionary sequences, and the rating of cultures. In R. Naroll & R. Cohn (Eds.), *A handbook of method in cultural anthropology* (pp. 834–871). New York, NY: Natural History Press.

Carson, S., Peterson, J. B., & Higgins, D. M. (2005). Reliability, validity, and factor structure of the Creative Achievement Questionnaire. *Creativity Research Journal, 17*, 37–50. doi:10 .1207/s15326934crj1701_4

Chambers, J. A. (1964). Relating personality and biographical factors to scientific creativity. *Psychological Monographs, 78*(7), 1–20. doi:10.1037/h0093862

Cole, J., & Cole, S. (1971). Measuring the quality of sociological research: Problems in the use of the "Science Citation Index." *American Sociologist, 6*, 23–29.

Cole, J., & Cole, S. (1972). The Ortega hypothesis. *Science, 178*, 368–375. doi:10.1126/science .178.4059.368

Cole, S. (1983). The hierarchy of the sciences? *American Journal of Sociology, 89*, 111–139. doi:10.1086/227835

Cole, S. (2004). Merton's contribution to the sociology of science. *Social Studies of Science, 34*, 829–844. doi:10.1177/0306312704048600

Cole, S., & Cole, J. R. (1967). Scientific output and recognition: A study in the operation of the reward system in science. *American Sociological Review, 32*, 377–390. doi:10.2307 /2091085

Comte, A. (1855). *The positive philosophy of Auguste Comte* (H. Martineau, Trans.). New York, NY: Blanchard. (Original work published 1839–1842.)

Constant, E. W., II. (1978). On the diversity of co-evolution of technological multiples: Steam turbines and Pelton water wheels. *Social Studies of Science, 8*, 183–210. doi:10.1177 /030631277800800202

Crane, D. (1965). Scientists at major and minor universities: A study of productivity and recognition. *American Sociological Review, 30*, 699–714. doi:10.2307/2091138

Crane, D. (1967). The gatekeepers of science: Some factors affecting the selection of articles for scientific journals. *American Sociologist, 2*, 195–201.

Crane, D. (1972). *Invisible colleges: Diffusion of knowledge in scientific communities.* Chicago, IL: University of Chicago Press.

Dennis, W. (1954). Productivity among American psychologists. *American Psychologist, 9*, 191–194. doi:10.1037/h0057477

Dennis, W. (1955). Variations in productivity among creative workers. *Scientific Monthly, 80*, 277–278.

Eagly, A. H., & Miller, D. K. (2016). Scientific eminence: Where are the women? *Perspectives on Psychological Science, 11*, 899–904. doi:10.1177/1745691616663918

Egghe, L. (2005). *Power laws in the information production process: Lotkaian informetrics.* Oxford, England: Elsevier.

Fanelli, D., & Glänzel, W. (2013). Bibliometric evidence for a hierarchy of the sciences. *PLoS One, 8*(6), e66938. doi:10.1371/journal.pone.0066938

Feist, G. J. (1993). A structural model of scientific eminence. *Psychological Science, 4*, 366–371. doi:10.1111/j.1467-9280.1993.tb00583.x

Feist, G. J. (1997). Quantity, quality, and depth of research as influences on scientific eminence: Is quantity most important? *Creativity Research Journal, 10*, 325–335. doi:10.1207/s15326934crj1004_4

Feist, G. J. (2014). Psychometric studies of scientific talent and eminence. In D. K. Simonton (Ed.), *The Wiley handbook of genius* (pp. 62–86). Oxford, England: Wiley.

Furnham, A., & Bonnett, C. (1992). British research productivity in psychology 1980–1989: Does the Lotka–Price law apply to university departments as it does to individuals? *Personality and Individual Differences, 13*, 1333–1341. doi:10.1016/0191-8869(92)90176-P

Garfield, E. (1987). Mapping the world of science: Is citation analysis a legitimate evaluation tool? In D. N. Jackson & J. P. Rushton (Eds.), *Scientific excellence: Origins and assessment* (pp. 98–128). Beverly Hills, CA: Sage.

Gibson, S. S. (1982). Scientific societies and exchange: A facet of the history of scientific communication. *Journal of Library History, 17*, 144–163.

Grosul, M., & Feist, G. J. (2014). The creative person in science. *Psychology of Aesthetics, Creativity, and the Arts, 8*, 30–43. doi:10.1037/a0034828

Haas, P. M. (1992). Introduction: Epistemic communities and international policy coordination. *International Organization, 46*, 1–35. doi:10.1017/S0020818300001442

Hagstrom, W. O. (1974). Competition in science. *American Sociological Review, 39*, 1–18. doi:10.2307/2094272

Hedges, L. V. (1987). How hard is hard science, how soft is soft science? *American Psychologist, 42*, 443–455. doi:10.1037/0003-066X.42.5.443

Hemlin, S. (1993). Scientific quality in the eyes of the scientist: A questionnaire study. *Scientometrics, 27*, 3–18. doi:10.1007/BF02017752

Hirsch, J. E. (2005). An index to quantify an individual's scientific research output. *Proceedings of the National Academy of Sciences, 102*, 16569–16572. doi:10.1073/pnas.0507655102

Hull, D. L. (1988). *Science as a process: An evolutionary account of the social and conceptual development of science.* Chicago, IL: University of Chicago Press.

Hull, D. L., Tessner, P. D., & Diamond, A. M. (1978). Planck's principle: Do younger scientists accept new scientific ideas with greater alacrity than older scientists? *Science, 202,* 717–723. doi:10.1126/science.202.4369.717

Hutchinson, E. G., & Zivney, T. L. (1995). The publication profile of economists. *Journal of Economic Education, 26,* 59–79. doi:10.1080/00220485.1995.10844857

Inhaber, H., & Przednowek, K. (1976). Quality of research and the Nobel prizes. *Social Studies of Science, 6,* 33–50. doi:10.1177/030631277600600102

Kaufman, A. B., & Kaufman, J. C. (Eds.) (2018). *Pseudoscience: The conspiracy against science.* Cambridge, MA: MIT Press.

Klavans, R., & Boyack, K. W. (2009). Toward a consensus map of science. *Journal of the American Society for Information Science and Technology, 60,* 455–476. doi:10.1002/asi .20991

Kornfeld, W., & Hewitt, C. E. (1981). The scientific community metaphor. *IEEE Transactions on Systems, Man, and Cybernetics, 11,* 24–33. doi:10.1109/TSMC.1981.4308575

Kuhn, T. S. (1970). *The structure of scientific revolutions* (2nd ed.). Chicago, IL: University of Chicago Press.

Kuhn, T. S. (2012). *The structure of scientific revolutions* (4th ed.). Chicago, IL: University of Chicago Press.

Lamb, D., & Easton, S. M. (1984). *Multiple discovery.* Avebury, England: Avebury.

Levin, S. G., Stephan, P. E., & Walker, M. B. (1995). Planck's principle revisited —A note. *Social Studies of Science, 25,* 35–55. doi:10.1177/030631295025002003

Lindsey, D. (1976). Distinction, achievement, and editorial board membership. *American Psychologist, 31,* 799–804. doi:10.1037/0003-066X.31.11.799

Lindsey, D. (1989). Using citation counts as a measure of quality in science: Measuring what's measurable rather than what's valid. *Scientometrics, 15,* 189–203. doi:10.1007/BF02017198

Lotka, A. J. (1926). The frequency distribution of scientific productivity. *Journal of the Washington Academy of Sciences, 16,* 317–323. Retrieved from www.dtic.mil/dtic/tr/fulltext/u2/a054425.pdf

Macfarlane, B., & Cheng, M. J. (2008). Communism, universalism and disinterestedness: Re-examining contemporary support among academics for Merton's scientific norms. *Journal of Academic Ethics, 6,* 67–78. doi:10.1007/s10805-008-9055-y

McDowell, J. M. (1982). Obsolescence of knowledge and career publication profiles: Some evidence of differences among fields in costs of interrupted careers. *American Economic Review, 72,* 752–768.

Merton, R. K. (1942). A note on science and democracy. Journal of Legal and Political Sociology, 1, 115–126. Retrieved from www.scribd.com/doc/270306844/A-Note-on-Science-and-Democracy-by-Robert-K-Merton

Merton, R. K. (1957). Priorities in scientific discovery: A chapter in the sociology of science. *American Sociological Review, 22,* 635–659. doi:10.2307/2089193

Merton, R. K. (1961a). The role of genius in scientific advance. *New Scientist, 12,* 306–308.

Merton, R. K. (1961b). Singletons and multiples in scientific discovery: A chapter in the sociology of science. In *Proceedings of the American Philosophical Society* (Vol. 105, pp. 470–486). Philadelphia, PA: American Philosophical Society.

Merton, R. K. (1968). The Matthew effect in science. *Science*, 159, 56–63. doi:10.1126/science.159.3810.56

Merton, R. K. (1973). *The sociology of science: Theoretical and empirical investigations*. Chicago, IL: University of Chicago Press.

Mitroff, I. I. (1974). Norms and counter-norms in a group of Apollo moon scientists: A case study in the ambivalence of scientists. *American Sociological Review*, 39, 579–595. doi:10.2307/2094423

Moravcsik, M. J., & Murugesan, P. (1975). Some results on the function and quality of citations. *Social Studies of Science*, 5, 86–92. doi:10.1177/030631277500500106

Mulkay, M. J. (1976). Norms and ideology in science. *Social Science Information*, 15, 637–656. doi:10.1177/053901847601500406

Myers, C. R. (1970). Journal citations and scientific eminence in contemporary psychology. *American Psychologist*, 25, 1041–1048. doi:10.1037/h0030149

O'Boyle, E., Jr., & Aguinas, H. (2012). The best and the rest: Revisiting the norm of normality of individual performance. *Personnel Psychology*, 65, 79–119. doi:10.1111/j.1744-6570.2011.01239.x

Ogburn, W. K., & Thomas, D. (1922). Are inventions inevitable? A note on social evolution. *Political Science Quarterly*, 37, 83–93. doi:10.2307/2142320

Open Science Collaboration (2015). Estimating the reproducibility of psychological science. *Science*, 349, aac4716. doi:10.1126/science.aac.4716

Patinkin, D. (1983). Multiple discoveries and the central message. *American Journal of Sociology*, 89, 306–323. doi:10.1086/227867

Planck, M. (1949). *Scientific autobiography and other papers* (F. Gaynor, Trans.). New York, NY: Philosophical Library.

Price, D. (1963). *Little science, big science*. New York, NY: Columbia University Press.

Price, D. (1976). A general theory of bibliometric and other cumulative advantage processes. *Journal of the American Society for Information Science*, 27, 292–306. doi:10.1002/asi.4630270505

Price, D. (1986). *Little science, big science ... and beyond* (2nd ed.). New York, NY: Columbia University Press.

Redner, S. (1998). How popular is your paper? An empirical study of the citation distribution. *European Physical Journal B*, 4, 131–134. doi:10.1007/s100510050359

Rodgers, R. C., & Maranto, C. L. (1989). Causal models of publishing productivity in psychology. *Journal of Applied Psychology*, 74, 636–649. doi:10.1037/0021-9010.74.4.636

Roeckelein, J. E. (1997). Psychology among the sciences: Comparisons of numbers of theories and laws cited in textbooks. *Psychological Reports*, 80, 131–141. doi:10.2466/PR0.80.1.131–141

Ruscio, J., Seaman, F., D'Oriano, C., Stremlo, E., & Mahalchik, K. (2012). Measuring scholarly impact using modern citation-based indices.

*Measurement: Interdisciplinary Research and Perspectives, 10,* 123–146. doi:10.1080/15366367.2012.711147

Schachter, S., Christenfeld, N., Ravina, B., & Bilous, R. (1991). Speech disfluency and the structure of knowledge. *Journal of Personality and Social Psychology, 60,* 362–367. doi:10.1037/0022-3514.60.3.362

Schaffer, S. (1986). Scientific discoveries and the end of natural philosophy. *Social Studies of Science, 16,* 387–420. doi:10.1177/030631286016003001

Schmookler, J. (1966). *Invention and economic growth.* Cambridge, MA: Harvard University Press.

Shadish, W. R., Jr., Tolliver, D., Gray, M., & Gupta, S. K. S. (1995). Author judgements about works they cite: Three studies from psychology journals. *Social Studies of Science, 25,* 477–498. doi:10.1177/030631295025003003

Simonton, D. K. (1979). Multiple discovery and invention: Zeitgeist, genius, or chance? *Journal of Personality and Social Psychology, 37,* 1603–1616. doi:10.1037/0022-3514.37.9.1603

Simonton, D. K. (1992a). Leaders of American psychology, 1879–1967: Career development, creative output, and professional achievement. *Journal of Personality and Social Psychology, 62,* 5–17. doi:10.1037/0022-3514.62.1.5

Simonton, D. K. (1992b). The social context of career success and course for 2,026 scientists and inventors. *Personality and Social Psychology Bulletin, 18,* 452–463. doi:10.1177 /0146167292184009

Simonton, D. K. (2003). Scientific creativity as constrained stochastic behavior: The integration of product, process, and person perspectives. *Psychological Bulletin, 129,* 475–494. doi:10.1037/0033-2909.129.4.475

Simonton, D. K. (2004). Psychology's status as a scientific discipline: Its empirical placement within an implicit hierarchy of the sciences. *Review of General Psychology, 8,* 59–67. doi:10.1037/1089-2680.8.1.59

Simonton, D. K. (2009). Varieties of (scientific) creativity: A hierarchical model of disposition, development, and achievement. *Perspectives on Psychological Science, 4,* 441–452. doi:10.1111/j.1745-6924.2009.01152.x

Simonton, D. K. (2010). Creativity as blind-variation and selective-retention: Combinatorial models of exceptional creativity. *Physics of Life Reviews, 7,* 156–179. doi:10.1016/j.plrev .2010.02.002

Simonton, D. K. (2013). Creative genius in science. In G. J. Feist & M. E. Gorman (Eds.), *Handbook of the psychology of science* (pp. 251–272). New York, NY: Springer.

Simonton, D. K. (2015). Psychology as a science within Comte's hypothesized hierarchy: Empirical investigations and conceptual implications. *Review of General Psychology, 19,* 334–344. doi:10.1037/gpr0000039

Sinatra, R., Wang, D., Deville, P., Song, C., & Barabási, A.-L. (2016). Quantifying the evolution of individual scientific impact. *Science, 354,* aaf5239. doi:10.1126/science.aaf5239

Smith, L. D., Best, L. A., Stubbs, D. A., Archibald, A. B., & Roberson-Nay, R. (2002). Constructing knowledge: The role of graphs and tables in hard and soft psychology. *American Psychologist, 57,* 749–761. doi:10.1037/0003-066X.57.10.749

Stewart, J. A. (1983). Achievement and ascriptive processes in the recognition of scientific articles. *Social Forces, 62*, 166–189. doi:10.1093/sf/62.1.166

Stewart, J. A. (1986). Drifting continents and colliding interests: A quantitative application of the interests perspective. *Social Studies of Science, 16*, 261–279. doi:10.1177/030631278601600200003

Sulloway, F. J. (2014). Openness to scientific innovation. In D. K. Simonton (Ed.), *The Wiley handbook of genius* (pp. 546–563). Oxford, England: Wiley.

Suls, J., & Fletcher, B. (1983). Social comparison in the social and physical sciences: An archival study. *Journal of Personality and Social Psychology, 44*, 575–580. doi:10.1037/0022-3514.44.3.575

Turner, S. (2007). Merton's "norms" in political and intellectual context. *Journal of Classical Sociology, 7*, 161–178. doi:10.1177/1468795X07078034

Walberg, H. J., Strykowski, B. F., Rovai, E., & Hung, S. S. (1984). Exceptional performance. *Review of Educational Research, 54*, 87–112. doi:10.2307/1170399

Wray, K. B. (2005). Rethinking scientific specialization. *Social Studies of Science, 35*, 151–164. doi:10.1177/0306312705045811

Wray, K. B. (2010). Rethinking the size of scientific specialties: Correcting Price's estimate. *Scientometrics, 83*, 471–476. doi:10.1007/s11192-009-0060-8

Zuckerman, H. (1977). *Scientific elite*. New York, NY: Free Press.

Zuckerman, H., & Merton, R. K. (1972). Age, aging, and age structure in science. In M. W. Riley, M. Johnson, & A. Foner (Eds.), *Aging and society: Vol 3. A sociology of age stratification* (pp. 292–356). New York, NY: Russell Sage Foundation.

# CHAPTER 9

# Genetic Engineering and Society

*Jessica Cavin Barnes, Elizabeth A. Pitts, S. Kathleen Barnhill-Dilling,
and Jason A. Delborne*

Genetic engineering disrupts assumed distinctions between nature and culture, between human and nonhuman, and between the production of knowledge and the production of commercially viable products. As a result, this area of technological development continues to inspire science and technology studies (STS) researchers not only to rethink theoretical paradigms, but also to test and retest a variety of ways to intervene in science and society.

Also referred to as genetic modification, *genetic engineering* involves inserting, deleting, or modifying an organism's deoxyribonucleic acid (DNA), ribonucleic acid (RNA), or proteins to change its characteristics, or *traits* (National Academies of Sciences, Engineering, and Medicine [NASEM], 2016b). Genetically engineered organisms are forms of *biotechnology*, a broad category that encompasses a variety of ways of altering biological materials and processes to make them more useful for human purposes. Although the selection of desirable traits in living organisms dates at least to the invention of agriculture, contemporary genetic approaches are particularly indebted to Darwin's (1859/2001) research on evolution and Mendel's (1866) study of heredity (NASEM, 2016b). Building on this work, in the early 1900s, scientists developed increasingly precise ways to alter the traits of plants and animals, first through new forms of selective breeding and then by applying chemicals or radiation to induce mutations (NASEM, 2016b). In 1962, the Nobel Prize in Physiology or Medicine was awarded to James Watson and Francis Crick for their discovery of the double helix structure of DNA. Although popular accounts typically position Watson and Crick as heroic geniuses working alone, a growing number of sources acknowledge that their accomplishment built on photographic evidence produced by Rosalind Franklin of King's College London, whose work was shared with Watson without her knowledge or permission (Maddox, 2002; Selya, 2003). In 1973, the foundation for contemporary genetic engineering was laid when Stanley

Cohen, Herbert Boyer, and colleagues described a set of techniques for extracting segments of DNA from one organism and inserting them into the DNA of another organism (Cohen, Chang, Booyer, & Helling, 1973; NASEM, 2016b). Scientists could now combine genetic material from different organisms, regardless of their species or genus (Cooper, 2008). The resulting *recombinant DNA (rDNA)* – or constructed DNA sequences not usually found in nature – remains a keystone of genetic engineering.

These and subsequent developments in genetic engineering inspired imaginations and the articulation of many potential uses in medicine, science, industry, and agriculture (e.g., Barton & Brill, 1983). Early applications of genetic engineering included the creation of ice-minus bacteria, a microorganism designed to be sprayed on strawberry fields to prevent damage from frost (Jasanoff, 2011a); the OncoMouse, a laboratory mouse that was made more susceptible to cancer (Haraway, 1997); and the FLAVR SAVR tomato, the first genetically modified (GM) crop, that expressed a trait for delayed softening of the fruit (Barben, 2010; Martineau, 2001). Although researchers have used genetic engineering widely in experiments in academic and industry laboratories since the 1980s, a relatively small number of products – many biomedical and a handful agricultural – are commercially available (NASEM, 2016b). Scientists have used genetically engineered microbes to produce a wide range of recombinant drugs, including hormones essential for human metabolism, growth, blood production, and fertility; vaccines; antibodies to prevent the rejection of organ transplants; and treatments for leukemia, hepatitis, fungal infections, cystic fibrosis, and other diseases (Avise, 2004). Agricultural applications of the technology are far less diverse, consisting primarily of plants engineered with herbicide and insect resistance. Agriculturalists have most commonly added these traits to four major crops: soybeans, cotton, corn, and canola (NASEM, 2016b). Virus-resistant papaya and summer squash, nonbrowning apples, and nonbruising potatoes that produce smaller quantities (compared to nonGM varieties) of acrylamide, a potentially carcinogenic chemical generated during frying, are also available (US Department of Agriculture, 2017). Some of these products dominate their markets. For example, most insulin used to treat Type 1 diabetes is now produced by bacteria or yeast that have been genetically engineered to carry a gene for human insulin. (Before this "human" insulin became the first recombinant drug to be approved for market in 1982, pharmaceutical insulin was typically extracted from the pancreases of pigs and cows; Barben, 2010; Reiss & Straughan, 1996.) Likewise, over 75 percent of the global land area planted with cotton and soybeans in 2015 was planted with GM herbicide- and insect-resistant varieties (James, 2014).

Although some of these technologies are now ubiquitous, their ascent was not always smooth. Critics – including activists, civil-society groups, religious and cultural leaders, organic and subsistence farmers, and scientists – have strongly opposed genetic engineering on a number of grounds (Delborne & Kinchy, 2008). Prominent among them have been concerns about unknown or unacceptable health risks (Hilbeck et al., 2015; Krimsky, 2015), potential environmental contamination (Delborne, 2008; Gustafsson, Agrawal, Lewenstein, & Wolf, 2015), the manipulation of ancestral or sacred organisms (McAfee, 2003a), lack of consumer choice and labelling of GM products (Herrick, 2005; Klintman, 2002), and consolidation and corporatization of control over global genetic resources (Schurman & Munro, 2010). Other problems have arisen from a mismatch between what was promised of genetic engineering and what has been delivered. Since the first visions of biotechnology, stakeholders have paired optimism about its potential with a sense of urgency to position it as an unparalleled solution to future problems associated with population growth, food scarcity, limited arable land, and environmental degradation (Bud, 1998; Jansen & Gupta, 2009). However, efforts to quantify the contribution of genetic engineering, especially in agriculture, to environmental health and human well-being have produced conflicting results; the social and economic benefits of GM crops are nuanced in all cases and contested in many (NASEM, 2016b). In the following sections, we highlight some ways in which scholarship in STS and adjoining fields makes sense of the troubled past, rapidly evolving present, and highly anticipated future of genetic engineering.

### 9.1   Genes and Genetic Engineering as Boundary Objects

Despite increasing knowledge about the structure and function of DNA and the advent of genetic maps that attempt to describe the physical arrangement of human and nonhuman genomes, the *gene* itself is a slippery concept. Generally defined as a distinct, heritable segment of a chromosome, scientists use the term not because DNA sequences are obviously or essentially discrete, but because describing particular genes as discrete entities makes it possible to accomplish particular goals (Keller, 2000; McAfee, 2003b). Perspectives from STS have facilitated the description of genes as *boundary objects* (Star & Griesemer, 1989, p. 393); that is, artifacts that can be interpreted flexibly, allowing individuals from different social worlds, such as scientists and policy makers, to communicate, despite attributing significantly different meanings to the object itself (Gottweis, 1998). Although boundary objects enable communication and even collaboration, their different interpretations also reinforce the distinctions made between scientific and nonscientific activity and between technical experts and nonexpert regulators, publics, and civil-society groups (Gottweis, 1998). STS scholars have referenced this process as *boundary work* (Gieryn, 1983, p. 782; Jasanoff, 1987).

Boundary work has been central in dismissing as irrational arguments that challenge the promise, benefits, or safety of genetically engineered organisms. The claim is that such arguments fall outside of what can be definitively or objectively studied. Because these concerns often rely on an understanding of genetic material and processes that differ from prevailing scientific perspectives, they have been relegated to the realms of ethics, culture, values, or politics (Gottweis, 1998). But although boundary objects and boundary work can create and maintain the lines drawn between experts and nonexperts – or between different ways of knowing – they can also be used to disrupt those lines. Cognizant of the demarcation and elevation of scientific notions of genes and gene flow, indigenous groups in Oaxaca, Mexico, have enrolled scientific expertise and evidence to communicate their concerns about the "contamination" of maize landraces with GM material (Kinchy, 2012). In this and other instances, activists have used boundary work to include their own ideas of risk in the boundaries of what counts as rational debate about genetic engineering.

In genetics research, the existence of multiple, sometimes competing interpretations of the gene dates at least as far back as the post-World War II effort to establish cybernetics as a universal science that would unite researchers from a broad variety of fields (Bowker, 1993). Defining information as discrete, quantifiable bits that could be transmitted immaterially (Shannon, 1948) enabled cybernetics researchers from a variety of disciplines to analogize mechanical and biological systems, using robots and living organisms as heuristics for one another (Aspray, 1985; Bowker, 1993; Hayles, 1999). Geneticists participating in these collaborations suggested that genes carried biological "messages," much as information was envisioned to carry messages across communication systems (Hayles, 1999; Keller, 1995, 2000). This type of *reductionism* has played a significant role in advancing the field of molecular biology (Fang & Casadevall, 2011). Today, the assumed equivalence of genetic codes and computer code is recontextualizing biological materials and processes as *biomedia*, enabling "a qualitatively different notion of the biological body – one that is technically articulated, and yet still fully 'biological'" (Thacker, 2003, p. 53; also see Thacker, 2004). However, the language of information is, in some key ways, an awkward fit for DNA and other biological material (Hayles, 1999; Kay, 2000; Keller, 1995, 2000). Although the term *information* suggests an abstract, standardized unit that functions in the same manner in any context, biologists have long emphasized that an organism's *genotype*, or genetic makeup, varies in relation to its material context. Furthermore, organisms with the same genotype may exhibit different *phenotypes* – observable characteristics – depending on their environment.

The boundaries of what counts as genetic engineering are as contested as the boundaries of the gene. For example, the biotech company Calgene argued that the FLAVR SAVR™ tomato, which it launched in the mid-1990s, was not transgenic because the company had simply inactivated the plant's own gene responsible for decay (Haraway, 1997). Others contended that the tomato was transgenic because, like many other GM organisms, it did carry inserted DNA that served as a marker to indicate that the desired modification had been made successfully (Haraway, 1997). Thus, whereas genetic science has been used to define categories of species, sex, gender, race, ethnicity, and ability (El-Haj, 2007; Hartzog, 2017; Law & Lien, 2013; Thompson, 2005), it has also blurred previously neat social and legal distinctions. Haraway (1997) aptly described transgenic organisms as a contested "border zone," writing that "transgressive border-crossing pollutes lineages – in a transgenic organism's case, the lineage of nature itself – transforming nature into its binary opposite, culture" (p. 60).

## 9.2 Genetic Knowledge as Subjective and Situated

Society has long equated scientific investigation with the objective description of reality and, in that frame, has understood genetic science as a neutral tool for understanding human and nonhuman bodies and populations. However, STS research has built on nearly a century of phenomenological and social constructionist thought to emphasize interconnectedness and relationality. In the early decades of the twentieth century, Husserl (1913/1962) and others advanced phenomenology as an alternative to the rationalism of modernity and, particularly, to naïve applications of the scientific method that sought "exact, quantifiable categories and objects, which subsequently become rigid and frozen, hiding any contingency they may contain" (Dorfman, 2009, p. 295). Phenomenologists, by contrast, were interested in the "real unity of the world as a whole" (Husserl, 1913/1962, p. 73). With respect to genetic engineering, this debate highlights the question of whether an organism should be understood as a compilation of standardized biological parts or as a complex whole that exhibits properties that cannot be fully predicted by inferences made from observing its component parts (Barrett, Peles, & Odum, 1997; Novikoff, 1945). From a phenomenological perspective, the problem with the parts-based approach is that its proponents take the objects of their investigation for granted (Deetz, 1992, p. 117). By contrast, phenomenologists argued that "my knowledge of the world, even my scientific knowledge, is gained from my own particular point of view, or from experience of the world without which the symbols of science would be meaningless" (Merleau-Ponty, 1962, p. viii).

Contemporary STS researchers have echoed this thinking by emphasizing the *coproduction* of science and society – in other words, the ways scientific knowledge reciprocally creates and is created by social structures and relations (Jasanoff, 2004b; Latour, 2012). Social and political systems often reorganize in response to science and technology, and scientific discoveries and technological developments are in no way predestined or determined; rather, they reflect and evolve in response to the material, cultural, and political resources of scientists and end users (Bijker, Hughes, & Pinch, 1987; Jasanoff, 2004b).

> In short, the ways in which we take note of new phenomena in the world are tied at all points – like the muscles on a skeleton or the springs on a cot frame – to the ways in which we have already chosen to live in it. (Jasanoff, 2004b, p. 32)

By reducing complex social and cultural power dynamics to technical problems that can be solved by reprogramming genetic codes (Jasanoff, 2011a), the expansion of genetic knowledge and technologies reorients how individuals – human or nonhuman – and interventions – medical or agricultural – are imagined.

The history of the eugenics movement illustrates the coproductive intertwining of scientific knowledge and social organization as well as the contestation and controversy that have surrounded the meaning of genetic science from the beginning (Gottweis, 1998). In the early decades of the twentieth century in the United States, Social Darwinists appropriated emerging genetics research, drawing on the selective breeding of plant and animal stock as a model for the deliberate "improvement" of the human race (Condit, 1999; Lombardo, 2008). The eugenics movement led to the forced sterilization of approximately 30,000 US citizens between 1900 and 1935, contributed to the 1924 restrictions on the ethnicities of immigrants who could be granted US citizenship, and was legitimated in the 1927 US Supreme Court case *Buck v. Bell*, which affirmed the State of Virginia's right to prevent individuals who were assumed to be genetically inferior from conceiving children (Condit, 1999, p. 27; Lombardo, 2003, p. 200). Soon after, in Germany, Nazis sterilized more than 300,000 people in the years leading up to the Holocaust, during which they executed 6 million people on the grounds that they were unfit to reproduce because of their religion, race, sexual orientation, or disability status (Condit, 1999, p. 27). In each of these cases, Nazis used emerging genetic science to support the discriminatory treatment of social groups that had already been deemed inferior (Condit, 1999).

STS scholars – in particular, those working in *feminist STS* – have used the notion of *subjectivity* in opposition to the claims of objectivity, insisting that researchers' identities and assumptions shape their scholarship and thereby shape science as a whole (Schnabel, Breitwieser, & Hawbaker, 2016). Because researchers and participants "are not singular, distinct individuals, and instead operate as interconnected beings within social-material entanglements" (Schnabel et al., 2016, p. 319), genetic scientists, genetic science, and genetic technologies are products of their time and space and can reproduce power relationships that were and are not inevitable. Feminist STS offers theoretical space to examine the power dynamics that characterize genetic science and its historical and contemporary applications, ranging from laboratory mice (Haraway, 1997) to reproductive technologies (Thompson, 2005). Rather than seeing eugenics as an unfortunate but natural byproduct of new knowledge about the genetic basis of physical and mental health and the nature of heredity, feminist STS scholars examined how genetic science has been used to perpetuate existing social inequities (Collins, 1999). This work demonstrates that ultimately, it was not science *per se*, but power that enabled the compulsory or coerced sterilization of poor, non-White, criminal, and mentally ill people, especially women.

Although the viability of eugenics as a scientific discipline crumbled as it came to be associated with the atrocities of Nazi Germany, the goal of selecting desirable traits through human reproduction and the notion that human abilities and disabilities are genetically controlled continued to inspire scientists, especially molecular biologists. This continuity in the prospect of engineering human bodies has caused some to caution that genetic engineering threatens a new form of eugenics that has shifted its focus from intervening in the human "gene pool" to altering the production of specific macromolecules in the cells of individual humans

(Gottweis, 1998). Today, traces of eugenic thinking are evident in contemporary transhumanism and related calls to draw on genetic engineering to improve on the evolution of humans as well as other species (Koch, 2010). A central critique of this perspective comes from the field of disability studies, which considers human-enhancement technologies through the theoretical lens of *ableism* (Wolbring, 2008, 2010). Ableism draws attention to the ways those in different cultures consider particular abilities more or less valuable. For example, valuing productivity and competitiveness over empathy, compassion, and kindness contributes to the positioning of various kinds of bodies as limited and in need of improvement (Wolbring, 2008).

Feminist STS scholars have used *standpoint theory* as an epistemology and methodology for understanding the ways genetic technologies embed social constructions of identity, including ability (Harding, 2004; Wajcman, 2009; Wylie & Sismondo, 2015). Standpoint theory holds that because knowledge is socially situated and reproduces dominant paradigms and power structures that may be invisible to those practicing science, the insights of groups historically excluded from scientific knowledge production should be solicited (Wylie & Sismondo, 2015). By extension, the imagined beneficiaries of human enhancement are perhaps uniquely positioned to exhume the power relationships and assumptions about ability embedded in this potential application of genetic engineering.

## 9.3   Neoliberalism and Genetic Engineering Technoscience

Genetic engineering blurs the line between knowledge production and the production of marketable products: scholars have thus discussed it as a *technoscience*. Introduced by philosophers to reference science that emerges from and produces technological artifacts, Latour (1987), Haraway (1990), and others took up the concept of technoscience in STS to more broadly describe the ways science ties to its technological and social milieux. Scholars in STS and other fields have drawn particular attention to the ways science and technology are coproduced with dominant political and economic ideologies. Critical social scientists have argued that genetic understanding and technologies also enabled and shaped the expansion of *neoliberalism*, an economic ideology and approach to capitalism that in many ways unfolded as a response to the abuses of power that characterized the nation-states of Nazism and communism (Busch, 2010).

Proponents of neoliberalism sought political freedom through economic freedom (Busch, 2010). By privileging market competition as the most efficient and rational processor of goods, services, and information, neoliberal policies aim to subsume the state in the service of the market; rather than distributing goods and services itself, the state is responsible for facilitating the persistence of markets and their expansion into new realms (Harvey, 2005; McCarthy & Prudham, 2004). Genetic science and genetic engineering have played a prominent role in this expansion by enabling the marketization of life in new ways (Busch, 2010; Cooper, 2008; Sunder Rajan, 2006). The reductionism of genetic science has facilitated enclosure and privatization, whereas genetic engineering has reduced the time and space required for the turnover of capital (Busch, 2010; McAfee, 2003b). Neoliberalism has reciprocally shaped many aspects of genetic engineering, from the way researchers conduct basic research in university laboratories to the commercialized products of genetic engineering (Lave, Mirowski, & Randalls, 2010). Sunder Rajan (2006) used the term *biocapital* to describe this intertwining of contemporary biotechnology and capitalism, especially in biomedicine.

In the 1970s, in the midst of a US economic recession, expiring chemical patents, and growing concerns about environmental and consumer protection – with the consequent imposition of tighter governmental regulations – pharmaceutical and petrochemical industries invested in emerging genetic science as a means of rebranding, aiming to associate themselves with "clean" life-science technologies and distance themselves from the chemical technologies recently discovered to be polluting human bodies and the environment (Cooper, 2008; Glover, 2010). Companies like Monsanto shifted their focus from the development of agricultural chemicals to the production of GM plants that would complement those chemicals, at once extending the lifetime of their previous investments and capturing new seed markets (Charles, 2001; Kloppenburg, 2004). A number of neoliberal policies instituted in the United States in the 1980s to encourage genetic science and its transfer from the laboratory to the market (Cooper, 2008) supported this speculative shift in agriculture and medicine. Federal funding for the life sciences dramatically increased, while the creation of new stock market exchanges facilitated private investment in high-risk biotechnology projects (Cooper, 2008). Intellectual property laws shifted with the passage of the Bayh–Dole Act, which allowed – and essentially required – universities, small businesses, and nonprofit organizations to patent their publicly funded research (Cooper, 2008). Collectively, these neoliberal reforms forged new relationships between science and business, creating academic laboratories beholden to commercial logics (Kleinman, 1998; Kleinman & Vallas, 2001; Krimsky, 1991).

The integration of neoliberal capitalism into agriculture preceded the emergence of genetic engineering, but genetically modified crops played a role in the ongoing erosion of the distinction between public and private research in plant breeding (Kloppenburg, 2004). As was the case with hybrid seed, expectations were high that agricultural applications of genetic engineering would be revolutionary and used for the benefit of the poor and hungry. Although visions of benevolent biotechnology are apparent in Monsanto's history and shaped the company's commercial strategies, they largely failed to shape the content or design of its products (Charles, 2001; Glover, 2010). Today, the vast majority of commercially available GM crops are useful in the context of large-scale industrial farming that characterizes the global North, not the subsistence systems in the global South (Glover, 2010). Furthermore, even GM products in development that purportedly aim to help the poor have been critiqued as mere technology transfer – attempts to repurpose the germplasm, agricultural techniques, and political economy of industrialized agricultural systems for small-holder farms (Brooks, 2015). The inconsistency between expectation and realization may reflect an intentional use of pro-poor rhetoric to promote genetic-engineering technologies (Kleinman & Kloppenburg, 1991), but Glover (2010) also explained it in the context of neoliberal pressures on Monsanto to develop products with market value.

The pressure to commercialize has more recently resulted in the emerging field of *synthetic biology,* an interdisciplinary science that aims "to make biology easier to engineer" (Endy, 2008). To increase the speed and efficiency of genetic engineering, synthetic biologists refashion laboratory work in the manner of engineering (Bennett, 2015) and, in so doing, shift the goal of this work from the production of knowledge to the production of novel, useful, or "synthetic" life forms. For example, synthetic biologist Carlson (2010) argued,

> Successful aeronautical engineers do not attempt to build aircraft with the complexity of a hawk, a hummingbird, or even a moth; they succeed by first reducing complexity to eliminate all the mechanisms they are unable to understand and reproduce. In comparison, even the simplest cell contains far more knobs, bells, and whistles than we can presently understand. No biological engineer will succeed in building a system de novo until most of that complexity is stripped away, leaving only the barest essentials. (p. 6)

The attempt to develop an engineering-driven approach to biology was a recurring theme in twentieth-century biology, even prior to the discovery of the double helical structure of DNA (Campos, 2009). The latest incarnation of this approach emerged as synthetic biology stems in part from the convergence of biology, engineering, and computation (Roco & Bainbridge, 2002); fields that sometimes coexist uncomfortably (Calvert, 2012; Frow & Calvert, 2013). Twenty-first-century synthetic biologists suggest that much as the standardization of screw threads helped facilitate the industrial revolution, the standardization of DNA will facilitate dramatic innovation (Knight, 2003). Specifically, synthetic biologists aim to develop a library of prefabricated DNA sequences called *standardized biological parts*, or BioBrick parts, that can be mixed and matched like LEGOs for the production of novel life forms (Balmer & Bulpin, 2013; Calvert, 2012; Campos, 2012; Carlson, 2010). The tension between standardization and biological variation is particularly evident in the *International Genetically Engineered Machine competition* for synthetic biologists, which invites teams of high school and university students, among others, to contribute BioBricks to an open source registry (Balmer & Bulpin, 2013; Frow & Calvert, 2013). These and other attempts to produce standardized biological parts present challenges that are simultaneously ontological and normative as the rhetoric of open source innovation intersects with intellectual property regulations (Pottage & Marris, 2012).

The effort to standardize and commercialize DNA sequences continues to allow the editing of genomes to become simpler and less expensive, facilitating not only economies of scale in academic and corporate science, but also the emergence of *do-it-yourself biology (DIY bio)*, an effort to advance open access to the tools and techniques of genetic engineering (Delfanti, 2013; Kelty, 2010; Kera, 2012; Landrain, Meyer, Perez, & Sussan, 2013). In the early years of the twenty-first century, biopunks or biohackers initially approached DIY bio as an individual pursuit, often working alone in their kitchens or garages (Anderson, 2009). In 2010, the first DIY bio laboratories were launched in Silicon Valley, California, and Brooklyn, New York, to facilitate the sharing of costs, equipment, and expertise. DIY biologists have been productively compared with outlaws in the Wild West, Victorian gentleman scientists, and contemporary software hackers (Kelty, 2010), although referring to them as "amateurs" (see Curry, 2014) may oversimplify their diverse areas of expertise. Although individuals with little formal training in biology often struggle with the unpredictable nature of living systems (Schyfter, Frow, & Calvert, 2013, p. 2), synthetic biology's modularized vision attracts individuals ranging from PhD-holding molecular biologists to professional artists, designers, engineers, entrepreneurs, and software programmers.

Standardization has also long been a prerequisite for patenting; for instance, in the early decades of the twentieth century, plant and animal breeders struggled to overcome legal requirements that their biological "inventions" were "disclosed specifically enough to be uniquely defined *and identically reproduced*" (Kevles, 1994, p. 113, italics added). Over time, individual scientists and academic and corporate entities have drawn on precedents set in plant and animal breeding to patent genetically engineered organisms ranging from bacteria to plants to rodents (Beauchamp, 2013; Kevles, 1994, 2008). North American and European patent law, a keystone of neoliberal governance, allows the patenting of plant products that were developed, but not those that were discovered; this distinction relies on the characterization of "genetic information as something that can be isolated and removed intact from the embodied context in which it is found" (Didur, 2003, p. 103). Leaning heavily on these intellectual property protections and continuing a consolidation process in agricultural biotechnology that began with the production of hybrid seed, a small and shrinking group of US and European transnational corporations now control significant portions of global food and pharmaceutical production (Cooper, 2008; Kloppenburg, 2004). Much of the opposition to GM crops has been a direct response to this corporate privatization of what once were subsistence or communal goods (Delborne & Kinchy, 2008; McAfee, 2003b).

## 9.4   Regulating Genetic Science

Scholarship in STS and related fields has shown that in addition to shaping the purposes and products of genetic engineering, a neoliberal political–economic context has influenced the regulation of genetic engineering at multiple scales (Hess, 2013). The Coordinated Framework for Regulation of Biotechnology, the comprehensive regulatory policy for the products of genetic engineering in the United States, was developed under the Reagan Administration in the 1980s, at the height of neoliberal reforms that reduced government control of natural resources and disassembled existing environmental regulations (Dryzek, 1996). Averse to the creation of additional policies, the Reagan Administration formulated the Coordinated Framework on the premise that genetically engineered products should be regulated in the same way as their non–genetically engineered counterparts and that the process through which these products were created should not alone merit the formulation of new laws (Kuzma & Tanji, 2010). Three agencies – the US Department of Agriculture, the Environmental Protection Agency, and the Food and Drug Administration – now draw on existing statutes to govern products of genetic engineering. These agencies must decide the regulatory status of GM products based solely on risk assessments using "sound science" (Jasanoff, 1995). The neoliberal attribution of scientific objectivity and rationality to an unfettered free market has prevented the inclusion of cultural, social, or economic considerations in the governance of biotechnology in the United States (Jasanoff, 1995; Kleinman & Kinchy, 2007).

In contrast, the Cartagena Protocol on Biosafety to the Convention on Biological Diversity – the most prominent international agreement pertaining to genetically engineered organisms – and the biotechnology policies of many other nations do allow for consideration of the potential socioeconomic consequences of living modified organisms (Kleinman & Kinchy, 2007). The Cartagena Protocol (2000) aims "to ensure the safe handling, transport and use of living modified organisms resulting from modern biotechnology that may have adverse effects on biological diversity, taking also into account risks to human health" (p. 3). Due to the structure of international negotiations around the Cartagena Protocol and the need for consensus, the final agreement allowed nations to regulate the products of genetic engineering even in the absence of definitive evidence of environmental or human health risks and on the basis of social or economic risks (Kleinman & Kinchy, 2007). In total, 170 nations adopted this agreement as of March 2017, although its parties do not include some nations with prominent biotechnology sectors such as the United States and Australia. The Protocol defined "modern biotechnology" as the application of *in vitro* nucleic acid techniques, including recombinant deoxyribonucleic acid (rDNA) and direct injection of nucleic acid into cells or organelles, or the fusion of cells beyond the taxonomic family that overcome natural physiological reproductive or recombination barriers and that are not techniques used in traditional breeding and selection (Cartagena Protocol, 2000, Article 3).

Although this definition may appear comprehensive, regulatory processes consistently involve contestation over the boundaries of what constitutes genetic engineering. For example, some ways of altering DNA, such as the use of *Wolbachia* bacteria, fall outside the scope of the Cartagena Protocol (Gilna, Kuzma, & Otts, 2014). *Wolbachia* function as parasites in the reproductive systems of some species of mosquitoes and, by injecting them into species that they do *not* normally infect, scientists have sought to curb the spread of dengue fever in Australia. This effort posed substantial challenges to existing regulatory structures because, although the mosquito species and the bacteria are native to Australia, the introduced bacterial infection produced a novel combination of the two, raising questions about how to define the natural in relation to the technological (De Barro, Murphy, Jansen, & Murray, 2011).

Under the notion of *bioconstitutionality*, Jasanoff (2011b) and colleagues examined moments in which the constitutions of life and law are reimagined in response to technoscientific developments, especially those that shuffle or subvert existing legal categories. Many new technologies emerge in an "institutional void" (Hajer, 2003) in which it is unclear which bodies should formulate policy or how new institutional arrangements should be established. Early developments in rDNA and subsequent techniques for gene transfer emerged without clear policies to regulate the science in laboratories or its application to commercializable products (Kuzma, 2013). Under the Coordinated Framework in the United States, the Plant Pest Act names the regulatory authority of the US Department of Agriculture over genetic engineering and thus hinges on the novel incorporation of a known or potential plant pest (Kokotovich & Kuzma, 2014). Many genetically engineered organisms have been created using *Agrobacterium tumefaciens*, a bacterium that causes crown gall disease in plants by incorporating a small segment of its own DNA into a chromosome of its host. This process has been widely coopted in genetic engineering as a vehicle for the insertion of desired genetic material into plant and animal genomes. However, a number of genetically engineered plants have been developed using molecular tools that do not involve *Agrobacterium*; these products, which include a loblolly pine tree transformed using biolistic methods (Firko, 2014), have thus evaded oversight under the Coordinated Framework.

Finding their work in an institutional void and realizing its disruptive potential, scientists who engage in genetic engineering have been among the first to call for limits on their own research and have, at times, taken it on themselves to formulate an approach to its governance. In 1974, the international molecular biology community imposed a moratorium on certain types of rDNA experiments to investigate concerns about "the possible unfortunate consequences of indiscriminate application of these techniques" for human and environmental health (Berg et al., 1974, p. 303). Scientists discussed these and related concerns at the February 1975 Asilomar Conference on Recombinant DNA, which drew researchers from the United States and twelve other countries (Frederickson, 1991). Although the organizers of Asilomar were honored with the Scientific Freedom and Responsibility Award from the American Association for the Advancement of Science, more cynical observers have criticized the event for being motivated as much by preempting public concerns and regulation (Berg & Singer, 1995) as by acting responsibly to ensure the safety of the technology (Capron & Schapiro, 2001).

Until policy makers reformulate policies to accommodate new technologies, debates and deliberation about them occur in the frames provided by existing legal notions. Jasanoff (2011b) suggested that law "is always already present as a conceptual and cultural resource, governing responsible human behavior and conditioning the terms in which people imagine the normative organization of their worlds" (p. 9). But genetic engineering is also an example of how science and technology can "overflow" the boundaries of the institutions and laws that exist to regulate them, due partially to limits in the ability of law to consider ethical issues and public concerns about the purpose of science (Callon, Lascoumes, & Barthe, 2009). Scientists at Asilomar confined their discussion on the risks of rDNA to the containment of engineered organisms in research. Ensuing global controversies over agricultural biotechnology drew attention to dimensions of genetic engineering not considered at that conference or in the risk-based regulation that followed (Jasanoff, Hurlbut, & Saha, 2015). The lens of coproduction has provided an understanding of these controversies as moments that not only reflect knowledge differences but also provide opportunities to reconstitute what counts as risk, evidence, and expertise.

## 9.5 Public Understanding of and Trust in Genetic Science

In the late 1990s and early 2000s, policy makers and scholars noted a broad crisis of trust in expertise-based governance in Western democracies, perhaps most notably in the UK (Attar & Genus, 2014). The potential for large-scale commercialization of GM foods emerged on the heels of the UK's Mad Cow scare and, with a series of well-publicized controversies with postmarket GM foods, public mistrust heightened such that policy makers could no longer ignore the risks of making food and agriculture decisions without public support (Attar & Genus, 2014; Rowe, Horlick-Jones, Walls, & Pidgeon, 2005). Efforts to address this crisis of confidence led to a relative increase in governance processes that sought to engage public audiences and helped give rise to scholarship in the *public understanding of science*, exploring links between knowledge, attitudes, and support for science and technological developments. This new field helped draw attention to the fundamental weaknesses associated with *the deficit model* of science communication, which assumes that increased knowledge results in increased support for scientific endeavors and, conversely, that opposition to science or technology is born primarily of a lack of knowledge about it (Brunk, 2006; Evans & Durant, 1995; Sturgis & Allum, 2004).

Although scholars and advocates working under the deficit model posited that improved understanding of genetic science and genetic engineering would garner greater consumer commitment to GM foods, substantial scholarship revealed that public attitudes about science are complex and informed by a range of sociocultural and political values (Sturgis & Allum, 2004; Wynne, 2005). These values are not easily measured by large-scale survey data, so new theories and methods were required to better describe, if not predict, how various publics respond to the application of genetic engineering, especially with respect to food (Sturgis & Allum, 2004; Sturgis, Cooper, & Fife-Schaw, 2005). Recognizing that factors other than knowledge influenced public attitudes about genetic engineering, *public engagement* – a practice motivated by the value of consensus – emerged as an effort to improve trust in science and scientific institutions (Attar & Genus, 2014; Pidgeon et al., 2005; Rowe et al., 2005). The assumption that increased public engagement is inherently positive undergirds the significant portion of scholarship on the public understanding of science, which advocates increased involvement in broader democratic deliberations that are meaningful, rather than mere mechanisms for selling science.

In 2003, the UK's newly formed Agriculture and Biotechnology Commission attempted such an exercise by organizing the "GM Nation?" debates with the expressed goal of debating in public and innovative ways about the potential commercial adoption of GM crops in the UK (Attar & Genus, 2014). "GM Nation?" ultimately triangulated vast amounts of mixed-method data to offer a comprehensive and nuanced account of the views of more than 36,000 UK citizens, bringing to light their deep concerns about the commercialization of GM foods (Pidgeon et al., 2005). Evaluation of the "GM Nation?" process also laid bare a number of questions, critiques, and concerns that apply broadly to public engagement in science and to genetic science in particular (Blok & Lemmens, 2015). These debates fostered academic and practical discussion about the purpose of public-engagement exercises; whereas the expressed goal is often to better understand dynamic and diverse public perceptions, concern persists that the real goal is to improve consumer confidence (Attar & Genus, 2014; Blok & Lemmens, 2015). Although efforts at inclusion in the "GM Nation?" debates were many, as were attempts to avoid bias, subsequent discursive analyses drew attention to some embedded neoliberal assumptions that underpinned these and other public-engagement mechanisms concerning genetic engineering. For example, the debate itself is often set in terms that couch participants as potential consumers of a product more readily than as citizens in a directly democratic process (Attar & Genus, 2014).

Additional concerns center on how problem framing dictates who is engaged in participatory processes (Powell, Colin, Kleinman, Delborne, & Anderson, 2011); whether or not public engagement actually improves decision-making (Rask & Worthington, 2015; Rask, Worthington, & Lammi, 2012); and how the outcomes of public-engagement exercises can be made policy relevant and impactful (Delborne, Schneider, Bal, Cozzens, & Worthington, 2013; Joss, 1998). Deliberative engagements tend to invite citizen input on how genetic engineering should be governed, positioning technological development as inevitable rather than opening the door to increased public input regarding the direction and priorities of scientific research. Furthermore, public participation "remains an empty word until procedures are set in place to make it real and effective" (DeMarchi, 2003, p. 174). As Seifert (2013) noted, "it remains to be seen whether public dialogues are capable of seriously challenging technology policies that are, first and foremost, geared to gain a competitive edge in the global high-tech race" (p. 79). Perhaps the most fundamental critique of deliberative exercises is that, in idealizing the notion of consensus, they ignore the ways any given decision necessarily privileges some voices over others (Mouffe, 2000). Especially in relation to the governance of genetic engineering and other environmental issues, it may be more productive to recognize "agreements reached through the political process as temporary configurations of power that are open to future dissent" (Peterson, Peterson, & Peterson, 2005, p. 766).

Feminist and postcolonial STS frameworks offer important theoretical bases for scholarship that addresses the ways power is inherent – but can be disrupted – in public-participation mechanisms and procedures. STS scholars have also articulated frameworks that offer practical space to enroll a broader range of voices in the governance of emerging technologies in genetic engineering, including real-time technology assessment (Guston & Sarewitz, 2002), upstream community engagement (Kuzma,

Romanchek, & Kokotovich, 2008; Lavery et al., 2010; Wilsdon & Willis, 2004), sociotechnical integration research (Fisher, Mahajan, & Mitcham, 2006; Schuurbiers & Fisher, 2009), anticipatory governance (Guston, 2014), and, perhaps most recently, responsible innovation (Stilgoe & Guston, 2017; Stilgoe, Owen, & Macnaghten, 2013). Some of these approaches, like responsible innovation, have been subject to critiques that echo those leveled at public engagement more broadly (Blok & Lemmens, 2015; van Oudheusden, 2014). However, by emphasizing the democratization of science production and governance – and by opening their own assumptions to investigation and inclusive deliberation (Stilgoe et al., 2013) – these frameworks may open spaces for public audiences to participate more intentionally in the coproduction and governance of genetic engineering.

## 9.6   Conclusion: The Ongoing Coproduction of Genetic Engineering Technoscience

The field of genetic engineering continues to evolve, with new methods and applications pushing the frontier of technological intervention in human and nonhuman bodies and the environment. In 2013, scientists coopted a natural system of acquired immunity in prokaryotes (Horvath & Barrangou, 2010) to develop a new method to alter DNA that is unprecedented in its efficiency, speed, low cost, and versatility. The method, clustered regularly interspaced short palindromic repeats (CRISPR, pronounced "crisper"), uses segments of DNA – CRISPRs and CRISPR-associated proteins – to identify and cut specific sequences of DNA, like molecular scissors (Horvath & Barrangou, 2010). In genetic engineering, the CRISPR system can be used for *gene editing*, the process of making changes – including insertions, deletions, mutations, and changes in gene expression – in the DNA of target organisms in specific locations in the genome (rather than random ones, as is the case with rDNA created using *Agrobacterium*, biolistic insertion, and other methods; Pennisi, 2013). Methods for gene editing were available before CRISPR, but in just a few years, the specificity and versatility of this technique has revolutionized basic research in genetic science and the potential to apply genome editing to problems in human health, agriculture, and biodiversity conservation (Ledford, 2015). CRISPR and other new genetic technologies are poised to reinforce and to disrupt patterns seen in earlier forms of genetic engineering, allowing STS concepts such as boundary objects and boundary work, subjectivity and coproduction, technoscience and biocapital, and public understanding and engagement to remain relevant and take on new meanings.

Although CRISPR technology garners a significant amount of attention in academic literature and the popular press, uncertainties persist about its functionality, potential consequences, and appropriate governance. For example, although CRISPR makes cuts in precise locations, it has been known to make off-target cuts as well, and it remains unclear how even small, intentional genomic changes might interact in complex ways with the genetic background and environmental conditions of the organism being edited (Montenegro, 2016). CRISPR and other tools for genome editing have also reignited debates about what counts as genetic engineering in regulation and public perception and have thus – like genes and genetic engineering more broadly – proved to be boundary objects. The first crop developed with gene editing – an oilseed rape line with herbicide tolerance – is considered a product of mutagenesis by the company that developed it and by US regulators; thus, the company explicitly markets it as non-GM (Ainsworth, 2015). The plant has been modified by scientists using molecular tools, but no genes were inserted into the plant's genome to cause the change in phenotype (Ainsworth, 2015). Like the technique used to create this oilseed rape, CRISPR allows researchers to alter an organism's DNA without necessarily introducing genetic material from a different species or even a different organism. Furthermore, unlike other forms of genetic engineering, CRISPR leaves behind few molecular traces, making it difficult to know whether an organism with a new trait has been modified using gene-editing technology or by other forms of mutation, natural or engineered (Ledford, 2015). This ability to create modified organisms without exogenous DNA or traces of the molecular machinery used to make edits could disrupt precedents for opposing, monitoring, and regulating the products of genetic engineering, based on the integration of novel genetic material (Ainsworth, 2015; Ledford, 2015).

The trouble with CRISPR's subtlety is heightened by expectations that the technology's low cost and ease of use will allow it to be used by a wide range of users and in many kinds of organisms (Ledford, 2015). Although the cost of other genetic-engineering techniques limits their application to products with high potential for financial returns, CRISPR may open possibilities for engineering plants and animals that would be more useful for subsistence and small farms around the world (Ledford, 2015). However, while farmers use CRISPR to develop pigs with immunity to African swine fever, a major problem for farmers in sub-Saharan Africa and Eastern Europe (Ainsworth, 2015), the bulk of CRISPR research in agriculture has focused on reversing herbicide resistance and creating live-stock with more muscle mass, positioning it, like its predecessors, as a technological solution for problems facing large industrial farms (Montenegro, 2016).

Neoliberal logics are also apparent in the anticipated use of CRISPR to edit human DNA. Medical researchers are currently using CRISPR in basic research to understand human diseases and may someday use CRISPR clinically to edit diseased cells – to remove HIV or cancer, for example (Cyranoski, 2016) – or to edit the human germline to create changes that are heritable (NASEM, 2017); these possibilities quickly spawned the formation of companies to develop the technology for these ends (Pennisi, 2013). Although CRISPR is revolutionary in some senses, this incarnation of genetic-engineering technoscience continues to be embedded in and coproduced with political and economic systems that prioritize certain applications and funding structures and undermine others.

Much like their predecessors at Asilomar, scientists working with CRISPR have called for self-imposed limits on the technology's deploy-ment to address questions of safety and regulatory oversight, among other issues. In 2015, a group of scientists, some of whom had attended the 1975 Asilomar conference, met in Napa, California, to discuss the scientific and social implications of genome editing, particularly in humans. They sub-sequently published recommendations for CRISPR research and public conversation about the technology, including the prohibition or cessation of human germline engineering until the risks could be evaluated and responsible uses determined (Baltimore et al., 2015). Other researchers proposed specific regulatory structures for the products of gene editing (Huang, Weigel, Beachy, & Li, 2016). STS scholars have warned that this academic discussion of CRISPR governance is repeating the errors of Asilomar by failing to include a diversity of voices (Jasanoff et al., 2015). Although those calling for the responsible development and deployment of gene-editing technologies have advocated transparency and dialogue with public audiences, scientific deliberation is already circumscribing the types of risk considered plausible and measurable and, thus, the topics that are appropriate for public discussion.

Importantly, CRISPR technology requires reimagining how to delimit the public audiences that should be included in such discussions because, in addition to making targeted genomic changes, CRISPR can be used in the development of *gene-drive* systems (Baltzegar et al., 2017). Unlike conventional or *Mendelian inheritance* patterns, which allow for a 50 percent chance that an organism will inherit a particular gene from one of its parents, gene drives bias inheritance so a particular engineered trait is more likely to be passed to future generations and to eventually be carried by a majority of the population (NASEM, 2016a). CRISPR has thus heightened the potential to modify – and in some cases, exterminate – entire species. No CRISPR-based gene-drive system has been tested or used outside the laboratory, but examples of gene-drive systems in development include efforts to curb the spread of malaria, dengue fever, and the Zika virus by either suppressing populations of the mosquitoes that spread these diseases or replacing them with mosquitoes that have been genetically engineered in a way that diminishes their ability to cause infection (Gantz et al., 2015). Other potential gene-drive applications include eliminating or suppressing invasive-species populations for conservation purposes (North Carolina State University, 2013) and altering insects, weeds, or other species that damage agricultural crops (Esvelt, Smidler, Catteruccia, & Church, 2014). The use of CRISPR to modify the genomes of a wide variety of species in the laboratory and the publication of the specific genetic constructs used in a number of gene-drive experiments (making them, in theory, replicable by many readers) drew attention to the urgent need for technical and regulatory mechanisms to contain gene-drive organisms and encourage public deliberation about their use (Esvelt et al., 2014; Oye et al., 2014). The ability of traits deployed using gene drives to spread through the landscape, including across sovereign borders, presents a challenge to existing structures for regulation, intellectual property protection, and public engagement concerning products of genetic engineering.

The uncertain but highly anticipated frontier of genetic engineering is challenging STS scholars to stretch their analyses in new ways and to reconsider modes of intervening in science and technology. STS researchers have broad interest not only in critiquing the relationship between science and society, but also in intervening constructively (Blok & Lemmens, 2015; Jasanoff, 2004a; Latour, 2004), particularly in genetic engineering. Gene editing, gene drives, and their application in realms as diverse as conservation and human enhancement currently exist in an institutional void (Hajer, 2003) very similar to that of the earliest rDNA technologies. This void provides opportunities for STS scholars to bridge "the gap between co-production as an analytic approach and co-production as a strategic instrument in the hands of knowledgeable social actors" (Jasanoff, 2004a, p. 281). STS thus remains an active force in the ongoing coproduction of genetic-engineering technoscience.

## REFERENCES

Ainsworth, C. (2015). Agriculture: A new breed of edits. *Nature, 528*, S15–S16.

Anderson, T. (2009, Summer). Darning genes: Biology for the homebody. *H+ Magazine, 3*, 34–36.

Aspray, W. F. (1985). The scientific conceptualization of information: A survey. *Annals of the History of Computing, 7*(2), 117–140. doi:10.1109/MAHC.1985.10018

Attar, A., & Genus, A. (2014). Framing public engagement: A critical discourse analysis of GM Nation? *Technological Forecasting & Social Change, 88*, 241–250. doi:10.1016/j.techfore.2014.07.005

Avise, J. C. (2004). *The hope, hype, and reality of genetic engineering: Remarkable stories from agriculture, industry, medicine, and the environment.* Oxford, England: Oxford University Press.

Balmer, A. S., & Bulpin, K. J. (2013). Left to their own devices: Post-ELSI, ethical equipment and the International Genetically Engineered Machine (iGEM) Competition. *BioSocieties, 8*, 311–335. doi:10.1057/biosoc.2013.13

Baltimore, D., Berg, P., Botchan, M., Carroll, D., Charo, R. A., Church, G., . . . Yamamoto, K. R. (2015). A prudent path forward for genomic engineering and germline gene modification. *Science, 348*, 36–38. doi:10.1126/science.aab1028

Baltzegar, J., Barnes, J. C., Elsensohn, J.E., Gutzmann, N., Jones, M. S., King, S., & Sudweeks, J. (2017). Anticipating complexity in the deployment of gene drive insects in agriculture. *Journal of Responsible Innovation, 5*, S81–97. doi:10.1080/23299460.2017.1407910

Barben, D. (2010). Analyzing acceptance politics: Towards an epistemological shift in the public understanding of science and technology. *Public Understanding of Science, 19*, 274–292. doi:10.1177/0963662509335459

Barrett, G. W., Peles, J. D., & Odum, E. P. (1997). Transcending processes and the levels-of-organization concept. *BioScience, 47*, 531–535. doi:10.2307/1313121

Barton, K. A., & Brill, W. J. (1983). Prospects in plant genetic engineering. *Science, 219*, 671–676. doi:10.1126/science.6297007

Beauchamp, C. (2013). Patenting nature: A problem of history. *Stanford Technology Law Review, 257*, 257–311. Retrieved from https://brooklynworks.brooklaw.edu/cgi/viewcontent.cgi?referer=www.google.com/&httpsredir=1&article=1460&context=faculty

Bennett, G. (2015). The moral economy of biotechnical facility. *Journal of Responsible Innovation, 2*, 128–132. doi:10.1080/23299460.2014.1002169

Berg, P., Baltimore, D., Boyer, H. W., Cohen, S. N., Davis, R. W., Hogness, D. S., . . . Zinder, N. D. (1974). Potential biohazards of recombinant DNA molecules. *Science, 185*, 303. doi:10.1126/science.185.4148.303

Berg, P., & Singer, M. (1995). The recombinant DNA controversy: Twenty years later. *Nature Biotechnology, 13*, 1132–1134. doi:10.1038/nbt1095-1132

Bijker, W. E., Hughes, T. P., & Pinch, T. J. (Eds.) (1987). *The social construction of technological systems: New directions in the sociology and history of technology.* Cambridge, MA: MIT Press.

Blok, V., & Lemmens, P. (2015). The emerging concept of responsible innovation: Three reasons why it is questionable and calls for a radical transformation of the concept of innovation. In B. J. Koops, I. Oosterlaken, H. Romijn, T. Swierstra, & J. van den Hoven (Eds.), *Responsible innovation 2: Concepts, approaches, and applications* (pp. 19–35). Berlin, Germany: Springer International. doi:10.1007/978-3-319-17308-5_2

Bowker, G. (1993). How to be universal: Some cybernetic strategies, 1943–70. *Social Studies of Science, 23,* 107–127. doi:10.1177/030631293023001004

Brooks, S. (2015). Philanthrocapitalism, "pro-poor" agricultural biotechnology and development. In B. Morvaridi (Ed.), *New philanthropy and social justice: Debating the conceptual and policy discourse* (pp. 101–116). Bristol, England: Policy Press.

Brunk, C. G. (2006). Public knowledge, public trust: Understanding the knowledge deficit. *Community Genetics, 9*(3), 178–183. doi:10.1159/000092654

Bud, R. 1998. Molecular biology and the long-term history of biotechnology. In A. Thackray (Ed.), *Private science: Biotechnology and the rise of the molecular sciences* (pp. 3–19). Philadelphia: University of Pennsylvania Press.

Busch, L. (2010). Can fairy tales come true? The surprising story of neoliberalism and world agriculture. *Sociologia Ruralis, 50,* 331–351. doi:10.1111/j.1467-9523.2010.00511.x

Callon, M., Lascoumes, P., & Barthe, Y. (2009). *Acting in an uncertain world: An essay on technical democracy.* Cambridge, MA: MIT Press.

Calvert, J. (2012). Ownership and sharing in synthetic biology: A "diverse ecology" of the open and the proprietary? *BioSocieties, 7,* 169–187. doi:10.1057/biosoc.2012.3

Campos, L. (2009). That was the synthetic biology that was. In M. Schmidt, A. Kelle, A. Ganguli-Mitra, & H. Vriend (Eds.), *Synthetic biology* (pp. 5–21). Dordrecht, Netherlands: Springer. doi:10.1007/978-90-481-2678-1_2

Campos, L. (2012). The BioBrick™ road. *BioSocieties, 7,* 115–139. doi:10.1057/biosoc.2012.6

Capron, A. M., & Schapiro, R. (2001). Remember Asilomar? Reexamining science's ethical and social responsibility. *Perspectives in Biology and Medicine, 44,* 162–169. doi:10.1353/pbm.2001.0022

Carlson, R. H. (2010). *Biology is technology: The promise, peril, and new business of engineering life.* Cambridge, MA: Harvard University Press.

Cartagena Protocol on Biosafety to the Convention on Biological Diversity, 2226 U.N.T.S. 208 (2000).

Charles, D. (2001). *Lords of the harvest: Biotech, big money, and the future of food.* Cambridge, MA: Basic Books.

Cohen, S. N., Chang, A. C. Y., Boyer, H., & Helling, R. B. (1973). Construction of biologically functional bacterial plasmids in vitro. *Proceedings of the National Academy of Sciences of the United States of America, 70,* 3240–3244. doi:10.1073/pnas.70.11.3240

Collins, P. H. (1999). Will the "real" mother please stand up? The logic of eugenics and American national family planning. In A. E. Clarke & V. Olesen (Eds.),

*Revisioning women, health and healing: Feminist, cultural and technoscience perspectives* (pp. 266–282). New York, NY: Routledge.

Condit, C. M. (1999). *The meanings of the gene: Public debates about human heredity.* Madison: University of Wisconsin Press.

Cooper, M. E. (2008). *Life as surplus: Biotechnology and capitalism in the neoliberal era.* Seattle: University of Washington Press.

Curry, H. A. (2014). From garden biotech to garage biotech: Amateur experimental biology in historical perspective. *British Journal for the History of Science, 47*(3), 539–565. doi:10.1017/S0007087413000411

Cyranoski, D. (2016). CRISPR gene-editing tested in a person for the first time. *Nature, 539,* 479. doi:10.1038/nature.2016.20988

Darwin, C. (2001). *On the origin of species by means of natural selection: or, The Preservation of favoured races in the struggle for life.* London, England: Electric Book. (Original work published 1859.)

De Barro, P. J., Murphy, B., Jansen, C. C., & Murray, J. (2011). The proposed release of the yellow fever mosquito, *Aedes aegypti* containing a naturally occurring strain of Wolbachia pipientis, a question of regulatory responsibility. *Journal Für Verbraucherschutz und Lebensmittelsicherheit, 6*(1), 33–40. doi:10.1007/s00003-011-0671-x

Deetz, S. (1992). *Democracy in an age of corporate colonization: Developments in communication and the politics of everyday life.* Albany: State University of New York Press.

Delborne, J. A. (2008). Transgenes and transgressions: Scientific dissent as heterogeneous practice. *Social Studies of Science, 38,* 509–541. doi:10.1177/0306312708089716

Delborne, J. A., & Kinchy, A. J. (2008). Genetically modified organisms. In S. Restivo & P. H. Denton (Eds.), *Battleground science and technology* (Vol. 1, pp. 182–195). Westport, CT: Greenwood Press.

Delborne, J. A., Schneider, J., Bal, R., Cozzens, S., & Worthington, R. (2013). Policy pathways, policy networks, and citizen deliberation: Disseminating the results of world wide views on global warming in the USA. *Science and Public Policy, 40,* 378–392. doi:10.1093/scipol/scs124

Delfanti, A. (2013). *Biohackers: The politics of open science.* London, England: Pluto Press.

DeMarchi, B. (2003). Public participation and risk governance. *Science and Public Policy, 30*(3), 171–176.

Didur, J. (2003). Re-embodying technoscientific fantasies: Posthumanism, genetically modified foods, and the colonization of life. *Cultural Critique, 53*(1), 98–115. doi:10.1353/cul.2003.0021

Dorfman, E. (2009). History of the lifeworld from Husserl to Merleau-Ponty. *Philosophy Today, 53,* 294–303. doi:10.5840/philtoday200953317

Dryzek, J. (1996). *Democracy in capitalist times: Ideals, limits, and struggles.* New York, NY: Oxford University Press.

El-Haj, N. A. (2007). The genetic reinscription of race. *Annual Review of Anthropology, 36,* 283–300. doi:10.1146/annurev.anthro.34.081804.120522

Endy, D. (2008). Engineering biology: A talk with Drew Endy. *Edge*, 237. Retrieved from http://edge.org/documents/archive/edge237.html#endy

Esvelt, K. M., Smidler, A. L., Catteruccia, F., & Church, G. M. (2014). Concerning RNA-guided gene drives for the alteration of wild populations. *eLife, 3*, e03401. doi:10.7554/eLife.03401

Evans, G., & Durant, J. (1995). The relationship between knowledge and attitudes in the public understanding of science in Britain. *Public Understanding of Science, 4*, 57–74. doi:10.1088/0963-6625/4/1/004

Fang, F. C., & Casadevall, A. (2011). Reductionistic and holistic science. *Infection and Immunity, 79*, 1401–1404. doi:10.1128/IAI.01343-10

Firko, M. (2014). *Request for confirmation that loblolly pine is not a regulated article. Letter to Dr. Les Pearson.* Retrieved from www.aphis.usda.gov/biotechnology/downloads/reg_loi/brs_resp_arborgen_loblolly_pine.pdf

Fisher, E., Mahajan, R. L., & Mitcham, C. (2006). Midstream modulation of technology: Governance from within. *Bulletin of Science, Technology & Society, 26*, 485–496. doi:10.1177/0270467606295402

Frederickson, D. S. (1991). Asilomar and recombinant DNA: The end of the beginning. In K. E. Hanna (Ed.), *Biomedical politics* (pp. 258–292). Washington, DC: National Academies Press. Retrieved from www.ncbi.nlm.nih.gov/books/NBK234217/

Frow, E., & Calvert, J. (2013). "Can simple biological systems be built from standardized interchangeable parts?" Negotiating biology and engineering in a synthetic biology competition. *Engineering Studies, 5*, 42–58. doi:10.1080/19378629.2013.764881

Gantz, V. M., Jasinskiene, N., Tatarenkova, O., Fazekas, A., Macias, V. M., Bier, E., & James, A. A. (2015). Highly efficient Cas9-mediated gene drive for population modification of the malaria vector mosquito Anopheles stephensi. *Proceedings of the National Academy of Sciences, 112*, E6736–E6743. doi:10.1073/pnas.1521077112

Gieryn, T. F. (1983). Boundary-work and the demarcation of science from non-science: Strains and interests in professional ideologies of scientists. *American Sociological Review, 48*, 781–795. doi:10.2307/2095325

Gilna, B., Kuzma, J., & Otts, S. S. (2014). Governance of genetic biocontrol technologies for invasive fish. *Biological Invasions, 16*, 1299–1312. doi:10.1007/s10530-012-0367-x

Glover, D. (2010). The corporate shaping of GM crops as a technology for the poor. *Journal of Peasant Studies, 37*(1), 67–90. doi:10.1080/03066150903498754

Gottweis, H. (1998). *Governing molecules: The discursive politics of genetic engineering in Europe and the United States.* Cambridge, MA: MIT Press.

Gustafsson, K. M., Agrawal, A. A., Lewenstein, B. V., & Wolf, S. A. (2015). The monarch butterfly through time and space: The social construction of an icon. *BioScience, 65*, 612–622. doi:10.1093/biosci/biv045

Guston, D. H. (2014). Understanding "anticipatory governance." *Social Studies of Science, 44*, 218–242. doi:10.1177/0306312713508669

Guston, D. H., & Sarewitz, D. (2002). Real-time technology assessment. *Technology in Society, 24*, 93–109. doi:10.1016/S0160-791X(01)00047-1

Hajer, M. (2003). Policy without polity? Policy analysis and the institutional void. *Policy Sciences, 36*, 175–195. doi:10.1023/A:1024834510939

Haraway, D. (1990). A manifesto for cyborgs: Science, technology and socialist feminism in the 1980s. In L. Nicholson (Ed.), *Feminism, postmodernism* (pp. 190–233). New York, NY: Routledge.

Haraway, D. (1997). *Modest_witness@secondmillennium.femaleman_meets_ OncoMouse: Feminism and technoscience*. New York, NY: Routledge.

Harding, S. G. (2004). *The feminist standpoint theory reader: Intellectual and political controversies*. New York, NY: Routledge.

Hartzog, M. (2017). Inventing mosquitoes: Tracing the topology of vectors for human disease. In L. Walsh & C. Boyle (Eds.), *Topologies as techniques for a post-critical rhetoric* (pp. 75–98). Cham, Switzerland: Palgrave Macmillan.

Harvey, D. (2005). *A brief history of neoliberalism*. New York, NY: Oxford University Press.

Hayles, K. (1999). *How we became posthuman: Virtual bodies in cybernetics, literature, and informatics*. Chicago, IL: University of Chicago Press.

Herrick, C. (2005). "Cultures of GM": Discourses of risk and labelling of GMOs in the UK and EU. *Area, 37*, 286–294. doi:10.1111/j.1475-4762.2005.00632.x

Hess, D. J. (2013). Neoliberalism and the history of STS theory: Toward a reflexive sociology. *Social Epistemology, 27*(2), 177–193.

Hilbeck, A., Binimelis, R., Defarge, N., Steinbrecher, R., Székács, A., Wickson, F., ... Wynne, B. (2015). No scientific consensus on GMO safety. *Environmental Sciences Europe, 27*, 4. doi:10.1186/s12302-014-0034-1

Horvath, P., & Barrangou, R. (2010). CRISPR/Cas, the immune system of bacteria and archaea. *Science, 327*, 17–70. doi:10.1126/science.1179555

Huang, S., Weigel, D., Beachy, R. N., & Li, J. (2016). A proposed regulatory framework for genome-edited crops. *Nature Genetics, 48*(2), 109–111. doi:10.1038/ng.3484

Husserl, E. (1962). *Ideas* (W. R. B. Gibson, Trans.). New York, NY: Collier. (Original work published 1913.)

James, C. (2014). *Global status of commercialized biotech/GM crops: 2014* (ISAAA Brief No. 49). Ithaca, NY: ISAAA.

Jansen, K., & Gupta, A. (2009). Anticipating the future: "Biotechnology for the poor" as unrealized promise? *Futures, 41*(7), 436–445.

Jasanoff, S. (1987). Contested boundaries in policy-relevant science. *Social Studies of Science, 17*, 195–230. doi:10.1177/030631287017002001

Jasanoff, S. (1995). Product, process, or programme: Three cultures and the regulation of biotechnology. In M. Bauer (Ed.), *Resistance to new technology: Nuclear power information technology and biotechnology* (pp. 311–331). Cambridge, England: Cambridge University Press.

Jasanoff, S. (2004a). Afterword. In S. Jasanoff (Ed.), *States of knowledge: The co-production of science and the social order* (pp. 274–282). London, England: Routledge.

Jasanoff, S. (2004b). Ordering knowledge, ordering society. In S. Jasanoff (Ed.), *States of knowledge: The co-production of science and the social order* (pp. 13–45). London, England: Routledge.

Jasanoff, S. (2011a). *Designs on nature: Science and democracy in Europe and the United States*. Princeton, NJ: Princeton University Press.

Jasanoff, S. (2011b). Introduction: Rewriting life, reframing rights. In *Reframing rights: Bioconstitutionalism in the genetic age* (pp. 1–27). Cambridge, MA: MIT Press.

Jasanoff, S., Hurlbut, J. B., & Saha, K. (2015). CRISPR democracy: Gene editing and the need for inclusive deliberation. *Issues in Science and Technology, 32*(1), 25–32.

Joss, S. (1998). Danish consensus conferences as a model of participatory technology assessment: An impact study of consensus conferences on Danish parliament and Danish public debate. *Science and Public Policy, 25*, 2–22.

Kay, L. E. (2000). *Who wrote the book of life? A history of the genetic code*. Stanford, CA: Stanford University Press.

Keller, E. F. (1995). *Refiguring life: Metaphors of twentieth-century biology*. New York, NY: Columbia University Press.

Keller, E. F. (2000). *Century of the gene*. Cambridge, MA: Harvard University Press.

Kelty, C. M. (2010). Outlaws, hackers, victorian amateurs: diagnosing public participation in the life sciences today. *Jcom, 9*(01), C03.

Kera, D. (2012). Hackerspaces and DIYbio in Asia: Connecting science and community with open data, kits and protocols. *Journal of Peer Production, 2*. Retrieved from http://peerproduction.net/issues/issue-2/peer-reviewed-papers/diybio-in-asia/

Kevles, D. J. (1994). Ananda Chakrabarty wins a patent: Biotechnology, law, and society, 1972–1980. *Historical Studies in the Physical and Biological Sciences, 25*, 111–135. doi:10.2307/27757736

Kevles, D. J. (2008). Protections, privileges, and patents: Intellectual property in American horticulture, the late nineteenth century to 1930. *Proceedings of the American Philosophical Society, 152*, 207–213.

Kinchy, A. (2012). *Seeds, science, and struggle: The global politics of transgenic crops*. Cambridge, MA: MIT Press.

Kleinman, D. L. (1998). Untangling context: Understanding a university laboratory in the commercial world. *Science, Technology, & Human Values, 23*, 285–314. doi:10.1177/016224399802300302

Kleinman, D. L., & Kinchy, A. J. (2007). Against the neoliberal steamroller? The biosafety protocol and the social regulation of agricultural biotechnologies. *Agriculture and Human Values, 24*, 195–206. doi:10.1007/s10460-006-9049-6

Kleinman, D. L., & Kloppenburg, J. R. (1991). Aiming for the discursive high ground: Monsanto and the biotechnology controversy. *Sociological Forum, 6*, 427–447. doi:10.1007/BF01114471

Kleinman, D. L., & Vallas, S. P. (2001). Science, capitalism, and the rise of the "knowledge worker": The changing structure of knowledge production in the United States. *Theory and Society, 30*, 451–492. doi:10.1023/A:1011815518959

Klintman, M. (2002). The genetically modified (GM) food labelling controversy: Ideological and epistemic crossovers. *Social Studies of Science, 32*, 71–91. doi:10.1177 /0306312702032001004

Kloppenburg, J. R. (2004). *First the seed: The political economy of plant biotechnology.* Madison: University of Wisconsin Press.

Knight, T. (2003). *Idempotent vector design for standard assembly of biobricks.* Retrieved from http://dspace.mit.edu/handle/1721.1/21168

Koch, T. (2010). Enhancing who? Enhancing what? Ethics, bioethics, and transhumanism. *Journal of Medicine and Philosophy, 35*, 685–699. doi:10.1093/ jmp/jhq051

Kokotovich, A., & Kuzma, J. (2014). Conflicting futures: Environmental regulation of plant targeted genetic modification. *Bulletin of Science, Technology & Society, 34*, 108–120. doi:10.1177/0270467614565695

Krimsky, S. (1991). *Biotechnics & society: The rise of industrial genetics.* New York, NY: Praeger.

Krimsky, S. (2015). An illusory consensus behind GMO health assessment. *Science, Technology & Human Values, 40*, 883–914. doi:10.1177/0162243915598381

Kuzma, J. (2013). Properly paced? Examining the past and present governance of GMOs in the United States. In G. E. Marchant, K. W. Abbott, & B. Allenby (Eds.), *Innovative governance models for emerging technologies* (pp. 176–197). Northampton, MA: Edward Elgar.

Kuzma, J., Romanchek, J., & Kokotovich, A. (2008). Upstream oversight assessment for agrifood nanotechnology: A case studies approach. *Risk Analysis, 28*, 1081–1098. doi:10.1111/j.1539-6924.2008.01071.x/pdf

Kuzma, J., & Tanji, T. (2010). *Unpackaging synthetic biology: Identification of policy problems and options* (SSRN Scholarly Paper No. ID 1451425). Rochester, NY: Social Science Research Network. Retrieved from http://papers.ssrn.com /abstract=1451425

Landrain, T., Meyer, M., Perez, A. M., & Sussan, R. (2013). Do-it-yourself biology: Challenges and promises for an open science and technology movement. *Systems and Synthetic Biology, 7*, 115–126. doi:10.1007/s11693-013-9116-4

Latour, B. (1987). *Science in action: How to follow scientists and engineers through society.* Cambridge, MA: Harvard University Press.

Latour, B. (2004). Why has critique run out of steam? From matters of fact to matters of concern. *Critical Inquiry, 30*, 225–248. doi:10.1086/421123

Latour, B. (2012). *We have never been modern.* Cambridge, MA: Harvard University Press.

Lave, R., Mirowski, P., & Randalls, S. (2010). Introduction: STS and neoliberal science. *Social Studies of Science, 40*, 659–675. doi:10.1177/0306312710378549

Lavery, J. V., Tinadana, P. O., Scott, T. W., Harrington, L. C., Ramsey, J. M., Ytuarte-Nuñez, C., & James, A. A. (2010). Towards a framework for community engagement in global health research. *Trends in Parasitology, 26*, 279–283. doi:10.1016/j.pt.2010.02.009

Law, J., & Lien, M. E. (2013). Slippery: Field notes in empirical ontology. *Social Studies of Science, 43*, 363–378. doi:10.1177/0306312712456947

Ledford, H. (2015). CRISPR, the disruptor. *Nature, 522,* 20–24. doi:10.1038/522020a

Lombardo, P. A. (2003). Taking eugenics seriously: Three generations of - are enough. *Florida State University Law Review, 30,* 191–218. doi:10.2139/ssrn.418102

Lombardo, P. A. (2008). *Three generations, no imbeciles: Eugenics, the Supreme Court, and Buck v. Bell.* Baltimore, MD: Johns Hopkins University Press.

Maddox, B. (2002). *Rosalind Franklin: The dark lady of DNA.* New York, NY: HarperCollins.

Martineau, B. (2001). *First fruit: The creation of the flavr savr tomato and the birth of biotech foods.* New York, NY: McGraw-Hill.

McAfee, K. (2003a). Corn culture and dangerous DNA: Real and imagined consequences of maize transgene flow in Oaxaca. *Journal of Latin American Geography, 2*(1), 18–42. doi:10.1353/lag.2004.0008

McAfee, K. (2003b). Neoliberalism on the molecular scale. Economic and genetic reductionism in biotechnology battles. *Geoforum, 34,* 203–219. doi:10.1016/S0016-7185(02)00089-1

McCarthy, J., & Prudham, W. S. (2004). Neoliberal nature and the nature of neoliberalism. *Geoforum, 35,* 275–283. doi:10.1016/j.geoforum.2003.07.003

Mendel, G. (1866). Versuche über Pflanzen-hybriden. *Verh. naturf. Ver. Briinn, 4,* 3–47.

Merleau-Ponty, M. (1962). *Phenomenology of perception.* New York, NY: Humanities Press.

Montenegro, M. (2016). Opinion: CRISPR is coming to agriculture—with big implications for food, farmers, consumers and nature. *Ensia.* Retrieved from http://ensia.com/voices/crispr-is-coming-to-agriculture-with-bigimplications-for-food-farmers-consumers-and-nature/

Mouffe, C. (2000). *The democratic paradox.* New York, NY: Verso.

National Academies of Sciences, Engineering, and Medicine (2016a). *Gene drives on the horizon: Advancing science, navigating uncertainty, and aligning research with public values.* Washington, DC: Author.

National Academies of Sciences, Engineering, and Medicine (2016b). *Genetically engineered crops: Experiences and prospects.* Washington, DC: Author.

National Academies of Sciences, Engineering, and Medicine (2017). *Human genome editing: Science, ethics, and governance.* Washington, DC: Author.

North Carolina State University Integrative Graduate Education and Research Traineeship Program (2013). *What can genetic engineering offer? Island mice: Conserving island biodiversity.* Retrieved from https://research.ncsu.edu/ges/ige rt/igert-research/island-mice-conserving-island-biodiversity/island-mice-what-can-genetic-engineering-offer/

Novikoff, A. B. (1945). The concept of integrative levels and biology. *Science, 101,* 209–215. doi:10.1126/science.101.2618.209

Oye, K. A., Esvelt, K., Appleton, E., Catteruccia, F., Church, G., Kuiken, T., . . . Collins, J. P. (2014). Regulating gene drives. *Science, 345,* 626–628. doi:10.1126/science.1254287

Pennisi, E. (2013). The CRISPR craze. *Science, 341*, 833–836. doi:10.1126/science.341.6148.833

Peterson, M. N., Peterson, M. J., & Peterson, T. R. (2005). Conservation and the myth of consensus. *Conservation Biology, 19*, 762–767. doi:10.1111/j.1523-1739.2005.00518.x

Pidgeon, N. F., Poortinga, W., Rowe, G., Horlick-Jones, T., Walls, J., & O'Riordan, T. (2005). Using surveys in public participation processes for risk decision making: The case of the 2003 British GM nation? Public debate. *Risk Analysis, 25*, 467–479. doi:10.1111/j.1539-6924.2005.00603.x

Pottage, A., & Marris, C. (2012). The cut that makes a part. *BioSocieties, 7*, 103–114. doi:10.1057/biosoc.2012.1

Powell, M., Colin, M., Kleinman, D. L., Delborne, J., & Anderson, A. (2011). Imagining ordinary citizens? Conceptualized and actual participants for deliberations on emerging technologies. *Science as Culture, 20*, 37–70. doi:10.1080/09505430903567741

Rask, M., & Worthington, R. (2015). *Governing biodiversity through democratic deliberation*. Abingdon, England: Routledge.

Rask, M., Worthington, R., & Lammi, M. (Eds.) (2012). *Citizen participation in global environmental governance*. London, England: Earthscan.

Reiss, M. J., & Straughan, R. (1996). *Improving nature? The science and ethics of genetic engineering*. Cambridge, England: Cambridge University Press.

Roco, M. C., & Bainbridge, W. S. (2002). *Converging technologies for improving human performance*. Dordrecht, Netherlands: National Science Foundation.

Rowe, G., Horlick-Jones, T., Walls, J., & Pidgeon, N. (2005). Difficulties in evaluating public engagement initiatives: Reflections on an evaluation of the UK GM Nation? Public debate about transgenic crops. *Public Understanding of Science, 14*, 331–352. doi:10.1177/0963662505056611

Schnabel, L., Breitwieser, L., & Hawbaker, A. (2016). Subjectivity in feminist science and technology studies: Implications and applications for sociological research. *Sociology Compass, 10*, 318–329. doi:10.1111/soc4.12364

Schurman, R., & Munro, W. A. (2010). *Fighting for the future of food: Activists versus agribusiness in the struggle over biotechnology*. Minneapolis: University of Minnesota Press.

Schuurbiers, D., & Fisher, E. (2009). Lab-scale intervention. *EMBO Reports, 10*, 424–427. doi:10.1038/embor.2009.80

Schyfter, P., Frow, E., & Calvert, J. (2013). Synthetic biology: Making biology into an engineering discipline. *Engineering Studies, 5*, 1–5. doi:10.1080/19378629.2013.763647

Seifert, F. (2013). Diffusion and policy learning in the nanotechnology field: Movement actors and public dialogues in Germany and France. In K. Konrad, C. Coenen, A. M. Dijkstra, C. Milburn, & H. van Lente (Eds.), *Shaping emerging technologies: Governance, innovation, discourse* (pp. 67–82). Amsterdam, Netherlands: IOS Press.

Selya, R. (2003). Essay review: Defined by DNA: The intertwined lives of James Watson and Rosalind Franklin. *Journal of the History of Biology, 36*, 591–597. doi:10.1023/B:HIST.0000004575.1

Shannon, C. E. (1948). A mathematical theory of communication. *Bell System Technical Journal, 27*, 379–423. doi:10.1002/j.1538-7305.1948.tb01338.x

Star, S. L., & Griesemer, J. R. (1989). Institutional ecology, "translations" and boundary objects: Amateurs and professionals in Berkeley's Museum of Vertebrate Zoology, 1907–39. *Social Studies of Science, 19*, 387–420. doi:10.1177/030631289019003001

Stilgoe, J., & Guston, D. (2017). Responsible research & innovation. In U. Felt, R. Fouche, C. A. Miller, & L. Smith-Doerr (Eds.), *The handbook of science and technology studies* (4th ed., pp. 407–434). Cambridge, MA: MIT Press.

Stilgoe, J., Owen, R., & Macnaghten, P. (2013). Developing a framework for responsible innovation. *Research Policy, 42*, 1568–1580. doi:10.1016/j.respol.2013.05.008

Sturgis, P., & Allum, N. (2004). Science in society: Re-evaluating the deficit model of public attitudes. *Public Understanding of Science, 13*, 55–74. doi:10.1177/0963662504042690

Sturgis, P., Cooper, H., & Fife-Schaw, C. (2005). Attitudes to biotechnology: Estimating the opinions of a better-informed public. *New Genetics and Society, 24*, 31–56. doi:10.1080/14636770500037693

Sunder Rajan, K. (2006). *Biocapital: The constitution of postgenomic life*. Durham, NC: Duke University Press.

Thacker, E. (2003). What is biomedia? *Configurations, 11*(1), 47–79. doi:10.1353/con.2004.0014

Thacker, E. (2004). *Biomedia*. Minneapolis: University of Minnesota Press.

Thompson, C. (2005). *Making parents: The ontological choreography of reproductive technologies*. Cambridge, MA: MIT Press.

US Department of Agriculture, Animal and Plant Health Inspection Service (2017). *Petitions for determination of nonregulated status*. Retrieved from www.aphis.usda.gov/aphis/ourfocus/biotechnology/permits-notifications-petitions/petitions/petition-status

Van Oudheusden, M. (2014). Where are the politics in responsible innovation? European governance, technology assessments, and beyond. *Journal of Responsible Innovation, 1*(1), 67–86.

Wajcman, J. (2009). Feminist theories of technology. *Cambridge Journal of Economics, 34*, 143–152. doi:10.1093/cje/ben057

Wilsdon, J., & Willis, R. (2004). *See-through science: Why public engagement needs to move upstream*. London, England: Demos.

Wolbring, G. (2008). The politics of ableism. *Development, 51*, 252–258. doi:10.1057/dev.2008.17

Wolbring, G. (2010). Human enhancement through the ableism lens. *Dilemata, 3*. Retrieved from www.dilemata.net/revista/index.php/dilemata/article/view/31

Wylie, A., & Sismondo, S. (2015). Standpoint theory, in science. In J. D. Wright (Ed.), *International encyclopedia of the social and behavioral sciences* (2nd ed., pp. 324–330). Oxford, England: Elsevier.

Wynne, B. (2005). Reflexing complexity post-genomic knowledge and reductionist returns in public science. *Theory, Culture & Society, 22*(5), 67–94. doi:10.1177/0263276405057192

# CHAPTER 10

# Technology Enables and Reduces Sex Differences in Society

### Jens Mazei[*]

Few topics have sparked as much interest, not only among scientists but also among politicians and the general public, as the topic of sex differences. In what specific psychological qualities and behaviors do women differ from men (Hyde, 2007, 2014) and how can such differences be explained (Eagly & Wood, 1999, 2013)? These issues are important because a thorough understanding of them would inform business practices and political debates (e.g., about the reasons for the lack of female top executives; Eagly & Carli, 2007; Eagly & Karau, 2002) and because they concern key decisions that people make in their private lives (e.g., about the qualities they look for in a mate or the level of income they seek; Tinsley, Howell, & Amanatullah, 2015; Zentner & Mitura, 2012).

People are also intrigued by the question of how technology and electronic media affect societies and individual behaviors. Scholars have examined many aspects of this question, such as how technological achievements enable information to be communicated and stored (Hilbert & López, 2011) and how the use of electronic media affects dyadic forms of interaction (Stuhlmacher & Citera, 2005) or group processes (Breuer, Hüffmeier, & Hertel, 2016).

My goal in this chapter is to connect these two streams of research by exploring how different forms of technology affect differences between women and men in society. More specifically, I explore how different forms of technology shape processes known to influence the emergence of sex differences. On one hand, it could be that certain technologies hinder the achievement of equality between women and men or, in other

[*] I would like to thank, in alphabetical order, Guido Hertel, Joachim Hüffmeier, and Alice F. Stuhlmacher for making me aware of important theoretical frameworks that shaped my thinking about the effects of technology. In the same vein, I would like to thank the research training group 1712/1 ('Trust and Communication in a Digitized World'), funded by the German Research Foundation. Finally, I would like to thank Julia B. Bear for collaborating on research projects that refined my thinking about gender in general.

words, *enable* sex differences to emerge; one example is the stereotypical and sexualized way the media depicts women and men (Karsay, Knoll, & Matthes, 2018; Lauzen, Dozier, & Horan, 2008). On the other hand, it could be that technology facilitates the achievement of equality or, in other words, helps *reduce* sex differences in a society. For example, in certain forms of online communication, people interact anonymously, which may mitigate pressure to adhere to traditional gender norms (cf. Stuhlmacher, Citera, & Willis, 2007). Combining these two points of view, technology may have multiple but *diverging* effects on sex differences (for a general discussion, see Postmes, Spears, & Lea, 1998).

To pave the way for my analysis on the effects of technology, I first provide an overview of insights from basic research on whether and how women and men differ in psychological attributes and behaviors (Hyde, 2007, 2014) and on why (Eagly & Wood, 1999, 2012). Then, on the basis of a well-substantiated theory of sex differences (Eagly & Wood, 1999, 2012; Wood & Eagly, 2002, 2012), I outline four avenues by which technology shapes processes that lead to sex differences: (a) advances in technology may shape the *division of labor* between women and men (Wood & Eagly, 2002, 2012); (b) exposure to media depictions of women and men can be part of the *socialization* process and may affect the content of *gender roles* (Smith & Mackie, 2007; Wood & Eagly, 2012); (c) communication through certain technologies can – at least sometimes – be anonymous and less personal (Postmes et al., 1998; Stuhlmacher et al., 2007), which may shape people's concerns that others will react with *backlash* (i.e., negative reactions to gender-role-inconsistent behaviors; Rudman, 1998; Rudman & Fairchild, 2004); and (d) the aforementioned characteristics of certain communication technologies may shape how *internalization* of gender roles (Eagly & Wood, 2012; Wood & Eagly, 2010) affects behavior (Postmes et al., 1998).

The question of how technology affects sex differences thus appears to defy a simple answer. Depending on its specific form, technology can either enable or reduce sex differences in society (see, e.g., Postmes et al., 1998; Wood & Eagly, 2010, 2012). To make these points, I incorporate a range of insights from the literature. Although researchers have examined the overarching issues of gender and technology from diverse vantage points (e.g., Bear & Collier, 2016; Lauzen et al., 2008; Wang & Degol, 2013; Whitley, 1997), my goal is not to describe the literature in its full breadth but to offer a helpful resource for researchers by providing a holistic and theory-driven perspective on the interplay of sex and technology.

## 10.1 Do Women and Men Differ in Their Psychological Attributes and Behavior?

Two key terms in this chapter – *sex* and *gender* – need to be clarified at the outset. As noted by Wood and Eagly (2002), *sex* typically "denotes the grouping of people into female and male *categories*" (p. 699, emphasis added). Thus, when describing comparisons between women and men as categorized by biological features, I am talking about comparisons between the sexes (Wood & Eagly, 2002, 2010). *Gender* typically denotes "the meanings that societies and individuals ascribe to female and male categories" (Wood & Eagly, 2002, p. 699; see also Bosson, Vandello, & Buckner, 2018). Please note that my use of a specific term (e.g., sex) should not be taken to mean that a certain mechanism (biology) underlies differences between men and women, a point frequently made in the literature (see Bosson et al., 2018; Wood & Eagly, 2002, 2010).

Researchers emphasized the role of meta-analysis (Borenstein, Hedges, Higgins, & Rothstein, 2009; Cooper, Hedges, & Valentine, 2009) as a method to examine sex differences (e.g., Eagly & Wood, 2013; Hyde, 2014). Hyde compiled a large number of meta-analytic estimates of sex differences in various domains of life (e.g., Hyde, 2007, 2014). The potentially unsatisfactory lesson regarding the question of whether the sexes differ is, it depends and it is complicated. Hyde (2007, 2014) found that approximately three-quarters of meta-analytically estimated sex differences are small – sometimes quite close to zero – in magnitude (as indicated by effect size). To give an example, Hyde (2014) noted that sex differences in mathematics performance are estimated at $-0.05 < d < 0.29$ and that sex differences in self-esteem amount to an estimated $d = 0.21$ (men had slightly higher self-esteem than women).

The finding that many sex differences are small (or even close to zero) invites discussion of whether it is appropriate to view – or portray – women and men as truly different (for a novel approach to examine this issue, see Carothers & Reis, 2013), a tendency that likely works to women's disadvantage (Tinsley & Ely, 2018). On the basis of Hyde's findings, it appears that women and men are typically not dramatically different from each other, which should make people hesitant to overemphasize any found differences. Yet, some small effects clearly matter in practice. As Eagly and Wood (2013) explained, "Even small differences can be important. The cumulative impact of small effects that occur repeatedly over occasions and situations can be considerable" (p. 343). Due to their *enduring* impact, then, small sex differences should not be mistaken for irrelevant sex differences.

In some domains, estimated sex differences appear to be larger (again as indicated by effect size). For instance, Hyde (2014) noted that sex differences in physical aggression were estimated at $d = 0.55$ (guess which sex was more physically aggressive) and that sex differences in interest in engineering amount to an estimated $d = 1.11$ (men were more interested than women). Thus, whether the sexes differ from each other is really a question of the *domain*.

An additional caveat is that, typically much *variability* emerged in effect size estimates, even for a single domain or activity (for a recent example, see Kugler, Reif, Kaschner, & Brodbeck, 2018; cf. Eagly & Wood, 2013; Hyde, 2007). That is, a given sex difference (e.g., in aggression) is typically not invariant across circumstances but rather is *moderated* by context conditions (for an example of a pertinent model that addresses this issue, see Deaux & Major, 1987). For example, although men tend to show more physical aggression than women on average, this sex difference vanishes in certain social situations (cf. Hyde, 2014). Sometimes a sex difference even reverses: For instance, women tend to show more *relational* aggression than men (cf. Hyde, 2014). Together, instead of asking whether women and men differ from each other, the better question is why the sexes differ from each other in certain *domains* and under certain *context conditions* (due to moderator effects).

## 10.2   Why Do Sex Differences Emerge?

Society theorizes markedly on the mechanisms that underlie sex differences. Theoretical accounts typically tend to emphasize either evolutionary and biological processes or social and cultural processes (e.g., Eagly & Wood, 1999, 2013; Hyde, 2014; Zentner & Mitura, 2012). Here, I build on Eagly and Wood's "biosocial model of the origins of sex differences" (Eagly & Wood, 2012; Wood & Eagly, 2002, 2012), an integrative theory with biological and social aspects that has been useful in explaining a number of phenomena (e.g., Koenig & Eagly, 2014; Kugler et al., 2018; Wood & Eagly, 2002).

The first key construct in this theory is the *division of labor* between women and men (Eagly, 1987; Eagly & Wood, 2012, 2013). When looking at different societies around the globe, women and men often do not engage in the same activities (Wood & Eagly, 2002). For example, women are often – though certainly not always – more likely to care for children, whereas men are often more likely to work full time or otherwise support a family (Eagly & Carli, 2007; Eagly & Wood, 2012; Wood & Eagly, 2002, 2010, 2012). Why might this be? In Eagly and Wood's theory, a society's division of labor results from the *interaction* between biological characteristics of women and men and the ecological, social, economic, and technological characteristics of the local environment (Eagly & Wood, 2012; Wood & Eagly, 2012). The contrasting biological characteristics of women and men (i.e., men are on average physically stronger, whereas only women can give birth to children; Eagly & Wood, 2012; Wood & Eagly, 2012) can lead to a division of labor characterized by female caretakers and male providers (e.g., Eagly & Carli, 2007), yet *only* to the extent to which the local environment – including its technological advances – does not allow for alternative divisions (Eagly & Wood, 2012; Wood & Eagly, 2002, 2010, 2012).

The division of labor gains relevance in Eagly and Wood's theory as the cause of *gender roles* (Eagly & Steffen, 1984; Eagly & Wood, 2012; Koenig & Eagly, 2014; Wood & Eagly, 2010). In a seminal book, Eagly (1987) conceptualized gender roles as "shared expectations (about appropriate qualities and behaviors) that apply to individuals on the basis of their socially identified gender" (p. 12). This definition stresses that gender roles entail *normative* expectations (see the notion of appropriateness; Eagly, 1987; Eagly & Karau, 2002; Rudman, Moss-Racusin, Phelan, & Nauts, 2012). Why do gender roles result from the division of labor? The presumed process that underlies the effect is *correspondent inference* (Gilbert & Malone, 1995), for instance, when people see that women are in charge of childcare and other caring behaviors (e.g., Eagly & Carli, 2007) and that men are in charge of gaining resources and being competitive at work, they attribute women's and men's observable behaviors to their dispositions. People thus *infer* that the qualities required by the activities – that is, being caring versus competitive – *correspond* to the qualities of the social groups engaging in them (Eagly & Steffen, 1984; Eagly & Wood, 2012; Wood & Eagly, 2010). As a result, people conceive of women as *communal* (e.g., caring or sensitive to others' needs) and of men as *agentic* (e.g., competitive or assertive; Eagly, 1987; Eagly & Wood, 2012; Rudman et al., 2012).

Once gender roles have emerged in a society, gendered expectations are passed on through *socialization* (Eagly & Wood, 2012; Wood & Eagly, 2012). Of relevance for this chapter, socialization occurs in part through technology (Bosson et al., 2018; Smith & Mackie, 2007), as TV shows and movies often portray women and men in distinct ways (Lauzen et al., 2008;

Wood & Eagly, 2012). Thus, electronic media provide people with ideas of the typical activities of women and men (Bosson et al., 2018; Lauzen et al., 2008; Smith & Mackie, 2007; as an example, consider the TV show *Mad Men*).

In turn, gender roles gain relevance in Eagly and Wood's theory as they affect behavior: First, they affect behavior due to their normativity (Eagly, 1987; Eagly & Wood, 2012; Wood & Eagly, 2010); that is, people react negatively to women and men whose behavior violates their gender roles (for overviews, see Moss-Racusin, 2014; Rudman & Phelan, 2008) – a phenomenon termed *backlash* (Rudman, 1998; Rudman & Fairchild, 2004). The threat of backlash motivates people to avoid role-violating behaviors and to engage in role-conforming behaviors (e.g., Amanatullah & Morris, 2010; Rudman & Fairchild, 2004). Second, gender roles affect behaviors as people *internalize* them (Eagly & Wood, 2012; Wood & Eagly, 2010). People often act on internalized ideas of appropriate behavior for women and men (Eagly & Wood, 2012; Judge & Livingston, 2008; Wood & Eagly, 2010). Third, gender roles presumably affect behavior through *biological processes* (e.g., the activation of hormones; Eagly & Wood, 2012; Wood & Eagly, 2010), but because such processes may be less influenced by technological advances, I will not delve more deeply into that mechanism here.

## 10.3    Avenues of Technology's Influence on Sex Differences

In the remainder of this chapter, I elaborate on how technology may shape the processes that lead to sex differences. Following the underlying theory just presented (Eagly, 1987; Eagly & Wood, 2012; Wood & Eagly, 2012), technological advances may affect (a) the division of labor (Wood & Eagly, 2002), (b) the observations people make about women and men, which are also part of the socialization process (Lauzen et al., 2008; Wood & Eagly, 2012), (c) the (perceived) risk of incurring backlash (Rudman & Fairchild, 2004; Stuhlmacher et al., 2007), and (d) how one's gender identity influences behavior (Postmes et al., 1998).

### *10.3.1    Technology and the Division of Labor*

One factor that quite obviously determines the division of labor between women and men is their biological characteristics; that is, differences in average physical strength and in ability to have and care for infants (Eagly & Wood, 2012; Wood & Eagly, 2002, 2012). Yet, the local environment with its specific characteristics, including available technologies, codetermines the division of labor (Eagly & Wood, 1999, 2012; Wood & Eagly, 2002, 2012). Thus, technological advances generally matter. Whether they *enable* or *reduce* a traditional division of labor – and, subsequently, the emergence of sex differences in psychological attributes and behavior – depends on a technology's specific characteristics. If using it requires great physical strength or is incompatible with childcare, men may enjoy certain advantages over women in a society, for example, if men become the main providers (see below, Eagly & Wood, 2012; Wood & Eagly, 2002). If, however, "technology eases the physical demands of many kinds of work" (Wood & Eagly, 2012, p. 62), men's advantages should be less pronounced or even be offset (e.g., Wood & Eagly, 2010).

An often-mentioned technology that has given an advantage to men is the plow (Eagly & Wood, 2012; Wood & Eagly, 2010, 2012). As Wood and Eagly (2002) pointed out, in largely agricultural societies, it would be a significant factor that men were better able to operate the plow, due to their greater physical strength, and that women had greater responsibilities for childcare. Being able to operate the plow, in turn, increased a person's status, due to the resulting marketable produce and the related economic gains (Wood & Eagly, 2002). Thus, the highly used and valued technology of the plow exacerbated the basic effects of women's and men's contrasting biological characteristics, so that the traditional division of labor could become more pronounced: men as main providers and women as main caretakers. The effect of technologies such as the plow, then, is that the sexes ultimately differ to a greater extent (see the described direct and indirect consequences of the division of labor; e.g., Eagly & Wood, 2012; Wood & Eagly, 2010).

Conversely, an often-discussed technology that has mitigated the impact of biological characteristics is contraceptives (Wood & Eagly, 2002, 2010). Wood and Eagly (2012,) reviewed findings suggesting that "in societies not practicing birth control, fertile women on average have a child every 3.7 years and nurse each child for 2.8 years" (p. 59). The availability of contraceptives in many contemporary societies, however, gives women greater control in the family planning process, so they need not engage in childcare – one aspect of the division of labor – until they wish (e.g., Wood & Eagly, 2002; note that the debate between "prochoice" and "prolife" is also relevant when considering the impact of the characteristics of the environment on the division of labor; when women have the legal right to choose, they again have greater control in the family planning process). Thus, certain technologies facilitate nontraditional divisions of labor by counteracting the impact of biological characteristics.

In a similar vein, the *workplace* as a social context has undergone much change in that physical strength is often not a job requirement (Wood & Eagly, 2002, 2010, 2012). As Eagly and Wood (2012) put it, we have gone through "a shift toward an occupational structure that favors brains over brawn" (p. 470). This shift renders men's greater physical strength less relevant and allows for alternative divisions of labor. Moreover, not only is physical strength less often required, but physical presence has also lost its status as a *condicio sine qua non* for work. Practices such as virtual teamwork (Breuer et al., 2016; Hertel, Geister, & Konradt, 2005) make it easier for women to reconcile family duties and workplace duties, again lessening the impact of biological characteristics.

However, despite the new opportunities provided by virtual work, it is still a long way until societies achieve true equality. One reason is that "beyond actual hours clocked, *perceptions of time spent in the office* can also suppress women's paychecks as well as their opportunities for bonuses and career growth – in hourly and salaried positions" (Gallup, 2016, p. 33, emphasis added). Thus, presence still matters, often to the disadvantage of women.

### 10.3.2   *Technology, Socialization, and the Emergence of Gender Roles*

Gender roles emerge as people learn and personally observe that women and men do different things in society (Eagly & Steffen, 1984; Gilbert & Malone, 1995; Koenig & Eagly, 2014). Such experiences are part of the socialization process by which children become prepared for their adult lives (Wood & Eagly, 2010, 2012). The key point in this chapter is that women and men are often portrayed as engaging in (stereo)typical activities in the electronic media (Bosson et al., 2018; Smith & Mackie, 2007; Wood & Eagly, 2012); that is, technology delivers observations that feed into gender roles.

For example, Lauzen and Dozier (2005) examined a sample of films to discern how they portrayed women and men of different ages. One noteworthy finding was that 72 percent of the characters in the films were men. Of the major characters, 73 percent. Such underrepresentation of women could send an unsettling message about the relative relevance of the two sexes. Another noteworthy finding was that, with increasing age, men – but not women – were more often portrayed in leadership positions (Lauzen & Dozier, 2005). This, too, sends an unsettling message about women's and men's roles in society.

Lauzen et al. (2008; cf. Wood & Eagly, 2010, 2012) explored the social roles assumed by women and men in TV programs. Once again, women were generally underrepresented; 60 percent of the major characters were men. Moreover, women were more often shown in interpersonal roles (e.g., a wife), whereas men were more often shown in work roles (Lauzen et al., 2008). Thus, films and TV often portray a traditional division of labor.

What people see in the media has consequences (Smith & Mackie, 2007; Wood & Eagly, 2012). A recent meta-analysis by Karsay, Knoll, and Matthes (2018) provided evidence. They examined the relationship between sexualizing media use and self-objectification. Self-objectification "involves adopting a third-person perspective of the body and is manifested by chronic attention to one's own physical appearance" (Karsay et al., 2018, p. 9). The meta-analysis not only included different research designs (correlational, longitudinal, and experimental) but – of interest for this chapter – also examined different types of media, including contemporary media such as video games and social networking sites. The authors found a robust positive relationship between sexualizing media use and self-objectification, estimated at $r = .19$. Moreover, the effect was stronger for the more contemporary media relative to TV. This research suggests that observations through technology – particularly contemporary technology – have an effect that matters (cf. Smith & Mackie, 2007; Wood & Eagly, 2012).

In sum, technology affects sex differences not only through its influence on the division of labor (Eagly & Wood, 2012; Wood & Eagly, 2002, 2012), but also through its influence on the socialization process and the content of gender roles. As Lauzen et al. (2008) put it, "the basic social roles assigned to female and male characters by storytellers are tremendously important contributors to the construction and maintenance of gender stereotypes" (p. 201). As I discuss in the next section, gender stereotypes or gender roles are very important drivers of behavior.

### 10.3.3    Technology and the Power of Gender Roles

According to socially shared gender roles (Eagly, 1987; Eagly & Karau, 2002), women are relatively communal whereas men are relatively agentic (Eagly, 1987; Eagly & Wood, 2012; Rudman et al., 2012; Wood & Eagly, 2010). Although such stereotypical – and perhaps simplistic – characterizations may at first invoke a negative visceral reaction, it is important to recognize that gender roles can nevertheless be a powerful driver of behavior (e.g., Amanatullah & Morris, 2010; Deaux & Major, 1987; Eagly &

Wood, 2012) by conveying normative expectations about the sexes (e.g., Eagly, 1987; Eagly & Karau, 2002) and by becoming part of one's self-concept (e.g., Eagly & Wood, 2012; Judge & Livingston, 2008).

**Backlash reactions and backlash concerns.** If it is true that gender roles are normative (Eagly, 1987; Eagly & Karau, 2002), people should react negatively to women and men who do not conform. In fact, such negative reactions, termed *backlash* (Rudman, 1998; Rudman & Fairchild, 2004), have been widely documented (for reviews, see Moss-Racusin, 2014; Rudman & Phelan, 2008; for a recent and nuanced meta-analysis, see Williams & Tiedens, 2016).

For example, Rudman and colleagues (2012, Study 2) examined reactions toward female and male job candidates applying for a full professor position. The candidates were described as either communal (consistent with the female gender role) or agentic (inconsistent with the female gender role), but always as competent. Agentic female candidates were found to be liked less than agentic male candidates; the effect was large ($d = 0.88$). Furthermore, agentic women were evaluated as less hirable than agentic men ($d = 0.72$) and this effect was mediated by the difference in liking. Such discriminating reactions are highly problematic, given their impact in practice.

Heilman and Wallen (2010) showed that men, too, face gender-role backlash (cf. Moss-Racusin, 2014). Participants evaluated male and female employees who either had a stereotypically male job (financial advisor) or a stereotypically female job (employee-relations counselor). In the study material, employees were always characterized as good at their job. The authors found that participants respected men who had a male-role-inconsistent job less than men who had a male-role-consistent job; the effect was sizable ($d = 1.28$; Heilman & Wallen, 2010).

In light of such repercussions for people who deviate from their gender role, people are often motivated to conform to their gender role, which ultimately results in behavioral sex differences (for a pertinent model, see Rudman & Fairchild, 2004). Amanatullah and Morris (2010), for instance, examined women's and men's behavior in salary negotiations. They found that women, fearing backlash for being seen as overly assertive, asked for lower salaries than did men. Thus, backlash reactions clearly matter – they affect behavior (e.g., Eagly & Wood, 2012; Rudman & Fairchild, 2004; Wood & Eagly, 2010). This study also highlights a second point: In further experimental conditions, women and men negotiated not their own salary but the *salary of a friend*. In that situation, women were less afraid of incurring backlash for behaving assertively, which led them to request a higher salary (Amanatullah & Morris, 2010). This intriguing finding reveals that people reflect on the situation and the likelihood of backlash for role deviations (Amanatullah & Morris, 2010). Amanatullah and Morris reasoned that women would expect less backlash when advocating for a friend because asserting oneself *for someone else's benefit* is not at odds with their communal role.

The question, then, is, when do people consider backlash to be unlikely? This is where technology comes into play. A pervasive notion is that communication through certain forms of technology, such as online platforms and chats, can be – or at least can feel – anonymous (e.g., Postmes et al., 1998; Postmes, Spears, Sakhel, & De Groot, 2001; Stuhlmacher & Citera, 2005). An interesting study by Moll, Pieschl, and Bromme (2014) makes a related point. The researchers examined adolescents' knowledge of their own Facebook activities. One key finding was that some did not accurately know *with whom exactly* they had shared something on Facebook (Moll et al., 2014). At least with certain pieces of information (such as their school and city), participants tended to *underestimate* the number of people who could see the information (Moll et al., 2014). Thus, some people thought that information about them could not be accessed by certain others. What, then, happens when people think information about them (e.g., their behavior) remains private or when they think that they are anonymous?

If people are, in fact, anonymous, one important consequence is that their gender-role-violating behaviors cannot trace back to them. As a result, backlash cannot be directed at a particular individual, which may render it less harmful. Hence, to the extent that the risk of incurring backlash underlies sex differences (yet see the section on internalization below), sex differences should diminish when people interact anonymously. As noted by Wood and Eagly (2012), "anonymity shields people from negative sanctions for their gender-incongruent behavior, and thereby increases such acts" (p. 80).

As an empirical example supporting this rationale, consider Evers, Fischer, Rodriguez Mosquera, and Manstead's (2005) study of anger expressions, specifically, people's willingness to give someone a certain amount of hot sauce. Participants were told either that they would later meet the "recipient" of their anger expression or that they would not. Thus, in the latter condition, participants were anonymous to the recipient. Even though women and men did not differ in their anger, they differed in their expression of it, such that men gave more hot sauce to another person than women did (Evers et al., 2005). However, the sexes only differed in their anger expression in the meet condition, not in the not-meet condition when they were anonymous (Evers et al., 2005).

Of even greater relevance to this chapter is a meta-analysis by Stuhlmacher and colleagues (2007) on the role of technology in the emergence of behavioral sex differences. The authors examined women's and men's behavior in negotiations conducted either face-to-face or through technologies such as telephone or e-mail. Virtual negotiations, such as those conducted by e-mail, offer fewer social cues about the other person, which not only may render one's sex less salient (Stuhlmacher et al., 2007; yet see below) but may also encourage the perception that one interacts anonymously (i.e., more so than in face-to-face interactions). Stuhlmacher et al. observed that it made a difference whether the negotiation was conducted face-to-face or virtually, as women became more competitive and hostile in their behavior – that is, *less* female-role congruent – in virtual negotiations. This effect was of medium size ($d$ = 0.64). All told, communicating through anonymous technologies can affect people's behavior and therefore affect observed sex differences.

Clearly, however, people are often not actually anonymous online (cf. Postmes et al., 1998). In fact, it is a key feature of contemporary technologies that information can be easily and enduringly *stored* (for a recent study of the effects of such documentation in a team context, see Breuer et al., 2016). Information storage has many important implications for individuals and for society. A relatively minor implication that is relevant to this chapter is that contemporary technologies allow the creation of a permanent record of one's gender-role deviations. Hence, an *enduring* risk for backlash, even for a single gender-role deviation, can result. Reflecting on such an enduring risk, people may carefully monitor their behavior to avoid not only present but future backlash. I am unaware of any study that has examined this rationale, but I think such a study would be particularly timely and relevant.

In summary, technology is – once again – a double-edged sword. On one hand, it can sometimes offer anonymity, which may reduce fear of backlash and thus reduce sex differences. On the other hand, technology creates the risk that one's role deviations will not be forgotten but permanently stored, which may bring about greater sex differences.

### 10.3.4 Internalization and Identity

Certain forms of technology-facilitated communication (e.g., Postmes et al., 1998, 2001; Stuhlmacher & Citera, 2005) *may* help reduce sex differences, but *must* they? Does anonymity guarantee equality? As it turns out, it is more complicated than that (Postmes & Spears, 2002; Postmes et al., 1998) because backlash is not the sole process by which gender roles affect behavior.

Another process is based on *internalization* of gender roles (e.g., Eagly & Wood, 2012; Judge & Livingston, 2008; Wood & Eagly, 2010, 2012). As explained by Eagly and Wood (2012), "gender roles influence people's self-concepts and thereby become *gender identities* – individuals' sense of themselves as female or male" (p. 468). What becomes part of people's self-concept is relevant because people *regulate* their behavior according to their self-concepts (e.g., Eagly & Wood, 2012; Wood & Eagly, 2010). That is, people check whether their behavior is in line with their gendered self-concept and, if it is not, try to align their behavior with their self-concept (e.g., Eagly & Wood, 2012; Wood & Eagly, 2010). If, for example, a businessman with traditional notions of agentic masculinity feels he was not assertive enough with subordinates, he may change his behavior afterward, making sure to be more assertive. Thus, people's *own views* of gender-appropriate behavior affect what they do, not only what they think what *other people* expect them to do (see backlash above; Eagly & Wood, 2012; Wood & Eagly, 2010, 2012).

What role might technology and anonymity play in all this? Research following the social identity model of deindividuation effects (Postmes & Spears, 1998, 2002; Postmes et al., 1998, 2001) has shown that anonymity does *not* necessarily counteract social processes such as stereotyping. On the contrary, when people interact by means of technology, they have relatively few cues about each other, which can render their individuality less salient; their impressions of each other become more "depersonalized" (e.g., Postmes et al., 1998, 2001). The flipside of this process is that they can also seem more similar to each other, highlighting their shared group membership, if there is one (e.g., Postmes et al., 1998, 2001). As Postmes and Spears (2002) observe, "provided a common identity is available, the inability to individuate members of a group ... increases the salience of group identity" (p. 1075). The norms and dynamics of the available shared group – which could be one's sex – can therefore become even *more* influential (Postmes & Spears, 2002; Postmes et al., 1998, 2001).

To illustrate: Imagine Paul, who is African American, and Mary, who is Caucasian, meet on an online platform for discussing political topics. The platform offers anonymity in that people are identified by random numbers, not by their real names. Thus, Paul (#54256) and Mary (#45663) lack any personal information about each other. From what they have posted on the platform, however, they can infer that they both support feminist political ideas. Thus, their shared group membership as feminists becomes salient. This shared group membership then increasingly influences their behavior such that Paul's and Mary's behaviors become even more aligned with the norms of the group. That is, their comments now *mainly* address feminist ideas, although they have also talked about political topics unrelated to feminism before (e.g., racism and education).

Postmes and Spears (2002) examined the implications of the social identity model of deindividuation effects for the emergence of sex differences in online discussions. In their research, participants – men and women – discussed a male and a female topic through a chat program. Prior to the discussions, gender stereotypes were activated or not. Moreover, either the discussants were depersonalized (relatively anonymous) or else individuating information (e.g., about their alleged biography and hobbies) was provided. The results were intriguing: Sex differences – men being more dominant than women when discussing the male topic – were most pronounced when gender stereotypes were activated *and people were depersonalized* (Postmes & Spears, 2002). Hence, following the social identity model of deindividuation effects (Postmes & Spears, 1998, 2002; Postmes et al., 1998, 2001), sex differences do not only occur in certain settings *despite* the fact that people are anonymous, but also *because* they are.

Overall, it appears that certain features of technology, such as anonymity, enable *and* reduce sex differences, depending on the specific process – such as internalization or backlash – by which gender roles affect behavior. Even anonymity cannot free us from sex differences.

## 10.4    Proposing Action

In this chapter, I aimed to show that technology triggers a multitude of processes that have *divergent* effects on differences between women and men (see Lauzen et al., 2008; Postmes et al., 1998; Stuhlmacher et al., 2007; Wood & Eagly, 2010, 2012). Condensing insights from the reviewed literature, I now summarize avenues by which technology can mitigate sex differences. I structured these potential interventions according to the underlying biosocial theory of Eagly and Wood (e.g., Eagly & Wood, 2012; Wood & Eagly, 2002, 2012), highlighting all interventions in italics.

First, if a society aims to promote equality, it should invest in technologies that facilitate nontraditional divisions of labor between the sexes. Specifically, as outlined above, societies can *increase the accessibility of contraceptives* (Wood & Eagly, 2002, 2010). Moreover, technologies can change workplace characteristics (Eagly & Wood 2012; Wood & Eagly, 2010) such that people can work remotely (see the rise of virtual teamwork; Hertel et al., 2005). Then, childcare (Eagly & Carli, 2007) should conflict less with women's work. For instance, employers could *invest more in flexible schedules and home-office opportunities*, aided by technology, if the work itself allows for such a change. Such developments, however, need to be accompanied with a "change of mind" such that being physically present at work is not taken as a sign of greater devotion to work (cf. Gallup, 2016).

Second, societies can pay more attention to the way women and men are depicted in the media (cf. Bosson et al., 2018; Smith & Mackie, 2007; Wood & Eagly, 2012). Women are currently underrepresented and, specifically, are shown less often in leadership roles (Lauzen & Dozier, 2005; Lauzen et al., 2008). To support equality between the sexes, creators of TV series and movies could *portray women and men in a more balanced manner.* As a consequence, gender roles should change (see Eagly & Steffen, 1984; Eagly & Wood, 2012; Gilbert & Malone, 1995; Lauzen et al., 2008) such that people do not conceive of women as relatively communal and men as relatively agentic (e.g., Rudman et al., 2012; Wood & Eagly, 2010).

Third, with regard to backlash (Rudman, 1998; Rudman & Fairchild, 2004), *procedures in the workplace and beyond could, when possible, be rendered anonymous.* For instance, in workplace discussions and focus groups, people may be able to interact through chat programs that conceal their personal characteristics. Then, women and men need not fear they appear overly agentic or communal, respectively, thereby triggering backlash (e.g., Moss-Racusin, 2014; Rudman & Phelan, 2008). Yet, the responsibility for change should not just be in the hands of the individuals who want to avoid backlash. Rather, workplace procedures could be redesigned such that people are unlikely to react with backlash. Specifically, whenever possible, *workplace procedures* (e.g., for hiring and promoting employees) *could be standardized* so that sex is ruled out as an influence. As a result, people can be freed from fear of backlash (see Amanatullah & Morris, 2010; Rudman & Fairchild, 2004, for research that examines the consequences of fear of backlash).

Finally, following the social identity model of deindividuation effects (e.g., Postmes et al., 1998, 2001), making sex the salient social identity should be avoided. As explained above, when interacting in a depersonalized manner, it is the available group that can become a powerful driver of behavior (see Postmes & Spears, 2002). Therefore, online interactions should be structured such that *alternative social groups are rendered salient.* The gender aspects of people's self-concept (e.g., Eagly & Wood, 2012; Wood & Eagly, 2010) should then become relatively less influential.

## 10.5  Concluding Remarks

In this chapter, my aim was to connect two streams of research – sex differences and the influence of technology on society – by exploring how technology shapes processes involved in the emergence of sex differences. As my theory-driven overview suggests, the question of how technology affects sex differences has no simple answer. Specifically, no *single* answer describes how technology affects sex differences. Some technologies enable sex differences and some reduce them. Thus, researchers and practitioners should pay attention to the specific features of a given technology and avoid allowing features that incite processes, such as backlash, that lead to sex differences to do so. In this way, people can support equality at home, at work, and in society as a whole.

## REFERENCES

Amanatullah, E. T., & Morris, M. W. (2010). Negotiating gender roles: Gender differences in assertive negotiating are mediated by women's fear of backlash and attenuated when negotiating on behalf of others. *Journal of Personality and Social Psychology, 98*, 256–267. doi:10.1037/a0017094

Bear, J. B., & Collier, B. (2016). Where are the women in Wikipedia? Understanding the different psychological experiences of men and women in Wikipedia. *Sex Roles, 74*, 254–265. doi:10.1007/s11199-015-0573-y

Borenstein, M., Hedges, L. V., Higgins, J. P. T., & Rothstein, H. R. (2009). *Introduction to meta-analysis.* Chichester, England: Wiley. doi:10.1002/9780470743386

Bosson, J. K., Vandello, J. A., & Buckner, C. E. (2018). *The psychology of sex and gender.* Thousand Oaks, CA: Sage.

Breuer, C., Hüffmeier, J., & Hertel, G. (2016). Does trust matter more in virtual teams? A meta-analysis of trust and team effectiveness considering virtuality and documentation as moderators. *Journal of Applied Psychology, 101*, 1151–1177. doi:10.1037/apl0000113

Carothers, B. J., & Reis, H. T. (2013). Men and women are from Earth: Examining the latent structure of gender. *Journal of Personality and Social Psychology, 104*, 385–407. doi:10.1037/a0030437

Cooper, H., Hedges, L. V., & Valentine, J. C. (2009). *The handbook of research synthesis and meta-analysis.* New York, NY: Russell Sage Foundation.

Deaux, K., & Major, B. (1987). Putting gender into context: An interactive model of gender related behavior. *Psychological Review, 94*, 369–389. doi:10.1037/0033-295X.94.3.369

Eagly, A. H. (1987). *Sex differences in social behavior: A social-role interpretation.* Hillsdale, NJ: Lawrence Erlbaum.

Eagly, A. H., & Carli, L. L. (2007). *Through the labyrinth: The truth about how women become leaders.* Boston, MA: Harvard Business School Press.

Eagly, A. H., & Karau, S. J. (2002). Role congruity theory of prejudice toward female leaders. *Psychological Review, 109,* 573–598. doi:10.1037//0033-295X.109.3.573

Eagly, A. H., & Steffen, V. J. (1984). Gender stereotypes stem from the distribution of women and men into social roles. *Journal of Personality and Social Psychology, 46,* 735–754. doi:10.1037/0022-3514.46.4.735

Eagly, A. H., & Wood, W. (1999). The origins of sex differences in human behavior: Evolved dispositions versus social roles. *American Psychologist, 54,* 408–423. doi:10.1037/0003-066X.54.6.408

Eagly, A. H., & Wood, W. (2012). Social role theory. In P. A. M. van Lange, A. W. Kruglanski, & E. T. Higgins (Eds.), *Handbook of theories of social psychology* (pp. 458–476). Thousand Oaks, CA: Sage.

Eagly, A. H., & Wood, W. (2013). The nature–nurture debates: 25 years of challenges in understanding the psychology of gender. *Perspectives on Psychological Science, 8,* 340–357. doi:10.1177/1745691613484767

Evers, C., Fischer, A. H., Rodriguez Mosquera, P. M., & Manstead, A. S. R. (2005). Anger and social appraisal: A "spicy" sex difference? *Emotion, 5,* 258–266. doi:10.1037/1528-3542.5.3.258

Gallup. (2016). *Women in America: Work and life well-lived.* Retrieved from www.gallup.com/reports/195359/women-america-work-life-lived-insights-business-leaders.aspx

Gilbert, D. T., & Malone, P. S. (1995). The correspondence bias. *Psychological Bulletin, 117,* 21–38. doi:10.1037/0033-2909.117.1.21

Heilman, M. E., & Wallen, A. S. (2010). Wimpy and undeserving of respect: Penalties for men's gender-inconsistent success. *Journal of Experimental Social Psychology, 46,* 664–667. doi:10.1016/j.jesp.2010.01.008

Hertel, G., Geister, S., & Konradt, U. (2005). Managing virtual teams: A review of current empirical research. *Human Resource Management Review, 15,* 69–95. doi:10.1016/j.hrmr.2005.01.002

Hilbert, M., & López, P. (2011). The world's technological capacity to store, communicate, and compute information. *Science, 332,* 60–65. doi:10.1126/science.1200970

Hyde, J. S. (2007). New directions in the study of gender similarities and differences. *Current Directions in Psychological Science, 16,* 259–263. doi:10.1111/j.1467-8721.2007.00516.x

Hyde, J. S. (2014). Gender similarities and differences. *Annual Review of Psychology, 65,* 373–398. doi:10.1146/annurev-psych-010213-115057

Judge, T. A., & Livingston, B. A. (2008). Is the gap more than gender? A longitudinal analysis of gender, gender role orientation, and earnings. *Journal of Applied Psychology, 93,* 994–1012. doi:10.1037/0021-9010.93.5.994

Karsay, K., Knoll, J., & Matthes, J. (2018). Sexualizing media use and self-objectification: A meta-analysis. *Psychology of Women Quarterly, 42,* 9–28. doi:10.1177/0361684317743019

Koenig, A. M., & Eagly, A. H. (2014). Evidence for the social role theory of stereotype content: observations of groups' roles shape stereotypes. *Journal of Personality and Social Psychology, 107,* 371–392. doi:10.1037/a0037215

Kugler, K. G., Reif, J. A. M., Kaschner, T., & Brodbeck, F. C. (2018). Gender differences in the initiation of negotiations: A meta-analysis. *Psychological Bulletin, 144,* 198–222. doi:10.1037/bul0000135

Lauzen, M. M., & Dozier, D. M. (2005). Maintaining the double standard: Portrayals of age and gender in popular films. *Sex Roles, 52,* 437–446. doi:10.1007/s11199-005-3710-1

Lauzen, M. M., Dozier, D. M., & Horan, N. (2008). Constructing gender stereotypes through social roles in prime-time television. *Journal of Broadcasting & Electronic Media, 52,* 200–214. doi:10.1080/08838150801991971

Moll, R., Pieschl, S., & Bromme, R. (2014). Competent or clueless? Users' knowledge and misconceptions about their online privacy management. *Computers in Human Behavior, 41,* 212–219. doi:10.1016/j.chb.2014.09.033

Moss-Racusin, C. A. (2014). Male backlash: penalties for men who violate gender stereotypes. In R. J. Burke, & D. A. Major (Eds.), *Gender in organizations: Are men allies or adversaries to women's career advancement?* (pp. 247–269). Cheltenham, England: Edward Elgar.

Postmes, T., & Spears, R. (1998). Deindividuation and antinormative behavior: A meta-analysis. *Psychological Bulletin, 123,* 238–259. doi:10.1037/0033-2909.123.3.238

Postmes, T., & Spears, R. (2002). Behavior online: Does anonymous computer communication reduce gender inequality? *Personality and Social Psychology Bulletin, 28,* 1073–1083. doi:10.1177/0146167202281006

Postmes, T., Spears, R., & Lea, M. (1998). Breaching or building social boundaries? SIDE-effects of computer-mediated communication. *Communication Research, 25,* 689–715. doi:10.1177/009365098025006006

Postmes, T., Spears, R., Sakhel, K., & De Groot, D. (2001). Social influence in computer-mediated communication: The effects of anonymity on group behavior. *Personality and Social Psychology Bulletin, 27,* 1243–1254. doi:10.1177/0146167201271001

Rudman, L. A. (1998). Self-promotion as a risk factor for women: The costs and benefits of counterstereotypical impression management. *Journal of Personality and Social Psychology, 74,* 629–645. doi:10.1037/0022-3514.74.3.629

Rudman, L. A., & Fairchild, K. (2004). Reactions to counterstereotypic behavior: The role of backlash in cultural stereotype maintenance. *Journal of Personality and Social Psychology, 87,* 157–176. doi:10.1037/0022-3514.87.2.157

Rudman, L. A., Moss-Racusin, C. A., Phelan, J. E., & Nauts, S. (2012). Status incongruity and backlash effects: Defending the gender hierarchy motivates prejudice against female leaders. *Journal of Experimental Social Psychology, 48,* 165–179. doi:10.1016/j.jesp.2011.10.008

Rudman, L. A., & Phelan, J. E. (2008). Backlash effects for disconfirming gender stereotypes in organizations. *Research in Organizational Behavior, 28*, 61–79. doi:10.1016/j.riob.2008.04.003

Smith, E. R., & Mackie, D. M. (2007). Perceiving groups. In *Social psychology* (3rd ed., pp. 155–202). New York, NY: Psychology Press.

Stuhlmacher, A. F., & Citera, M. (2005). Hostile behavior and profit in virtual negotiation: A meta-analysis. *Journal of Business and Psychology, 20*, 69–93. doi:10.1007/s10869-005-6984-y

Stuhlmacher, A. F., Citera, M., & Willis, T. (2007). Gender differences in virtual negotiation: Theory and research. *Sex Roles, 57*, 329–339. doi:10.1007/s11199-007-9252-y

Tinsley, C. H., & Ely, R. J. (2018). What most people get wrong about men and women. *Harvard Business Review*, May–June, 114–121. Retrieved from https://hbr.org/2018/05/what-most-people-get-wrong-about-men-and-women

Tinsley, C. H., Howell, T. M., & Amanatullah, E. T. (2015). Who should bring home the bacon? How deterministic views of gender constrain spousal wage preferences. *Organizational Behavior and Human Decision Processes, 126*(1), 37–48. doi:10.1016/j.obhdp.2014.09.003

Wang, M. T., & Degol, J. (2013). Motivational pathways to STEM career choices: Using expectancy–value perspective to understand individual and gender differences in STEM fields. *Developmental Review, 33*, 304–340. doi:10.1016/j.dr.2013.08.001

Whitley, B. E., Jr. (1997). Gender differences in computer-related attitudes and behavior: A meta-analysis. *Computers in Human Behavior, 13*, 1–22. doi:10.1016/S0747-5632(96)00026-X

Williams, M. J., & Tiedens, L. Z. (2016). The subtle suspension of backlash: A meta-analysis of penalties for women's implicit and explicit dominance behavior. *Psychological Bulletin, 142*, 165–197. doi:10.1037/bul0000039

Wood, W., & Eagly, A. H. (2002). A cross-cultural analysis of the behavior of women and men: Implications for the origins of sex differences. *Psychological Bulletin, 128*, 699–727. doi:10.1037//0033-2909.128.5.699

Wood, W., & Eagly, A. H. (2010). Gender. In S. T. Fiske, D. T. Gilbert, & G. Lindzey (Eds.), *Handbook of social psychology* (5th ed., pp. 629–667). Hoboken, NJ: Wiley.

Wood, W., & Eagly, A. H. (2012). Biosocial construction of sex differences and similarities in behavior. In J. M. Olson, & M. P. Zanna (Eds.), *Advances in experimental social psychology* (Vol. 46, pp. 55–123). Burlington, MA: Academic Press. doi:10.1016/B978-0-12-394281-4.00002-7

Zentner, M., & Mitura, K. (2012). Stepping out of the caveman's shadow: Nations' gender gap predicts degree of sex differentiation in mate preferences. *Psychological Science, 23*, 1176–1185. doi:10.1177/0956797612441004

# CHAPTER 11

# Technology for Society

## Todd L. Pittinsky

This concluding chapter considers criteria for the social benefits society should demand from the explosion of ever-newer technologies. The term "technology for society" references technology that, whether or not it amazes and revolutionizes society, and whether or not it is provided by the private or public sector – will serve most worthy desires for safety, health, well-being, companionship, community, peace, and justice.

## 11.1  Whose Side Is the Technology Revolution On?

The *technology revolution* is a mix of marvels and aggravations. Cell phones have saved lives and made it possible for poor farmers and others in Third World countries to connect with wider markets, negotiate better prices, and so on. At the same time, Pew estimates that 67 percent of US cell owners check for messages, alerts, or calls even when the phone is not ringing, and 44 percent have slept with their phone next to their beds to ensure they did not miss anything. In South Korea, roughly 72 percent of children will own a smartphone by the age of twelve and will spend up to 5.4 hours a day on their phone; South Korean adults will spend 3.8 hours *on their phones* (Jeong, Kim, Yum, & Hwang, 2016).

## 11.2  We Can Shrug Our Shoulders, Laugh or Get Angry or Simply Scratch Our Heads

The development of pesticides and high-yield grains may have saved over a billion people from starvation yet may also bequeath superweeds and superbugs. Antibiotics have saved millions of lives, yet in doing so they promote the evolution of even stronger bacteria. Cars have become safer as they become "smarter," but smart cars can be hacked. A study finds that, almost like a villain in a James Bond movie, someone with a laptop could remotely open one's car door just as they are changing lanes on the highway. A blind person can now wear a "smart shoe." Guided by voice commands, the shoe will work with the GPS in a smartphone to guide the blind user with simple vibrations felt in the shoe (Collins, 2014). But how long until these, too, are hacked?

A few years ago, someone had the idea to hire homeless people to walk around at conventions and fairs wearing Wi-Fi transmitters so visitors would have all the internet access and bandwidth they desired (Wortham, 2012). Some observers considered this exploitive and elitist, although the homeless people themselves considered it a good way to make some money with the perk of getting to be around people and talk to them.

## 11.3   Can We Do Better?

Great technology has had downsides since fire and the wheel, but what is new is the increasing sophistication and speed with which new technologies appear and spread, especially digital/information technologies. A particularly useful or delightful piece of software can be everywhere before society has had time to consider its downsides. Even a physical device, such as the smartphone, can be almost ubiquitous much more quickly than has ever been the case before.

It is therefore an encouraging and a daunting aspect of our time that it seems possible for technology to affect the quality of one's own and other people's lives in so many important and even profound ways, described in Table 11.1.

It is a long list, and could likely be longer, but so many people work with technology all over the world, and information technology, in particular, is so versatile that all these aspects of life and more may be seriously affected. Much of human life is subject to whatever technology someone manages to invent and someone else manages to sell. Who is making the decisions?

### 11.3.1   *From Reaction to Road Map*

So far, business and military interests largely have guided the technology revolution. Of course, individual brilliance and ambition is an unpredictable, but even those largely channel into business and military interests. Twitter, for example, became a commercial enterprise, not a public utility. Individuals interested in the social impacts of technology therefore find themselves reacting and giving chase, especially when a "successful" – that is, moneymaking – new technology bumps up against something that deeply matters to people, such as their pride (e.g., robot nursing home

Table 11.1 *Ways technology affects quality of humans' lives*

| | |
|---|---|
| Care and safety of children | Human-centered buildings and cities |
| Career development | Legal and social justice |
| Civic virtues | Life expectancy |
| Climate and environment | Love |
| Community life | Material well-being |
| Crime and prisons | Mental health |
| Culture and art | Mutual support |
| Education | Peace between nations |
| Employment | Physical health |
| Ethnic and racial equality and allophilia | Political freedom |
| Family life | Political stability |
| Freedom from fear and threat | Safe food |
| Freedom from terrorism | Social integration in multicultural |
| Friendship | societies |
| Gender equality | Spiritual and religious life |
| | Transportation and infrastructure |

aides), their morals (e.g., internet porn), their privacy (e.g., Google), or their very being (e.g., human embryo genetic editing).

Facebook, for example, found itself addressing a series of suicides about which Facebook "friends" knew but did nothing to *stop*. The company formed a partnership with the US National Suicide Hotline to enable users to report suicidal content with one click and help get the suicidal person immediate services from a network of 161 brick-and-mortar crisis centers operating 24/7. Now, the digital equivalent of bystanders who see a person about to jump from a tall building can become upstanders who actively intervene. Precisely because Facebook's technology affects such an important part of its users' lives – their connections to other people – the company seems gradually to acknowledge that it will continually have to react to unintended side effects, from stalking to cyberbullying to government surveillance. But sadly, even despite these efforts, Facebook live murder and suicide videos may be increasing online (Harper & Mullin, 2018).

It is not just the technology providers who have to give chase. So do all kinds of social and civic institutions. A school superintendent, recently asked what was most exciting about the job, said her district was supplying every teacher and student with an iPad. When a researcher in the audience asked how the idea had come to the superintendent, the response was that the school board requested it. When one of those board members was asked why the board was championing it, it was because another district was doing it. To what extent will this sort of reactive thinking be driving not only the adoption of new forms of technologies for education, but also new technologies for warfare – goaded by "well, they've got it" thinking? To what extent will reactive thinking drive the adoption of techniques for making "designer" babies, goaded by, "well, they've got one" thinking?

Missing are roadmaps for how technology could serve people's most worthy wishes *for their own sakes and* informed by broader and more diverse constituencies. Because business and defense are core parts of the web of technology and society, they will be important players in any efforts to channel technology *for* society. Indeed they are. For example, many of Google/Alphabet's "moonshots" – new projects that live in the "gray area between audacious technology and pure science fiction" are efforts to create a social good, although emanating from – and ultimately being beholden and answerable to – a commercial enterprise. So the concept of "technology for society" is not inherently hostile to corporate and military interests, but neither does it privilege them as businesses and the military themselves would do.

Decisions about the greater good of society involve important, uncertain, and divisive issues and therefore call for leadership. We do not each get to choose whether we want to live in the Age of Technology or the Information Age. Decisions are already in process, but they are generally made ad hoc by the sellers and buyers of products: essentially equally self-serving parties. Elements of the government are also making important decisions, from schools to the military and intelligence services. These decisions are not ad hoc, but neither are they generally made for the greater good of all humankind.

One cannot predict what sort of leadership will emerge to influence where technology goes on behalf of more benevolent purposes, or if there will ever be any such leadership, given the obvious conflict of such an idea with the idea of free markets. Considering the speed of today's technical progress and what already appears to be a huge lead, it might be too late. In a little over 30 years, cyberspace has gone from being a science fiction writer's neologism to official status as the "fifth domain" for warfare, along with land, sea, air, and space ("Cyberwar," 2010). The hacker organization called Anonymous has already won several notable battles against national governments with no weapon but keyboard strokes.

One symptom of the lack of leadership is the increasingly strong divide between *technoenthusiasts* – "Genetically modified plants can end starvation!" "The Internet can bring the whole world together!" – and *technophobes* – "Genetically modified plants are taking over just so big agribusinesses can make even more money!" "The Internet is creating a generation that doesn't know how to relate to other people in real life!" Of course, leadership does not eliminate disagreement, unless the leadership is a dictatorship. But it can counterbalance toward more consensus. Often society can eliminate disagreement by providing a common direction, so that even when people disagree on the means, they have wide agreement on the ends. What is needed, then, is a set of detailed roadmaps; that is, a set of destinations and the directions to get there. Providing a destination and the directions to get there is, of course, a good working definition of leadership.

### *11.3.2 What Exactly Is the Greater Good?*

How can such direction emerge? Rather than categorize various manifestations of technology as *good* or *evil*, a good first step would be to ask: "What are the greatest goods we humans seek? What do we want most to improve about our collective human life?" Then it would make sense to ask: "How can the technology of today or tomorrow help us have these goods we seek?" Judgment of current technologies is not really the point, though it might sometimes be a starting point.

What does it mean to think about technology *for* society rather than simply technology *and* society? Very broadly, it means examining a technology's contribution over time to the quantity and distribution of physical health and safety, emotional happiness and well-being, art and culture, personal relationships, physiological needs, love, and belonging.

How can one measure – or even be sure one sees – such contributions? It certainly will not be easy, but neither is it impossible. First, to avoid false precision, one must acknowledge that "society" is:

- *Diverse*: Societies are different, and the people in any particular society are different.
- *Amorphous and protean*: Society is an open system, constantly interacting with other forces (the personal and individual, the natural world).
- *Multilayered*: People experience multiple layers of society, from their neighborhood to their country to the entire world. Even at the most compact level – say, a neighborhood – society is heterogeneous and rarely reaches full consensus on any particular issue.

Even if a society largely agreed on the probable implications of a new technology, different people would prioritize them differently and even such consensus as might be reached will and should change or dissolve over time.

In some sense, this is the Aristotelian task of defining eudaimonia, the highest human good and human flourishing. But with an urgency and accountability of a business plan, to consider (and also experience) what the impacts will really be. It is common for technology companies to spin a bragging narrative of social transformation – increasingly people need to hold them accountable for the specific ways, and the anticipated and unanticipated effects.

What could be the criteria by which to judge that a technology is *for* society? Such a technology will promote one or more of the following:

1  *Good relationships*: People have high-quality relationships with their family, friends, and acquaintances. The larger groups of which we are part – our towns and countries – feel coherent and harmonious. Communities accomplish things together and help each other, neighbors know each other, coworkers feel connected. Children are parented effectively in caring and nurturing environments. People, whether they know each other or not, treat each other with civility and respect. *Do social media platforms like Facebook in their current form accomplish this? In alternative forms and implementations, might they do so more effectively?*

2  *Economic and material well-being*: Work pays enough to support workers and their families. It offers potential for growth and development and does not force workers to neglect their own well-being, families, and other relationships. *Do robot and artificial intelligence technologies help this? In alternative forms and implementations, might they do so more effectively?*

3  *Healthy natural and built environment*: The natural environment is sustainable, not endangered and polluted. The built environment – the cities and towns and their infrastructure – is safe, effective, and pleasant to use or live in. *Do smart building or smart city provide this for the great majority? In alternative forms and implementations, might they do so more effectively?*

4  *Health*: People have healthy food and good healthcare; freedom from toxins in the food, water, ground, and air; and an expectation of a long and largely healthy life with an ending that is neither hideous nor debilitating. *Do the trajectories of genomic and biotechnology advances accomplish this? In alternative forms and implementations, might they do so more effectively?*

5 *Peace and security*: People are free from crime, war, political instability, and terrorism. *Does cybersecurity provide this? In alternative forms and implementations, might it do so more effectively?*

6 *Culture and leisure*: People have access to and an understanding of rich and rewarding culture, high and popular. They also have time for and access to rewarding leisure activities. *Do gaming and virtual reality accomplish this? In alternative forms and implementations, might they do so more effectively?*

7 *Spirituality, religion, and ethics*: People having access to religious, spiritual, and philosophical teachings and the freedom to practice them. They are encouraged to think about more than how to make a living and how to spend earnings. *Does the current crop of mobile apps provide this? How might they do so more effectively?*

8 *Good education*: People can get an education that encourages intellectual inquiry and growth and develops the ability to think rationally about the choices one faces as a private individual and as a citizen. *Do open educational resources and massive open online courses movements provide this? How might they do so, more effectively?*

9 *Good governance*: There are democratic governments,[1] with political empowerment for all genders and for all ethnic and religious groups and widespread participation. The government rules with fairness, justice, compassion, and freedom of thought and expression. *Do current "e-gov" and social media provide this? How might they do so more effectively?*

By "technology *for* society," then, we mean technology that helps more people have more of the things on the list above.

### 11.3.3 Technology for the Greater Good

Having listed the ends, what of the technological means? Science fiction writers have sometimes envisioned societies in which robots are so powerfully programmed to "serve and protect" human beings that they end up creating a nanny tyranny, barring their human charges from anything that might endanger or inconvenience them.[2] Whether or not one fears this

---

[1] General agreement may no longer exist that democratic government is, as Churchill said, "the worst form of government, except for all the others." If autocracy becomes the world ideal, then perhaps many things about this list will change, though even then it will be necessary (for someone) to ask "What do want and how can technology help us get it?"

[2] A classic of this theme is "With Folded Hands" by Jack Williamson (1947). (See, e.g., Bova, 1973.)

particular outcome, it suggests that general criteria exist for technology that is *for* society, even if people do not know what any specific technology will do or how it will work. Such technology will be:

1   *Positively ambitious*: The concept of "technology for society" inherently recognizes its opposite – the dangerous or aggravating sides of the technology revolution. But the goal is never just to halt progress. The goal is always to point technology toward the greater good of everyone and then travel forward. Examples are creating social networking sites with algorithms to promote diversity rather than homogeneity, so that it neutralizes an echo-chamber effect (see Colleoni, Rozza, & Arvidsson, 2014; Vaccari et al., 2016) or news sites designed to feed back ideologically diverse and intellectually and not only comforting coverage of a topic or issue (Pittinsky, 2012).

2   *Balanced*: The alternative to positive ambition is to remain aware that any technology effective enough to be "for society" is bound to have some downsides, too. "Technology for society" examines both, tries to balance them realistically, and seeks to create the most good with the least harm. So far, with business interests driving much of the integration of technology into society, society has given too little consideration to downsides until they are *faits accomplis*. For example, some corporations do put gender, race, and ethnicity into their machine-learning models. These decisions, albeit yielding in some narrow ways more "accurate" predictions, may concurrently lead to unfair and biased outcomes, particularly for underrepresented minorities (see O'Neil, 2016).

3   *Keeps humans front and center*: Technology often replaces human roles (human labor and human judgment) without consideration of what that will mean for the people involved. Ordinarily, technology developers believe this is not their problem. Developers of "technology for society," however, must consider it their problem, as their goal must always be the greater good of all people, not just the greater good of those who will enjoy a lower price or greater convenience. For example, they may create robots not to replace workers, but rather to help them do their work more efficiently.

4   *Universal*: The technology must consider the quantity of goodness not just for some, but for wide constituencies, if not for all. For example, technology producers should attempt to incorporate more assisting languages, not merely centered on English and other major European languages. This attempt will enable more societies across cultures to use the technology easily and reap its benefits.

5 *Intergenerational*: The reduction in costs and the improvement of benefits extends across generations. "Technology for society" tries not to leave booby-traps for the future. For example, technology to promote the use of renewable energy that is much better for the environment than fuel-based energy is intrinsically more valuable, impacting across generations.

6 *Well-timed*: People tend to think new technologies arrive when they arrive as a matter of chance and individual creativity. In fact, it is not that simple and not always that outside people's control. Companies, for example, choose when to focus on a particular problem. Federal agencies make choices about what lines of research and development to support. Timing, therefore, is a criterion of "technology for society." For example, is a particular technology arriving – and having its impact – too soon or too late? For example, in developing countries such as Indonesia, the presence of ride-hailing services may have come too early; it disturbed the existing markets and even led to conflicts between traditional players and newcomers (Cochrane, 2016) and extracted great human suffering from the dislocation. It may even threaten the ongoing development of Indonesia's mass rapid public transportation as it siphons out of public transpiration a segment of the population that, if it rode public transportation, would help subsidize the system's investments in accessibility for larger swatches of Indonesian society.

7 *Open to evolution and reevaluation*: Society's norms evolve. Technology that is truly "for society" should have the capacity to evolve with the people. For example, more and more social media now have a privacy feature that allows users to download and delete all personal information from their server. In the past, once users registered on a social media platform, their personal information would remain on the server for good. This approach reflects how social media platforms can move in the direction of meeting individuals' need for privacy.

In any given case, some of these factors will be interdependent. Some may even conflict. The analysis therefore cannot be inflexibly bound to a checklist of criteria. Rather these criteria should serve as a foundation for reflection, prioritization, and wise judgments.

### 11.3.4   Technology for Society

One does not have to be a technophile to see that technology, in its various physical and digital forms, can do worlds of good. Devices, especially computers, already have. As a whole, the human race suffers far less than it did in the past, not only from hunger and disease, but from ignorance and isolation. Nor does one have to be a technophobe to fear some of the current and looming impacts of some advanced technologies. Irrespective of one's starting point, people do not have to be quite as passive as we have been, letting the benefits and the harms tumble willy-nilly from the cornucopia of human inventiveness and marketing. It is time to move discussions of technology and society to ones of technology for society, with all the messiness, work, and potential for good the charge implies.

## REFERENCES

Bova, B. (Ed.) (1973). *The science fiction hall of fame* (Vol. 2A). New York, NY: Doubleday.

Cochrane, J. (2016, March 22). Protest in Indonesia against ride-hailing apps turns violent. *New York Times*. Retrieved from www.nytimes.com/2016/03/23/world/asia/indonesia-jakarta-taxi-uber-grabcar.html

Colleoni, E., Rozza, A., & Arvidsson, A. (2014). Echo chamber or public sphere? Predicting political orientation and measuring political homophily in Twitter using big data. *Journal of Communication, 64*, 317–332. doi:10.1111/jcom.12084

Collins, K. (2014, July 24). Smart shoes guide runners and the blind with vibrations, *Wired*. Retrieved from www.wired.co.uk/article/lechal-smart-shoes

Cyberwar: War in the fifth domain (2010, July 1). *Economist*. Retrieved from www.economist.com/briefing/2010/07/01/war-in-the-fifth-domain

Harper, P., & Mullin, G. (2018, February 28). How FacebookLive murder and suicide videos are spreading online and what you should do if you spot inappropriate content. *Sun*. Retrieved from www.thesun.co.uk/news/3426352/facebook-live-clips-murder-suicide-shootings-report/

Jeong, S., Kim, H., Yum, J., & Hwang, Y. (2016). What type of content are smartphone users addicted to? SNS vs. games. *Computers in Human Behavior, 54*, 10–17. doi:10.1016/j.chb.2015.07.035

O'Neil, C. (2016). *Weapons of math destruction: How big data increases inequality and threatens democracy*. New York, NY: Crown.

Pittinsky, T. L. (2012). *Us plus them: Tapping the positive power of difference*. Boston, MA: Harvard Business School Press.

Vaccari, C., Valeriani, A., Barberá, P., Jost, J. T., Nagler, J., & Tucker, J. A. (2016). Of echo chambers and contrarian clubs: Exposure to political disagreement among German and Italian users of Twitter. *Social Media + Society, 3*, 1–24. doi:10.1177/2056305116664221

Williamson, J. (1947). *With folded hands*. Reading, PA: Fantasy Press.

Wortham, J. (2012, March 12). Use of homeless as Internet hot spots backfires on marketer. *New York Times*. Retrieved from www.nytimes.com/2012/03/13/technology/homeless-as-wi-fi-transmitters-creates-a-stir-in-austin.html

# Index